Tibetan Buddhist Philosophy of Mind and Nature

Tibetan Buddhist Philosophy of Mind and Nature

DOUGLAS S. DUCKWORTH

OXFORD
UNIVERSITY PRESS

OXFORD
UNIVERSITY PRESS

Oxford University Press is a department of the University of Oxford. It furthers the University's objective of excellence in research, scholarship, and education by publishing worldwide. Oxford is a registered trade mark of Oxford University Press in the UK and certain other countries.

Published in the United States of America by Oxford University Press
198 Madison Avenue, New York, NY 10016, United States of America.

First issued as an Oxford University Press paperback, 2022

Library of Congress Cataloging-in-Publication Data
Names: Duckworth, Douglas S., 1971– author.
Title: Tibetan Buddhist philosophy of mind and nature / by Douglas S. Duckworth.
Description: New York, NY : Oxford University Press, [2019] |
Includes bibliographical references and index.
Identifiers: LCCN 2018010436 | ISBN 9780190883959 (hardcover) |
ISBN 9780197616598 (paperback) | ISBN 9780190883973 (epub) |
ISBN 9780190883980 (online resource)
Subjects: LCSH: Buddhist philosophy. | Buddhism—China—Tibet Autonomous Region—Doctrines. | Madhyamika (Buddhism)
Classification: LCC B162.D83 2019 | DDC 181/.043923—dc23
LC record available at https://lccn.loc.gov/2018010436

For my dear mother and mothers everywhere

Contents

Acknowledgments

THOSE WHO HAVE contributed to this book are too numerous to enumerate. Yet I would like to acknowledge some of them here. A big thanks goes to the late Aku Rapkyé, Chökyi Nyima Rinpoché, Drupön Thinley Ningpo, Jeffrey Hopkins, Khenpo Sherap Dorjé, Khenpo Tsültrim Dargyé, Thrangu Rinpoché, and Tulku Nyima Gyeltsen for teaching me about topics in this book and more. Also, feedback on drafts of this book were invaluable, including the input of Marcus Bingenheimer, José Cabezón, George Cardona, David Carpenter, Ryan Conlon, Catherine Dalton, Thomas Doctor, Georges Dreyfus, Jay Garfield, Jeffrey Hopkins, Gerd Klintschar, Karin Meyers, Gail Stenstad, Rolf Truhitte, and Philippe Turenne. I wish to thank them all. Paul Hackett's Buddhist Canon's Research Database has also been a wonderful resource for my work. Elizabeth Callahan and Marcus Perman also assisted me in locating Tibetan texts. Research for this book was enabled by a Humanities and Arts Research Program Grant, as well as a College of Liberal Arts Research Award, both from Temple University.

Tibetan Buddhist Philosophy of Mind and Nature

Introduction

THIS BOOK IS a thematic survey of Tibetan Buddhist thought. It provides a theoretic framework to introduce a wide range of intersecting ideas. With many informed studies and translations of Tibetan traditions now available in English, I feel that the time is right to survey the intellectual terrain of Tibetan Buddhist thought with a wide-angle lens. What follows is my attempt to provide this lens and to map the terrain both descriptively and creatively. I do not base my framework around particular schools or sectarian traditions, but attempt to focus on issues and themes that structure the philosophical conversations within and among the schools. While doing so, I draw freely from European and American philosophical traditions to engage with and elaborate upon Buddhist thought and practice in Tibet. A central theme of Tibetan philosophy I draw out is the intertwining of mind, language, and world.

Understanding Buddhism in India is fundamental to understanding Buddhism in Tibet. Tibetan Buddhists played an essential role in preserving Indian Buddhist culture, not only by carrying on the traditions of study and practice from India into the present, long after their demise in India, but also by preserving Indian Buddhist texts in translation. Most Buddhist texts of the mature era of Indian Buddhist literature (fifth to eleventh centuries) are no longer extant in any language other than in Tibetan translation. Buddhist texts and traditions entered the Tibetan plateau from India from the eighth to eleventh centuries, just before living Buddhist traditions died out on the Indian subcontinent under the weight of Muslim incursions. After the eleventh century, Buddhist monastic institutions in India were left in rubbles, and Buddhist popular traditions came to be assimilated into Hindu traditions.

Given the importance of the Indian subcontinent for Tibetan Buddhism, I begin with a fair amount of discussion of Indian sources. The first chapter begins by looking to Nāgārjuna, an influential second-century Indian Buddhist thinker, and his articulation of emptiness and interrelation. Emptiness is the ultimate truth in Mahāyāna Buddhism: the truth which, when known, sets you free. I highlight how the ultimate truth in Mahāyāna Buddhism comes to be interpreted along two main lines: as indicative of an inconceivable reality or as an absence of intrinsic nature. The former interpretation characterizes what comes to be known as "Mind-Only" in Tibet (or Yogācāra), while the latter characterizes Madhyamaka, "the Middle Way." These two traditions represent competing interpretations of the ultimate truth and the Perfection of Wisdom (*prajñāpāramitā*) Sūtras. Further, Tibetans hold Mind-Only and Madhyamaka to represent two main schools of interpretation elucidated within the two "great chariot traditions" (*shing rta chen po*) of Mahāyāna Buddhism. While Tibetans use these terms to characterize distinct strands of interpretation of the meaning of the Buddha's message, we should keep in mind that these terms do not refer to individual schools or bounded canons of texts.

Also, what Tibetans refer to by the terms "Middle Way" and "Mind-Only" can be quite different, with usages that are highly charged within specific contexts of sectarian traditions and preferred interpretations of one's own school. In order to dislodge these terms from a single tradition's interpretive claims, for the purposes of this book I will use them differently. In my usage, "Mind-Only" highlights a particular phenomenological style of interpretation and orientation to contemplative practice. I use Madhyamaka, "the Middle Way," to highlight a critical orientation and deconstructive ontology. These terms, and the "schools" associated with them, are highly contested and polysemic, yet I appropriate them as a heuristic and to convey an intimate relationship between two intertwined trajectories of interpretation. I feel that the problems I create by continuing to use these terms, with the distinctive meanings I have assigned them, are less severe than the problems of avoiding them altogether or narrowly constraining them to definitions tied into a single sectarian tradition's interpretation.

With the interplay of these two trajectories I attempt to sustain a tension between two contrasting readings of Buddhist thought, as both are viable and widely attested interpretations of Mahāyāna Buddhist literature and practice. One reading is commonly found in the works of academic philosophers attuned to ontological analyses and the Madhyamaka tradition of the Geluk (*dge lugs*) school of Tibetan Buddhism. Another interpretation that I keep in play is a phenomenological reading that appeals to the irreducibility and inexpressibility of the lived world as experienced. I use "phenomenology" to represent this latter trajectory of interpretation, and while it may not be a perfect fit, the style of doing philosophy in phenomenological traditions clearly resonates here, and certainly shares a family resemblance with an important dimension of Mind-Only, which I shall highlight in chapter 1.

The relationship between these two orientations, of Madhyamaka and Mind-Only, or ontology and phenomenology, reiterates some of the problems and popular associations of a contrast between stereotypical "analytic" and "continental" ways of doing philosophy. That is, these two modalities are imperfect and simplistic caricatures of a complex and internally diverse relation of ideas. I take them to be co-constituted, like the first- and third-person perspectives on the world and the methodologies that grow out of these ways of reflection. In other words, what I characterize as ontological and phenomenological orientations are two dimensions of how a single individual relates to what is meaningful and true.

In chapter 2 I consider the ways that Madhyamaka and Mind-Only can be seen to offer distinct depictions of the world, framed in terms of a relationship between ontology and phenomenology. I suggest that the perspectives offered by ontology and phenomenology can be understood as taking their starting points in object-oriented and subject-oriented modes of inquiry, respectively. Mind-Only highlights the subjective orientations to a world; Madhyamaka undermines the finality of any object-ive world picture by highlighting the contingency of all object-ifying constructions. I show how these perspectives are mutually entailed, and thus can be seen to share a common ground.

I have struggled with how to convey these two orientations, for "Madhyamaka" and "Mind-Only," along with its closely allied "Yogācāra," are problematic and polysemic terms. Another alternative I considered was to represent the two orientations I aim to convey exclusively with the terms "ontology" and "phenomenology." Yet since this book is primarily rooted in Buddhist thought, rather than discuss Buddhist ideas solely in foreign terms imported from another culture, I opted to keep Buddhist terminology. Also, "phenomenology" is just as polysemic as Yogācāra, so it does not solve the dilemma in the end. I have also thought about this issue with another pair of terms, "constructivism" and "realism." While these terms are relevant to this topic, they both fall into ontological orientations, and both trajectories of thought I am concerned with participate in each side of a constructivist-realist dichotomy; they are not actually distinct, but intertwined. For these reasons, rather than introduce a neologism, I continue to use "Madhyamaka" and "Mind-Only," following the Tibetans, to flag two orientations of interpretation that are entangled in such a way that each one supplements the other.

After aligning the axis of this book around these two orientations, in the next three chapters, I touch on mind, language, and world as a loose thematic framework. I begin with a theory of mind and a closely paired notion—self-awareness (*svasaṃvedana*)—in chapter 3. I show that the status of self-awareness is a wedge issue between the descriptive ontology of Madhyamaka and the phenomenological orientation of Mind-Only. Awareness can be understood as Janus-faced; it does "double-duty" as subject and object, as internal and external. This hybrid structure sets the stage for what I call *objective idealism*—a world in which perceiver and perceived take place in an internal relation. With the term "objective idealism" I aim to represent how subject and object are simply polarities within a higher structure that transcends (and includes) this duality. While the language of substance and idealism is anathema to Madhyamaka, the interrelation of perceiver and perceived I wish to convey is not an ordinary subjective idealism; here there is no internal subject reigning over objects, the *relata* are not separate and relation itself is internal and not a real (external) relation. Thus, without an external world, there can be no internal world either (nor a world in between). The nonduality I seek to convey is not only the stuff of metaphysics, but also exemplifies the creative interplay of inner and outer worlds.

Chapter 4 turns to language. I show how many philosophical disputes revolve around linguistic disputes, prompted by competing conceptions of language. I also discuss the relation between concepts and percepts. Here again we can see the collapse of yet another dichotomy—like the one between ontology and phenomenology, subject and object—as percepts and concepts are interdependent. While a dichotomy of percepts and concepts is central to the epistemological edifice of proponents of Yogācāra such as the seventh-century Indian, Dharmakīrti, I show how this dichotomy falls apart in two main ways: conception collapses into perception (with nondual self-awareness in Mind-Only) and perception collapses into conception (with the thoroughgoing conceptuality of radical contingency and universal mediation emphasized in Madhyamaka). In both cases, we see the collapse of a percept-concept dichotomy, and language plays an important role in shaping both sides of this apparent divide.

In chapter 5 I consider the contemplative traditions of tantra. While mind (gnosis) and speech (mantra) are undoubtedly important in this context, too, here we also turn to the body (deity). The body, like speech and mind, exemplifies another intertwining, as it too is both perceiver and perceived. The body is the organ of the universe, the *flesh* of the world, and the dynamic substance of objective idealism. The objective idealism I have in mind here is not a simplistic notion of subjective idealism,[1] but the irreducibility of the relationally constituted whole. This nonduality is a dynamic unity that comprises everything—the uni-verse (one and many). It is not a static, metaphysical absolutism, but one that is participatory; it is enacted in the contemplative practices of tantra, as well as Mahāmudrā and the Great Perfection (*rdzogs chen*), the culmination and transcendence of Tibetan tantric traditions. These traditions can be seen as performances of this nonduality, fostering freedom through re-cognition and creative enaction, while undermining sedimentary, reified conceptions of mind and nature (that delimit and/or superimpose the way the world is and must be).

In four appendices I include translated excerpts from Tibetan texts that illustrate and expand upon some of the issues I raise in the chapters of this book. Each translation represents a distinctive tradition and genre of philosophical writing, and demonstrates to some extent the diversity and complexity of Buddhist philosophical literature. It is also noteworthy that all four of these texts represent a part of a living Buddhist culture; each of these texts can be found among texts currently studied and practiced in different Tibetan Buddhist communities across Asia today. This goes to show that the Tibetan Buddhist philosophy represented here is not only a vibrant and diverse tradition, but a living one, too.

In what follows, I take a broad view of what I see to be some of the most important philosophical issues at stake across Tibetan traditions, and try to avoid getting too bogged down within an exegesis on any particular tradition. This approach is admittedly ambitious and invites real dangers

1. On the difference between subjective and absolute idealisms, see Fredrick Beiser, *German Idealism: The Struggle Against Subjectivism, 1781–1801* (Cambridge: Harvard University Press, 2002), 370–372. For a discussion of "idealism" in Yogācāra, see Mario D'Amato, *Maitreya's Distinguishing the Middle from the Extremes* (New York: Columbia University Press, 2012), 20–23.

of overgeneralization (when fine-grained particularities are ignored) and superimposition (when personal preference overshadows an impartial description). Yet a thematic overview like this also can enable some insights into Tibetan forms of Buddhism that may not be visible when any single tradition is considered in isolation.

It is needless to mention that my interpretation of Buddhism is inflected by the European and American traditions I have inherited, but I should also acknowledge that the interpretation I offer here is influenced by the legacy of a nineteenth-century tradition stemming from eastern Tibet that has been called the "Gemang (*dge mang*) movement," named after the place where it flourished.[2] In contrast to an allegedly "nonsectarian movement" (*ris med*) that is antagonistic toward the Geluk tradition or incompatible with it, the Gemang movement is marked by an integration of Geluk and Nyingma (*rnying ma*) traditions of scholarship and practice in a way that they are configured to be mutually illuminating. That is to say, this Gemang tradition is neither tied to Geluk sectarianism nor to a sectarian identity built upon what is incompatible with the Geluk school. Rather, it is characterized by hybridity and integration, with an eye on practice.

While I try to steer away from adopting a single sectarian voice on Buddhist thought in this book, to a certain extent the "Gemang movement," like my academic training, has shaped the way I represent this subject matter. I acknowledge that the kind of hybrid tradition that informs my interpretation and methodology may be no more objective or value-free than any other; nevertheless, I believe (with Gadamer) that the influence of some tradition is necessary when any standpoint is taken on a subject matter. That said, contortions, distortions, and creations inevitably take place when a methodological lens is used to convey a domain of knowledge. It is my hope that what is enabled by my approach outweighs the problems that this methodology introduces.

In this book I aim to communicate important facets of Tibetan tradition neither by parroting it nor by standing over it with domineering academic hubris. Rather, my agenda is to convey a way to think about (and with) Tibetan Buddhist philosophy of mind and nature. In outlining these aspects of Buddhist thought, I do not censure my own perspectives on the material and also draw freely from a range of Indian, European, and

2. E. Gene Smith, *Among Tibetan Texts* (Boston: Wisdom Publications, 2001), 23–24.

American philosophical traditions to explain and elaborate key issues in Buddhist Tibet. To date there is no such overview of Tibetan philosophical culture, as most scholarly texts and translations of Tibetan thought are embedded within the structure of a particular sectarian tradition. I aim to provide an alternative way to access the subject matter so scholars and interested nonspecialists can relate to Tibetan thought outside the confines of a single sectarian voice or a one-dimensional philosophical stance. This book is intended as a bridge, both for Buddhists who seek to enrich their knowledge in conversation with Northwestern European and American philosophical traditions, and for those more familiar with these philosophical traditions to engage with Tibetan Buddhist thought.

Nonspecialists can use this book to gain a perspective on Tibetan philosophy, a place from which to find points of departure and threads of conversation from the intellectual worlds they inhabit. Specialists, on the other hand, can use this book to contextualize their particular areas of expertise. They may also feel compelled to highlight places that fall out of this frame, fill it out, or provide alternative frameworks to challenge or supplement the one I offer here. This book is a first step, not the last, to framing Tibetan Buddhism philosophically, and I hope readers will dig further into studies on topics that I outline here in broad strokes.

I

Between Construction and Immediacy

I pay homage to the best of speakers, the perfectly awakened one who taught dependent arising—the pacification of conceptual constructs—without ceasing or arising, not annihilated nor eternal, neither coming nor going, and neither different nor the same.

—NĀGĀRJUNA, prologue to *Fundamental Verses of the Middle Way* (*Mūlamadhyamakakārikā*)

Introduction

A key question in philosophy—and one that drives two predominant strands of Buddhist thought—is the question of immediacy: is there anything meaningful that is nonlinguistic and nonconceptual or is everything that is meaningful mediated by language and concepts? The way this question is answered is tied into fundamental assumptions about the world. Exposing these presuppositions is critical to the interpretation of key Buddhist notions such as emptiness and liberation. One interpretation stresses the ways in which every act of knowledge is mediated, and is vigilantly suspicious of ideas about nonconceptual content. Another highlights the centrality of nonconceptual content, foregrounding an unconstructed, nonconceptual ground within or upon which conceptions necessarily take place.

Buddhist philosophy falls on both sides along this spectrum (and in/between). On one end, emphasis is placed on the contexts in which concepts permeate experience, such that the status of reality is only ever conventional or contingent; there is no ultimate story about the reality we inhabit and *that* is the meaning of the ultimate truth—emptiness. At the other end, emphasis is placed on meditative contexts in which ultimate reality is known in a way that is inconceivable and not bound to any conceptual system; ultimate truth can be experienced, but is beyond thought. The difference between the two polarities of this spectrum is that an ultimate reality tends to be denied at one end whereas it is affirmed at the other. A contemporary analytic philosopher, Mark Siderits, aligns the latter interpretation with "realism," arguing that the distinction between these two interpretations is the difference between Yogācāra realism and Madhyamaka anti-realism:

> It is important to understand that the view that ultimate reality is beyond conceptualization is itself a variety of realism. From this it follows that the claim that there is no such thing as the ultimate nature of reality is not equivalent to the claim that reality is beyond conceptualization. The difference here is, I claim, just the difference between the Madhyamaka and the Yogācāra conceptions of emptiness.[1]

These competing interpretations of ultimate truth represent the views of Madhyamaka and Yogācāra.

The juncture between conceptuality and nonconceptuality is a point at which Mind-Only and Madhyamaka meet because this juncture is where the two truths (the relative and ultimate) diverge. Two roads can be taken at this juncture: one that embraces a nonconceptual ultimate and another that denies any concept as ultimate (or any concept of an ultimate). That is, two diverging interpretations of emptiness reflect what is at stake in the issues surrounding constructed versus unconstructed meaning, the nature of experience, and the possibilities and limits of knowledge. Although on the surface these two interpretations are diametrically opposed, this chapter probes the way they can be seen to share a deeper affinity or common ground between them, particularly when they are framed against the backdrop of the Buddhist contemplative practices in which they are embedded.

Emptying Emptiness

A central theme in Tibetan philosophy coalesces around two broad streams of interpretation—construction versus immediacy—which are reflected in

1. Mark Siderits, "Causation and Emptiness in Early Madhyamaka," *Journal of Indian Philosophy* 32 (2004): 414n6.

two ways of interpreting the import of ultimate truth. The tension between these two ways of relating to truth, as conceptually constituted (determinate all the way down) or nonconceptual at its core (undetermined and immediate), is reflected in conflicting interpretations of language, another issue that is relevant to this topic. The place of language in the constitution of meaning comes into clear focus when we consider the case of negation. In Buddhist thought, negations (like no-self) have a distinctive role in breaking through stultifying habits of mind, and Buddhists are masters of negation.

Emptiness is a prototypical negation. The ultimate truth of emptiness is at times described as a positive truth to be known, and at times an absence that is known only *via negativa*, that is to say, by knowing what is not. The difference between a contentful and contentless emptiness can be likened to the ways of knowing silence: as knowing the *presence* of silence as opposed to knowing the *absence* of sound. In the former sense, knowledge of emptiness can be said to be knowledge of an ineffable reality. In the latter, the content of knowledge is simply an absence. In both cases, ultimate knowledge of emptiness is not directly describable; yet paradoxically, it is through this knowledge that liberation is presumed a possibility for Buddhists.

An important point in understanding "emptiness" in Buddhism is that it does not simply mean nothingness. In fact, emptiness can carry many meanings. In addition to meaning simply a lack of intrinsic identity (*svabhāva*), it can also refer to the fact that things are intertwined, in the way that words and concepts are only ever abstracted from, or superimposed upon, a dynamically entangled and inexpressible matrix or field of reality. For instance, we may say (or think), "I am drinking tea." Yet when we try to discern any discrete element in this sentence (or reality), there is no individual part that can be said to have a real existence in isolation from the interrelated field. For instance, where or when is the action of "drinking"? Is it in the "already drank," the "moment of drinking" or the "yet to have drunk"? Where is the "I," the agent of the act of drinking separate from that action?[2] And how can a singular agent, or anything else, really exist separately from the multiple constituents of a changing process? As for "tea," there is no singular tea apart from water and leaves; it

2. For a parallel analysis regarding motion, see Nāgārjuna, *Fundamental Verses of the Middle Way* (*Madhyamakakārikā*), chapter II.

is a cultural product, not the underlying nature of reality. The underlying nature of reality is empty. Thinking that such things as "tea" or anything else exists otherwise, as more than abstractions or superimposition, is what the twentieth-century mathematician and philosopher, Alfred North Whitehead, called "the fallacy of misplaced concreteness,"[3] mistaking cultural products for an immediate and unconditioned nature. Reminiscent of Nāgārjuna's negation of intrinsic nature, Whitehead claimed:

> The misconception which has haunted philosophic literature throughout the centuries is the notion of "independent existence." There is no such mode of existence; every entity is only to be understood in terms of the way in which it is interwoven with the rest of the Universe.[4]

While seeming to represent the natural constitution of the world, concepts (like "tea") simultaneously distort and disclose. In other words, concepts disclose a window through which to see the world precisely by limiting possibilities (by delimiting boundaries). Yet the presumed boundaries—such as those between existence and nonexistence, self and other—are not natural categories but are contingent, conceptual constructions. Conceptual constructs allow for stories to be woven out of conceptual threads, but there are no hard and fast boundaries among the things that concepts shape. Concepts may seem to innocently and directly represent what is already there, yet they are always tied to a particular purpose or agenda, and have no independent reality outside of this matrix of relations.

The notion of emptiness constantly undermines any attempt to pin anything down (emptiness included). In one sense, it can work as a purgative, when the view of emptiness (along with all other views) is expelled together with the ignorance that it subverts. We might say in this case that "emptiness empties," reflecting (or prefiguring) Heidegger.[5] In another sense, the matrix of dependent relationships

---

3. See Whitehead, *Science and the Modern World* (Cambridge: Cambridge University Press, 2011), 64–70, 72.

4. Whitehead, "Immortality," in *The Philosophy of Alfred North Whitehead*, ed. Paul Schilpp (Evanston, Ill: Northwestern University Press, 1941), vol. 3, 687.

5. In his essay, "What Is Metaphysics?" Heidegger said, "the nothing nothings." See English translation in *Heidegger: Basic Writings*, ed. David Krell (New York: Harper & Row, 1977), 105. In his characteristically abstruse and provocative way, Heidegger also claimed that "science wants to know nothing of the nothing" (98).

that is the world itself can be understood as emptiness, signifying the indeterminate nature of any discrete thing. The meaning of dependent origination also involves the mind and language's inability to pin down anything with an intrinsic nature (*svabhāva*), a truly independent essence. The closer you look, the harder it is to determine what you are searching for. This is not only a problem that Heisenberg pointed to on the quantum level (with the uncertainty principle), but also pertains to any level of such analysis.

Moreover, relation is only possible when there are separate things, but since a single, independent identity fails as reality, relation does too. That is, relationships imply difference, and there can be no real difference (or sameness) when nothing has any real (independent) identity. Since things are not really separate, in the final analysis they cannot even be said to be related because a real, concrete relation implies at least two things and reality is not (even) one! In short, emptiness and interdependence cannot be reduced to any isolated component of a complex network of relations; the concept of emptiness is empty, and the concept of relationality is relational, too.

Emptiness Enframed and Unenframed

While there are many different interpretations of the import of emptiness among Buddhist traditions, for our purposes I will begin by outlining two, which I will refer to as the "enframed" and "unenframed" interpretations, respectively.[6] These two interpretations follow the distinct interpretations offered by Gorampa (1429–1489), an influential Sakya (*sa skya*) scholar, and Tsongkhapa (1357–1419), the forefather of the Geluk tradition.[7] These two figures represent two prominent streams of Madhyamaka thought in Tibet. In order to introduce the difference between their interpretations, I will use the logical form of the tetralemma—the four alternatives of existence, nonexistence, both, and neither—as a model. Framing negation through the four alternatives of the tetralemma is a device that is

6. The "enframed" and "unenframed" interpretations of emptiness are further discussed in Douglas Duckworth, "Madhyamaka in Tibet: Thinking Through the Ultimate Truth," *Critical Review of Buddhist Studies* 20 (2016): 171–197.

7. For a discussion of the difference between these two interpreters on the negation of the tetralemma, see Constance Kassor, "Gorampa Sonam Senge on the Refutation of the Four Extremes," *Revue d'Etudes Tibétaines* 22 (2011): 121–137.

commonly used to express the meaning of emptiness, and two trajectories of interpretation come into clear focus when we consider the interpretations of emptiness in this way.

I will first lay out the unenframed interpretation, which directly challenges the ability of a conceptual or linguistic system to adequately account for emptiness. Then I will describe the "enframed" interpretation, which seeks to forge an interpretative structure within which emptiness can be clearly apprehended and described. This distinctive feature of the enframed interpretation clearly contrasts with the unenframed interpretation, for which emptiness acts as a purgative and all attempts of systematic enframement within the structures of language and concepts fail.

The negation of the first lemma is a negation of existence. As the first negation, this is the most important, particularly given the fact that for Buddhists, holding on to reified notions of things like selves is what binds us to suffering. Thus, the denial of the true existence of such things is paramount. It is significant that the denial of the first lemma of existence is effectively the same in both the enframed and unenframed interpretations of negation. This is a shared feature despite the differences in what are otherwise divergent interpretations.

To deny existence in the context of an ontological analysis in Madhyamaka is to deny that there is an intrinsic identity in things. As Śāntarakṣita, the eighth-century scholar who visited Tibet from India, begins the verses of his *Ornament of the Middle Way*: "All entities—asserted by Buddhists or otherwise—lack intrinsic nature because ultimately they are neither one nor many, like a reflection."[8] When anything is analyzed in terms of its essence, there is nothing singular, independent, or enduring found at all. Thus, everything is said to lack intrinsic nature, appearing like an illusion, reflection, or a dream.

In the negation of the second lemma, it is not just existence, but nonexistence is denied as well. In the unenframed interpretation, this is because things are not simply nonexistent; they are not really nonexistent either. In other words, the denial of nonexistence means that nonexistence is no more real than existence, as Nāgārjuna said, "If the existent is not established, then the nonexistent is not established either."[9] The fact that nonexistence is denied is one reason why Madhyamaka is not a nihilistic

---

8. Śāntarakṣita, *Ornament of the Middle Way* (*Madhyamakālaṃkāra*), v. 1.

9. Nāgārjuna, *Fundamental Verses of the Middle Way*, XV.5.

view that embraces the reality of nonexistence. Illustrating this denial with an example, Śāntideva, the eighth-century Indian author of the celebrated *Way of the Bodhisattva*, stated, "Thus, when a child dies in a dream, the thought 'he does not exist' counteracts the thought that he does exist, but it too is false."[10] In other words, a dream where the child you never had dies is not a real child's death: if a child (existence) was never really born, there is never a real death (nonexistence), either.

This denial of nonexistence overcomes metaphysical nihilism, countering the tendency toward reification for those who substantialize the "reality" of nonexistence. The Indian philosopher Candrakīrti (*ca.* 7th c.) illustrated this with a wonderful example of a man who went to a store where the storekeeper said, "We have nothing for sale," and is met with the customer's response, "Give me some of that 'nothing!' "[11] The denial of the second lemma deflects a tendency to reify emptiness into some kind of thesis of metaphysical absence, as nihilists and essentialists are prone to do. Indeed, "the extreme of nonexistence" is just as bad as "the extreme of existence"; in fact it is worse. As Saraha, the eighth-century Indian master, is alleged to have said, "To hold on to things as real is to be stupid like a cow. To hold on to things as unreal is to be even more stupid!"[12]

The denial of the third lemma undermines the idea that things are *both* existent and nonexistent, for if each conjunct has been negated individually, the conjunction fails too. Simply stated, if something is not existent nor is it nonexistent, then you can't have it both ways; it is not both. Yet we may wonder, is the law of noncontradiction, that something cannot be both A and not A, a feature of a system of logic (a mere cultural product) or reality? Different answers to this question are found in competing interpretations of the negation of the fourth lemma, *not either*.

The denial of the fourth lemma, that of neither existence nor nonexistence, can be seen as simply a restatement of each of the former denials (as we will see in the enframed interpretation) and is consistent with the (presumably) invariable rules of a classical logic (like the law of noncontradiction). It can also be taken to be a repudiation of the whole structure of the conceptual and linguistic project, rendering it doomed from the start

---

10. Śāntideva, *Way of the Bodhisattva* (*Bodhicaryāvatāra*), IX.141.

11. Candrakīrti, *Clear Words* (*Prasannapadā*) commentary on *Fundamental Verses of the Middle Way*, XIII.8 (D. 3860, vol. 102), 83b.

12. Kongtrül, *Encyclopedia of Knowledge* (Beijing: Nationalities Press, 2002), 144.

by pointing to the false premises upon which the very notions of existence and nonexistence rest. This latter (unenframed) interpretation points to the way that language is fundamentally inhabited by reifying distortions, specifically when static essences are presumed to be the referents of linguistic signs. That is to say, the denial of neither shows that the notion of *neither* existence nor nonexistence suffers from a presupposition failure, a vacuous premise, just like the death of the dream-child denied in the second lemma. The negation is like a denial of wife-beating when asked, "Have you stopped beating your wife?" The denial presupposes an unwanted premise embedded within the question—that you did beat your wife (or that you even have a wife). Yet without presupposing the reality of existence or nonexistence (or wives or wife-beating), there is nothing really that a denial of either could be. The limits of language and extra-linguistic reality are issues at stake here, and the unenframed interpretation highlights the contingent and distorting ways of language and concepts.

In contrast to the "unenframed interpretation" sketched above, we find another interpretation of negation in the tetralemma articulated in the Geluk tradition inspired by Tsongkhapa.[13] Rather than appealing to the nature of reality as nonconceptual, the "enframed interpretation" appeals to the power of thought. It thus represents the function of negation in the tetralemma differently, whereby the negation of existence and nonexistence toggles between two parameters of value: ultimate and conventional. That is to say, the negation of existence is the negation of *ultimate* existence (the idea that things exist really or ultimately is negated); the negation of nonexistence is the negation of *conventional* nonexistence (the idea that things like cups and tables do not exist at all, even conventionally, is negated); the negation of both is simply a restatement of the first two lemmas (the idea that things both ultimately exist and conventionally do not exist is negated); and the negation of neither reiterates this again (the idea that things neither ultimately do not exist nor conventionally exist is negated). In this way, rather than imploding the system by appealing to language and thought's inability to adequately represent reality, the enframed interpretation appeals to their *ability*, in terms of formulating a clearly delimited meaning of emptiness: the lack, or nonexistence, of *ultimate* existence; and a clear delineation of existence: existence means *conventional* existence.

---

13. On Tsongkhapa's interpretation of negation in the tetralemma, see Thupten Jinpa, *Self, Reality and Reason in Tibetan Philosophy* (London: RoutledgeCurzon, 2002), 38–41.

The enframed interpretation uses reason as a tool to construct a system rather than just to deconstruct; it empowers language and thought to clearly convey the meaning of emptiness. In other words, in an enframed interpretation, there is no denial of the whole conceptual framework. Rather, another register of conceptual meaning—conventional existence—is carved out to account for the (empty/illusory) world. Thus, the parameters *conventionally* and *ultimately* are added to assertions of (conventional) existence and (ultimate) nonexistence, and the contradiction of affirming both existence and nonexistence is avoided. Moreover, in this interpretation a view is clearly asserted: to exist is to exist *conventionally*. Emptiness, too, is a thesis about the ultimate nature of reality: nothing *ultimately* exists and emptiness is *conventionally* existent (just like this thesis, and any other existent thing for that matter, is *conventionally* existent). Thus, it represents a clear system of truth.

The four lemmas—is, is not, is both, is neither—are all negated in Madhyamaka, but the import of the negations of the second (not nonexistent) and fourth (not either) lemmas, in the two distinct enframed and unenframed interpretations in particular, exemplifies a pivotal moment in Buddhist theory and practice. These competing interpretations mark the boundary between conceptually framed and nonconceptual interpretations of meaning. That is to say, the different ways that "not nonexistent" and "not either" are interpreted—as conceptually bound denials and/or as an indictment on the entire conceptual project—rest on different understandings of the extension of negation and the function of language in the disclosure of nonconceptual meaning. We will consider further the implications of these interpretations of emptiness next.

Emptiness as Performative and Propositional

Negations and paradoxes crop up in moments of self-reference, when language and minds turn on themselves at their limits, such as we see in attempts to understand and articulate what is inconceivable and inexpressible.[14] Such paradoxes reveal important facets of the nature of language, mind, and world. Consider the case of the predication of the impredicable, for instance, as in the statement "Brahman is impredicable." Nāgārjuna's

14. See Graham Priest, *Beyond the Limits of Thought* (Oxford: Oxford University Press, 2002); Bimal Krishna Matilal, "Mysticism and Ineffability: Some Issues of Logic and Language," in *Mysticism and Language*, ed. Steven Katz (Oxford: Oxford University Press, 1992), 154–155.

infamous thesis in *Dispelling Disputes*, "I have no thesis,"[15] exemplifies this principle as well. Are such statements meaningless (or perhaps deceptively meaningful), or only meaningful statements within certain parameters (e.g., "I have no *truly existent* or ultimate thesis—but this is a *conventional* claim")? Or, are these statements meaningful in a way that they express what goes beyond direct reference?

A relevant point here is the distinction between a non-implicative negation (*med dgag, prasajya-pratiṣedha*) and an implicative negation (*ma yin dgag, paryudāsa*). Non-implicative negations do not imply anything else in their denial of linguistic meaning; they merely point to absence. Period. An example of a non-implicative negation is "Don't drink and drive." Nothing more is implied here other than a negation. Implicative negations, in contrast, implicate something else beyond what is explicitly stated, for example, "That fat boy never eats during the day," which implies something unsaid: that he eats at night.

A non-implicative negation has been defined as an explicit negation that does not implicate any phenomena by dint of the negation.[16] In the influential Geluk tradition of Tibet, this kind of negation is the ultimate truth of emptiness, which is an absence of intrinsic existence. In contrast, emptiness in Mind-Only-inspired contemplative traditions, such as the Jonang (*jo nang*), are often said to be implicative negations, since what an ultimate negation implies is not simply an absence, but what is beyond the mind.[17] If a negation implies a phenomenon, or any idea like "nonduality," "unity," or "wholeness," it is an implicative negation. The import of a non-implicative negation, in contrast, is *only* negation.

The distinction between these two types of negation frames two broad trajectories of Buddhist philosophy in Tibet. One side can be represented by the Madhyamaka tradition of the Geluk school, for which the ultimate truth of emptiness is interpreted as only a non-implicative negation. The other side is represented by Mind-Only and Yogācāra-inflected traditions in

---

15. Nāgārjuna, *Dispelling Disputes* (*Vigrahavyāvartanī*), v. 29: "If I had a thesis, I would have fault; since I have no thesis, I am only faultless."

16. See Tsongkhapa, *Thoroughly Illuminating the Viewpoint* (*dgongs pa rab gsal*) (Xining, China: Nationalities Press, 1998), 536; Künzang Sönam, *Overview of the Wisdom Chapter: A Lamp Completely Illuminating the Profound Reality of Interdependence*, in Tupten Chödrak (Beijing, China: China's Tibet Publishing House, 2007 [1993]), 802.

17. See, for instance, Dölpopa, *Ocean of Definitive Meaning*, 88; see also Duckworth, *Mipam on Buddha-Nature: The Ground of the Nyingma Tradition* (Albany, NY: SUNY Press, 2008), 58–59.

Tibet, as found in the Kagyü (*bka' brgyud*) and certain strands of Nyingma (*rnying ma*). Another important Tibetan school is the Sakya, yet since there is a lot of diversity within this school (as is the case with the others as well), I do not think it is helpful to chart them here monolithically. Also, since this book is structured around philosophical issues and not sectarian traditions, I do not feel it is helpful or necessary to feign comprehensiveness (the internal dynamics within Tibetan schools are complex), nor do I think it is helpful to draw lines between philosophies with direct correspondences to sectarian identities.[18]

In any case, negation (as in no-self or emptiness) has an important role to play in all Buddhist traditions. Despite the important role of absence in the Geluk tradition, emptiness—the absence of essence—does not refer to total negation in this tradition, but refers in particular to the negation of the *ultimate* status of any phenomenon. That is, conventional phenomena are denied existence ultimately, not conventionally. Significantly, in this interpretation the denial of self, too, does not mean the denial of the "mere self" (*bdag tsam*) or the conventionally existent self.[19] The mere self (trimmed away of metaphysical baggage or reification) is unapologetically affirmed in the Geluk tradition. That is, the characteristically Buddhist denial of self is interpreted to refer only to mistaken conceptions of self—such as that of a permanent, singular, or truly existing entity—not the self *simpliciter*. The mere self, like the *mere* table or chair (i.e., the table or chair apprehended without the overlay of true existence), is unequivocally claimed to exist. Conventional existence, what "makes sense" within a pre-theoretical, transactional world, is never negated. To negate it is nihilism. Rather, it is the reification of true existence that is to be negated.

All Tibetan Buddhist traditions claim to represent "the middle way" of Madhyamaka between the two extremes, yet they do so in quite different ways. In presentations of Madhyamaka, emptiness is commonly said to undermine the extreme of existence, while appearance is said to

18. Consider, for instance, the wide differences between the views of Gorampa, Śākya Chokden, and Taktsang, all associated with the Sakya school in the fifteenth century. A similar range of views can be found in other schools, across historical periods and places. The spectrum is vast. We can see this when we consider the differences between Rangjung Dorjé and Mikyö Dorjé, for instance, in the Karma Kagyü school; Rongzom, Longchenpa, Dampa Deshek, Khenpo Pemavajra, and Dodrupchen Tenpé Nyima in the Nyingma; Dölpopa, Bamda Gelek, and Tsoknyi Gyatso in the Jonang; the Fifth Dalai Lama and Pabongka, etc. in the Geluk. For this reason, I find it more helpful to organize this book thematically in terms of philosophical ideas rather than in terms of schools.

19. Jinpa, *Self, Reality and Reason in Tibetan Philosophy*, 71.

undermine the extreme of nonexistence. Yet Tsongkhapa says just the opposite in his *Three Principal Aspects of the Path*: "Appearance eliminates the extreme of existence and emptiness eliminates the extreme of nonexistence."[20] This conveys that appearance simply means conventional appearances (without intrinsic nature) for Tsongkhapa; thus, appearance eliminates (reified) existence. As for emptiness, it eliminates the extreme of nonexistence because it does not mean anything like the total denial of appearance. Rather, emptiness means simply the lack of intrinsic existence. Thus, the extreme of nonexistence is eliminated by this kind of emptiness (not an emptiness that is a mere, unqualified void or simply a lack of concepts). Outlining his interpretation of Candrakīrti, Tsongkhapa said:

> The glorious Candrakīrti distinguished between essential existence and existence, he also distinguished between essential nonexistence and nonexistence. Until you understand this, you will no doubt fall into both extremes, and thus will not know the meaning of Madhyamaka free from extremes.[21]

Here Tsongkhapa makes a distinction between *essential* existence and existence, suggesting the way that *essential* existence (and *essential* nonexistence) is the reified type, whereas *mere* nonexistence (phenomena's lack of true nature) and *mere* existence (phenomena without true nature) are affirmed.

In contrast to the certain parameters delimited in Tsongkhapa's interpretation, metaphor, or suggestion, plays a prominent role in other (e.g., Yogācāra) interpretations of emptiness. In particular, suggestion is explicitly at play in the interpretation of emptiness as an implicative negation, a negation that implies something else. Unlike abstract, propositional denials, emptiness here can create trajectories of thought that resonate with nondenotable meanings, negative statements that boast the power to signify the impossible—transcendence, otherness. That is, this metaphorical usage of language is like a work of art in that it can open up worlds through evoking

---

20. Tsongkhapa, *Three Principal Aspects of the Path* (*lam gyi gtso bo rnam gsum*), 7 (Xining, China: *sku 'bum byams pa gling*, 2001).

21. Tsongkhapa, *Great Exposition of the Stages of the Path* (Xining, China: Nationalities Press, 2000), 594–595; English trans. adapted from Joshua W. C. Cutler (ed.), *The Great Treatise on the Stages of the Path to Enlightenment*, vols. 1–3 (Ithaca, NY: Snow Lion Publications, 2000–2004), 142–143.

meaning. In a significant way, metaphors do not simply re-present; they dis-close. They do not only work within the closures of presumptions; they also function to disrupt and transcend them. Thereby, they can transform and disclose not just *objects* of reference but *ways* of relating to the world.

In this light, negations not only are taken to determine absence, but are also interpreted to have a potential to point beyond the linguistic system. This radical function of language opens the semantic range of ultimate truth beyond the notion of a predetermined absence. Relating to language in this way, as we see in Mahāmudrā or the Great Perfection, enables a bypass of conceptually delimited significance, with the import that neither a positive thing nor an absence is held in mind as a result. As Mipam (1846–1912) says in his *Beacon of Certainty*, a work of philosophical poetry that integrates elements of Madhyamaka with the Great Perfection:

> Since gnosis transcends the mind,
> It is inconceivable by an extrinsic thought.
> Since it is not an object of language or thought
> There is no partiality for non-implicative negations or implicative negations,
> Difference, appearance or emptiness, etc.[22]

And furthermore:

> From the perspective of the great gnosis of unity,
> The elimination of the object of negation by "nonexistent"
> Implies neither a mere existential absence (*med*) nor a predicative negation (*ma yin*)—
> What other phenomenon is there to imply by negation?
> Both of these are merely mental imputations;
> I assert neither as the [consummate] meaning.[23]

He argues that the ultimate meaning of emptiness is nonconceptual, going beyond not only expressions that are affirmations, but both kinds of negations as well. Some recent Tibetan commentators have described the

22. Mipam, *Beacon of Certainty* (*'ju mi pham rgya mtsho*, 1846–1912), *nges shes sgron me rtsa 'grel* (Sichuan: Nationalities Press, 1997), 49; see also Duckworth, *Mipam on Buddha-Nature*, 86.

23. Mipam, *Beacon of Certainty*, 5; see also Duckworth, *Mipam on Buddha-Nature*, 87.

distinction between two interpretations of emptiness by making a distinction between two types of non-implicative negation: (1) a non-implicative negation that is free from one extreme, the extreme of existence, and (2) a non-implicative negation that is free from all extremes.[24] The latter more fully represents the indeterminate (or undetermined) meaning of emptiness, which is not solely an absence of true existence, but is free from all conceptual frameworks (existence, nonexistence, both, and neither). Others have shown this distinction to be between two types of freedom from constructs: (1) a freedom from constructs that is a non-implicative negation and (2) a *genuine* freedom from constructs (that is beyond all constructs of negation, affirmation, and so on).[25] The latter shows the radical nature of emptiness, which is not even a non-implicative negation.

A negation can be seen to be no different from an affirmation, as the inversion of an affirmation that simply functions as a negative proposition rather than a positive one. Yet another way of interpreting a negation is as an activity, a performance. That is, to negate is not simply to *say* something, but to *do* something. As an activity of denial, a negation can open new vistas of reality by disclosing something—like a background or frame—that is not directly representable by any kind of proposition. This function of language, as showing and *presenting* rather than denoting, reflects an important dimension of Buddhist discourses on ultimate truth.[26] In particular it conveys a (nonconceptual) mode of

---

24. Khenpo Namdröl (*mkhan po rnam grol*, b. 1953) stated this in a recorded oral commentary on Mipam's *Beacon of Certainty*.

25. Khenpo Chökhyap (*chos dbyings khyab brdal*, 1920–1997) stated this in a recorded oral commentary on *Distinguishing the Views and Philosophies*, a text composed by his teacher, Bötrül (1898–1959).

26. For instance, Mipam describes the role of thought and language in relation to the experience of the ultimate as follows: "Since there is no language or thought that *directly* engages the ultimate, it is not a direct object of language or thought. As is taught, the ultimate is beyond demonstration and analogy. However, language and thoughts can engage the ultimate *indirectly* because it is appropriate to perceive the ultimate through the power of an act of meditation that evokes the certainty of the meaning of the ineffable nature of the distinctive self-awareness gained through the scriptures and reasons that ascertain the nonconceptual ultimate." Mipam, *Shedding Light on Thusness*, in *spyod 'jug sher 'grel ke ta ka* (Sichuan: Nationalities Press, 1993), 382. In an appeal to the ultimate as an experience, Mipam describes the words such as "basic nature," "self-existing gnosis," "perfection of wisdom," "ultimate," etc. as simply a gateway for entering the nameless basic nature, which itself is beyond words and solely what is known through self-awareness. He addresses objections to the status of what is inexpressible being expressed by saying that such a view is like seeing the tip of the finger that points to the moon, but not seeing the moon. See Mipam, *Shedding Light on Thusness*, 423–424.

meditative understanding. Further, both kinds of negation (implicative and non-implicative), and affirmations, can function in this performative way: when what is implied by language is not an object, but a *way* an object is to be encountered—a mode of subjectivity or receptivity—that is evoked by words or signs.[27]

In this light, to deny the self need not always be to affirm no-self, particularly when the denial is interpreted as performative and not propositional. Yet when emptiness is understood solely as a proposition, divorced from its performative dimensions, it can become programmatic and doctrinal—Buddhist dogma. As simply a proposition—a static, determinate truth that one is only to capture and pin down, certify and quantify—emptiness can become reduced to an object of conquest, an object that cannot be an indeterminate mystery, an open horizon of possibilities, or something to which one is to attune. Emptiness, as simply an *object* of knowledge, can also become a sterile statement of the truth of the world.

Yet emptiness not only evokes some *thing* to be known but can include and impel an orientation to the world, which includes a performative, phenomenological dimension. Emptiness in this light, inclusive of an orientation, encompasses embodied participation and cognitive comportment toward the world. It can be akin to knowledge of the environment or nature; that is to say, it is not known as something one can stand apart from and observe in a "spectatorial epistemology," but only (and necessarily) can be seen from within it.[28] Here we can see why emptiness can be understood not simply as a propositional or representational truth, but as what calls for attunement and performance. Also, knowing emptiness in this way entails transformation.[29]

An important point here is that meaning need not be solely denotative or object-oriented. Rather, the sense of words like "emptiness" and "mind-nature" can move beyond objective referents and point to a participatory encounter, in a way similar to what Paul Ricoeur has suggested by the

---

27. For further discussion of this topic, see Duckworth, "Onto-theology and Emptiness: The Nature of Buddha-Nature," *Journal of the American Academy of Religion* 82, no. 4 (2014): 1070–1090.

28. See John Wylie, *Landscape* (New York: Routledge, 2007), 145–149.

29. For further discussion of this issue, see Duckworth, "Non-Representational Language in Mipam's Re-presentation of Other-Emptiness," *Philosophy East & West* 64, no. 4 (2014): 920–932.

"non-ostensive reference" or "depth semantics" of a text.[30] In such a case, meaning is found in modes of subjectivity—or interactions—rather than being hooked up to static referents or essences "out there." In this light, meaning is not "out there," nor is it inside, but it lies in the interactions of mind, language, and world. In the following chapters, we will unpack the meaning of this in more detail.

Conclusion

For Buddhists in Tibet, the ultimate truth is understood to be emptiness, but the meaning of emptiness is interpreted in different ways. It can be understood as a statement about reality, the undermining of any statements about reality, and/or a way of attuning to reality. Thus, the ultimate truth in Buddhism has been interpreted with different emphases, as an inconceivable nature of reality (e.g., Yogācāra) or as an absence of intrinsic nature (e.g., Madhyamaka). However it is interpreted, knowledge of the ultimate truth is important for Buddhists because it undermines ignorance, the source of suffering.

This chapter began with a discussion of emptiness and introduced two broad streams of interpretation of the import of negation, the "enframed" and "unenframed" interpretations. The enframed interpretation emphasizes the value of language and thought in the discovery of ultimate truth, while the unenframed interpretation emphasizes the way that language and thought impede this discovery. Both interpretations claim to represent the view of Madhyamaka, the middle way between the extremes of essentialism and nihilism.

The Geluk tradition of Madhyamaka emphasizes the interpretation of emptiness as an absence of true existence. In this school, in an important sense, a statement of emptiness is a true statement about the world. We can see how emptiness plays a role as a proposition in this tradition, yet

30. See Paul Ricoeur, *Interpretation Theory: Discourse and the Surplus of Meaning* (Fort Worth: Texas University Press, 1976), 87. For a further discussion on differences between modern conceptions of knowledge and Buddhism, see Duckworth, "Echoes of Tsültrim Lodrö: An Indigenous Voice from Contemporary Tibet on the 'Buddhism and Science Dialogue,'" *Journal of Contemporary Buddhism* 16, no. 2 (2015), 7–8.

its meaning is also participatory and performative, since the meaning of emptiness is to be cultivated through meditation, which leads to transformation. In Mind-Only and Yogācāra-inflected traditions like the Kagyü and Nyingma, the experiential or phenomenological dimension of emptiness is emphasized, whereby emptiness is inclusive of a participatory (or cognitive) orientation and is not typically framed as an object or solely the (object-ive) nature of things. Here, we often find interpretations of emptiness contrasted with its meaning held as merely a conceptual or propositional truth.

Yet depending on the particular context—describing or evoking a meditative equipoise on emptiness, for oneself or for another—we find both kinds of interpretation, propositional and performative, in play in both Madhyamaka and Yogācāra trajectories of interpretation in Tibet, across different Buddhist traditions such as the Geluk, Sakya, Kagyü, and Nyingma. Thus, rather than thinking of Tibetan Buddhist philosophy as a spectrum of views, perhaps a better metaphor is a circle, such that the ends of the spectrum, which take different points of departure, come back around and meet each other. The image of a circle illustrates the way that both trajectories share a common orbit or common ground. I will address the issue of this complementarity further in a discussion of the relationship between Mind-Only and Madhyamaka in the next chapter.

2

Nonduality of Madhyamaka and Yogācāra

Kāśyapa, the mind is not inside nor is it outside. It is not in both nor is it observed. Kāśyapa, the mind is formless, indemonstrable, unobstructed.

—SŪTRA OF THE KĀŚYAPA CHAPTER (*Kāśyapaparivartasūtra*)

Introduction

This chapter introduces the ways that different interpretations of emptiness relate to the intertwined domains of ontology (what is) and phenomenology (how things appear). I will begin by discussing how a fusion of ontology (the structure of reality) and phenomenology (the structure of experience) comes into play in the traditions of Madhyamaka and Mind-Only, which will lead into a discussion (in chapters 4 and 5) of how each of these traditions plays a significant role in shaping the philosophical foundations of major contemplative practices that flourished in Tibet.

It can be helpful to broadly outline two forms of analyses in Mahāyāna Buddhism, ontological and phenomenological. Ontological arguments characterize Madhyamaka's focus on the deconstruction of essence. These arguments are oriented toward objects, that is, they take a circumscribed object as a site of analysis and attempt to determine (and thereby undermine) the ontological status of that object. Phenomenological analyses, in contrast, are emphasized in Mind-Only, as well as in traditions of the "Great Perfection" and the "Great Seal" (Mahāmudrā). These types of inquiry are oriented toward the experiential dimension of a subject rather than objects, and purport to lead a subject into a different orientation beyond (enframed) objective and even subjective orientations. In other words, Buddhist phenomenological analyses are concerned with ways of relating to experience, whereas ontological analyses aim to determine, and undermine, the status of objects.

Phenomenology is supposedly not concerned with ontology; that is to say, phenomenological analyses putatively address not what is, but what appears. Brentano even referred to the object of mind as *inexistent*, which purportedly avoids commitment to an ontological status of objects existing or not.[1] In contrast to ontological analyses, phenomenology is geared toward the way we experience the world. Phenomenology does not delimit the semantic range of truth to mental ideas, or representations, as is the case with object-oriented analyses. It is primarily an inquiry into the nature of subjectivity and experience rather than being saddled to only object-ifying analysis. When ontological questions of existence are left out, Mind-Only can be understood as a phenomenological inquiry.

Ontology and Phenomenology

The following two ways of relating to the mind characterize the distinctive ways of framing the world ontologically and phenomenologically: relating to the mind as an object and relating to the mind as a subject. Treated as an object, the mind is just like everything else; in the Buddhist context it is empty because its essence is not discoverable upon looking for it. Also, the mind as an object does not have a privileged status among entities. The mind is fully dependent upon other objects for its existence in a way that is no different from the way that objects are dependent on the mind (and each other) for their existence. In this light, the mind exists, just like conventional objects, merely as an imputed entity abstracted from a matrix of interrelations.

In phenomenology, by contrast, the mind as *subject* is ascribed a unique status. As constitutive of an experiential, lived reality, the mind is an irreducible part of the world. As a non-object or non-thing, the realm of the mind or the mental constitutes the phenomenal character and qualitative perspective unique to subjects of experience. Subjectivity here is unique, and not even unique among things because it is not taken as a thing. It is not a *thing* because it is precisely the opposite of an objectified thing, and it

1. See Franz Brentano, *Psychology from an Empirical Standpoint* (New York: Routledge, 1995 [1874]), 68–69.

cannot be reduced to a thing because it is integral to the structure by which things are known.

Awareness cannot be reduced to an object (in phenomenology *not* ontology) because it is fundamentally different in nature. It is not different in its nature in terms of what is absent (intrinsic reality understood as essence) but is different in terms of what is present (the lived or living dimension). In this sense, awareness has (or rather is) intrinsic nature, just not an intrinsic essence that can be adequately conceived; it must be lived in or through, as a contemporary phenomenologist, Evan Thompson, states: "Consciousness is something we live, not something we have."[2]

In contrast to a distinctively phenomenological analysis, the weight of ontological analyses falls on objects. Through the ontological analyses of Madhyamaka, all objects are determined to be empty, or stated otherwise, all phenomena are determined to be indeterminate. While this kind of ontological analysis is a powerful tool to undercut reification, the role of the subject, or awareness, in these kinds of analysis is treated in the same way as an object. This kind of impartiality—that treats all phenomena the same way—gives arguments explanatory power but also limits their import. It gives arguments power because the mind is not given a privileged place; everything without exception is subjected to a deconstructive analysis and is determined to be empty. However, awareness is not an object, or not *just* an object, and this presents a challenge to the universality of ontological analyses, for treating awareness as an object is arguably making a category mistake. Mistaking the nature of the subject as an object is not simply a mistake that is on the order of mixing apples and oranges, but of taking infinity as a geometric object. Apples and oranges are both fruit, yet while infinity *can* be treated as a geometric object, it is not *just* a geometric object, and it also is not *only* that object. In the same way, subjectivity *can* be treated like an object (as in Madhyamaka ontological analyses), but it is not delimited solely by such analysis.

Just as a stance that ignores the world of subjects can be a powerful tool to provide a new lens on the world (as in the case of the methodology of scientific realism to overcome subjective prejudices), a stance that "brackets" the world of objects can be a powerful lens on the world, too (by overcoming prejudices about object-ivity, that is, preconceptions about objects). This is the appeal of phenomenology. Although the analyses of

---

2. Evan Thompson, *Waking, Dreaming, Being: Self and Consciousness in Neuroscience, Meditation, and Philosophy* (New York: Columbia University Press, 2015), 100.

phenomenology are purported to be simply about experience, devoid of the trappings of ontology and metaphysics, are they really? This is a central question that comes up in philosophy, Buddhist or otherwise.

As an integral part of experience, the cognitive dimension of reality can be acknowledged to be an ontological reality in addition to a phenomenological one. By making a move to ontology by affirming the ultimacy of nondual gnosis, for instance, Mind-Only or Yogācāra theories are commonly accused by Mādhyamikas of reifying the mind and asserting a form of subjective idealism.[3] Yogācāra can be seen to blend ontology into phenomenology in a position stigmatized as the "Mind-Only" philosophical system (*grub mtha'*), as proponents of Yogācāra are charged with being nihilists about the "mere" world of appearing objects and being essentialists about mind.[4] The inverse of this problem has been directed at the Geluk interpretation of Madhyamaka: they have been accused of being essentialist about conventionally existent objects and nihilist about ultimate reality.[5] When you fall from the middle way to one extreme (of nihilism or essentialism regarding the conventional or ultimate truths), you tend to fall to both.

An important distinction to be made in phenomenology is between an idealist position that reifies a subjective pole of experience and a position that sees the subjective pole as simply a component in a dynamically interconnected structure. This is a distinction between subjective idealism on the one hand, and nonduality or interdependence (objective idealism) on the other. The distinction is important for phenomenological traditions, and for Mind-Only as well.

---

3. See, for instance, Mipam, *Overview: Essential Nature of Luminous Clarity*, in *bka' brgyad rnam bshad dang spyi don 'od gsal snying po yang dag grub pa'i tshig 'grel bcas bzhugs* (Sichuan: Nationalities Press, 2000), 407. See also Douglas Duckworth, *Mipam on Buddha-Nature: The Ground of the Nyingma Tradition* (Albany, NY: SUNY Press, 2008), 46.

4. See, for instance, Künzang Sönam, *Overview of the Wisdom Chapter*, 697.

5. For instance, Gorampa characterized Tsongkhapa's position on the Middle Way as "nihilism" (*chad mtha'*). Gorampa, *Distinguishing the Views* (*lta ba'i shan 'byed*), (Sarnath: Sakya Students' Union, 1988), 3; English translation in José Cabezón and Geshe Lobsang Dargyay, *Freedom from Extremes: Gorampa's "Distinguishing the Views" and the Polemics of Emptiness* (Boston: Wisdom Publications, 2007). Changkya Rolpé Dorjé (*lcang skya rol pa'i rdo rje*, 1717–1786) criticized his own Geluk Madhyamaka tradition for a tendency toward essentialism regarding the conventional truth in his *Song of the View*; see Changkya's text with Mipam's commentary in Mipam, [*Commentary on Changkya's*] *"Song of the View"* (*lta ba'i mgur ma*), *Mipam's Collected Works*, vol. 4 (*pa*), 838–839; English translation of Changkya's text with Mipam's commentary in Karl Brunnhölzl, *Straight from the Heart: Buddhist Pith Instructions* (Ithaca: Snow Lion Publications, 2007), 409–410.

I wish to argue that Mind-Only is not necessarily a form of subjective idealism. For a subjective idealist, mind is necessary whereas objects are contingent. A realist, however, presuming a mind-independent world, claims just the opposite: that the mind is contingent whereas objective reality is necessary. In Madhyamaka, both subject and object are equally contingent, being dependent upon each other; as Candrakīrti said, "Just as knowable objects do not exist, the mind does not exist, either."[6] In contrast, Mind-Only traditions highlight that there can be no contemplation of objects without awareness.[7]

When read strictly as subjective idealism (as in the philosophical system), Mind-Only is not so interesting, as it invites the well-known problems of solipsism and lacks a workable ethical dimension. Other readings, such as objective idealism, are more consistent with a Buddhist ethos of interdependence and can also provide a viable framework for ethics. Objective idealism is clearly distinct from subjective idealism, for subjective idealism collapses objects into a subject. In contrast to the dualistic framework implicit in subjective idealism, in objective idealism, external relations (like those between subject and object) are unreal as they are subsumed by the whole (a "whole" that eludes direct representation within a conceptual or linguistic framework). Also, neither mind nor matter need have a privileged place in a (nondual) relational ontology where the world is constituted by relations.

Notably, the way questions are posed along phenomenological or ontological lines structures the way truth is oriented.[8] The tradition of Madhyamaka, for instance, can be seen to emphasize questions of ontology. In this tradition, all metaphysical foundations are denied and

---

6. Candrakīrti, *Introduction to the Middle Way* (*Madhyamakāvatāra*), VI. 71.

7. For instance, Dharmakīrti's argued in *Ascertaining Sources of Knowledge* (*Pramāṇaviniścaya*) that objects are necessarily perceived objects (*sahopalambhaniyama*). Dharmakīrti, *Ascertaining Sources of Knowledge*, I.55ab (D. 4211, vol. 174), 166a. Sakya Paṇḍita follows this when stating two main reasons for the view that the world has a cognitive nature: (1) all objects of cognitions are cognitive because it is impossible for an object of cognition to lack clarity and awareness, and (2) objects are always necessarily observed together with cognitions (*lhan cig dmigs nges*). Sakya Paṇḍita (*sa skya paṇḍita kun dga' rgyal mtshan*, 1182–1251). *Treasury of Epistemology, tshad ma rigs gter*) (Beijing, China: Nationalities Press, 1989), 55. Mipam also gives these reasons in *Words that Delight Guru Mañjughoṣa: Commentary on the "Ornament of the Middle Way" (dbu ma rgyan gyi rnam bshad 'jam byangs bla ma dgyes pa'i zhal lung)*, in *dbu ma rgyan rtsa 'grel* (Sichuan: Nationalities Press, 1990), 263–264.

8. I have addressed two models of the two truths, the ontological and phenomenological, in an article called, "Two Models of the Two Truths: Ontological and Phenomenological Approaches," *Journal of Indian Philosophy* 38, no. 5 (2010): 519–527.

ultimate truth is framed in terms of absence. Some contemporary philosophers, like Mark Siderits and Dan Arnold, even interpret the phenomenological projects of Abhidharma and Yogācāra as ontological ones, whereas the quest to understand our experience of the world without distortion is taken as a quest for essential ontological primitives.[9] Another way to interpret the projects of Abhidharma and Yogācāra is simply to take them as endeavors in phenomenology.[10] In this light, the categories of experience (like the aggregates) are not ontological primitives, but are mere modalities of experience—*ways* things appear rather than *what* structures reality. Thus understood, the starting point for Abhidharma and Yogācāra analyses can be seen to be rooted in phenomenological analysis.

In his book, *Buddhism as Philosophy,* Mark Siderits outlined two models of the two truths in what he called a *metaphysical* model and a *semantic* model:

> There are two types of interpretation of the doctrine of emptiness, metaphysical and semantic. A metaphysical interpretation takes the doctrine to be an account of the ultimate nature of reality . . . On the semantic interpretation, the doctrine of emptiness is the rejection of the idea of ultimate truth.[11]

What Siderits refers to as a *metaphysical* model accepts only one truth—the ultimate truth—and interprets emptiness as the ultimate ground of reality. This model represents the two truths as an appearance-reality distinction. In this model, the conventional (or relative) truth is denied as an illusion because things do not exist the way they appear. In his latter model, which he refers to as the *semantic* interpretation, only one truth is acknowledged, too, but this time it is the conventional truth, not the ultimate. The ultimate truth here is simply the denial of ultimate truths; that is, the denial of the illusion that there is more than conventional truth.

---

9. See, for instance, Dan Arnold, "Nāgārjuna's 'Middle Way': A Non-Eliminative Understanding of Selflessness," *Revue Internationale de Philosophie* 64, no. 253 (3) (2010): 373–374.

10. See, for instance, Richard King, "*Vijñaptimātratā* and the Abhidharma Context of Early Yogācāra," *Asian Philosophy* 8, no. 1 (1998): 5–17.

11. Mark Siderits, *Buddhism as Philosophy: An Introduction* (Indianapolis: Hackett Publishing Co., 2007), 182.

While Siderits draws an important distinction between two different ontological approaches to the two truths, *both* of his representations are metaphysical. That is, in light of a phenomenological analysis, an alternative that he avoids, both of the models he lays out deal with questions of what the world is (i.e., metaphysics). In this way, he frames the possibilities of truth within metaphysics. Siderits discounts the role of phenomenology in these two models by pigeonholing phenomenology into metaphysics, a typical move made by critics of phenomenology, portraying phenomenology as bad metaphysics. In light of this, it comes as no surprise that he interprets Yogācāra as metaphysical idealism, a straw man, as other Madhyamaka traditions have done.

Despite the one-sidedness of his portrayal, Siderits makes an important point in clarifying the radically anti-realist ontology of Madhyamaka. Many philosophical mistakes are made when the domains of phenomenology (*snang tshul*) and ontology (*gnas tshul*) are not clearly delineated, or rather, when they slide together unnoticed. A key Madhyamaka insight is that there are only appearances; that is, there is nothing *behind* what appears. There may seem to be a reality beyond appearances, or appearances may seem to be more than what they are, but there is no further reality.

Nevertheless, the rebounding collapse of *what is* and *what appears* inevitably emerges when the limits of ontological analysis are reached—when the lines that had supposedly (or methodologically) divided the separate domains of two truths come to be breached (intentionally or not). In this case, emptiness (the ultimate truth) appears and appearance (the conventional truth) is empty, without separation. In this light, both Madhyamaka's ontology and Mind-Only's phenomenology do not necessarily diverge in the end, as both wind up with a kind of nonduality. It is not surprising that these two traditions would share a common ground due to the fact that they represent two different interpretations of the meaning of emptiness in the Perfection of Wisdom Sūtras.

When pressure is put on the structure of truth in either orientation (phenomenological or ontological), the dual structure collapses in the end. Mādhyamikas shut down the two-truth model and claim that there is only one. That is, everything dependently arisen is derivative to something else—all the way down—and there is nothing whatsoever, no-thing or emptiness, behind the interplay of interdependent relations. As emptiness is the meaning of dependently arisen phenomena, the two truths are not separate. Without understanding either truth, one cannot understand the other. So the two truths can be said to be "neither the same nor different"[12] or described as "essentially the same while conceptually distinct."[13]

Mind-Only gets to nonduality through a different route. Mind-Only denies the reality of subject-object duality and asserts nondual cognition, which is the way things are (known) when reality is seen as it is. Since there is no real object, there is no real subject, either; and without a real subject, there is no real subject-object duality. Rather than starting with questions about ontology and then moving into phenomenology, by starting with concerns of phenomenology (how things appear) and then moving to ontology, a similar conclusion (nonduality) can be reached. That is, by seeing the appearance of subject-object duality as false, proponents of Mind-Only assert what is—nondual experiential reality—as the ultimate truth. Even though this reality cannot be directly described or denoted—because any such claim to reality presupposes a grammar of thought and language that is distortive, dualistic, and presupposing of essences—nonduality can be (indirectly) indicated and (experientially) known. Like the relational dynamic of interdependence in Madhyamaka's nondualism, the end of Mind-Only is not limited to a static monism (e.g., subjective idealism), but can be a relational dynamic of nonduality as well.

In certain ways the status attributed to awareness in the phenomenology of Mind-Only is not unlike the role of the "self" in the Advaita Vedānta tradition.[14] Wolfgang Fasching describes how in this tradition consciousness is not an object:

> The point is that the *experiencing itself*—consciousness—is *not* a structural moment of what is given, but is *the very taking place*

---

12. Bötrül, *Ornament of Mañjughoṣa's Viewpoint*, 141; English trans. in Bötrül, *Distinguishing the Views and Philosophies*, translated, annotated, and introduced by Douglas Duckworth (Albany: SUNY Press), 2011, 148.

13. Tsongkhapa, *Thoroughly Illuminating the Viewpoint, Tsongkhapa's Collected Works* (*zhol* ed.), vol. 16 (Xining, China: Nationalities Press, 1998), 554: *ngo bo gcig la ldog pa tha dad pa byas pa dang mi rtag pa lta bu*.

14. In the *Gauḍapādīyakārikā*, an early Vedānta text addressing the doctrine of nondualism (*advaitavāda*), there are statements that are very similar to those of Nāgārjuna and the discourse of Mahāyāna Buddhism. The influence of Mahāyāna Buddhism is blatantly evident. In fact, one verse in this text proclaims the doctrine of non-origination (*ajātivāda*) in a way that is nearly identical to the opening verse of the first chapter of Nāgārjuna's *magnum opus*—the *Mūlamadhyamakakārikā* I.1: "Not from self, nor from other, not from both, nor without cause; no entity whatsoever has ever arisen anywhere." Compare *Gauḍapādīyakārikā* IV.22: "Nothing (*vastu*) whatsoever is originated either from itself or from something else; nothing whatsoever existent, nonexistent, or both existent and nonexistent is originated." Cited and trans. from Richard King, *Early Advaita Vedānta and Buddhism: The Mahāyāna*

> *of givenness itself.* The whole inner/outer (self/not-self) distinction constitutes itself within the realm of experiential contents—and consequently experiencing itself is not located within some 'inner sphere'. My consciousness is not to be found on one side of this inner-outer distinction in which what we experience is necessarily structured, but is, again, the taking place of experience itself. The viewpoint is part of the structure of the field of presence and therefore not presupposed, but constituted by it.[15]

If the self is identified as a discrete essence, an enduring entity (among things), and singular (in contrast to multiplicity), it is subject to negation. But awareness, the self, or rather, who we really are, is not an object. This is explicitly laid out in Fasching's depiction of Advaita Vedānta:

> The presence itself of what is present can never be an observable *object*, yet at the same time it is the most familiar thing in the world: It is that wherein everything we experience has its being-experienced, the medium of all phenomena (the taking place of their phenomenality). And the soteriological aim of Advaita Vedānta—the realization of *ātman*—is nothing but simply becoming explicitly aware of this taking place of presence as such.[16]

In this description of Advaita Vedānta, conscious experience is not an internal space as opposed to external objects, but is a non-thetic presence, the condition for the possibility of subjects and objects that cannot be adequately represented by objective description. According to Fasching, this "witness consciousness" is not an internal subject as opposed to an object, but is the pure horizon of experience and subject/object disclosure, "the pure 'subject' that underlies all subject/object distinctions"[17] as

---

Context of the Gauḍapādīya-kārikā (New York: SUNY, 1995), 127. See also *Gauḍapādīyakārikā* IV.56: "All is born according to the conventional; therefore, there is no eternal. In terms of reality, all is unborn; thus, there is no annihilated." Trans. in King, 256–257.

15. Wofgang Fasching, "I am of the Nature of Seeing," in *Self, No Self? Perspectives from Analytical, Phenomenological, & Indian Traditions*, ed. Mark Siderits, Evan Thompson, and Dan Zahavi (Oxford: Oxford University Press, 2011), 210.

16. Fasching, "I am of the Nature of Seeing," 209.

17. Deutsch (1969), 49. Cited in Fasching, "I am of the Nature of Seeing," 211.

Eliot Deutsch said, or "the 'field' of consciousness/being within which the knower/knowing/known arise."[18]

Madhyamaka arguments target this kind of entity, a conscious principle that takes on a unique (independent) status, as well any notion of an independent reality. According to Madhyamaka, the mind, like everything else, is empty. We can say that the one thing really worth knowing for a Mādhyamika is emptiness; that is, emptiness is the truth that sets you free. Or in other words, since emptiness is the nature of reality, there is no true nature of things to really know (positively); there is only false consciousness to be removed (negatively): the false attribution of true nature. For Mind-Only, however, the one thing worth knowing (or the truth that sets you free) is the mind (or rather, the nature of mind). The nature of mind is to be known positively (although not known in the way that *things* are known). That is, the realization of the nature of mind is not known like an object is known by a subject, for it must be realized by living through it—constitutively or reflexively—"from within." Moreover, since mind-nature is what is and what you are most fundamentally, it is held to be immediately accessible.

Mind-Only seeks to know the nature of mind and Madhyamaka the nature of phenomena, and both claim a window into the nature of reality. For this reason, the nature of mind and reality is not simply empty because its emptiness entails its appearance. The very structure of emptiness is appearance (and the inverse is true, too: the structure of appearance is emptiness). In both cases, the nondual contains and transcends the dual; it does not simply annul it. Thus, this interpretation is different from the dualism of an illusory world and a singularly monistic (and static) ultimate truth (as we commonly see in Advaita Vedānta).

The appeal to the unity of emptiness and appearance is shared in Madhyamaka and Mind-Only, but there is an important aspect that distinguishes these distinctive approaches. While Madhyamaka emphasizes an ontological orientation that represents the unity of appearance and emptiness intersubjectively (or third-personally), Mind-Only emphasizes a phenomenological orientation that relates to the unity of appearance and emptiness *from within* (that is subjectively, first-personally or rather, zero-personally or *suprapersonally*—beyond subject-ivity and object-ivity). While the nature of mind is descriptively empty in Madhyamaka, it is

---

18. Fort (1984), 278. Cited in Fasching, "I am of the Nature of Seeing," 211.

experientially devoid of duality according to Mind-Only and thus must be known from within as an experiential reality of nonduality.

Yet Madhyamaka also has a phenomenological dimension (emptiness is known) just as an ontological dimension (nonduality) is present in Mind-Only. The experiential orientation is a vital part of Madhyamaka, too, and Tsongkhapa shares this sentiment near the end of his *Three Principal Aspects of the Path:*

> As long as the two - the ineluctable appearance of dependent
> arising and
> The understanding of emptiness free from assertions - are
> seen to be separate,
> One has still not understood the intent of the Buddha.
> When they are seen to be in invariable, dependent relation,
> As simultaneous without alternation,
> All apprehensions of determinate objects dissolve -
> One has perfected the analysis of the view.[19]

Thus, a distinctive phenomenological analysis begins where the ontological analysis of Madhyamaka ends. That is, Madhyamaka sets up a provisional distinction between the two truths of what is and what appears. When these two collapse, and what is (empty) is understood as what appears, there is an irreducible unity of empty appearance or appearing emptiness. The two truths become one, or rather nondual (not two). This nondual truth—or in other words, what remains in emptiness—is the domain of contemplative practice. When awareness is acknowledged as an integral part of the equation of an appearance of objects, rather than simply being empty (which implicates another side of a dichotomy—such as "appearance" or the "non-empty"), nonduality can be a starting point (and endpoint) of analysis. This trajectory is also apparent in the Nyingma tradition, for instance, which extends a hierarchy of Buddhist philosophical views beyond Madhyamaka to tantra (see translation in Appendix C). In chapter 5, we will look to the ways in which the contemplative practices of tantra are informed by both Mind-Only and Madhyamaka.

While Mind-Only analyses probe the nature of experience, Madhayamaka analyses, when taken to their limit, probe the nature of

19. Tsongkhapa, *Three Principal Aspects of the Path*, 6–7.

experience, too. This is because emptiness, to be meaningful at all, is always something *known*. To know emptiness is to experience it. Unlike any other object of knowledge, emptiness infuses experience, so ideally an *experience* of emptiness is the end of Madhyamaka analysis, an analysis that begins with *objects* of experience, and proceeds to include experience itself, unstructured by any real separation between subjects and objects.

For Mādhyamikas, there is no real subject-object duality because the subject is dependent upon the object, just like objects are dependent upon subjects for their (perceived) reality. For proponents of Mind-Only, too, the subject (understood as object) is empty, just like all other things. This is because all things are, as Mādhyamikas have consistently shown, empty of true nature. Things are empty because their existence is dependent on what they are not—causes, parts, and imputations. The identity of anything is inhabited by what it is not, just as a flower is not a flower without sunlight, water, earth, etc. Minds, too, are empty just like everything else.

The phenomenological and ontological analyses we see in Mind-Only and Madhyamaka thus can be seen to represent opposite ends of a spectrum. Yet the spectrum I seek to chart is not on a straight line, but forms a circle; each endpoint collapses into the other, for neither is really separate from the other. In other words, phenomenology and ontology—or an analysis of the way things appear (*snang tshul*) and the way things are (*gnas tshul*)—are different starting points for analysis, but in the end, they are infused. That is to say, they are only virtually or provisionally distinguished for the purpose of inquiry, but are never actually separable.

Yet there is an important difference in the respective approaches of Mind-Only and Madhyamaka. In Mind-Only, the mind *as subject*—or rather, the cognitive dimension of reality—is not negated in the same way as an object, and arguably cannot be negated in this way because awareness is constitutive of experience as the condition for the possibility of anything we can know. Madhyamaka's ontology evens out the asymmetrical relationship between awareness and objects; that is, not only is the presence of a subject necessary for there to be an object, but an object is the condition for the possibility of a subject, too: an awareness (of an object) and an object (of awareness) are symmetrical. Neither has a privileged status as more real.

In the next section I will describe the object-oriented ontological analyses of Madhyamaka, and then outline some of the Mind-Only modes of analysis that engage phenomenological orientations as well. Later we will see the way that both kinds of these analyses inform Buddhist contemplative practices in Tibet.

Critical Ontology in Madhyamaka Arguments

This section outlines the contours of the Madhyamaka critique of intrinsic nature. I present Madhyamaka arguments in two broad categories of critique: in terms of time and space. In systematic presentations of Madhyamaka analyses, sometimes there are four or five kinds of argument enumerated,[20] and Longchenpa, a fourteenth-century Tibetan in the Nyingma tradition, speaks of eight in his auto-commentary on the *Wish-Fulfilling Treasury*.[21] Most Madhyamaka arguments fall within one of two rubrics: (1) analysis of causality and (2) part/whole analysis. In other words, the arguments go after reified notions of time and space; they are deconstructions of diachronic and synchronic essence, respectively. I will briefly enumerate and summarize Madhyamaka styles of argumentation within these two rubrics. If you are familiar with the basic contours of Madhyamaka analysis, you may wish to skip to the next section on Prāsaṅgika-Madhyamaka.

One kind of analysis, called "the argument of the diamond shards" (*rdo rje gzegs ma'i gtan tshigs*), systematically addresses production in terms of four possibilities: self-production, production from other, production

20. Five arguments that will be discussed are (1) the argument of lacking singularity or plurality (*gcig du bral gyi gtan tshigs*), which analyzes the essence (*ngo bo la dpyod pa*); (2) the argument of the diamond shards (*rdo rje gzegs ma'i gtan tshigs*), which analyzes the cause (*rgyu la dpyod pa*); (3) the argument refuting the four alternatives of production (*mu bzhi skye 'gog pa'i gtan tshigs*), which analyzes the effect (*'bras bu la dpyod pa*); (4) the argument refuting the production of an existent or nonexistent thing (*yod med skye 'gog pa'i gtan tshigs*), which analyzes both the cause and the effect (*rgyu 'bras gnyis ka la dpyod pa*); and (5) the argument of dependent arising (*rten 'brel gyi gtan tshigs*), which analyzes everything (*thams cad la dpyod pa*). For references to these arguments accepted by both Prāsaṅgikas and Svātantrikas, see José Cabezón and Geshe Lobsang Dargyay, *Freedom from Extremes: Gorampa's "Distinguishing the Views" and the Polemics of Emptiness* (Boston: Wisdom Publications, 2007), 213, 331n380.

21. In addition to five Madhyamaka arguments, Longchenpa adds the argument of lacking permanence or disintegration (*rtag 'jig med*), the argument of neither changing nor not changing (*'gyur mi 'gyur*), and the argument refuting the four properties (*chos bzhi 'gog pa*). His fivefold enumeration replaces the argument refuting the four alternatives of production (*mu bzhi skye 'gog pa'i gtan tshigs*) with an argument refuting the performance of a function. See Longchenpa, *White Lotus, Autocommentary on the "Precious Wish-Fulfilling Treasury,"* in *Seven Treasuries* (*mdzod bdun*), vol. 7, ed. Tarthang Tulku (Sichuan, China, 1996), 1144–1154; Mipam, *Concise Summary of Philosophies from the "Wish-Fulfilling Treasury,"* in *Mipam's Collected Works*, vol. 21, 484–486. See Appendix C.

from both (self and other), and causeless production.[22] The logic follows purportedly exhaustive possibilities of a real causal process to show the absurd conclusions of each. First, self-production is said to be unreasonable because it serves no purpose: what already exists does not need to be produced. Also, an existent entity would be endlessly self-produced. For instance, there would be an endless perpetuation of self-replicating seeds if the entirety of causes necessary for production were already present in a single entity itself. As Buddhapālita said in his commentary on Nāgārjuna's *Fundamental Verses of the Middle Way*: "Entities do not arise from their own natures because their arising would thereby be pointless and absurd."[23] Other-production is not reasonable either. If simply being other were sufficient for production, it would absurdly follow that light would be the cause of darkness because it meets the criterion for being its cause—it is other. As Candrakīrti said, "If something can arise based on what is other than itself, then dense darkness could arise from the tongue of a flame, and anything could arise from anything because all that is not a means of production is the same in being other."[24] Succinctly, he said: "no thing is produced from what is other, because there is no other."[25]

The notion of production from both self and other is said to have the problems of both self-production and production from other. Also, production from both self and other is premised on the dichotomous conception of one thing standing against another as an unproblematic given, a presumption that these are natural boundaries that structure discrete, autonomous entities. Nāgārjuna has consistently shown the problem with this kind of notion by pointing to the contingent nature of such categorical entities: "Without intrinsic nature, how could there be extrinsic nature?"[26]

Causeless production, the last of the four alternatives, is absurd because if this were the case, anything could arise from anything, and there

---

22. This is found in the first verse of the first chapter of Nāgārjuna's classic, the *Fundamental Verses of the Middle Way*, and is developed by Candrakīrti in his commentaries on that text, his "meaning commentary" (*don 'grel*), *Introduction to the Middle Way* (in chapter VI), and in his "word-commentary" (*tshig 'grel*), the *Clear Words* (chapter I).

23. Buddhapālita, *Buddhapālita's Commentary on the "Fundamental Verses of the Middle Way"* (*Buddhapālitamūlamadhyamakavṛtti*), (D. 3842), 161b.

24. Candrakīrti, *Introduction to the Middle Way*, VI.14.

25. Candrakīrti, *Clear Words* (D. 3860, vol. 102), 11b.

26. Nāgārjuna, *Fundamental Verses of the Middle Way*, XV.3.

would be no point for farmers to toil in fields if crops were causeless.[27] Since none of the four causal descriptions account for production, and these are said to exhaust the possibilities of a real causal account, it is argued that there is no real production. It is important to keep in mind that the lack of *real* production is not an absolute denial of production; it denies production above and beyond the conventions and practices of the world, the idea of "production" being nothing other than a cultural product, a convention of consensus.

A second Madhyamaka argument, the argument refuting the four alternatives of production (*mu bzhi skye 'gog*), similarly addresses causality. This time, the argument is pitched in terms of a *reductio ad absurdum* within another fourfold account of the real production of an effect, in terms of: (1) a single effect produced from a single cause, (2) a single effect produced from numerous causes, (3) numerous effects produced from a single cause, and (4) numerous effects produced from numerous causes.[28] It is claimed that none of these four possibilities of singularity or multiplicity (one or many), account for real production; hence, there is no such production.

Another argument targeting a real causal process is the argument refuting the production of an existent or a nonexistent thing. Nāgārjuna succinctly presents this when he states:

> If an effect were essentially existent,
> Then what would a cause produce?
> If an effect were essentially nonexistent,
> Then what would a cause produce?[29]

The argument can be understood like this: if a cause produces an effect and impinges upon an *existing* effect, then it would absurdly follow that the cause and the effect exist at the same time. However, the cause cannot impinge upon a nonexistent effect because what exists cannot be related to what does not exist, just as an (existing) sprout can neither help, nor harm, the (nonexistent) hair of a turtle. These three arguments critique a

---

27. Candrakīrti, *Introduction to the Middle Way*, VI.99.

28. This argument is found in Jñānagarbha's *Distinguishing the Two Truths*, v. 14: (*du mas dngos po gcig mi byed/ du mas du ma byed ma yin/ gcig gis du ma'i dngos mi byed/ gcig gis gcig byed pa'ang ma yin*). (D. 3881, vol. 104), 2a–2b.

29. Nāgārjuna, *Fundamental Verses of the Middle Way*, XX.21.

reified notion of causality. Nāgārjuna concisely undermines a real causal process as follows:

> It cannot be the case that cause and effect are one;
> It cannot be the case that cause and effect are different.
> If cause and effect were one, producer and produced would be the same;
> If cause and effect were different, cause and non-cause would be the same.[30]

In contrast to a causal analysis in terms of time, space is also the site of a second type of Madhyamaka analysis, part/whole analysis. These arguments reveal the interdependence of part and whole, and likewise how any delimited identity is necessarily constituted by what it is not. There are two arguments that fall under the rubric of part/whole analyses. The first is the argument of lacking singularity or plurality, which states that nothing is truly singular because everything has multiple parts. Therefore, nothing is truly plural either because without "one" there is no "many."[31] Another version of the part/whole analysis is "the sevenfold chariot reasoning."[32] The seven aspects of this argument concern the relationship of a chariot to its parts, and analogously, the relationship of the self to the psycho-physical constituents (*phung po, skandha*): (1) a chariot is not the same as its parts, (2) a chariot is not different from its parts, (3) a chariot does not depend upon its parts, (4) the parts do not depend upon the chariot, (5) a chariot does not possess its parts, (6) a chariot is not the collection of its parts, (7) a chariot is not the shape of its parts. Like a chariot, it is argued that the self cannot be found when analyzed in this way. The "self" is simply a designation with no real basis, like a "chariot."

The last form of argument I will mention falls under both of the rubrics of causal and part/whole analysis—the reason of dependent origination. Nāgārjuna put this succinctly: "Because of being dependently arisen, all things lack intrinsic nature; because they lack intrinsic nature, they are

---

30. Nāgārjuna, *Fundamental Verses of the Middle Way*, XX.19–20.

31. This reason is found in the eighteenth chapter of Nāgārjuna's *Fundamental Verses of the Middle Way*. This is also the central reasoning of Śāntarakṣita's *Ornament of the Middle Way* (*Madhyamakālaṃkāra*), v. 1.

32. See Candrakīrti, *Introduction to the Middle Way*, VI.150–158.

empty."[33] This argument can be stated as follows: things arise dependently and are thus causally produced, but not in a way that they are intrinsically existent. Since all phenomena are necessarily dependent on something extrinsic—what they are not—a singular substance cannot be extracted from this network as a truly autonomous, ontological entity. In other words, an entity is *always already* bound up within, and defined by, its role in a network of relations; hence, all things are empty. It is important to keep in mind that all these Madhyamaka arguments are used in a Buddhist context to contend against the existence of real entities and not to undermine causality completely.

Prāsaṅgika-Madhyamaka and Radical Deconstruction

A further subdivision of Madhyamaka arguments stems from the way that the formal features of an argument can implicitly carry unwanted ontological presuppositions. This insight comes from what is known in Tibet as Prāsaṅgika-Madhyamaka, as distinct from Svātantrika-Madhyamaka. In the first chapter of his *Clear Words* (*Prasannapadā*), Candrakīrti famously defended Buddhapālita against Bhāviveka's criticism that he had failed to formulate Nāgārjuna's critique of causality in terms of a probative argument, but rather left the argument in the form of a *reductio*. This debate is well known to be the starting point of the "Prāsaṅgika-Madhyamaka" interpretation in Tibet. "Prāsaṅgika-Madhyamaka," like "Madhyamaka" and "Buddhist," is a fraught term with multiple, contested meanings.[34] Here I simply outline an important dimension of the characteristic Prāsaṅgika method, one that implicates a distinct ontological view.

One way to understand the distinction between a probative argument and a *reductio* is as a formal distinction. That is, these are two ways of expressing the same idea: both prove something, like emptiness. Yet another way is to see the way that probative arguments carry implicit, ontological commitments that are unwanted in the context of describing the way

33. Nāgārjuna, *Dispelling Disputes* under v. 22: *pratītyasamutpannatvān niḥsvabhāvaṃ niḥsvabhāvāt śūnyam iti upapannaṃ*. Published in E. H. Johnson and Kanst, *The Dialectical Method of Nāgārjuna* (Delhi: Motilal Banarsidass, 1986 [1978]), 11.

34. For more on the range of interpretations of Prāsaṅgika, see Sara McClintock and Georges Dreyfus (eds.), *The Svāntantrika-Prāsaṅgika Distinction* (Boston: Wisdom Publications, 2003).

things are. If all things are empty, then emptiness is empty, too, and thus the truth of emptiness is not something to be once and for all proven.

We can see this difference when we consider the fact that negating one thing need not commit you to the affirmation of the alternative. For instance, when an unmarried man denies that he has stopped beating his wife, he need not affirm that he ever did beat her (or that he even has a wife). In the case of denying intrinsic existence, too, the logical subject (like a bachelor's wife) is unreal, so denying intrinsic existence need not commit oneself to affirming the opposite—*intrinsic absence*—just as a bachelor need not be committed to affirming that he has now stopped beating his wife. Thus, unlike a probative argument, a *reductio* can avoid commitments to the subject of debate, along with anything that is "proven."

Probative arguments are fine in contexts of describing the world in a discursive conventional mode, like when saying, "there is smoke there on that hill, so there is fire," or that "the chair is impermanent because it is a product." Yet these claims, and the logical relations that hold them together, are not asserted from a Prāsaṅgika's own perspective in the context of ascertaining the nature of things because doing so implicates an ontological commitment about the world that is antithetical to the anti-realism (or non-realism)[35] of a consistent Mādhyamika's final "position," which is positionlessness. At least this is how Longchenpa characterizes Prāsaṅgika.[36]

I should mention that there are many interpretations of Prāsaṅgika in Tibet, and some present it to have none of its own claims, even about conventional reality.[37] Others (e.g., Tsongkhapa) characterize it quite differently, with distinct claims to conventional and ultimate truth. Tsongkhapa's interpretation is unique, and is an influential outlier from most other interpretations in Tibet. For this reason I will discuss Tsongkhapa's distinctive interpretation of Prāsaṅgika separately in chapters 3 and 4. Rather than outline different views of Prāsaṅgika, here I will begin with Candrakīrti

35. I distinguish "non-realism" from "anti-realism" here to highlight how an interpretation of Prāsaṅgika (without assertions) parallels the distinction between "non-theism" and "atheism." Atheism is the denial of God; non-theism does not entertain the denial (or affirmation) of God.

36. See Longchenpa's discussion of the contexts of assertion in Prāsaṅgika-Madhyamaka, in *White Lotus*, 1166–1167.

37. See, for instance, Kongtrül, *Encyclopedia of Knowledge* (Beijing: Nationalities Press, 2002), 552, 559.

to highlight in broad strokes some issues that are raised in light of a Prāsaṅgika interpretation.

Consider the case of Buddhapālita's *reductio* that "Entities do not arise from their own natures because their arising would thereby be pointless and absurd."[38] Bhāviveka criticized Buddhapālita, saying that he failed to formulate a proper inference, thus leaving an ambiguity in place, that an opponent might presume that the contraposition of this statement were true; namely, that something like a sprout is self-produced because its production has a point and is not endless. Yet in his defense of Buddhapālita, Candrakīrti sheds light on a subtle point: that it is not necessary to formulate the inference in this case, not simply because its form is implicit in the *reductio* and its implications will be understood by a clever debater, but *because the formal structure itself is premised upon a realist ontology*.

In this light, even the claim, "the chair is empty because it is a dependent arising" is not a claim that a Prāsaṅgika must accept in her own perspective because there are no chairs, emptinesses, or dependent arisings in the way things really are. Using inferences to show that phenomena like chairs lack intrinsic natures may help one move into this Prāsaṅgika perspective, but such claims are only a step in the anti-realist direction; they cannot be claims made from a Prāsaṅgika's own stance on the nature of things. In terms of the way things are, a Prāsaṅgika maintains a noble silence (not to be confused with just "silence," which may or may not coincide with the correct view of how things are).

Significantly, a Prāsaṅgika need not assent to commonly appearing logical subjects, an issue addressed in Candrakīrti's response to Bhāviveka in *Clear Words*. Bhāviveka had claimed that *unqualified sound* must be used as the subject of a debate when a Buddhist proves sound to be impermanent to a non-Buddhist, because sound is understood in incompatible ways by non-Buddhists (e.g., as a quality of space) and Buddhists (as a transformation of physical elements). Thus, according to Bhāviveka, *mere sound*—stripped of all ontological baggage—must be used in order for the two competing parties to share an ontologically neutral, common subject matter of debate. Yet Candrakīrti showed that Bhāviveka's project is misguided and impossible because the subject matter of debate for a realist is not shared with an anti-realist. There is still ontological baggage on board in the notion of a "mere sound."

38. Buddhapālita, *Buddhapālita's Commentary on "Fundamental Verses of the Middle Way,"* (D. 3842), 161b.

That is to say, the claim that a logical subject, like "*mere* sound," is epistemically warranted (by a full-fledged *pramāṇa*) commits one to a noninferential *given*, precisely the type of realist presumption that a Prāsaṅgika denies. Whether it be a conceptually theorized sound or a perceptually delivered *given*, there are no neutral, untheorized grounds to proceed upon in a debate between realists and anti-realists. In fact, appealing to a perceptual given like *mere sound*, rather than a conceptually-qualified one, simply shifts the weight of a realist's ontological baggage onto percepts rather than concepts; it still carries the heavy implicit assumptions of realism.

Avoiding all ontological commitments implicit in a realist presumption is precisely the reason why *reductios* are preferred over probative arguments for a Prāsaṅgika in the context of demonstrating how things really are. With a *reductio* there are no commitments to *the way things are*. In a uniquely Prāsaṅgika context, no claims need be made other than those made through the anthropologist's gaze, assenting to the ways the people of the world talk in whatever ways they do—in terms of "Homeric gods," "tables," "quarks," etc.—while not assenting to the ontologies of these claims. Autonomous probative arguments, however, presuppose a world that is ontologically given independent of the ways it is conceived and described, a real world confirmed by epistemic warrants (*pramāṇa*), shared subjects, and natural relations between them. Prāsaṅgikas will have none of this (nor even their denial in some interpretations),[39] in their own final perspective on the way things are.

In particular, "four arguments unique to Prāsaṅgika-Madhyamaka"[40] are distinguished from formal (autonomous) arguments, which are seen to carry implicit ontological presumptions when understood in a context of ascertaining the ultimate truth. The four Prāsaṅgika arguments correlate with the reasons against the four accounts of production (self-, other-, both, causeless) in the first verse of chapter one of Nāgārjuna's *Fundamental Verses of the Middle Way*: (1) a consequence expressing contradiction, such as "it absurdly follows that production is pointless because the product is already there" (for those who claim that an effect is self-produced);[41] (2) a parallel absurd consequence following from the same

39. See Kongtrül, *Encyclopedia of Knowledge*, 715.

40. See Kongtrül, *Encyclopedia of Knowledge*, 559.

41. Or alternatively, "It follows that you eat excrement because you eat food" (for those who claim that an effect is self-caused, being the same as the cause).

reasoning, such as "it absurdly follows that light arises from darkness" (for those who claim that an effect arises from what is other); (3) pointing out that one's reasoning is circular or begs the question (in response to the claim that things arise from both self and other when neither has been established, as in the circular logic of a claim like "God is powerful because He is the Creator"); and (4) inference that is acknowledged by others, such as "farmers toil in fields to produce crops" (in response to the claim that production is causeless).

It is noteworthy that among these four types of argument, three exclusively negate; the fourth explicitly appeals to what is acknowledged by others. For Longchenpa, Prāsaṅgika-Madhyamaka is chiefly concerned with undermining mistaken views of reality, not affirming its own:

> The Prāsaṅgika's way of eliminating constructs . . . is not like the Svātantrikas, who establish the relative as false through negating its truth, and establish a lack of constructs through negating constructs regarding the ultimate. Rather, Prāsaṅgikas explicitly negate whatever is held onto while not implicitly establishing anything at all; thus, they avert the misconceptions of others.[42]

In this interpretation, a Prāsaṅgika does not establish a system. Rather, a Prāsaṅgika simply undermines any and all attempts to establish "reality" by undermining the realist presuppositions upon which such a project necessarily plays out. Thus, a Prāsaṅgika's own final position about the way things are in this portrayal is always only silence (expressed as "inexpressiblity"), because reality is beyond conceptual proliferations (i.e., the unenframed ultimate). This interpretation follows the "unenframed" interpretation of emptiness (mentioned in chapter 1). When making assertions about conventional truths, to follow simply the (unreflective) empirical stance of "what is acknowledged by the world" (like the claim that "seeds produce sprouts"), without appealing to an ultimate causal story or

42. Longchenpa, *Precious Treasury of Philosophical Systems*, in *Seven Treasuries* (*mdzod bdun*), ed. Tarthang Tulku (Sichuan, China, 1996), 812. Kongtrül as well stated: "Prāsaṅgikas negate the assemblages of constructs by means of many kinds of reasoning; however, they do not establish a freedom from constructs. See Kongtrül, *Encyclopedia of Knowledge*, 715.

deeper description of how things really are conventionally, is a manner of assertion unique to this Prāsaṅgika tradition.[43]

Kongtrül (1813–1899), who apparently follows an interpretation of Madhyamaka from the Eighth Karmapa, Mikyö Dorjé (1507–1554), portrays Prāsaṅgika as not only making conventional assertions from others' perspectives, but ultimate assertions of emptiness and unreality are made in this way, too; this is a difference from Svātantrikas, who he says accept emptiness as an assertion of their own system.[44] Thus, he explains that when a Prāsaṅgika claims anything, positive or negative in the context of establishing the ultimate, it is done solely *from the perspective of others*. That the nature of things is not even said to be empty is found in Nāgārjuna:

> If there were something non-empty, then there would be
> something empty.
> Since there is nothing that is non-empty, how can there be
> something empty?"[45]

The move to negate even emptiness is significant because there is no ultimate reality affirmed from a Prāsaṅgika's own perspective in this interpretation, so even a claim of emptiness, or an argument like "the table is empty because it is neither one nor many" is not a claim that a Prāsaṅgika herself affirms from her own perspective. This is because any claim to the ultimate, even one of emptiness, implicates reification: for such a claim reifies emptiness (and the table) as ontological realities, whereas even emptiness is empty and cannot be captured linguistically or conceptually. Here, emptiness is performative, not a metaphysical thesis. For this reason, this interpretation puts forward that *no assertions are made from a Prāsaṅgika's own perspective in the context of ascertaining the ultimate.*

---

43. For instance, Mipam says, "The unique way that Prāsaṅgikas present the conventional is as dependently arisen appearances that do not withstand [ontological] analysis—the appearances that accord with all the world, oneself and others—through engaging in accord with the world of mere appearances without [ontological] analysis." Mipam, *Light of the Sun*, 408: *brten nas 'byung ba'i snang ba brtag mi bzod pa 'di rang gzhan 'jig rten thams cad la mthun par snang ba tsam la ma brtags par 'jig rten thun mong dang mthun par 'jug pa ni thal 'gyur ba'i tha snyad thun min byed tshul yin.* See English trans. in Padmakara Translation Group, *The Wisdom Chapter*, 208.

44. Kongtrül, *Encyclopedia of Knowledge*, 552; 559.

45. Nāgārjuna, *Fundamental Verses of the Middle Way*, XIII.7.

This interpretation is not unique to Madhyamaka commentarial traditions, for we see this suggested in words of Buddhist sūtras as well, like the *Verse Summary of the Perfection of Wisdom*: "Even if bodhisattvas conceive 'this aggregate is empty,' they are coursing in signs and do not have faith in the domain of the unborn."[46] We will return to an alternative interpretation of Prāsaṅgika offered by Tsongkhapa, a subtle and influential one with a quite different portrayal of the nature of emptiness, in chapters 3 and 4. First we will turn to introduce the phenomenological analyses of Mind-Only.

Phenomenological Analyses in Mind-Only

The critical first step in phenomenological analysis is to understand that everything known is known in experience, that there is nothing that can be known outside or separate from an experiential context. We see this in Husserl's *epoché*, his "bracketing" of the world as it is ordinarily understood, a suspension of judgment in order to probe the deeper structure of experience.[47] In Mind-Only, we find a related process of probing the nature of experience and reality. Mind-Only texts also present a number of arguments against the reality of a mind-independent world, such as the dream argument (that our perceptions of external objects are as mistaken in waking perception as they are in dreams), arguments that objects are observer-dependent (e.g., water appears differently to fish and humans), and that objects are always accompanied by cognitions (objects are always *known* objects).

Other arguments found in Indian Yogācāra texts attack the very notion of materiality, such as Vasubandhu's arguments against partless particles constituting extended phenomena,[48] Dignāga's argument that neither external particles nor their combinations can provide an account of the perception of phenomena,[49] and Dharmakīrti's argument that perceived objects are not real because they are neither singular nor plural: "That

46. *Condensed Perfection of Wisdom* (*Prajñāpāramitā-sañcayagāthā*), H. 17, vol. 34, 189b–190a.

47. This method is developed by Husserl in his *Ideas I*. See *Ideas Pertaining to a Pure Phenomenology and to a Phenomenological Philosophy—First Book: General Introduction to a Pure Phenomenology*, trans. F. Kersten (The Hague: Nijhoff, 1982).

48. Vasubandhu, *Twenty Verses* (*Viṃśatikā*), v. 11–14.

49. Dignāga, *Investigation of the Percept* (*Ālambanaparīkṣā*) v. 1–5; English trans. in Duckworth et al., *Dignāga's Investigation of the Percept* (Oxford: Oxford University Press, 2016), 38–39.

form in which entities are perceived does not exist in reality, for these (things) have neither a unitary nor a multiple form."[50] In his commentary on Dharmakīrti, Prajñākaragupta clearly and concisely conveys the problem with the claim to an external world: "If blue is perceived, then how can it be called 'external'? And, if it is not perceived, how can it be called 'external'?[51]

Vasubandhu is the godfather of arguments against external realism. He pointed out a central problem of emergence: that we cannot get extended objects from what is not extended. Dignāga pointed out a further problem with a dualistic metaphysic, namely, substance dualism's inability to provide a coherent account of the phenomenal world. Both of these figures raised problems of emergence and supervenience, in terms of the relationship between what is the (indivisibly) small and the (macroscopically) large.

Dignāga's arguments shed light on the problem in terms of (1) the relation between extended things and what is not extended, and (2) the relationship between mind and matter. For the first problem, Dignāga echoes Vasubandhu's argument in the *Twenty Stanzas* that extended objects cannot be constituted by indivisible particles that lack extension.[52] The second problem—the relationship not between macro-objects and micro-objects, but between cognition and matter—is known as the "hard problem" of consciousness. It is a version of the mind-body problem that addresses the question: how can experience arise from matter, which does not share its nature? This problem is set up by the presumptions of a mental-physical dualism, but can be answered with monism. Dignāga's answer is not, however, a physicalist monism (which is left with an explanatory gap that fails to address experiential reality), nor the monism of subjective idealism (which collapses everything into a subjective mind). Rather, his monism is relational; it is the nonduality of objective idealism.

---

50. Dharmakīrti, *Commentary on Epistemology* (*Pramāṇavārttika*), III. 359: *bhāvā yena nirūpyante tad rūpaṃ nāsti tattvataḥ / yasmād ekam anekaṃ vā rūpaṃ teṣāṃ na vidyate.* Citation and translation from Ernst Steinkellner, "Is Dharmakīrti a Mādhyamika?" in *Earliest Buddhism and Madhyamaka*, ed. David Seyfort Ruegg and Lambert Schmithausen (Leiden: E. J. Brill, 1990), 78.

51. Prajñākāragupta in *Pramāṇavarttikālaṃkāra*, 366, 17 (III v. 718). Cited in Yuichi Kajiyama, *An Introduction to Buddhist Philosophy: An Annotated Translation of the Tarkābhāṣa of Mokṣākaragupta*, 140: *yadi saṃvedyate nīlaṃ kathaṃ bāhyaṃ tad ucyate / na cet saṃvedyate nīlaṃ kathaṃ bāhyaṃ tad ucyate* (Kyoto University: Memoirs of the Faculty of Letters, 1966).

52. Vasubandhu, *Twenty Verses*, vv. 11–14.

Dignāga challenged the idea that there can be a coherent account of perception in terms of external objects. He argued that it is incoherent to maintain that the content of perception is fundamental particles because these particles are not perceived: what is perceived is never particles; we always perceive macro-objects, not micro-ones.[53] To appeal to fundamental particles to explain the content of perception is to beg the question; their existence is only presumed from the divisible constitution of the macro-objects that we seem to interact with.

Dignāga also attacked a position that maintains that, rather than particles, *compounds* (*'dus pa*) are what we really perceive. He argued that compounds of particles cannot be the content of perception because the unities attributed to them are simply imputations—conceptual constructs—without substance.[54] Reflecting the way that Buddhists have critiqued the reality of universals, the integrity of compounds as singularities (like a forest or a garland) are claimed to not inhere in entities, but to be held together by conceptual and linguistic designation. Thus, he argued that the appearance of extended external objects does not come from an external world.

We might think that the position he argues for is one that holds that the mind-matter relation must be between two like things, that mind and matter could not impinge upon each other without a shared nature. In this case, in order for matter to impinge upon the mind, it must share its nature; that is, matter must be, in some sense, mental. Even if this is the case, the content of mental perception need not be solely a mental projection, as in subjective idealism, for the subjective mental image, along with the objective mental image, can be seen to be a product or manifestation of something else that is neither a subjective mind nor an external object. As in objective idealism, the subjective and the objective phenomenal features can constitute two parts of a larger whole. Indeed, we will see in the next chapter how the subjective and objective features of self-awareness form such a structural whole, which can be referred to as the "shape" of objective and absolute forms of idealism.

There are different accounts of how Buddhists have dealt with mental-physical interaction. Some have offered a representationalist

---

53. Dignāga, *Investigation of the Percept*, v. 1; English trans. in Duckworth et al., *Dignāga's Investigation of the Percept*, 38.

54. See Dignāga, *Autocommentary on "Investigation of the Percept"*(*Ālambanaparīkṣāvṛtti*) under v. 2; English trans. in Duckworth et al., *Dignāga's Investigation of the Percept*, 42.

answer, holding that the external world is known through a cognitive image (*ākāra*), a representation in the mind. That is, what we directly interact with is not matter, but the mental image in our minds that corresponds to the physical world. Dignāga has shown that the status of an external world is not necessary with such an account. This is because a causal account of perception can function just the same without positing anything extrinsic to the mind, for the representationalist account has already deemed what is outside the mind irrelevant for phenomenal appearance.[55]

A distinctive feature of Dignāga's system is that he makes external realism compatible with idealism—the same principles that guide a coherent causal process in terms of external entities can function without those entities as well. That is, we might call something "matter" or a "configuration of energy" and presume a causal story around that entity we designate. We can presume that matter is external and separate from mind, or we can presume that matter (or energy) is the same kind of stuff as the mind and still have the same regularity of causal processes that external realism demands. Furthermore, the process need not be initiated by mind (as in the "top-down" causation of subjective idealism) or by matter (the "bottom-up" causation of physicalism) but by means of a third entity, which is neither external nor internal but the cause of both. In fact, this third alternative, as a form of neutral monism that is neither mental nor physical but shares properties of, or is the cause of both, is another possibility (e.g., Bohm's implicate order).

The status of the world, as either subjective idealism or objective idealism, is another level of ambiguity at play in Dignāga's Yogācāra philosophy (in addition to the one between external realism and subjective idealism). The difference is one between *subjective* idealism (where everything that exists is mind) and *objective* idealism (where there is nothing outside a unitary structure within which subjective and objective features are simply instances of internal relation). In subjective idealism, the mind is constitutive of the world. In the latter case of objective idealism, the mind is inextricably intertwined with the world, too; however, it is entangled in such a way that an internal mind cannot actually be separable from

55. See Dignāga, *Autocommentary on "Investigation of the Percept"*(*Ālambanaparīkṣāvṛtti*) under v. 8; English trans. in Duckworth et al., *Dignāga's Investigation of the Percept*, 45.

an external world, nor need it be identical with it. In both cases of subjective and objective idealism, there is nothing outside the mind.[56]

Dignāga might be called an idealist, given that he refers to the content of perception as "the nature of an internal cognitive object" (*nang gi shes bya'i ngo bo*).[57] Yet Dignāga's explanation does not simply reduce cognition to the *subject*, as in the simplistic caricatures of "Mind-Only" in which objective percepts are simply the products of a *subjective* mind. Rather, there is a more complex and arguably more nuanced causal story. Even while appearing within a duality of an inner mind and outer object, the way things appear is not the way they are. The content of perception is not really separate from the mind.

Dignāga's account of perception entails a temporal, self-generating and self-regulating process of conscious experience, which is driven by a feedback loop of predisposition and habituation. That is, he says that the capacities for perception reside in cognition and cognition arises from these capacities.[58] In this way, the cognitive process is autopoietic: it is a self-organizing, self-perpetuating system. It exemplifies the cognitive coupling of agent and environment, which mutually co-operate to create a life-world. In his system, moreover, both the dualist's and physicalist's problem of emergence—how mind arises from matter—is skirted, because the transcendental structure of the world is not spatially located *in here* or *out there*, so is not bound by the temporality that it shapes. Thus, the process is said to have been there since beginningless time.[59]

We can discern a tension in this Mind-Only description, namely, a tension between subjective idealism and objective idealism, as seen in the respective meanings ascribed to subjectivity, internality, and cognition. The nature of cognition and subjectivity is in question because cognition is not just a subject here, at least it is not held to be only a subject delimited within the structure of a subject-object duality. Cognition is also said to be reflexive, disclosed in a process through which it presents itself as subject

56. For a further discussion of idealism and Yogācāra, see Duckworth, "The Other Side of Realism: Panpsychism and Yogācāra," in *Buddhist Philosophy: A Comparative Approach*, ed. Steven Emmanuel (Hoboken, N J: Wiley-Blackwell, 2017), 29–43.

57. Dignāga, *Investigation of the Percept*, v. 6; English trans. in Duckworth et al., *Dignāga's Investigation of the Percept*, 39.

58. Dignāga, *Autocommentary on "Investigation of the Percept"*(*Ālambanaparīkṣāvṛtti*) under v. 8; English trans. in Duckworth et al., *Dignāga's Investigation of the Percept*, 45–46.

59. See Dignāga, *Investigation of the Percept*, v. 8; English trans. in Duckworth et al., *Dignāga's Investigation of the Percept*, 39.

and object. Given that cognition is said to be "internal," the meaning of *internality*—retained as something distinct from subjectivity, and particularly in the absence of external objects—is left as a further question for the commentarial literature that frames this philosophy. For Mādhyamikas like Tsongkhapa, the independent reality of an "internal" mind falls into Mind-Only's error of subjective (and by implication, absolute) idealism, one that is corrected by Candrakīrti's Prāsaṅgika-Madhyamaka.

Cognitive Grounds

In addition to self-awareness, another central notion in Mind-Only through which the structure of the world is articulated is the basic consciousness (*ālayavijñāna*). While the basic consciousness, being nominally a "consciousness" (*vijñāna*), may be identified with the subjective pole of perception, it is the source of not only the subjective representations of mind, but also of objective representations of bodies, environments, and materials as well. The *Descent to Laṅka Sūtra* states: "Mahāmati, the basic consciousness simultaneously reveals forms of body, place, and material objects (*longs spyod*) appearing to mind."[60] Also, Asaṅga in his *Compendium of Mahāyāna* states: "The nature of the basic consciousness is the resultant cognition with all potentialities; it comprises all bodies of the three realms and all existences."[61] Thus, the function of the basic consciousness can be seen to support a form of *panpsychism*—that all is mind, mind-like, or mind-dependent—or neutral monism (that the causal matrix is neither mind nor matter, but the ground of both). This is because, rather than a subjective idealism that simply collapses objects into subjects, the basic consciousness is a structure that shapes subjectivity as well as the configuration of an external world.

The way the basic consciousness constitutes the world can be represented diachronically and synchronically. The basic consciousness as the cause of the world is the aspect of the seeds or potentials from the past; the aspect of maturation is the manifest content of the body, materials, and environments that are used and inhabited now. While it may be likened to an access consciousness, the basic consciousness (in its aspect of potentials)

---

60. *Descent to Laṅka Sūtra* (*Laṅkāvatārasūtra*), (D. 0107), 77a. See also Asaṅga, *Stages of Yoga Practice* (*Yogācārabhūmi*), D.4038, 7a; English trans. in Waldron, *The Buddhist Unconscious*, 185. See also Mipam, *Gateway to Scholarship*, 21.

61. Asaṅga, *Compendium of Mahāyāna* (*Mahāyānasaṃgraha*) I.21 (D. 4048), 7a.

is not accessible, only its matured aspect is manifest. The basic consciousness is thus not only behind the scenes, working the causal story of the appearing world (like a projector in an old cinema hall), but is also part of the cognitive structure of appearances that are manifest (the immersive experience of the film). The mysterious, causal functioning of the basic consciousness is the aspect of its potentials ("the Buddhist unconscious"), yet the phenomenal world is the manifest aspect of the basic consciousness—its aspect of maturation.[62] The basic consciousness is neither the same nor different than phenomenal consciousness;[63] these dual attributes articulate a dynamic interrelation of conscious and subconscious processes.

The basic consciousness is thus twofold in (1) its aspect of maturation, which is its structure of manifest, dependently arisen phenomena, and (2) its aspect of potentials, which is its structuring, or causal aspect, that is not manifest, but consisting in potential in predispositions from beginningless time. These twin aspects—result and cause, form and structure—are interdependent. The former is completely consistent with the Buddhist notion of dependent arising, as an interdependent matrix of the synchronic world. It is the latter articulation of a diachronic causal process that is a unique assertion of Yogācāra extending Abhidharma causal theory. The notion of the basic consciousness can be seen as a direct response to problems embedded in early Abhidharma theory by serving to connect the dots in a causal story of momentary events.

---

62. These two dimensions can be seen in Vasubandhu's work in parallel with Dignāga's treatment of the *ālambana*, the cause and content of perception (Dignāga did not speak of the *ālayavijñāna*). A relevant passage in Vasubandhu's *Concise Elucidation of the Secret Meaning* (*Vivṛtagūḍhārthapiṇḍavyākhyā*), a commentary on the *Compendium of Mahāyāna*, makes this connection with a distinction between an "indirect" and a "direct" causal story of perception: "[The *ālambana*] is twofold in another way: there is the directly perceived *ālambana* and the one perceived indirectly. The direct *ālambana* is the phenomenal form of what is apprehended (*grāhyākāra*). The indirect *ālambana* is the *ālayavijñāna* because due to it, [a consciousness] appears with the phenomenal form of what is apprehended." (D. 4052), 329b: *mngon sum du dmigs pa dang brgyud pa'i sgo nas gzhan du rnam pa gnyis te / de la mngon sum gyi dmigs pa ni gzung ba'i rnam pa gang yin pa'o // brgyud pa'i dmigs pa ni kun gzhi'i rnam par shes pa ste / de'i dbang gis gzung ba'i rnam par snang ba'i phyir ro*. This passage is cited in Schmithausen, "On the Problem of the External World in the Ch'eng wei shih lun," 44–45 (translation mine).

63. Asaṅga states this in his *Compendium of Mahāyāna*: "Both the basic consciousness [and the engaged consciousnesses] are conditions for each other," he follows this statement with a citation from the Abhidharma, saying: "All phenomena are conjoined with consciousness, and those [consciousnesses] are likewise [conjoined with phenomena]. They are constantly paired as cause and effect of each other." Asaṅga, *Compendium of Mahāyāna* I.27 (D. 4048), 7b.

Unlike the way that discrete entities are denied (as is the case with explicit reference to emptiness), the notion of the basic consciousness is part of a rich causal account of the structure within which a world takes place—where subjects and objects not only fall together, but rise together too (as mutually substantiating). Like the notions of emptiness and interdependence in Madhyamaka, the basic consciousness is neither one nor many. It is not a single cosmic consciousness, nor is it the isolated continuum of a single mind. It is also not the matrix of a world of discretely bound, disconnected individuals.[64] Rather, it is an intertwined network, the source and substance of unity-in-diversity, or emptiness. In other words, the basic consciousness represents a structure of the world where discrete boundaries are shaped and where they dissolve.

The status of the external world is clear in Mind-Only: there is none. Yet what constitutes reality is ambiguous: is it all mind or not? An answer to this question may be found in the status of the *dependent nature* (*paratantra*) among the Yogācāra theory of three natures. The three natures is another way the world is articulated in Yogācāra texts. The three natures are: the *imagined nature* (*parikalpita*), the *dependent nature*, and the *consummate nature* (*pariniṣpanna*). There are many interpretations of the three natures (as is the case with the two truths of Madhyamaka), yet for our purposes the three natures can be represented in the following way, stemming from the way they are laid out in an influential sūtra, the *Sūtra Explaining the Intent* (*Saṃdhinirmocanasūtra*).[65]

Conceptual construction is the *imagined nature*: what we impute as the reality of things like trees, selves, and tables, and the concepts we use to capture these entities. We hold these things to be real and a natural part of reality, when they are in fact cultural artifacts; that is to say, they are not separate from our conceptual constructions. The real world is not the way we construct it to be: that is the *consummate nature*, reality's emptiness of

64. Asaṅga, *Compendium of Mahāyāna* I.60: "When it is shared (*sādhāraṇa*), the basic-consciousness is the seed of the world-receptacle (*bhājanaloka*); when it is unshared (*asādhāraṇa*), it is the seed of the individual bases of consciousness (*prātyātmikāyatana*)." *Compendium of Mahāyāna* (D. 4048), 12a.

65. A metaphor for the three natures used in the sixth chapter the *Sūtra Explaining the Intent* is a colorless crystal. See p. 134. Tibetan edition and English translation in Powers, *Wisdom of Buddha*, 84–87. Vasubandhu also composed a treatise on the three natures, where he concisely presents the three natures in the first three verses. See Vasubandhu, *Treatise on the Three Natures* vv. 1–3; English trans. in Gold, *Paving the Great Way, Vasubandhu's Unifying Buddhist Philosophy* (New York: Columbia University Press, 2015), 223.

constructions. The causal process of appearances is the *dependent nature,* the basis of our false conceptions, which is the casual matrix of relation and inexpressible field of (cognitive) reality.

Like the two truths in Madhyamaka, the three natures in Yogācāra comprehensively apply to all things, including themselves. Just as is the case with a statement that emptiness is empty (as we see in Nāgārjuna's Madhyamaka), a statement about any of the three natures entails them all. In the *Compendium of Mahāyāna,* Asaṅga shows how the three natures refer to themselves as well as other things:

> In one sense, the dependent nature is dependent; in another sense, it is imagined; and in yet another sense, it is consummate. In what sense is the dependent nature called "dependent"? It is dependent in that it originates from the seeds of dependent propensities. In what sense is it called "imagined"? Because it is both the cause of imagination and what is imagined by it. In what sense is it called "consummate"? Because it does not at all exist in the way it is imagined.[66]

In this way, each and every phenomenon, including each of the three natures, has all three natures.

Like the basic consciousness, the dependent nature is structured by dependent arising and has been identified with a distorted mode of cognition,[67] yet this cognitive process is not necessarily one that is only internal. Rather, it is the structure of subjective and objective worlds: the world in dynamic interaction of cognitions, faculties, and objects. The dependent nature of this process can be illustrated with an example of the appearance

---

66. Asaṅga, *Compendium of Mahāyāna* II.17 (P. 5549), 18b.5–8. Trans. adapted from Karl Brunnhölzl, *Center of a Sunlit Sky: Madhyamaka in the Kagyü Tradition* (Ithaca, NY: Snow Lion Publications, 2004), 486.

67. For instance, Asaṅga characterized the dependent nature as follows in the *Mahāyānasaṃgraha* I.21: "What is the characteristic of the dependent nature? It is a cognition comprised by unreal imagination concerning the basic consciousness potentiality." Asaṅga, *Compendium of Mahāyāna* (D. 4048), 13a. In Tibet, Mipam also described the dependent nature in cognitive terms: "In the perspective of thoroughgoing conceptuality, while there is dualistic appearance, the awareness that exclusively appears as such, but is not established in duality, is called 'the dependent nature.' It is the basis for the arising of distortion, the imagined nature." Mipam, *Garland of Light Rays: Commentary on "Distinguishing the Middle and the Extremes" (dbu dang mtha' rnam par 'byed pa'i bstan bcos kyi 'grel pa 'od zer phreng ba), Mipam's Collected Works,* vol. 4 (*pa*), 669. See also Duckworth, *Mipam on Buddha-Nature,* 48.

of a rainbow. For a rainbow to appear we need at least three things in place: white light (e.g., the sun), a refracting medium (e.g., water), and a receptor of light (e.g., eyes). Of course the eyes have to be looking in the right direction, and the light coming to the eyes at the right angle (between 40–42 degrees) to be visibly refracted, too. Without any of these things (light, water, eyes) properly configured, no rainbow appears. It is not that the rainbow is "out there" in the world, nor is the rainbow only "in here" in our eyes or minds. Rather, the appearing rainbow is the result of an intricate relational structure in which the perceiving eye is intertwined. Just as the eyes are integral to the perception of a rainbow, we need not be subjective idealists to affirm that the mind is constitutive of the world. In other words, "beauty is in the eye of the beholder" does not necessarily mean that beauty is totally subjective, as if it were "all in our heads," but it can simply mean that the subject is an integral part of the dynamic process by which beauty takes place. This distinction, as with the distinction within idealisms (subjective or epistemic on one hand, and objective or absolute on the other), is often overlooked.

Mind-Only is better described in terms of objective idealism rather than subjective idealism because objective idealism not only captures the fact that the basic consciousness is a consciousness and the content of object-presentation, but also conveys that the basic consciousness is the content of the presentation as subjectivity, too. In this way, the reality of a *subject* determined by its subject-object presentation can be denied while affirming the conscious process, just as when the mere flow of consciousness is affirmed in a causal story that denies any enduring entity like a unified self. This emergent process comes from something that is not itself a *subjective* consciousness, but from what is said to be an "internal consciousness" nonetheless. In contrast, describing mind-independent objects is a metaphysical project, and Mind-Only at its best is phenomenology, not metaphysics. Or better yet, it is a "liberation phenomenology" oriented toward freedom, the pragmatic foundation of all Buddhist philosophies.

Mind-Only is often harnessed with the label "(subjective) idealism," and thus saddled with the problems associated with it—such as those of solipsism, there being an asymmetry between a (real) mind and an (unreal) object, and there being no way to drive a wedge between an "internal" mind and an "external" object (the wedge upon which subjective idealism depends—since there is no place to stand outside of a subject-object relation to split those up and privilege the former). Yet the importance of Mind-Only analyses is often overlooked in caricatures of this tradition.

In the eighth century, the influential exponent of Advaita Vedānta, Śaṅkara, challenged the Yogācāra refutation of an external world by arguing that the existence of externality itself is presupposed in its denial.[68] Similarly, Nāgārjuna's critics have argued that his claim to emptiness was a performative contradiction.[69] Nāgārjuna responded that emptiness is empty, too. As is the case with the "emptiness of emptiness" in Madhyamaka, understanding how the three natures apply to themselves as well shows how these arguments against them are inconclusive. That is, there is no need for anything to be real or external for things to appear as if they existed that way—just as nothing is independent despite appearing that way. Moreover, in reality, things are neither unreal (in Madhyamaka) nor internal (in Mind-Only) either, so these critiques fail.

In fact, seeing the mental nature of appearances is only one stage of Mind-Only analysis, and this first step need not be the only or final one. There are other analyses in the Mind-Only tradition that undermine not only external realism but also subjective idealism. For instance, the reduction of objects to mind is found as the first step of a four-stage process, or one of four practices (*prayoga*) of an inquiry that goes deeper than just undermining the mistaken notion of an external, material world.

Haribhadra's (8th c.) commentary on the *Ornament of Clear Realization* (v. 20), for instance, explains a four-stage process in which the first stage of analysis is the deconstruction of the concept of a personal self. The self that is an enduring, singular essence is not real because it is not found in the psycho-physical constituents (*skandhas*), which are impersonal, multiple, dependent on other things, and always in flux. The second stage determines how what is apprehended is dependent on an apprehender, and thus how apprehended objects can have no independent reality apart from apprehending subjects. It is important to note that this stage undermines the reality of objects *phenomenologically*, through an analysis of how things are experienced, rather than *ontologically*, as we saw in analyses that conclude that objects have no real currency when sought in terms of their parts or wholes, etc.

---

68. See Saṅkara, *Brahmasūtrabhāṣya* under II Adhyāya, 2 Pāda, 28; English trans. in Thibaut, *Vedānta Sūtras*, Sacred Books of the East, Part I, vol. 34 (Delhi: Motilal Banarsidass, 1998 [1904]), 421.

69. For Buddhists' and non-Buddhists' critiques of Madhyamaka, see Jan Westerhoff, "On the Nihilist Interpretation of Madhyamaka," *Journal of Indian Philosophy* 44:2 (2016), 340–357.

The third stage of Haribhadra's analysis is that without a real object, a real subject does not exist either. This is the critical stage that undermines subjective idealism. Since an isolated internal subject makes no sense without reference to externality, the critique of an internal subject follows after arguments against an external world (since there can be nothing internal without anything external and *vice versa*).[70] Vasubandhu expresses this in his *Thirty Verses:* "When cognition does not observe any objects, it abides in mere consciousness, since there is no apprehender without something apprehended."[71] This step in the analysis resembles Heidegger's critique of Husserl's transcendental ego. That is, the move to criticize the entire dualistic structure of internal-external orientation reflects Heidegger's move to criticize early Husserlian idealism, which is seen to privilege the subject (transcendental ego), while extending his phenomenological project by collapsing the subject (and object) into the relationally constituted identity of "being-in-the world."

For Haribhadra, it is in the fourth stage that we come to know what is free from all conceptual extremes, experientially. This stage parallels a crucial point in the negation of the tetralemma in the unenframed interpretation of Madhayamaka: the shift from the negation of the third lemma (not both) to the negation of the fourth lemma (not either). The fourth stage undermines the whole structure of duality upon which the analysis is premised. In this last phase, the analysis turns on itself, and is no longer representational, but performative.

Another variation of the fourfold phenomenological analysis can be found in Vasubandhu's *Treatise on the Three Natures:*[72]

> As a result of perception of mind only, there is no perception of cognitive objects. As a result of no perception of cognitive objects, there can be no perception of mind. As a result of no perception of duality, there is perception of the basic field of reality (*dharmadhātu*). As a result of perception of the basic field of reality, there can be perception of liberation.

70. See, for instance, Haribhadra, *Clear Meaning* (*Sphuṭārtha*) (D. 3793), 124b–125a; English trans. in Komarovski, *Visions of Unity* (Albany: SUNY Press, 2011), 152.

71. Vasubandhu, *Thirty Verses* (*Triṃśikā*) v. 28 (D. 4050), 3a.

72. Vasubandhu, *Treatise on the Three Natures* (*Trisvabhāvanirdeṣa*), vv. 36–37. See also comments and English trans. in Gold, "No Outside, No Inside: Duality, Reality and Vasubandhu's Illusory Elephant," *Asian Philosophy* 16, no. 1 (2006): 25.

The insights into the later stages are premised on the preceding analyses that determine that appearances are mental and that the subject is not real. After objects are discerned as mind—as mentally constituted—the mind is discerned to be unreal, too. Indeed, there is no real subject because there is no real object; thus, the subject (mind) does not have a privileged status as real because it too is empty. This fourth stage, like the negation of the fourth lemma of the tetralemma, overcomes duality; it is the culmination, and dissolution, of analysis.[73]

These four stages are taken up in other Mahāyāna texts as well, such as the *Ornament of the Mahāyana Sutrās*, which states:

> Becoming aware that there is nothing apart from the mind,
> They realize that also the mind does not exist at all.
> Having seen that the two do not exist, the intelligent ones abide
> In the basic field of reality, which does not contain that.[74]

In late nineteenth-century Tibet, Mipam offered the following commentary on these verses:

> Bodhisattvas understand that the phenomena appearing as perceived aspects are not external objects apart from mind; they are just like dream-objects manifesting in the mind itself. Their minds then genuinely abide in the nature of mind only. They realize that the perceived lacks a nature—and this is one part of reality free from perceived and perceiver . . . Then they directly realize the basic field of reality, free from the characteristics of perceived and perceiver, which is the attainment of the path of seeing. How does this happen? During the phase of forbearance (*bzod pa*), they understand that there are no external objects, that there is nothing perceived other than mind. They [bodhisattvas] then realize that

73. An excellent summary of these four stages can be found in A. Lutz, J. Dunne, and R. Davidson, "Meditation and the Neuroscience of Consciousness: An Introduction," in *Cambridge Handbook of Consciousness*, ed. P. D. Zelazo, Morris Moscovitch, and Evan Thompson (Cambridge: Cambridge University Press, 2007), 513–515. Mipam also discusses four stages; see Duckworth, *Mipam on Buddha-Nature*, 40–42. For another discussion of these four phases, see Karl Brunnhölzl, *Gone Beyond*, vol. 2 (Ithaca, NY: Snow Lion Publications, 2011–2012), 223–226.

74. *Ornament of the Great Vehicle Sūtras* (*Mahāyanasutrālaṃkāra*) VII.8 (D. 4020, vol. 123), 6b; English trans. in Dharmachakra Translation Committee, *Ornament of the Great Vehicle Sūtras* (Boston: Snow Lion Publications, 2014), 138.

> if there is no perceived, then there is also no mind that perceives because the perceived and the perceiver mutually depend on each other. The realization that there is no perceiver when there is no perceived is the meditative equipoise of the supreme property (*chos mchog*), immediately preceding the path of seeing. Right after this, when the intelligent ones become aware that both the perceived and the perceiver lack a nature, they actualize nonconceptual gnosis. They abide with individual, self-awareness, directly cognizing the basic field of reality free from the attributes of the dualistic phenomena of perceived and perceiver.[75]

Another text of the "five treatises of Maitreya," *Distinguishing the Middle and the Extremes*, lays out the four stages as follows:

> Based on observation,
> Non-observation comes to be
> Based on non-observation,
> Non-observation takes place.[76]

In fifteenth-century Tibet, Gö Lotsāwa (1392–1481) correlated these four stages with the four yogas of Mahāmudrā.[77] He said:

> The first [mahāmudrā yoga, *single-pointedness*] is to look inward and to observe mind only. The second, that there is nothing external, is the [mahāmudrā yoga of] *freedom from constructs*, which is the realization that all phenomena that are objects of mind lack any foundation. The realization that external appearances and the internal mind are free from constructs and *one taste* is [the third mahāmudrā yoga,] the practice (*sbyor ba, prayoga*) of the non-observation of

75. Mipam, *A Feast on the Nectar of the Supreme Vehicle*, 108–109; English trans. in Dharmachakra Translation Committee, *Ornament of the Great Vehicle Sūtras*, 141.

76. Maitreya, *Distinguishing the Middle and the Extremes* (*Madhyāntavibhāga*) I.6; English trans. in Dharmachakra Translation Group, *Middle Beyond Extremes* (Ithaca: Snow Lion Publications, 2006), 31.

77. Gö Lotsāwa, *Mirror That Completely Illuminates Reality* (*theg pa chen po rgyud bla ma'i bstan bcos kyi 'grel bshad de kho na nyid rab tu gsal ba'i me long*), 465. See Klaus-Dieter Mathes, "Gos Lo tsā ba Gzhon nu dpal's Commentary on the *Dharmatā* Chapter of the *Dharmadharmatāvibhāgakārikās*," *Studies in Indian Philosophy and Buddhism* (University of Tokyo, 2005), 17.

observation. Not meditating with deliberate observation on that nonduality of subject and object is called *non-meditation*, the fourth [mahāmudrā] yoga.[78]

These stages, in which "mind-only" idealism serves as an important propaedeutic that is later transcended, appear not only in commentarial treatises (*śāstras*), but in sūtras as well. For instance, the *Descent to Laṅkā Sūtra* states:

> Relying on mind-only,
> One does not imagine external objects.
> Relying on non-appearance,
> One passes beyond mind-only.
> Relying on authentic observation,
> One passes beyond non-appearance.
> Yogis who dwell in non-appearance,
> Do not see the Great Vehicle.[79]

Dölpopa (1292–1361), the forefather of the Jonang tradition in Tibet, glossed this passage as follows:

> For the time being, one is taught mind-only, but finally having fully passed beyond that, one is taught Madhyamaka without appearance, and then, having also passed beyond that, one is taught Madhyamaka with appearance, and if one does not arrive there, one does not see the profound meaning of the Great Vehicle.[80]

Dölpopa explained that first one is taught mind-only, that objects are mind-dependent, and then one learns about "Madhyamaka without appearance," that the subject, too, is not real like the object. This is the Madhyamaka of "self-emptiness," which is the mere absence of true existence. After

---

78. Gö Lotsāwa, *Mirror That Completely Illuminates Reality*, 465. See Mathes, *A Direct Path to the Buddha Within* (Sommerville, MA: Wisdom Publications, 2008), 382–386. Mathes mistranslates this last phase, as "Perceiving again in a special way . . ." yet what Mathes translates as "special way" is the deliberate observation (*thad du dmigs pa*) that is precisely what is denied, not affirmed.

79. *Descent to Laṅka Sūtra* (*Laṅkāvatārasūtra*), X.256–257 (H. 111, vol. 51), 270a.

80. Dölpopa, *Ocean of Definitive Meaning, Dölpopa's Collected Works* (*'dzam thang* ed.), vol. 3, 396.

understanding the way objects and subjects are absent, lacking intrinsic nature, one then proceeds to the presence of nonduality in "Madhyamaka with appearance." This is the domain of "other-emptiness" (*gzhan stong*), the appearance of ultimate nonduality. This positive characterization of ultimate gnosis and its domain is also a prominent topic in the theory and practice of tantra, which we will turn to in chapter 5.

Conclusion

Despite the rhetoric of difference, phenomenology and ontology can be seen to mutually entail each other. We have seen these two styles of analysis exemplified in a contrast between Madhyamaka and Mind-Only. A Madhyamaka analysis highlights an ontological dimension, that all objects are empty. The analyses of Mind-Only highlights a phenomenological dimension, with a focus on subjective mind. Both of these styles of analysis can be seen to have different points of departure, while ending up with the same conclusion (nonduality). Also, it is important to recognize that both traditions utilize both styles of analysis.

The culmination of the deconstructive analyses of Madhyamaka can be found in Prāsaṅgika-Madhyamaka, when no claims are held concerning the final nature of reality and nothing is acknowledged beyond mundane convention. Yet when all becomes mere appearance, the subject matter of Madhyamaka shifts from ontology to phenomenology. Conversely, Mind-Only analyses take their point of departure in a phenomenological inquiry into the nature of appearance. Yet the phenomenological analysis of Mind-Only turns toward ontology when a cognitive ground is formulated as the basis of the lived world.

As phenomenology presumes ontology for Mind-Only, ontology presumes phenomenology for Madhyamaka. In Mind-Only, the ultimate truth has content, "what remains in emptiness." For Mādhyamikas, too, emptiness appears. There is no separate emptiness other than an appearance's lack of intrinsic identity, so the phenomenal presentation of an entity itself instantiates emptiness (e.g., the table instantiates the table's emptiness). This is because emptiness in Madhyamaka's ontology means nothing other than a phenomenon's lack of true identity. Thus, both Mind-Only and Madhyamaka can be seen to assert a common ground—the unity of appearance and emptiness—that is the structure of reality.

For both traditions, this structure is constituted by nonduality, and thus cannot be fully represented. It cannot be adequately represented objectively because nonduality is integrally cognitive. It cannot be adequately represented subjectively either because there are objective constraints; it is relationally constituted (empty) and nondual. For these Buddhist traditions, a relational (dualistic) structure is how things come to appear, but in reality the structure itself is beyond duality (and beyond singularity). Thus in these traditions, the "structure" of nonduality cannot be directly stated, but can be known, like the way that (the performative) emptiness cannot be directly stated, but can be shown.

3

Self-Awareness and the Subject-Object

Hey! This is self-aware gnosis!
It is beyond words and is not the domain of mind.
I, Tilopa, have nothing to teach.
Know it as it is presented in self-awareness itself.
—TILOPA, in Wangchuk Gyeltsen, *Biography of Nāropa*, 96

Introduction

Self-awareness (*svasaṃvedana*) is the linchpin of a system of Buddhist epistemology (*pramāṇa*) formulated by Dignāga in the sixth century and developed by Dharmakīrti in the seventh. In this epistemology, self-awareness can be seen to function not only as the precondition for knowledge, but also as the pinnacle of knowledge. The status of "self-awareness" has a central place in the discourses of modern phenomenology, too, and carries a number of different connotations.

Many phenomenologists since Husserl have argued that without self-awareness—the pre-theoretical grounding in a first-personal, privileged access to experience (e.g., I undoubtedly know that I am undergoing an experience)—knowledge lacks a foundation. These phenomenologists claim that there is no way to build a coherent theory of experience—in the humanities or the natural sciences—without self-awareness. Opponents of self-awareness, however, argue that knowledge needs no foundation. Dennett even argues that phenomenology is based in the mistaken intuitions of folk psychology.[1]

1. Apparently for Dennett, phenomenology is only relevant as a form of public discourse. That is, for him there is only talk of phenomenology that can be an object of study; he calls it "heterophenomenology." In other words, phenomenology functions for him similar to the way theology functions for an atheist: there is just talk of God (theology), yet it is the God-talk, not God, which can potentially yield knowledge. See Daniel Dennett, *Consciousness Explained* (Boston: Back Bay Books, 1991), 72–98.

Many philosophers, East (Candrakīrti, Tsongkhapa) and West (Dennett), have challenged the assumption that self-awareness is foundational, along with the reliability of introspection. Some Buddhist scholars have argued that there is no warrant for believing that our intuitive knowledge of ourselves is any less distorted than our intuitions about the world. That is, we are just as mistaken about the reality of the objects of our experience (e.g., object constancy amidst a flux of experience) as we our about our self-identity. Thus, it is argued that the presumed "immediacy" of self-awareness is also just another construction.

In this chapter, I discuss various interpretations of self-awareness, including its meaning as the beginning and culmination of Mind-Only's phenomenological analysis. I also discuss the ways this notion has been criticized as simply another conceptual construct. Self-awareness plays a pivotal role in Buddhist epistemology, and whether it is accepted or not can be seen as a litmus test for the distinction between constructivism and realism and the domains of ontology and phenomenology.

Types of Self-Awareness

Self-awareness can be taken to be many things, including the awareness of a self, the quality of subjective consciousness in an awareness of an object, and the structure of intentionality. The awareness of a *self* (at least a self that is understood as an object) is of course denied by Buddhists across India and Tibet. A second meaning, as the quality of subjective consciousness, can refer to the feature of awareness that is embedded in the awareness of any object. Here self-awareness is first-personal access to experience—the quality of being aware *as an experiential subject* when aware of something. This is the self-awareness commonly claimed by modern phenomenologists, and connotes the *phenomenal feel* of experience, its experienced dimension, as opposed to an objective fact that is representational, representable, or demonstrable. Self-awareness in this case is held to always accompany all object-awarenesses. It is important to keep in mind that the *self* in this sense of *self*-awareness is not a substantive self, but should be understood as a reflexive pronoun in an non-egological way, as in "self-generating" or "self-propelled," rather than "generator of a self" or "propeller of a self."

A third interpretation of self-awareness takes it to consist in a special intransitivity of awareness, as opposed to an intentional awareness that is a consciousness *of an object*. Self-awareness in this sense can be taken to be both the structure of experience and the structure of reality as well. This interpretation can be seen in the Yogācāra tradition stemming from Dignāga and Dharmakīrti, which describes self-awareness as the way that the mind presents itself in the phenomenal features (*ākāra*) of an object and a subject. Here, self-awareness is not simply the subjective aspect of an apprehension, but is the unified field of a subject-object presentation of the world. Dharmakīrti expressed the nature of this awareness as follows: "Awareness is undifferentiated, but its appearance is differentiated into two. That being the case, that dualistic appearance must be cognitive confusion."[2] That is, while awareness is undifferentiated, it presents itself in the phenomenal features of a subject and object. Self-awareness in this context is not only the means by which experience arises but also its content: everything, subjects and objects, arise in and as awareness. In this kind of interpretation, experiential reality is nothing but awareness; the world is singular (or rather, nondual) even though it presents itself as a duality of subjects and objects.[3]

All three of these interpretations of self-awareness are related. The first, self-awareness as the awareness of self, is, according to some thinkers, implicated by the latter two.[4] Indeed, the relationship between a mistaken sense of self and the second and third types of self-awareness is a topic around which there is a lot of debate and there is much at stake.[5] The second meaning—self-awareness as the subjective feel of experience—can be considered to be a self, a subtle self or minimal self as the bare sense of being a subject of experience. The third sense of self-awareness, as the structure of reality, can be identified with the self, too, albeit a cosmic self, in the sense of the self as universe or a boundless, ecological self. Of

---

2. Dharmakīrti, *Commentary on Epistemology* III.212, translation from John Dunne, *Foundations of Dharmakīrti's Philosophy* (Boston: Wisdom Publications, 2004), 406.

3. Topics addressed in this section are further discussed in Duckworth, "Self-Awareness and the Integration of Pramāṇa and Madhyamaka," *Asian Philosophy* 25, no. 2 (2015): 207–215.

4. Buddhists such as Tsongkhapa, as well as non-Buddhists such as Rāmakaṇṭha Bhaṭṭa, argue this. For Tsongkhapa's position, see the discussion that follows; for Rāmakaṇṭha Bhaṭṭa's, see Alex Watson, *The Self's Awareness of Itself: Rāmakaṇṭha Bhaṭṭa's Arguments Against the Buddhist Doctrine of No-Self* (Wien: De Nobili, 2006).

5. See, for instance, Siderits et al. (eds.), *Self, No Self? Perspectives from Analytical, Phenomenological, and Indian Traditions* (Oxford: Oxford University Press, 2011); see also Jay Garfield, "The Conventional Status of Reflexive Awareness: What's at Stake in a Tibetan Debate?," *Philosophy East & West*, 56, no. 2 (2006): 201–228.

course this is not a self among others, but is an all-embracing unity, the source and substance of reality.

The first type, an egological view (self-awareness as *awareness of* self), is something Buddhists explicitly negate, but what about the second or third? The fact that self-awareness implicates an ultimate ground, or a mistaken notion of self, has been argued by Tsongkhapa, and is the reason why he denies it. Yet the meaning of self-awareness is complex, and theorists in India and Tibet have come down on a range of views on this key topic.

Two main ways that self-awareness has been represented in India and Tibet can be clarified as the difference between a *reflective* self-awareness and a *pre-reflective* self-awareness.[6] This distinction highlights the contrast between self-awareness understood to be reflective (or introspective) in the former case and *pre-reflective* (or reflexive) in the latter. While a reflective quality of mind is tied to an intentional, transitive structure, a pre-reflective one is not. A reflective self-awareness takes as its object another cognition; it is a higher order thought or perception, such as what we see in the works of David Armstrong and David Rosenthal.[7] That is, reflective self-awareness is a second-order awareness or introspective cognition. Moreover, reflective self-awareness has the structure of the first type of self-awareness—as a directed, intentional consciousness, an *awareness of* something. Pre-reflective self-awareness, however, is a different story. It is an intransitive cognition without a direct object, not an *awareness of* something. Heidegger expressed this kind of pre-reflective awareness as "disclosure" in contrast to (reflective) "apprehension": "The self is there . . . *before* all reflection. Reflection, in the sense of turning back, is only a mode of self-*apprehension,* but not the mode of primary self-disclosure."[8] For Heidegger, self-disclosure is prior to a reflective self-apprehension.

---

6. This difference has been articulated clearly by Matthew MacKenzie. See MacKenzie, "The Illumination of Consciousness: Approaches to Self-Awareness in the Indian and Western Traditions," *Philosophy East & West* 57 (2007): 41–42.

7. See David Armstrong, *A Materialist Theory of the Mind* (London: Routledge, 1968) and David Rosenthal, *Consciousness and Mind* (Oxford: Oxford University Press, 2005).

8. Martin Heidegger, *The Basic Problems of Phenomenology*, trans. by Albert Hofstadter (Bloomington: Indiana University Press, 1988 [1982]), 159.

As described by the eighth-century Indian scholar, Śāntarakṣita, prereflective self-awareness is the nature of awareness: "Consciousness is the opposite of matter; this immateriality is nothing but its self-awareness."[9] Self-awareness as an *intransitive* awareness is an important feature of this awareness for Śāntarakṣita: "Being singular without parts, it cannot be divided into three [the knower, the known, and the knowing]. This self-awareness is not constituted by action and agent."[10] This prereflective self-awareness is thus not something that is partitioned into a separate known and knower. Such a view of self-awareness, as part in parcel with awareness itself, can be found in Yogācāra texts,[11] the phenomenological tradition of Husserl, the works of Sartre, and has been recently explicated by Dan Zahavi.[12] As Zahavi and Parnas describe their own theory:

> Consciousness is self-luminous. It is characterized by intentionality, but being intentionally aware of objects, it is simultaneously self-aware through and in itself. Its self-awareness is not due to a secondary act or reflex but is a constitutive moment of the experience itself, and consciousness can consequently be compared to a flame, which illuminates other things, and itself as well.[13]

Here it is argued that self-awareness is built into awareness, acting like a flame that illuminates itself as it illuminates other things. It is significant

---

9. Śāntarakṣita, *Ornament of the Middle Way*, v. 16: *vijñānaṃ jaḍarūpebhyo vyāvṛttam upajāyate iyam evātmasaṃvittir asya yā 'jaḍarūpatā*. See Masamichi Ichigo, *Madhyamakālaṃkāra of Śāntarakṣita with His Own Commentary or Vṛtti and with the Subcommentary or Pañjikā of Kamalaśīla* (Kyoto: Sangyo University, 1985), 70n1.

10. Śāntarakṣita, *Ornament of the Middle Way*, v. 17.

11. See Dignāga, *Compendium of Epistemology* (*Pramāṇasamuccaya*), I.10; translated in Masaaki Hattori, *Dignāga on Perception* (Cambridge, MA: Harvard University Press, 1968), 29. See also Sakya Paṇḍita, *Treasury of Epistemology* (Beijing, China: Nationalities Press, 1989), 245; Śākya Chokden, *Commentary on "Treasury of Epistemology,"* in *Śākya Chokden's Collected Works*, vol. 19, 479; Yaroslav Komarovski, *Visions of Unity* (Albany: SUNY Press, 2011), 246.

12. See Dan Zahavi, *Subjectivity and Selfhood: Investigating the First-Person Perspective* (Cambridge: MIT Press, 2005), 20–22.

13. Dan Zahavi and Josef Parnas, "Phenomenal Consciousness and Self-Awareness: A Phenomenological Critique of Representational Theory," *Journal of Consciousness Studies* 5, nos. 5–6 (1998), 696.

that Nāgārjuna rejected the flame analogy for self-illumination several times.[14] Since phenomenologists typically argue in this way that the quality of self-awareness is an intrinsic property of awareness, (pre-reflective) self-awareness is primary and foundational; it serves as a ground for undeniable knowledge or *acquaintance*.[15] Dan Zahavi further characterizes self-awareness as the "acquaintance consciousness has with *itself* and *not* as an awareness of an experiencing *self*."[16] As Zahavi and Parnas claim:

> The basic self-awareness of an experience is not mediated by any foreign elements such as concepts and classificatory criteria. It is an immediate and intrinsic *self-acquaintance* which is characterized by being completely *irrelational*.[17]

It is precisely because self-awareness is presumed to have this kind of feature—as an intrinsic, non-relational property of awareness with a unique status among kinds of knowledge—that it is rejected by Tsongkhapa. Tsongkhapa consistently refused to privilege the mind's access to itself over its access to objects. Tsongkhapa thus put self-awareness on par with object-awareness—and for him, all such cognitions are only conceptual constructions. For a Mādhyamika like Tsongkhapa, everything is relational and subject to critique, in contrast to a phenomenological foundationalism that holds there to be bedrocks for indubitable knowledge.

Zahavi and Parnas claim that "it is doubtful whether one could account for the immediacy, unity and infallibility of self-awareness (particularly its so-called *immunity to the error of misidentification*), if it were in any way a

---

14. Nāgārjuna, *Fundamental Verses of the Middle Way* VII.8–12, *Dispelling Disputes* vv. 34–39, and *Finely Woven Scripture* (D. 3826), 23a.

15. We find this language of acquaintance in Bertrand Russell as well, who said: "All of knowledge, both knowledge of things and knowledge of truths, rests upon acquaintance as its foundation." Russell, *The Problems of Philosophy* (Oxford: Oxford University Press, 1997 [1912]), 48.

16. Zahavi, *Subjectivity and Selfhood*, 100. Yet the question remains as to how exactly "acquaintance" with awareness constitutes a type of knowledge. This question has led the Naiyāyikas and Tsongkhapa to deny self-awareness as a type of knowledge because, by definition; if it does not know anything, it does not qualify to be counted as a type of cognition. See, for instance, Vātsyāyana's commentary on Gautama's characterization of perceptual cognition in *Nyāya Sūtra*, 1.1.4. Gautama, *Nyāya Sūtra*, in *Gautamīyanyāyadarśana with Bhāṣya of Vātsyāyana*, ed. Anantalal Thakur (Delhi: Indian Council of Philosophical Research, 1997), 10.

17. Zahavi and Parnas, "Phenomenal Consciousness and Self-Awareness," 696.

mediated process."[18] In contrast to the presumption of this modern phenomenology, Madhyamaka is based on an error-theory—and *nothing is immune to error* in the experiences of an ordinary being—even our most cherished ideas about self-identity and "first-personal givenness" is shot through with innate ignorance.[19] Everything, apart from a buddha's cognition and emptiness known in a sublime being's meditative equipoise, is infected by this ignorance. Thus, these kinds of ontological or epistemological foundations are not secure. In Tsongkhapa's system of Madhyamaka, self-awareness is not a reliable means of knowledge because it appears in a way that conflicts with the way it is (like an object-awareness).

A third meaning of self-awareness, the dual-aspected nature of self-awareness in Mind-Only, is not only pre-reflective, but resembles the substance of Spinoza's dual-aspect monism. Like Spinoza, who used thought and extension as examples of *attributes* of substance, Dignāga and Dharmakīrti outlined subjective and objective features of self-awareness. In his *Ascertaining Sources of Knowledge* (*Pramāṇaviniścaya*), Dharmakīrti claimed that "what is experienced by cognition is not different [from it]."[20] Self-awareness in this case is thus both the means and content of knowledge, similar to Spinoza's notion of substance, which he defined as "what is in itself and is conceived through itself."[21] Spinoza also supported the case that subjects and objects only appear to be distinct but in fact are not by following the principle that unlike things cannot be causally related,[22] like Dharmakīrti.[23]

---

18. Zahavi and Parnas, "Phenomenal Consciousness and Self-Awareness," 696.

19. See Tsongkhapa, *Middling Stages of the Path (byang chub lam rim 'bring ba'i sa bcad kha skong dang bcas pa)* (Byllakuppe, India: Sera Je, 2005), 343; English translation in Hopkins, *Tsong-kha-pa's Final Exposition of Wisdom*, 117.

20. Dharmakīrti, *Ascertaining Sources of Knowledge* (*Pramāṇaviniścaya*), I.38a: *nānyo 'nubhāvyo buddhyāsti*. See Keria, *Mādhyamika and Epistemology* (Wien: Arbeitskreis für Tibetische und Buddhistische Studien, 2004), 40n75.

21. Spinoza, *Ethics* 1, Definition 3, in *Spinoza: Complete Works*, trans. Samuel Shirley, ed. Michael Morgan (Indianapolis: Hackett Publishing, 2002), 217.

22. Spinoza claimed that "If things have nothing in common with one another, one of them cannot be the cause of the other" (Spinoza, *Ethics* 1, Proposition 3). Also, he added that "although two attributes may be conceived to be really distinct (i.e., one may be conceived without the aid of the other), we still cannot infer from that that they constitute two beings, *or* two different substances" Spinoza, *Ethics*, Scholium to Proposition 10.

23. See Dharmakīrti on self-awareness, in *Commentary on Epistemology* III.326–327; and on causes "of the same type" (*sajāti*), in *Commentary on Epistemology* II.36. See also Dan Arnold, *Brains, Buddhas, and Belief* (New York: Columbia University Press, 2012), 33.

This third kind of self-awareness, as the transcendental structure of experience, is a form of objective or absolute idealism. There is certainly a parallel between self-awareness in the second sense (of subjectivity being built into an awareness of objects) and the third sense (in which self-awareness is the structure of the world), but we find the difference accentuated in the works of Mind-Only and Yogācāra-inflected Tibetan traditions such as the Nyingma, the works of Dölpopa's Jonang tradition, the Kagyü, and Śākya Chokden's Sakya tradition. Unlike the Geluk tradition, these traditions make a distinction between *conventional* self-awareness, that is the ordinary mind, and *ultimate* self-awareness, that is gnosis.

Mind and Gnosis

A modified version of this third type of self-awareness, as the ultimate substance or truth, is found in the works of the Sakya scholar, Śākya Chokden (1428–1507). Self-awareness for Śākya Chokden is *sui generis*, like Spinoza's substance (a.k.a. God). In the way that for Spinoza, mind and matter are nothing but attributes of the one (infinite) substance of God,[24] Śākya Chokden claims that the only thing that is real is self-awareness, and that this self-awareness is the ultimate reality—the real ground for the unreal subject-object presentation of duality. Yet the self-awareness that Śākya Chokden claims to be real is impermanent. Also, it is exclusively a nondual awareness, not ordinary (conventional) self-awareness, for he denies the reality of any awareness that perceives duality.[25] Real self-awareness for him is of another order than ordinary cognitions. Śākya Chokden thus creates a third category for self-awareness, beyond dualistic subjectivity and objectivity. This self-awareness is thus a kind of supermind, or gnosis (*ye shes*), as opposed to ordinary consciousness (*rnam shes*).

The distinction that Śākya Chokden draws between two types of self-awareness is similar to the distinction in the Great Perfection between

24. Spinoza stated in Proposition 15 of the *Ethics:* "Whatever is, is in God, and nothing can be or be conceived without God."

25. Śākya Chokden, *Enjoyment Ocean of the Seven Treatises,* in *Śākya Chokden's Collected Works* (Thimphu, Bhutan: Kunzang Tobgey, 1975), vol. 19, 477–478; see also Komarovski, *Visions of Unity,* 163–164.

self-awareness (*rang rig*) in Mind-Only and the gnosis of self-awareness (*so sor rang rig pa'i ye shes*), which is awareness (*rig pa*).[26] Many Tibetan traditions make a distinction between (ultimate) self-awareness that is nonconceptual gnosis and (relative) self-awareness that is conceptual consciousness. In his writings on the Great Perfection, for instance, Longchenpa's distinction between the basic consciousness (*kun gzhi*) and the Truth Body (*chos sku*) can be said to be articulating the same fundamental difference: the distinction between a distorted, *egological* subject and an unbounded, *ecological* subject. In fact, Longchenpa distinguishes his view of the Great Perfection from that of "Mind-Only" with the claim that:

> Proponents of Mind-Only assert a changeless permanence and mere [ordinary] awareness as self-illuminating, but this position differs because we assert the unconditioned spontaneous presence beyond permanence and annihilation, and the spontaneously present qualities of the basic element."[27]

In this way, Longchenpa appeals to the presence of an unconditioned awareness that transcends ordinary conditioned states of mind, and by doing so, distinguishes his assertion by saying that the claims of the proponents of Mind-Only are caught within a reified world of conceptual constructs. Thus, he draws a clear distinction between self-aware mind and self-aware gnosis. Longchenpa distinguishes the mind (*blo*) as relative and thus distorted, whereas "the essence of the ultimate is the domain of self-aware gnosis beyond conceptual extremes . . . self-awareness (*so so rang gi rig pa*) is undistorted gnosis beyond thought, words, and expression."[28] This is also similar to the way the Jonang distinguish their tradition from Mind-Only.[29] Dölpopa used the same criteria to distinguish "relative mind-only" (*kun rdzob kyi sems tsam*), which he rejects, from the "ultimate mind-only"

---

26. See Matthew Kapstein, "We Are All Gzhan stong pas," *Journal of Buddhist Ethics* 7 (2000): 109–115.

27. Longchenpa, *White Lotus: Autocommentary on the "Precious Wish-Fulfilling Treasury,"* in *Seven Treasuries*, vol. 7, ed. Tarthang Tulku (Sichuan, China, 1996), 1420.

28. See Longchenpa, *White Lotus*, 1155–1156.

29. See Khenpo Lodrö Drakpa, *Roar of the Fearless Lion* (Dharamsala: Library of Tibetan Works and Archives, 1993), 63; 214–223; see also Duckworth, *Mipam on Buddha-Nature: The Ground of the Nyingma Tradition* (Albany, NY: SUNY Press, 2008), 64–65.

(*don dam pa'i sems tsam*) that he endorses.[30] (See Appendix A for a Jonang presentation of the relationship between Mind-Only and Madhyamaka.)

Dölpopa distinguished ultimate self-awareness from its relative counterpart as follows: "The difference between knower and known is [a property of] relative object-awareness (*kun rdzob gzhan rig*); for ultimate self-awareness (*don dam rang rig*), the knower and known are the same."[31] Another Jonang scholar, Tāranātha (1575–1634), contrasted Dölpopa's and Śākya Chokden's views in a text outlining twenty-one key points of distinction. He claimed that Śākya Chokden treats the relative and ultimate self-awareness as the same *in terms of their reflexivity*, whereas Dölpopa makes a radical distinction between the two, with no overlap.[32] Indeed, Śākya Chokden himself does describe the ultimate in a way that resembles the phenomenality of the dualistic mind. He depicts ultimate self-awareness as the "phenomenal feature of an apprehender" (*'dzin rnam*),[33] in the way that he describes ordinary self-awareness, and similarly characterizes it as internal, "inward looking" (*kha nang lta*) as opposed to outward looking.[34] In this way, he draws on the unique quality of subjectivity in *pre-reflective self-awareness*, the second type of (ordinary) self-awareness, as an analogue for ultimate self-awareness. Thus, the way a unique status is given to subjectivity in the immediacy of first-personal perception parallels the status of self-awareness as the ultimate, incontrovertible truth of objective or absolute idealism.

This type of self-awareness is refuted by Mādhyamikas like Candrakīrti and Tsongkhapa because it is seen as representing a form of subjective idealism or absolute idealism, which reifies a self.[35] Indeed, a self-awareness

30. Dölpopa, *The Mountain Doctrine: Ocean of Definitive Meaning, Dölpopa's Collected Works*, vol. 3, 396–398.

31. Dölpopa, *The Mountain Doctrine: Ocean of Definitive Meaning*, 601.

32. Tāranātha, *Twenty-One Profound Points* (*'dzam thang* ed.) *Tāranātha's Collected Works*, vol. 18, 214; English trans. in Mathes, *Journal of the International Association of Buddhist Studies* 27, no. 2 (2004): 302.

33. It has been suggested that ordinary self-awareness resembles this gnosis, in the sense that "analogical luminous clarity" (*dpe'i 'od gsal*) resembles "actual luminous clarity" (*don gyi 'od gsal*). See Dreyfus, "Would the True Prāsaṅgika Please Stand? The Case of 'Ju Mipham," in *The Svātantrika-Prāsaṅgika Distinction*, ed. Georges Dreyfus and Sara McClintock (Boston: Wisdom Publications, 2003), 346n33.

34. Śākya Chokden, *Unprecedented Sun*, in *Śākya Chokden's Collected Works* (Thimphu, Bhutan: Kunzang Tobgey, 1975), vol. 13, 122; see also Komarovski, *Visions of Unity*, 249.

35. Tsongkhapa characterizes a reified nondual self-awareness as a type of self. See Tsongkhapa, *Middling Stages of the Path*, 300; English trans. in Hopkins, *Tsong-kha-pa's Final*

that is an internal mind and an independent substance explicitly contradicts the Buddhist doctrine of interdependence. Yet Śākya Chokden denies the subjective idealist claim to the reality of an internal mind as opposed to an external world because he denies the reality of all dualistic cognitions. Since he agrees with the (Madhyamaka) claim that nothing taken as an object sustains ontological analysis (including this ultimate mind), he asserts that the reality of self-awareness is of a different order than truths that result from these kinds of ontological analyses.[36] For Mādhyamikas like Tsongkhapa, of course, there are no different orders of ultimate analysis in this way; all is equally empty. Yet Śākya Chokden maintains a special place for nondual self-awareness, claiming that it is the only thing that is real.[37]

Śākya Chokden, with the subjective idealists, does not postulate a metaphysical notion of matter independent of experiential reality. Since the "stuff" of the world for him is cognitive, and structurally similar to ordinary self-awareness, the primary material of the world is not completely opaque to cognition, unlike a physicalist's mysterious (metaphysical) notion of "matter." Yet Śākya Chokden claims that nondual self-awareness is the transcendental condition for dualistic mind. He says, "Without primordial gnosis, adventitious consciousness does not arise as distorted appearances. Nevertheless, we do not accept that it is possible for a common ground of the two."[38] He thus draws on a distinction between gnosis and consciousness similar to one we find made in the distinction between pantheism and *panentheism* ("all is God" *vs.* "all is in God")—a distinction that collapses God into nature on the one hand and maintains a hierarchy with the transcendent status of the divine on the other. Without the theological language, we can draw out his distinction by distinguishing between the subjective idealism of his portrayal of Mind-Only (e.g., "proponents of true representations" (*rnam bden pa*), who collapse matter into mind) and

---

Exposition of Wisdom (Ithaca, NY: Snow Lion Publications, 2008), 46. See also Candrakīrti, *Introduction to the Middle Way* VI.72.

36. This sentiment is shared by the Seventh Karmapa, Chödrak Gyatso. See his *Ocean of Epistemological Scriptures and Reasoning* (*tshad ma rigs gzhung rgya mtsho*), (Varanasi: Nithartha International, 1999), vol. 1, 350–351.

37. Śākya Chokden says, "The gnosis that is the basic field of reality is truly real." Śākya Chokden, *Splendor of the Sun*, in *Śākya Chokden's Collected Works*, vol. 19, 118: (*chos kyi dbyings kyi ye shes bden par grub*). See also Komarovski, *Visions of Unity*, 220–225; 241.

38. Śākya Chokden, *Unprecedented Sun*, in *Śākya Chokden's Collected Works*, vol. 13, 121. See also Komarovski, *Visions of Unity*, 239–240.

the absolute idealism of what he refers to as Madhyamaka (e.g., "proponents of false representations" (*rnam mrdzun pa*), who deny both ordinary mind and matter, but claim that everything takes place by means of a transcendent, mind-like substance—gnosis). Thus, like the role of the ultimate ground of awareness in the Nyingma, he asserts a kind of supermind (*ye shes*) or third category that is the substrate of both matter and mind.

Another model for affirming a cognitive ground of reality is found in the Jonang tradition. For Dölpopa, the cognitive ground of gnosis is the ultimate: "The ultimate mind is the mind that exists within the abiding reality; relative mind is a mind that does not exist within the abiding reality."[39] In other words, gnosis is real; consciousness is not. Furthermore, Dölpopa conveys the epistemological implications of this: "Since the relative does not exist in reality, it is self-empty. It appears to consciousness, but not to gnosis. Since the ultimate exists in reality, it is not empty of itself but is other-empty. It appears to gnosis but never to consciousness."[40] In this way, consciousness and what appears to it are self-empty; while gnosis and its domain are other-empty.

For Dölpopa, the relationship between ultimate reality and the relative world is similar to that of God and world in classical theology: it is a *hierarchical* dichotomy and the primacy of the former element in the dichotomy is the necessary condition for the latter. For the Jonang, this asymmetrical dichotomy is also similar to the relationship between *brahman* and *māyā* in Śaṅkara's eighth-century systemization of Advaita Vedānta. We can see this in the way that Dölpopa depicts nirvana in relation to samsara, as well as the ultimate truth in relation to the relative truth—buddha and sentient being, gnosis (*ye shes*) and consciousness (*rnam shes*), the other-empty and the self-empty, etc. The two form a strict dichotomy and the former is a necessary condition for the latter *but not vice versa*. To uphold his hierarchical and dualistic system, Dölpopa contends that other-emptiness is superior to self-emptiness.[41]

The duality of the two truths in Dölpopa's Jonang tradition is based on an appearance-reality distinction. It is hierarchical, not reciprocal.

---

39. Dölpopa, *The Mountain Doctrine: Ocean of Definitive Meaning*, 581: *don dam gyi sems ni gnas lugs la yod pa'i sems so/ /kun rdzob kyi sems ni gnas lugs la med pa'i sems so.*

40. Dölpopa, *The Sun Elucidating the Two Truths*, in *Dölpopa's Collected Works*, vol. 6, 697.

41. The topics in this section are discussed further in Duckworth, "Other-Emptiness in the Jonang: The Theo-logic of Buddhist Dualism," *Philosophy East & West* 65, no. 2 (2015): 485–497.

What is unconditioned is the ground of the conditioned, not *vice versa*. Thus, it is not the case that by eliminating samsara that you thereby eliminate nirvana, or by eliminating sentient beings you eliminate buddhas.[42] Consequently, the two elements in the dichotomy do not co-exist in mutual co-dependence like left/right or up/down. Moreover, a permanent nirvana that Dölpopa contrasts with impermanence is a permanence that is an eternal ground. It is transcendent and unchanging. Thus, the unconditioned is not a permanence that is co-dependent with impermanence nor is it eliminated by eliminating impermanence. The permanent, unconditioned reality is also self-arisen (or self-existing), so it is not produced like something that is "other-arisen" (which is a product and thus impermanent and conditioned).[43] Thus, he says that the ultimate truth is beyond dependently arisen phenomena.[44]

Dölpopa also refers to this ultimate truth (or reality) as "the supreme self" (*bdag mchog*) and "purity" (*gtsang*), which he says is beyond the relative dichotomies of self/no-self, pure/impure, and permanence/impermanence.[45] In this way, the ultimate is distinguished as the supreme "other" (*gzhan*) beyond the inner and outer, the internal and external. This is the "other" of "other-emptiness," which functions as a third category beyond conventional dichotomies (*phung po gsum*). Other-emptiness, reflecting the "other" beyond the dichotomy of "inner" and "outer," is certainly amenable to a philosophically articulated view of tantra, which we will visit in chapter 5. Such affirmations of a pure reality, *behind* the empirical reality of changing appearance or *within* that reality, contrast with the way the ultimate truth is represented in singularly negating discourses in Madhyamaka.

Such a characterization is not limited to the Jonang. The presence of an unbounded awareness (beyond subjectivity) is the basis of the awareness/mind distinction made in the Great Perfection and the consciousness/

---

42. Dölpopa, *The Categories of the Possible and the Impossible*, in *Dölpopa's Collected Works* (*'dzam thang* ed.), vol. 6, 306–307.

43. Dölpopa makes a distinction between self-existing (or self-arisen) gnosis and other-arisen gnosis: the former is the unconditioned ultimate truth, while the latter, which is newly arisen as the result of cultivating the path, is conditioned. Dölpopa, *The Mountain Doctrine: Ocean of Definitive Meaning*, 314.

44. Dölpopa, *The Mountain Doctrine: Ocean of Definitive Meaning*, 505.

45. Dölpopa, *The Mountain Doctrine: Ocean of Definitive Meaning*, 523–524.

gnosis distinction that is the bedrock of the traditions affirming "other-emptiness." We thus find influential figures in the Kagyü schools, for instance, who make this all-important distinction between consciousness and gnosis.[46] In Advaita Vedānta, too, *jñāna* is similarly distinguished from the *vṛtti-jñānas*,[47] or nondual gnosis is different from dualistic consciousness. This dichotomy reflects what we see in the Kagyü works of the Third Karmapa, Rangjung Dorjé (1284–1339), the works of Longchenpa in the Nyingma, Dölpopa in the Jonang, and Śākya Chokden in the Sakya tradition. The exception is the Geluk.

While Tibetan scholastic traditions tend to reject Mind-Only as inferior to Madhyamaka, key ideas from Mind-Only—like self-awareness and a foundational, cognitive ground—are found in tantric traditions, including Mahāmudrā and the Great Perfection. This direction of thought and practice in Tibet lies in contrast to the orientation of critical anti-realism in Madhyamaka, the apotheosis of which is found in the Geluk tradition.

The Critical Gaze of Geluk Prāsaṅgika

While the "basic consciousness" (*ālayavijñāna*) and self-awareness (*svasaṃvedana*) are keystones for some systems of Buddhist philosophy to get beyond what is merely conventional, the Prāsaṅgika-Madhyamaka, as interpreted by the Geluk tradition, does not follow suit. In fact, foundationalists and idealists that deny the reality of an external world are targets of the Geluk tradition's Prāsaṅgika.

Prāsaṅgika-Madhyamaka squarely rejects idealism in its absolute and subjective forms, and does not assent to any independent means to verify the claims of idealism (or physicalism for that matter). Rather than denying an external world, external objects are acknowledged to exist as long as internal minds are counterposed with them.[48] Thus, neither objects nor

46. See, for instance, Rangjung Dorjé, *Treatise Distinguishing Consciousness and Gnosis*; English trans. in Karl Brunnhölzl, *Luminous Heart: The Third Karmapa on Consciousness, Wisdom, and Buddha-Nature* (Ithaca, NY: Snow Lion Publications, 2009), 361–366.

47. See Wolfgang Fasching, "'I am the Nature of Seeing,' Phenomenological Reflections on the Indian Notion of Witness-Consciousness," in *Self, No Self?*, ed. Mark Siderits et al., 200–201.

48. The necessity of asserting external objects as one asserts cognitions is one of Tsongkhapa's eight unique assertions of Prāsaṅgika, which can be found in his *Thoroughly Illuminating the Viewpoint*, 585. The eight listed there are the unique manners of (1) refuting a basic

minds have a privileged status in this tradition. Yet even while Tsongkhapa explicitly affirms external objects along with internal minds, since these two opposed notions are co-constituting, conceptual constructs, it is important to keep in mind that neither the external nor the internal are ultimately real for him.

We have seen that self-awareness, as distinct from object-awareness, ascribes to the mental a unique way that a mind knows itself, a way that is different from the way a mind knows any other object. The radically deconstructive logic of Prāsaṅgika-Madhyamaka denies any special status to self-awareness; the mind is simply a dependently arisen phenomenon, just like any other one. Moreover, since ordinary experience is fundamentally erroneous—that is, nothing appears the way it really is to an ordinary being[49]—the Geluk tradition does not partake in ordinary phenomenology. Instead, it is primarily concerned with Madhyamaka's critical ontology, or what we could call a form of "ontological deflationism," in that it aims to undermine the foundations of the entire ontological project.[50]

For the Geluk tradition following Tsongkhapa, self-awareness is rejected as a notion that attributes to the mind a special status as an independently existent entity, and this idea is seen as one that hypostasizes the mind. One reason for this is that a unique, first-personal access to self-awareness, being simply given in experience, presumes that there are grounds for immediate access to truth, and nothing has that status for Tsongkhapa. For his Geluk tradition, conventional truths are always mediated and contingent. Geluk scholars argue that self-awareness, understood

consciousness distinct from the six consciousnesses; (2) refuting self-awareness; (3) not asserting that autonomous arguments (*rang rgyud kyi sbyor ba, svatantraprayoga*) generate the view of thusness in the continuum of an opponent; (4) the necessity of asserting external objects as one asserts cognitions; (5) the assertion that Disciples and Self-Realized Ones realize the selflessness of phenomena; (6) the assertion that apprehending the self of phenomena is an affliction; (7) the assertion that disintegration is an entity; and (8) the consequent unique presentation of the three times. Tsongkhapa also lists a different set of unique assertions in his *bka' gnas brgyad kyi zin bris*. See David Ruegg, *Two Prolegomena to Madhyamaka Philosophy* (Wien: Arbeitskreis für Tibetische und Buddhistische Studien, 2002), 144–147. For a discussion of the unique assertions of Prāsaṅgika according to the Geluk tradition, see Dan Cozort, *Unique Tenets of the Middle Way Consequence School* (Ithaca: Snow Lion Publications, 1998).

49. See Tsongkhapa, *Middling Stages of the Path*, 318; English trans. in Hopkins, *Tsong-kha-pa's Final Exposition of Wisdom*, 76; see also Jamyang Zhepa translated in Hopkins, *Maps of the Profound* (Ithaca: Snow Lion Publications, 2003), 930.

50. See Matthew MacKenzie, "Ontological Deflationism in Madhyamaka," *Contemporary Buddhism* 9, no. 2 (2008): 197.

as a form of epistemologically primary, private knowledge, is not necessary to account for mental experience and memory, which are often evoked in arguments for self-awareness.[51] This Prāsaṅgika-Madhyamaka tradition does not entertain the notion of self-awareness understood phenomenologically either, as some sort of non-thetic, intransitive cognition, as this concept is seen as simply another reification. Moreover, such a notion of self-awareness does not produce knowledge; it offers no explanatory power in the realms of either the conventional or ultimate truth.

The constriction of the import of knowledge to explicability, however, has been challenged by a contemporary analytic philosopher, Galen Strawson, who stated that self-awareness—as a knowledge by acquaintance—is the condition for the possibility of knowledge:

> There's a narrow, philosophically popular, independent-justification-stressing conception of knowledge that makes it hard for some to see this [self-knowledge by acquaintance] is really knowledge, but the claim doesn't really need defence. Rather the reverse: this particular case of knowledge, self-knowledge in non-thetic self-awareness, shows the inadequacy of the narrow conception of knowledge. This general point is backed up, most formidably, by the fact that knowledge of this kind must lie behind all knowledge of the narrower justification-involving sort, as a condition of its possibility. This is because it's a necessary truth that all justification of knowledge claims is relative to something already taken as given.[52]

Contending that non-thetic self-awareness is the condition for the possibility of knowledge, Strawson claims that knowledge cannot be delimited to justification. Thus, he argues that there is a domain of knowledge more primary and fundamental than the narrowly construed and propositional "space of reasons."[53] We see a different approach to knowledge

---

51. See, for instance, Künzang Sönam, *Overview of the Wisdom Chapter: Lamp Completely Illuminating the Profound Reality of Interdependence*, in Tupten Chödrak (Beijing, China: China's Tibet Publishing House, 2007 [1993]), 711.

52. Strawson, "Radical Self-Awareness," in *Self, No-Self?*, ed. Siderits et al., 288.

53. Wilfred Sellars used this phrase to qualify what constitutes knowledge when he said: "The essential point is that in characterizing an episode or a state as that of *knowing*, we are not giving an empirical description of that episode or state; we are placing it in the logical space of reasons, of justifying and being able to justify what one says." Sellars, *Empiricism and the Philosophy of Mind* (Cambridge: Harvard University, 1997 [1956]), 76.

in the works of Tsongkhapa, who rejects the idea of self-awareness as an extraneous metaphysical posit.

Not only does Tsongkhapa deny the existence of self-awareness, but also the notion of a "basic consciousness" separate from mental consciousness. For Tsongkhapa, the basic consciousness (like self-awareness) serves as a substrate for the self, one that reifies personal identity. Tsongkhapa dispenses with this notion of a substrate consciousness and sees it as simply another reification, another conceptually constructed essence that masquerades as the primary reality of the self. Instead of a basic consciousness, Tsongkhapa posits "the entity of disintegration" (*zhig pa'i dngos po*) to account for causality.[54] The "entity of disintegration" is his attempt to offer a coherent causal process in the absence of real entities.

The impetus for his theory of the entity of disintegration, or so it seems, is to provide an account for causality in the absence of foundations. That is, "disintegration" is said to function like other entities in the absence of *real* entities. With no real entities, an entity's disintegration—which is typically held within Buddhist philosophical systems to be a non-entity—is thus attributed with the same status as an efficacious entity (nominal). That is, both an entity and its disintegration are nothing more than nominal designations. While injecting disintegration with causal power is an attempt to preserve a nominalist theory of causality, this theory invites other problems, such as the reification of absence (i.e., treating emptiness as a "thing"), which has been a frequent target for critics of the Geluk tradition. Others have argued that the notion of an entity of disintegration goes against the Prāsaṅgika commitment to accord with mundane convention renowned in the world.[55]

Among the unique features of Tsongkhapa's portrayal of Prāsaṅgika, along with positing the "entity of disintegration," a basic consciousness and self-awareness are not only denied ultimate existence, but are held to not exist *even conventionally*. Conventional truths are always subject to rational analysis; when conventional status is analyzed, no such

54. See, for instance, Tsongkhapa, *Ocean of Reason* (*dbu ma rtsa ba'i tshig le'ur byas pa shes rab ces bya ba'i rnam bshad rigs pa'i rgya mtsho*), in *Tsongkhapa's Collected Works*, vol. 15 (*ba*) (Xining, China: Nationalities Press, 1998), 117; English trans. in Jay Garfield and Geshe Ngawang Samten, *Ocean of Reasoning* (Oxford: Oxford University Press, 2006), 203.

55. See, for instance, Mipam, *Light of the Sun* (*nyin byed snang ba*), 489; English trans. in Padmakara Translation Group, *The Wisdom Chapter*, 292.

self-awareness or basic consciousness is analytically found, and when analyzed in terms of their ultimate status, they are found to be groundless like every other phenomenon.

Further, Tsongkhapa claims that the denial of true existence even conventionally is a unique feature of Prāsaṅgika-Madhyamaka.[56] This is because he holds that the claim to uncover a deeper foundation of conventional existence beyond transactional truth is a back door to essentialist *ultimate* presuppositions. For Tsongkhapa, reifying the conventional entails misconceiving the ultimate, just as reifying the ultimate entails misconceiving conventional truth. Both truths, which are essentially the same, rise and fall together. Thus, not only ultimate foundations, but even *conventional* foundational theories are repudiated in his Prāsaṅgika-Madhyamaka.

A key point to Tsongkhapa's Prāsaṅgika-Madhyamaka is that nothing exists on its own *even conventionally*.[57] Thereby, there is no need to ground conventions in any deeper foundation. Without the need for conventional foundations—like a dependent nature, a basic consciousness, or self-awareness—there is no need for ultimate foundations, either, as if a *real* ultimate were needed to ground *unreal* conventions. When there is nothing but groundless conventions—all the way up and all the way down—the ultimate and the conventional are no longer separate; the two truths are none other than two aspects of the same thing. Thereby, the two truths are not only without contradiction, but are mutually supportive, and this is a key to Tsongkhapa's interpretation of Prāsaṅgika-Madhyamaka.

Another essential point of Tsongkhapa's Prāsaṅgika view is that distinctions within the conventional—between truth and falsity, existence and nonexistence, real and unreal—are not objective; that is, they are not determined from objects themselves. Conventional distinctions between what is real and unreal are made *in terms of the world*. That is to say, these distinctions are not made based on any real differences in objects themselves; rather, what constitutes what is real and unreal is *intersubjective*. Significantly, what is intersubjective necessarily incorporates a subjective dimension.

One might think that if a Prāsaṅgika does not accept objective distinctions, then this position would not be different from the subjective

56. See Cozort, *The Unique Tenets of the Middle Way Consequence School*, 60.

57. Tsongkhapa stated that things not existing on their own even conventionally is the basis of unique Prāsaṅgika assertions such as their being no basic consciousness or self-awareness,

idealism of the "Mind-Only" school. Rather than claim that the mind is independently real in contrast to unreal external objects (like a subjective idealist), a Mādhyamika explicitly affirms the interdependency of minds and objects. Following Candrakīrti, Künzang Sönam (1823–1905) unpacks Tsongkhapa's Prāsaṅgika interpretation when he describes how minds and external objects are equally existent in worldly convention (and in Abhidharma) and equally nonexistent when their nature is sought in analysis (and in a sublime being's meditative equipoise). He goes on to show how Prāsaṅgikas accept external objects conventionally because the coextensive presence and absence of objects and cognitions undermines the claim that even conventionally there are no external objects. That is, when there are external objects, there are internal cognitions, and when there are internal cognitions, there are external objects; cognitions and objects are paired and thus rise and fall together. He reiterates this point by saying that not only does no *conventional* analysis negate external objects, but that conventional analysis undermines the absence of externality.[58]

Elaborating on the difference between Madhyamaka and Mind-Only, Künzang Sönam says that "the distinction of whether or not external objects are asserted or not conventionally comes down to the acceptance of something existing on its own (*rang mtshan gyis grub pa*)."[59] This is the main issue for his Prāsaṅgika interpretation and undergirds Tsongkhapa's unique Prāsaṅgika claims. He argues that proponents of Mind-Only are not satisfied with assenting to the external world as it is proclaimed by the world; they think that if there were external objects, they would have to be the types of things that would be findable upon analysis, and existing separately from cognition.[60] Yet since there are no such things, they deny them. Prāsaṅgikas, in contrast, assert external objects without these criteria, namely, without there being any objective basis of designation for these claims. Thus, Prāsaṅgikas simply assent to external objects in accord with mundane convention, and this is due to the fact that they do not

---

even conventionally. Tsongkhapa, *Thoroughly Illuminating the Viewpoint*, 585; see also Künzang Sönam, *Overview of the Wisdom Chapter*, 715.

58. Künzang Sönam, *Overview of the Wisdom Chapter*, 706–707.

59. Künzang Sönam, *Overview of the Wisdom Chapter*, 707.

60. Künzang Sönam, *Overview of the Wisdom Chapter*, 707.

accept anything existing on its own, neither an external nor an internal world, even conventionally.[61]

Künzang Sönam clarifies Tsongkhapa's claim that Prāsaṅgikas assert external objects by arguing that it is not at all like the assertions of those who come to affirm external objects based on analysis (like Vaibhāṣikas and Sautrāntikas). This is because Prāsaṅgikas reject the kind of realism that is implicated by the acceptance of an analytically determined external world. Rather, Prāsaṅgikas simply accept external objects (conventionally) in accord with the ways of the world, without (ontological) analysis.[62] There is a subtle distinction to be made here that can easily be overlooked.

One might think that since the external world is affirmed in this Prāsaṅgika tradition, then it is one that accepts external realism. Perhaps some may fall into this camp (just as some may interpret Mind-Only as subjective idealism), but this need not be the case, particularly when the Prāsaṅgika affirmation of an external world is understood as an assertion that a Prāsaṅgika makes not from her own perspective on the status of an external world in reality. Rather, the Prāsaṅgika's assent to external reality can be understood simply as a claim that conforms to intersubjective agreement determined by mundane convention. In any case, ultimately there is no external world for Prāsaṅgikas, so while they may not be idealists, they are certainly not external realists, either. That is, Prāsaṅgikas are not external realists despite claiming the reality of an external world because they acknowledge that the external world does not stand on its own, even conventionally; like minds and objects, an external world rises and falls together with an internal world. (See Appendix B for a translation highlighting the unique character of Prāsaṅgika in this tradition).

Conclusion

We have seen how self-awareness is a flash point around which competing lines of interpretation of Mahāyāna Buddhism are drawn. Self-awareness can refer to an intransitive cognition and an intrinsic property of all awarenesses. It can also take the form of an objective or absolute idealism, as a metaphysical claim. Self-awareness has an important place in the Yogācāra tradition of Dignāga and Dharmakīrti, and it functions as a precondition for knowledge. Some Tibetans like Śākya Chokden took up this trajectory

61. Künzang Sönam, *Overview of the Wisdom Chapter*, 707.

62. Künzang Sönam, *Overview of the Wisdom Chapter*, 707.

of Buddhist epistemology to affirm self-awareness as ultimate gnosis, the ultimate source of knowledge.[63] In contrast, Tsongkhapa followed Candrakīrti in denying self-awareness. He did not build his Buddhist system upon this kind of epistemology or phenomenology. Rather, his system is driven by the critical ontology of Madhyamaka.

In fact, in the Prāsaṅgika-Madhyamaka tradition as articulated by Tsongkhapa, self-awareness is anathema to the correct view of reality. There is no place for self-awareness in Tsongkhapa's own tradition of Madhyamaka, as either an ultimate or a conventional truth. For him, it is simply a conceptual projection, and is held to be a false idea of the self and world that binds one to samsara.

Despite the explicit differences between these distinct Buddhist theories of self-awareness, the differences can be seen to coincide with Mādhyamika and Yogācāra attempts to articulate nonduality from different vantage points: from the outside and inside, respectively. While Tsongkhapa lays out a nondual *substructure* by evoking the primordiality (or primacy) of the unreflective stance of mundane convention, and by claiming that there is no mind without an object just as there is no object without a mind, proponents of self-awareness like Śākya Chokden collapse the dichotomy of subject and object in another way: by sublating the duality of subject and object to a nondual *superstructure*, primordial gnosis. Further, Tsongkhapa gives a relational account of nonduality by collapsing the ontological distinction between two truths. In contrast, an alternative approach (absolute idealism) offers a unified account of nonduality from a point of departure of nonconceptual gnosis, or ultimate self-awareness.

Yet the way this kind of nondual gnosis functions as a third category that is neither an ordinary subject nor an object creates a philosophical problem as to how this supermind relates to the ordinary world of mind and matter, which is another iteration of the mind-body duality problem, writ large. Tsongkhapa skirts this issue by not taking up with the nature of mind or matter in this way, but by turning to the two truths of Madhyamaka—ontological deconstruction and unreflective convention—as a solution.

Do proponents of a nondual gnosis, in attempt to solve a philosophical problem of duality by explicitly denying external realism and subjective idealism, only defer this problem by claiming a transcendent ground of

63. See Komarovski, *Visions of Unity*, 220–223.

gnosis rather than simply a common ground (that is relationally constituted) for both? That is, despite explicit claims to nonduality, is duality not implicitly left in place? The anti-foundationalist proposal of Tsongkhapa's Madhyamaka offers an alternative to nonduality framed within a singular structure like an ultimate, nondual awareness. That is, by unrelentingly affirming the duality of external objects and internal minds, Tsongkhapa implicitly collapses this duality, too. He does so by showing that internality cannot exist without externality, and thus that the notions of an internal mind and an external world are both co-constituting, conceptual constructions. We will see in the next two chapters how two styles of contemplative practice, rooted in Mind-Only and Madhyamaka, are informed by these two perspectives.

4

Concepts and the Nonconceptual

Mañjuśrī, what is there to root the baseless? All phenomena abide upon the root of the baseless.

—VIMALAKĪRTI SŪTRA (H. 177, vol. 60), 328a

Introduction

This chapter discusses two theories of Buddhist knowledge: one based in a Yogācāra tradition inspired by Dharmakīrti and one based in a Madhyamaka tradition stemming from the works of Nāgārjuna and Candrakīrti. In the Buddhist world, Tibet is unique in that both traditions of epistemology (*pramāṇa*) and Prāsaṅgika-Madhyamaka, as found in the works of Dharmakīrti and Candrakīrti, took root there. It is hard to underestimate the significance of this fact, and the enormous influence this convergence had upon the unique forms of philosophical and contemplative practices that flourished in Tibet. Southeast Asian traditions did not share in these developments of Mahāyāna Buddhism. Although the tradition of Mahāyāna came to dominate Buddhist thought in China, since Buddhist texts had been translated there long before Dharmakīrti and Candrakīrti lived, their works did not gain prominence in China. As a result, they were not transmitted in Korea or Japan, either. In Tibet, however, the intersection of Dharmakīrti's epistemology and Candrakīrti's Madhyamaka led to a vibrant philosophical tradition.

In Dharmakīrti's epistemology, rather than linguistic entities or objects of thought, perceptual experience is emphasized as the primary medium of undistorted truth. Inference also plays a key role, particularly as we see in Madhyamaka's critical ontology—where analysis, not pre-reflective self-awareness, leads the way to liberating knowledge. In Yogācāra and Madhyamaka, both inference and perception have important roles to play, so we can see once again how both traditions interpenetrate, as each of them has phenomenological and ontological modalities or contexts where inference or perception is paramount.

When these traditions come together in Tibet, there are two main ways in which the path to awakening is laid out. One path is based on a developmental, "gradualist model," as when yogic perception (which for Dharmakīrti is conceptually engineered) becomes knowledge in the sense of an embodied skill. Here, the perceptual assimilation of conception comes to carry soteriological force, as perception plays an active role in ascertainment (of truths like the four noble truths and emptiness). In another model, perception carries soteriological force in an innatist path of direct realization, or in what comes to be a "discovery model" of pre-reflective self-awareness—the model of nondual gnosis. We find this in several Tibetan traditions. Further, in Sakya, Nyingma, and Kagyü traditions, we will see how a pre-reflective self-awareness acts as the ground of liberation, playing the soteriological role of yogic perception as well as serving as a bridge between conception and perception. Before exploring these issues in this chapter, we will first discuss the linguistic roots of these topics.

Language and the Roots of Knowledge

As critiques of the ontology of substance, Buddhist arguments have a clear precedent in Sanskritic explanations of grammar and meaning—whether meaning resides in the parts (phonemes or words) or in the whole (sentences or language), and whether meaning is produced by a determinable causal process or within an irreducible flash of understanding (*pratibhā*). In this section we will explore some competing theories about language and ontology from India to expose a reciprocal relationship between a philosophy of language and an ontological view. Such an inquiry sheds light upon how a specific linguistic theory reveals not only the foundation for what is meaningful in a system, but what ontological and metaphysical presuppositions are at work within a system (explicitly or implicitly). Although this is not a context to treat this topic with the sustained in-depth inquiry it deserves, I feel that this detour can provide a useful explanatory model that sheds light on an important issue in Buddhist philosophy, and philosophy in general.

We will begin with the question of where meaning lies, a linguistic issue that resonates with ontological import. In the *Mahābhāṣya*, a second-century BCE discussion of Pāṇini's grammar, Patañjali stated that phonemes are meaningless with the example of a chariot:

> Just as the parts of a chariot, taken apart, are, each on its own, incapable of the action of moving, but the group of these [parts]—the chariot—is capable of it, like that the group of these phonemes have meaning (*artha*), the parts (i.e., the isolated phonemes) are meaningless (*anarthaka*).[1]

Here we see a precedent for Candrakīrti's "chariot reasoning" that critiques the notion of a real self in relation to the aggregates. Yet in contrast to Candrakīrti's critique of wholes and parts, Patañjali, prefiguring his commentator Bhartṛhari, depicts meaningless parts as subordinate to a meaningful whole. In fact, Bhartṛhari's holism is quite opposite to the atomistic view of the Abhidharma Buddhist notion that holds that constituent parts (*dharmas*) are real, never wholes, which are always only conceptual constructs.

An atomistic theory of meaning is found in Śabara (*ca.* 4th c.), the first commentator on Jaimini's seminal *Mīmāṃsāsūtra*. His words show a Mīmāṃsaka interpretation that does not attribute the existence of meaning beyond phonemes: "Now what is the word (*śabda*) "cow" (*gauḥ*)? 'The phonemes '*ga*', '*au*', and '*ḥ*' constitute the word'...There is nothing which is apart from these (phonemes) and is called a "word" (*pada*)."[2] The correlation between an atomistic philosophy of language and an atomistic ontology in the Mīmāṃsaka view is made explicit by Kumārila (*ca.* 7th c.):

> Just as it is only when the atoms are eternal that it is possible for the jars, etc. to be made out of them, it is only when the phonemes are [eternal] that there is an appearance of an order [of phonemes] based on conventional usage. Since without the phonemes there would be no substratum, in the absence of these [phonemes] we could not have any arrangement. And it has already been proven that there are no parts to phonemes, as atoms [have no parts].[3]

---

1. Patañjali, *Mahābhāṣya* 1.2.45: *yathā tarhi rathāṅgāni vihṛtāni pratyekaṃ vrajikriyāṃ pratyasamamarthāni bhavanti tatsamudāyaś ca rathaḥ samartha evam eṣāṃ varṇānāṃ samudāyā arthavanto 'vayavā anarthakā iti.* Cited from and trans. by Jan E. M. Houben, *The Saṃbandha-Samuddeśa and Bhartṛhari's Philosophy of Language* (Groningen: E. Forsten, 1995), 44.

2. Śabara, *Śābarabhāṣya* under *Mīmāṃsā Sūtra* 1.1.5; translation adapted from Ganganatha Jha, *Śābara-bhāṣya*, vol. 1 (Baroda: Oriental Institute, 1973), 19.

3. Kumārila, *Ślokavārttika, śabdanityatādhikaraṇa* 292–293. Translation adapted from Jha, *Ślokavārttika* (Calcutta: The Asiatic Society 1985 [1908]), 461.

The atomism of this Mīmāṃsā view of language is mirrored by their ontology: just as partless phonemes are the real substrate of language, likewise, partless atoms are the real substrate of objects. This kind of atomistic view was one of Nāgārjuna's targets of his Madhyamaka analyses, as in the Abhidharma, where indivisible material particles and indivisible conscious moments are held to be the building blocks of phenomenal reality.

Another atomistic vision of reality is found in the system of Nyāya. In the Naiyāyika account of atomism, objects of common sense are given a privileged role in presentations of ontology and language. While the Naiyāyikas accept the reality of partless atoms, they emphasize the ontological primacy of wholes: "If the existence of the whole (*avayavin*) is denied, then there can be no knowledge of anything."[4] The kinds of "wholes" that the Naiyāyikas refer to, as opposed to Bhartṛhari's or a Vedāntin's metaphysical "Whole" (*brahman*), are the objects of common sense. That is, Nyāya ontology is grounded in common sense notions of what is real.[5] Distinctive approaches to language and ontology in Buddhist Tibet correspond in significant ways with those of the Nyāya (esp. the common-sense realism of the Geluk Prāsaṅgika) and Bhartṛhari (esp. in the Mind-Only and Yogācāra-inflected tantric traditions, where ultimate self-awareness is primary, primordial, and irreducible).

In contrast to the Mīmāṃsaka notion of the phoneme as the constituent unit of meaning, Bhartṛhari (*ca.* 5th c.) depicted meaning as irreducibly whole. Also, unlike the Nyāya-Vaiśeṣikas, who describe language as a conventional representation *corresponding* to a physical reality, the *constructive* role of language in Bhartṛhari reflects his underlying metaphysical system. For Bhartṛhari, meaning is irreducible, like his ontology of the whole—Brahman. Thus, he claims that meaning is not reducible to its parts:

---

4. Gautama, *Nyāyasūtra* 2.1.34: *sarvāgrahaṇamavayavyasiddheḥ*, in *Gautamīyanyāyadarśana with Bhāṣya of Vātsyāyana*, ed. Anantalal Thakur (Delhi: Indian Council of Philosophical Research, 1997), 75.

5. Naiyāyika responses to logical skepticism consistently show a subordination of logic to common sense, as in *Nyāyasūtra* 4.2.25, where a response to an opponent's claim that partless atoms have parts is denied because that view would entail an infinite regress (*anavasthā*); and in *Nyāyasūtra* 4.2.15, where the critique of the Nyāya notion of universals existing in particulars (neither partially nor wholly) is discredited by the response that (without such inherence of universals) there would be a similar (unwanted) consequence of annihilation (*pralaya*) (of common sense realism).

> When the meanings (of the individual words) have been understood separately, another presence of understanding takes place. This is called the meaning of the sentence, brought about by the meanings of the individual words. Although it is known to occur in an individual, it cannot be described as "that is this" even by the one who perceives it.[6]

It is significant that Bhartṛhari claims here that the experience of sentence meaning itself is not denotable. Meaning here is an inexpressible, irreducible whole. What is real for Bhartṛhari, too, is the whole, the indivisible holistic reality of the language-principle (*śabdabrahman*).[7] Bhartṛhari's ontology is mirrored in his philosophy of language; his presentation of language and reality directly contrasts with a Mīmāṃsā notion that attributes reality to the constituent parts.

Bhartṛhari depicted the reality of substance as the absolute nature of reality and the true referent of words. The status of an enduring substance behind what is perceived as changing qualities is an ontological issue that is met with varied responses in the philosophical traditions of India. Buddhists have consistently critiqued the notion of an enduring substance behind the fluctuating mass of perceptible qualities. Bhartṛhari, on the other hand, represents the true reality as an absolute monism; everything else (the level of reality where there is differentiation and apparent change) is a second order of reality. Reflecting the two truths of Buddhism, Bhartṛhari described the former of these two levels as the "primary truth"

---

6. Bhartṛhari, *Vākyapadīya* II.143–144, in Subramania Iyer, ed. *Vākyapadīya of Bhartṛhari, Containing the Ṭīkā of Puṇyarāja and the Ancient Vṛtti*, Kāṇḍa II (Delhi: Motilal Banarsidass, 1983), 65: *vicchedagrahaṇe 'rthānāṃ pratibhā 'nyaiva jāyate / vākyārtha iti tāmāhuḥ padārthairupapāditām // idaṃ taditi sānyeṣāmanākhyeyā kathañcana / pratyātmavṛttisiddhā sā kartrāpi na nirūpyate*. Translation adapted from Subramania Iyer, trans., *The Vākyapadīya of Bhartṛhari, Kaṇḍa II: English Translation with Exegetical Notes* (Delhi: Motilal Banarsidass, 1977), 60–61.

7. We can see a parallel with the irreducible unity in Bhartṛhari's holistic language-principle in the notion of self-awareness, discussed in the last chapter. Like the two aspects of self-awareness, Bhartṛhari describes language, like a lamp, as having two properties: being what is apprehended and being the apprehender. See Bhartṛhari, *Vākyapadīya*, I.55, in Subramania Iyer, ed. *The Vākyapadīya of Bhartṛhari with the Vṛtti and the Paddhati of Vṛṣabhadeva*, Kaṇḍa I (Poona: Deccan College Monograph Series 32, 1966), 115; English trans. in Subramania Iyer, trans., *The Vākyapadīya of Bhartṛhari with the Vṛtti, Chapter I* (Poona: Deccan College, 1965), 61.

(*mukhyasattā* or *sampratisattā*) and the latter as the "metaphorical truth" (*upacārasattā*).[8]

Bhartṛhari's distinction between two substances, and two realms of discourse, reflects an ontological distinction between two truths. Correspondingly, he delineates language as twofold: (1) as a grammatical system that can be analyzed in terms of syntax and parts, and (2) as an irreducible semantics of meaningfulness that is being itself. The former is the realm of dialectical inquiry, and the latter is the monistic foundation of reality. This appeal to a foundation of reality appears to be at odds with the dialectical inquiry of the former, but is held to be the transcendental condition for its existence.

The claim to an underlying foundation of reality contrasts with Madhyamaka critiques of a substance lying behind the phenomenal world. We can see an ontological parallel in discussions of language, and how substance, or a realm of semantic value, is related to syntax. An appeal to a realm of meaning, or pure semantics, beyond syntax is characteristic of a holistic strand of philosophy found in Bhartṛhari. A suspicion of substance, and skepticism about the metaphysics of a real meaning *behind words*, characterizes the analytic critiques in Madhyamaka, where all meaning is relational. In distinction to the critiques of substance typical of the negative dialectics of Madhyamaka, an indivisible and pure substance underlying reality is a feature of Bhartṛhari's and Vedānta's metaphysics.

The presence of this metaphysical substance correlates with the role of "presence" (*pratibhā*) in Bhartṛhari's linguistic theory. *Pratibhā* is the experience of the unity of meaning. Meaning as *pratibhā* is an *event* of understanding that is irreducible and inexplicable. Of a second-order are the explanations of the *objects* of knowledge, which treat meaning as an abstraction apart from the dynamic moment of lived reality. As an object, meaning becomes delimited to data conforming to predetermined linguistic and thought structures that are imposed upon reality and in turn, predetermine the limits of the comprehensible world. Such an approach to meaning confines meaning to explicability. In contrast to such *object*-oriented meanings, affirming the irreducibility of meaning attributes a distinct status to *subjectivity* in the constitution of meaning. The theory of *pratibhā*, acknowledging the participatory role of the subject, accords more

8. Subramania Iyer, *Bhartṛhari: A Study of the Vākyapadīya in the Light of the Ancient Commentaries* (Poona: Deccan College, 1969), 209.

with the subject-oriented (phenomenological) discourse of Mind-Only, in contrast to the discourses that presume objective *facts* grounded in a pluralistic ontology.

In contrast to the theory of *pratibhā*, where meaning is affirmed as an irreducible whole, Dignāga and Dharmakīrti put forward the theory of *apoha*. *Apoha* is a linguistic theory of concept acquisition through "exclusion" (*apoha*), involving cognition through the means of excluding everything that is not that concept. The process of concept formation is through a double negative; thus, the notion of "pot" is held to be known *via not non-pot*. *Apoha* is a Buddhist explanation that denies that words denote real universals, and is based on the assumption that language is a fundamentally deceptive construction that necessarily misrepresents reality (rather than disclosing it as it is). Dharmakīrti developed Dignāga's *apoha* theory in defense of his epistemological system from the objections of the Naiyāyikas, as an attempt to uphold a non-essentialist philosophy of language that does not attribute ontological status to linguistic referents.[9]

Conception and Perception

Dharmakīrti's epistemology had a big impact on Buddhist philosophy in Tibet, so I will say a bit more about his tradition. Dharmakīrti developed Dignāga's system of mutually exclusive categories of reliable sources of knowledge: nonconceptual perception and conceptual inference. Dharmakīrti characterized the "conceptual" as a cognition for which word and object appear as suitable to be mixed.[10] Such conception is necessarily distorted. The contents of perception, in contrast to linguistic content that is distorted, are ineffable particulars. The notion of ineffable particulars undermines the idea that concepts of things with spatial and temporal extension (universals) are ultimately real. By eliminating any real unity to things like selves—synchronically (through identifying the plurality of the self's supposed identity with the five aggregates) and diachronically (through identifying the momentary nature of the causal flow of experience)—no real substances are explicitly held to exist behind a fluctuating process.

9. For more on the complicated subject matter of *apoha*, see *Apoha: Buddhist Nominalism and Human Cognition*, ed. Mark Siderits et al. (New York: Columbia University Press, 2011).

10. Dharmakīrti, *Drop of Reason* (*Nyāyabindu*), I.5: *abhilāpasaṃsargayogyapratibhāsapratītiḥ kalpanāḥ*.

Dharmakīrti's epistemological system is based on a distinction between conceptual mind and nonconceptual perception. Yet with this distinction, perception on its own is, for all intents and purposes, meaningless without the aid of a mental consciousness's interpretation, which amounts to a reliance upon conceptual ascertainment (*nges pa, niścaya*). Conceptual ascertainment, however, is by nature mistaken, yet only a perception where ascertainment takes place can be ascribed knowledge. Thus, while perceptual cognition may be the best candidate to ground knowledge, this grounding is a dubious one because an implication of it being nonconceptual is its lack of determinacy and communicability. That is, it is not *knowledge about* anything.

The price paid for consistency in one place of Dharmakīrti's system leaves an inconsistency in another, for how then does conception relate to nonconceptual perception? And if perception is nonconceptual, how can it be meaningful? One attempt to smooth the rift between perception and conception is found in innovations of the role of ascertainment or judgment (*niścaya*) in making the link between them. Others have also tried to mend the relationship between perception and conception with the mediating role of mental perception (*mānasapratyakṣa*).[11] Another trajectory of interpretation marks more of a paradigm shift than simply a patchwork on an unstable dichotomous structure. This trajectory was taken by Buddhist traditions that articulate the irreducibility of self-awareness. We will briefly consider how the relation between conception and perception has been addressed by some of Dharmakīrti's interpreters.

One way to relate the conceptual and the nonconceptual is through "mental perception." Dharmottara, one of Dharmakīrti's commentators in India, described this as what accounts for the connection between perception and conception.[12] In a move familiar to twentieth-century sense-data theorists like Bertrand Russell, Dharmottara asserts a temporal gap between perception and conception, such that after the first moment of a bare (nonconceptual) perceptual encounter with the *raw feels* or sense data of ineffable particulars, in the following moment mental perception forms a judgment. Thus, sense perception, to the extent that it can be said to deliver knowledge, must be mediated by mental perception.

---

11. See Dreyfus, *Recognizing Reality: Dharmakīrti's Philosophy and Its Tibetan Interpretations* (Albany, NY: SUNY Press, 1997), 359–363.

12. See Dreyfus, *Recognizing Reality*, 354–364.

The distinction between sense perception and mental perception, the "sixth sense," can be expressed as the difference between, for instance: knowing blue versus knowing *that* "it is blue."[13] What makes the difference between *seeing* and *seeing as* can be seen in the role of mental perception, which is posited as that which interprets the raw data of particulars and converts this into knowledge. Commenting on Dharmakīrti, Prajñākāragupta defined mental perception as follows: "A mental perception is a cognition that apprehends its object as 'this.'"[14] Mental perception is thus one attempt to reconcile conception and perception.

Another way that a link is made between the nonconceptual and conceptual is through the notion of self-awareness. Following Dharmakīrti, the thirteenth-century Tibetan scholar, Sakya Paṇḍita, maintained perception to be nonconceptual and passive, that is, without judgment (*nges pa*). Judgments, in contrast, for him are always conceptual. Also, Sakya Paṇḍita presented self-awareness as what bridges the gap between nonconceptual perception and conceptual cognition, illustrated by the analogy of an interlocutor (self-awareness) introducing a blind speaker (conception) to a mute seer (perception).[15] In this way, he put forward self-awareness as a bridge between the nonconceptual and the conceptual.

Dharmottara's interpretation of mental perception gets taken up in Tibet, too, particularly in the Geluk tradition, which apparently comes down through the twelfth-century Tibetan scholar, Chapa.[16] In contrast to Sakya Paṇḍita, for Chapa a perceptual source of knowledge is not held to be a passive reception, but entails judgment or ascertainment, whereas he categorized "perception without ascertainment" (*snang la ma nges pa*) as an unreliable source of knowledge. Following Chapa, who described perception as a constructive cognitive process rather than a passive, receptive

---

13. Dignāga, *Compendium of Epistemology*, under v. 4; English trans. in Masaaki Hattori, *Dignāga on Perception* (Cambridge, MA: Harvard University Press, 1968), 26.

14. Prajñākāragupta, *Pramāṇavarttikālaṃkāra*, 305, 4–5. Cited in Hisayasu Kobayashi, "Self-Awareness and Mental Perception," *Journal of Indian Philosophy* 38 (2010): 240.

15. Sakya Paṇḍita, *Treasury of Epistemology* (*tshad ma rigs gter*) (Beijing, China: Nationalities Press, 1989), 10.

16. See Paul Hackett, "On the Epistemological Distinction between Sautrāntika and Cittamātra in Tsong-kha-pa's *Legs bshad snying po*," in *Vimalakīrti's House: A Festschrift in Honor of Robert A. F. Thurman on the Occasion of his 70th Birthday*, ed. Christian Wedemeyer et al. (New York: AIBS, 2015), 354–360.

one,[17] the Geluk tradition includes ascertainment (*nges pa*) in perception. Rather than perception being a passive, nonconceptual encounter, a key part of the way that the Geluk tradition overcomes the disjunction between perception and conception is through this attribution of ascertainment, or judgment, to perception. Unlike Sakya Paṇḍita, who described a disjunction between perception and conception (following Dharmakīrti) and bridged it with self-awareness, in the Geluk tradition, there is no such radical disjunction between concept and percept.[18]

The blurred lines between concept and percept in the Geluk tradition depart from Dharmakīrti's radical dichotomy, and reflect their interpretation of Dharmakīrti's epistemology as what has been described as a "semi-realist" approach to universals, where universals exist and common-sense objects (extended in time and space) are directly perceived.[19] Moreover, this feature of Geluk epistemology flirts with a non-Buddhist, Nyāya model of the perception of wholes, which was contested by Dharmakīrti.

In any case, the fact that Dharmakīrti's arguments against real unities on one level leave a disjunction on another is a driving force for interpretations of his work. Dignāga and Dharmakīrti's works (in)famously engage different registers of truth that resonate with both external realism and epistemic idealism, which inspired the hermeneutical principal of "ascending scales."[20] The perspectival shifts of an "ascending scales" interpretation allows the tradition to not settle on one level of analysis (by either affirming a plurality of functional particulars or denying external objects while affirming a dualistically presenting, "internal" mind). Instead, to serve different purposes, analysis can move along a context-dependent, fluid dynamic that continues on a trajectory—from objects to subjects, and beyond subjectivity.

---

17. See Pascale Hugon, "Phywa pa chos kyi seng ge's Views on Perception," in *Religion and Logic in Buddhist Philosophical Analysis: Proceedings of the Fourth International Dharmakīrti Conference*, ed. H. Krasser et al. (Vienna: Verlag der Österreichischen Akademie der Wisschenschaften, 2005), 174.

18. For references to the way Candrakīrti collapses perception and conception, too, see Tom Tillemans, "Serious, Lightweight, or Neither: Should Madhyamaka Go to Canberra?" in *How Do Mādhyamikas Think? And Other Essays on the Buddhist Philosophy of the Middle* (Boston: Wisdom Publications, 2016), 237–238n11.

19. For citations from several Geluk scholars, including Tsongkhapa, on a realist stance regarding universals, see Dreyfus, *Recognizing Reality*, 173.

20. I take this term from Georges Dreyfus. See his discussion of this topic in *Recognizing Reality*, 89–91; 99. See also discussion in John Dunne, *Foundations of Dharmakīrti's Philosophy* (Boston: Wisdom Publications, 2004), 53–79.

For instance, Dharmakīrti affirmed the reality of what has causal efficacy (*arthakriyāśakti*) within a framework of external realism, yet this framework can be seen to be sublated within the framework of Yogācāra's epistemic idealism. This is suggested by the fact that he denies several types of relations (such as inherence) in favor of only two (causal and identity relations) in one context, but then rejects the reality of even these relations ultimately, when he critiques the reality of relations all together.[21] Dharmakīrti's "final position," as taken up by some traditions in Tibet, extends the implications of his arguments such that they do not stop at epistemic idealism, but necessitate embracing an absolute idealism (or nondualism) as well (for better or for worse).[22]

While Dharmakīrti claims perception to be "nonconceptual" (in the way he defined "conceptual" as linguistic cognition), perception can be said to be conceptual in other ways. Another kind of conceptuality is not limited to simply linguistic understanding, but is present as a characteristic of all dualistic experiences.[23] For instance, Dharmakīrti described the innate misconception of duality as the "internal distortion" (*antarupaplava*).[24] Although Dharmakīrti goes to great lengths to put forward perception as nonconceptual, in the end the perception he promotes is *always already* bound up within a distorted conceptual construction that is dualistically presented consciousness. It is only a reliable means of knowledge as long as samsara remains in place.[25]

---

21. See, for instance, Dharmakīrti's *Investigation of Relation* (*Sambandhaparīkṣā, 'bral ba brtag pa rab tu byed pa*) (D. 4214), where he denies the reality of the relations he affirms in other contexts.

22. His final position as absolute idealism is pushed upon him by Mādhyamikas like Tsongkhapa, who wish to negate it. Yet he is also pushed there, favorably, by figures like the Seventh Karmapa, Chödrak Gyatso (*chos grags rgya mtsho*, 1454–1506), and Śākya Chokden. See Dreyfus, *Recognizing Reality*, 431–432.

23. Utpaladeva, a tenth-century Śaiva influenced by Dharmakīrti, defined concepts in terms of duality: "A concept is an act of ascertainment (*viniścayaḥ*) presenting a duality (*dvayākṣepī*). Utpaladeva, *Īśvarapratyabhijñākārikā* I.6.1; translation adapted from Rafaelle Torella, ed. and trans. (Rome: IsMEO, 1994), 128.

24. Dharmakīrti *Commentary on Epistemology* III.359–362. See Dunne, *Foundations of Dharmakīrti's Philosophy*, 89n57.

25. Dharmakīrti, *Ascertaining Sources of Knowledge, ad* I.59; English trans. in Dunne, *Foundations of Dharmakīrti's Philosophy*, 315–316; see also discussion in H. Kasser, "Are Buddhist Pramāṇavādins non-Buddhistic? Dignāga and Dharmakīrti on the Impact of Logic and Epistemology On Emancipation," *Hōrin* 11 (2004), 142–144.

A related notion of conceptuality is expressed in the *Sublime Continuum*, where cognitive obscuration (*shes bya'i sgrib pa*) is depicted as the conception of the "three spheres" (subject, object, action).[26] Such a grammar of thought reflects an intimate relationship between thought, obscuration, and the grammar of language. This form of conceptuality encompasses all (ordinary) knowledge, as *Distinguishing the Middle and the Extremes* states as well: "The three realms of mind and mental states is unreal imagination."[27]

The shifting referents of "concept" (*rtog pa*) are sharpened in Mipam's delineation of three types of conceptuality: (1) gross concepts, (2) concepts apprehending word and object as suitable to be mixed, and (3) essential conceptuality (*ngo bo nyid kyi rtog pa*).[28] The first type, gross concepts, refers to concepts as depicted in the Abhidharma: the mental state of determination (*rtog pa, vitarka*) as opposed to discernment (*dpyod pa, vicāra*).[29] The second type of conceptuality, apprehending word and object as (suitable to be) mixed, stems from the Buddhist epistemological tradition of Dharmakīrti. The third type of conception, essential conceptuality, implicates concepts to be an essential part of even (ordinary) perceptions. This third type replaces the radical dichotomy of the second (conception and perception) with a dichotomy of ordinary versus extraordinary cognition (gnosis), and plays an important role in Mind-Only and Yogācāra-inspired contemplative traditions such as tantra.

The conceptuality of perception can also be seen in Tsongkhapa's Madhyamaka, and in terms of his delineation of three types of "intrinsic characteristics" (*rang mtshan*) that prefigures and parallels Mipam's threefold delineation of "concepts." In his *Essence of Eloquence*, Tsongkhapa laid out his threefold typology, where he delineates the third type as the unique object of negation in Prāsaṅgika-Madhyamaka, and the first and

---

26. Maitreya, *Sublime Continuum* (*Uttaratantra*), V.14: "Concepts of the three spheres are asserted as cognitive obscurations" (*'khor gsum rnam par rtog pa gang/ de ni shes bya'i sgrib par 'brjod*). The other obscuration, afflictive obscuration (*nyon sgrib*) is defined in the *Sublime Continuum* as afflictions such as stinginess.

27. Maitreya, *Distinguishing the Middle and the Extremes*, I.8ab (*yang dag ma yin kun rtog ni/ sems dang sems byung khams gsum pa*), in *dbu mtha' rnam 'byed rtsa 'grel*, 3; English trans. in Dharmachakra Translation Group, *Middle Beyond Extremes* (Ithaca: Snow Lion Publications, 2006), 32.

28. See Mipam, *Light of the Sun*, 477–478; English trans. in Padmakara Translation Group, *The Wisdom Chapter*, 206.

29. See Vasubandhu, *Treasury of Metaphysics* (*Abhidharmakośa*), I.33.

second as related to Abhidharma and epistemology (*pramāṇa*), respectively. Like Mipam's first category of concept (*rtog pa*) as *determination* drawn from Abhidharma, Tsongkhapa demarcates an Abhidharma notion of *self-characteristic* (*rang mtshan*), as contrasted with *general characteristic* (*spyi mtshan*). The difference between these two is seen in the difference between a particular trope and a general type. An example of this distinction is the heat of fire (particular characteristic) and fire as a material form (general characteristic). He described a second kind of intrinsic characteristic as a *unique particular*, "a functional particular (*rang mtshan*) in the tradition of the logicians (*rtog ge*)." This second type comes straight out of Dharmakīrti's epistemology of causally efficacious particulars, which are unique in terms of time, place, and form.[30] As for the third type, again reflected in Mipam's "essential conceptuality" above (or the notion of "mere dualistic appearance" as a concept[31]), we find the subtlest form of *intrinsic characteristic* (*rang mtshan*) for Tsongkhapa. This type of intrinsic characteristic is presupposed in the mistaken imputation of intrinsic nature to objects. The negation of this third type is the subtle object of negation of Prāsaṅgika-Madhyamaka—phenomena not existing "by virtue of their intrinsic characteristics" (or "on their own") *even conventionally*.[32]

In both Mipam's and Tsongkhapa's treatment of a third category (of "conceptuality" and "intrinsic characteristics," respectively), we see the false attribution of essence as laying the framework for beings in samsara;

---

30. See, for instance, Mokṣākāragupta, *Discourse on Logic* (*Tarkābhāṣa*), 22; English trans. in Yuichi Kajiyama, *An Introduction to Buddhist Philosophy* (Kyoto University: Memoirs of the Faculty of Letters, 1966), 56.

31. A Nyingma scholar, Bötrül (1898–1959), delineated three types of conceptuality: (1) concepts of true existence, (2) concepts of reified signs, or objectification, and (3) concepts that are mere dualistic appearances. Each one is progressively subtler: he states that the first is manifest for ordinary beings, the second is manifest in the postmeditations of bodhisattvas on the "impure grounds" (grounds 1–7), and the third is sometimes manifest for bodhisattvas on the "pure grounds" (grounds 8–10). See Bötrül, *Ornament of Mañjughoṣa's Viewpoint*, *Bötrül's Collected Works*, vol. 1, 230–231; English trans. in Bötrül, *Distinguishing the Views and Philosophies*, trans. Duckworth (Albany: SUNY Press, 2011), 227–228. Tsongkhapa discusses constructs of true existence (*bden pa'i spros pa*) and constructs of dualistic appearance (*snang ba'i spros pa*) in *Middling Stages of the Path* (Byllakuppe: Sera Je, 2005), 358; English trans. in Hopkins, *Tsong-kha-pa's Final Exposition of Wisdom* (Ithaca, NY: Snow Lion Publications, 1998), 142; see also Thupten Jinpa, *Self, Reality, and Reason in Tibetan Philosophy* (London: RoutledgeCurzon, 2002, 61, 202–203n71.

32. See Tsongkhapa, *Essence of Eloquence* (*drang ba dang nges pa'i don rnam par phye ba'i bstan bcos legs bshad snying po*), in *Tsongkhapa's Collected Works*, vol. 14 (*pha*) (Xining, China: Nationalities Press, 2015 [2008]), 425–426; English trans. in Thurman, *The Speech of Gold*, 292.

it is an endemic tendency embedded within distorted modes of being. This is a dualistic, reified structuring of experience; as Dharmakīrti stated, "conceptuality is ignorance."[33] Mind-Only and Madhyamaka are contemplative practices geared toward finding a way out of the snare of this conceptually enframed experience.

In contrast to the threefold typology of conceptuality, *Distinguishing Phenomena and the Basic Nature* also mentions five types of "nonconceptuality," which are distinguished from the genuine nonconceptuality of nonconceptual gnosis:

> [Nonconceptual gnosis] has the character of being free from the five types: (1) mental non-engagement, (2) complete transcendence, (3) quietism, (4) essential meaning, and (5) premeditated signs.[34]

In his commentary on this text, Vasubandhu explains the first type, mental non-engagement, as not nonconceptual gnosis because even babies have this.[35] Mipam comments that babies do not mix word and object but apprehend word and object as *suitable* to be mixed.[36] Vasubandhu explains that the second type of nonconceptuality concerns determination and discernment, which are transcended on the second of the four meditative absorptions (in the Form Realm). This becomes what Tibetan commentators like Mipam claimed to be nonconceptuality in the context of the Abhidharma. Vasubandhu explains the third type of nonconceptuality as referring to the nonconceptuality of "quietism" in unconscious states, such as sleep or fainting; the fourth, he describes as the non-thought of insentient objects that essentially have no thoughts; and the fifth, "premeditated signs," he depicts as a contrived thought of non-thought, an artificial nonconceptuality.[37] These five are examples of what may be said to be

---

33. Dharmakīrti, PVSV on PV1.98–99ab. Cited from Dunne, *Foundations of Dharmakīrti's Philosophy*, 61n17.

34. Maitreya, *Distinguishing Phenomena and the Basic Nature* (*Dharmadharmatāvibhāga*), v. 42.

35. Vasubandhu, *Commentary on "Distinguishing Phenomena and the Basic Nature,"* 35a.

36. Mipam, *Light of Wisdom*, 644.

37. Vasubandhu, *Commentary on "Distinguishing Phenomena and the Basic Nature,"* 35a. Thrangu Rinpoché, a contemporary Buddhist teacher, glosses this last one in a depiction of the Chinese Buddhist Heshang Moheyen. See Thrangu Rinpoché, *Distinguishing Dharma and Dharmatā*, trans. by Jules Levinson (Delhi: Sri Satguru Publications, 2001), 72–74. It is evident from Vasubandhu that a notion of "bad nonconceptuality" was present in India long before the Tibetan representations of the Chinese Buddhism of Heshang.

"nonconceptual" but are *not* nonconceptual gnosis. Indeed, there is more to nonconceptual gnosis than simply being generically "nonconceptual," as Tsongkhapa consistently emphasized.[38] Also, nonconceptual gnosis, as distinguished from conceptual mind, is important for Yogācāra-inflected Buddhist traditions in Tibet, as we saw in the last chapter.

Prāsaṅgika-Madhyamaka and Conventional Foundations

A pre-theoretic or pre-reflective scheme plays an important role in Tsongkhapa's system; that is, the "non-philosophical" stance of naïve realism (one that is *not* so naïve and that *is* philosophical) is fundamental. For his Geluk tradition, this stance is filled with objects—extended, external, everyday objects—like tables and chairs. Likewise, for the traditions of Mind-Only, including the Great Perfection, the "stuff" of the world is disclosed in pre-reflective awareness, the primordiality of the unconditioned world. The primordiality of the world here is not one depicted as cultural artifacts to which we return (as is the case with Tsongkhapa's portrayal of *mere* conventions). Rather, after distorted conceptions of intrinsic existence (along with their appearance) are overcome, what remains is described in terms of the transformation of the basic consciousness (in Mind-Only) or the manifestation of gnosis (in the Great Perfection); the display of awareness (*rig pa*) remains in/as emptiness. Yet for Tsongkhapa, the fabric of the world is not disclosed as something else—something beyond the conventional, commonsense world. In fact, the recovery of the conventional world of *mere* existence is a crucial axis around which his system turns, as it is the basis for his ethics.

In a way parallel to phenomenology's claim to bypass ontology, Tsongkhapa aimed to forge an epistemology that has no real ontological commitments. To do so, he outlined one of his criteria for conventional truth as that which is immune to ontological reasoning:

> We hold that what exists conventionally is: (1) acknowledged by a conventional cognition [i.e., consensus], (2) not undermined by

38. Tsongkhapa, *Great Exposition of the Stages of the Path*, 787–788; English trans. in Cutler (ed.), *The Great Treatise*, vols. 1–3 (Ithaca, NY: Snow Lion Publications, 2000–2004), 343–344. See also Tsongkhapa, *Middling Stages of the Path* (Byllakuppe: Sera Je, 2005), 295–296; 307–308; English trans. in Hopkins, *Tsong-kha-pa's Final Exposition of Wisdom*, 38; 57.

> another conventional source of knowledge knowing it to be that way, and (3) not undermined by reason that correctly analyzes its [ontological] reality, that is, whether it intrinsically exists or not.[39]

Despite one criterion for conventional truth to be worldy consensus, Tsongkhapa's theory of the "entity of disintegration" articulates a causal story that departs from consensus. In Tibetan traditions generally and Tsongkhapa's system in particular, we find a tension between the truth of consensus (in Prāsaṅgika-Madhyamaka) and a revision or reform of this consensus (with *pramāṇa*).[40] Indeed, the ways in which the relationship between Prāsaṅgika (i.e., Candrakīrti) and epistemology (i.e., Dharmakīrti) are configured guide and shape Tibetan philosophical traditions.

For Tsongkhapa, conventionally existent phenomena like "mere tables" function as the causal story of the world, and there is no other "real" causal story to be told beyond nominal conventions. While Tsongkhapa evokes an unreflective stance of commonsense to avoid unwanted foundational assumptions of epistemology, he arguably reinserts the conventional as foundational in the same breath.

Similar to a robust realism where things do in fact exist the way they appear, Tsongkapa's epistemology offers what can be seen as a kind of correspondence theory of truth. This is because for him, a *mere* object (like a tree)—despite appearing to intrinsically exist while it does not—in a sense *corresponds* to the (conventional) reality (of the tree). In other words, an appearing object (*snang yul*) like a phenomenal tree is deceptive, yet the object engaged (*'jug yul*)—the shade-giving tree—accurately corresponds with (conventional) reality.[41] Thus, the world pre- and post-realization remains, in an important sense, fundamentally the same for Tsongkhapa's Prāsaṅgika, the only difference is that the added layer of intrinsic existence no longer exists when realization is actualized.

Thus, the conventional truth for Tsongkhapa's Geluk tradition can be seen to function in parallel with the dependent nature (*paratantra*) in Yogācāra, which is imputed with an imagined nature (*parikalpita*) that

---

39. Tsongkhapa, *Great Exposition of the Stages of the Path*, 627; English trans. in Cutler (ed.), *The Great Treatise*, 178.

40. On this issue, see The Cowherds, *Moonshadows* (Oxford: Oxford University Press, 2011).

41. See Tsongkhapa, *Great Exposition of the Stages of the Path*, 625; English trans. in Cutler (ed.), *The Great Treatise*, 174–175; see also Tsongkhapa, *Thoroughly Illuminating the Viewpoint*, in *Tsongkhapa's Collected Works*, vol. 16 (Xining, China: Nationalities Press, 1998), 558.

it does not have.[42] In contrast to the revisionist program of Yogācāra, Tsongkhapa's account hinges on there being no radical disjunction between things as they are and conceptual construction. This is because in significant ways, according to him a *mere* table looks a lot like the (falsely conceived) *intrinsically existent* table (after all, they are both *tables*), even while neither of them is ultimately real and only one conventionally exists. In Yogācāra, by contrast, the dependent nature, when seen as it is, is quite different from the imagined nature, which is a distorted, conceptual construction. The fact of this disjunction calls for a radical revision of the world, not just a confirmation of the "natural attitude" or the consensus of "what is acknowledged by the world." For this reason, Mind-Only and Yogācāra-inflected traditions in Tibet posit a "pure dependent nature" (*dag pa'i gzhan dbang*),[43] an "ultimate self-awareness," or a gnosis that transcends the strictures of dualistic consciousness, and thus do not simply affirm a conventionally existent world of mere tables and chairs. In doing so, they contradict the conventional world of consensus and the ontological austerity of Prāsaṅgika-Madhyamaka, and thus according to Tsongkhapa's system, tend toward nihilism (by denying the conventional) and realism (with claims to the existence of what is more than just conventional).

Tsongkhapa collapses the distinction between conventional fact and ultimate fiction when he qualifies conventional truths with the ontologically rich term "mere" (*tsam*)—in the way he distinguishes, for instance, the "mere self" (*bdag tsam*) from an "intrinsically existent [self]" (*rang bzhin gyis yod pa['i bdag]*). For instance, he states:

> There are two senses of 'self': (1) one that is conceived with a nature that is essentially real and (2) one that is held in mind with the mere thought 'I am'. The former is an object of negation by reasoning and the latter is not negated, for it is maintained conventionally.[44]

---

42. For an explicit description of the three natures based in the interpretative framework of Tsongkhapa's Prāsaṅgika-Madhyamaka, see Künzang Sönam, *Overview of the Wisdom Chapter*, in Tupten Chödrak (Beijing, China: China's Tibet Publishing House, 2007 [1993]), 691–692.

43. See, for instance, Longchenpa, *Precious Treasury of Philosophical Systems*, in *Seven Treasuries* (*mdzod bdun*), ed. by Tarthang Tulku. Sichuan, China, 1996, 746–747.

44. Tsongkhapa, *Great Exposition of the Stages of the Path*, 663; see Jinpa, *Self, Reality and Reason in Tibetan Philosophy*, 71.

Thus, Tsongkhapa maintains that the ontologically neutral apprehension of a "mere self" looks a lot like the ontologically reified one that is perceived to be intrinsically existent, even though the latter is a fundamentally mistaken perception. That is, the ontologically neutral "mere self" is what turns out in the end to be a correct perception, as the appearance of a self without intrinsic existence. He states: "The merely conventionally posited term *mere* excludes real intrinsic existence, but not valid establishment."[45]

Yet an ontologically neutral phenomenon like a "mere self" for him is supplanted by the ontologically rich "mere self" that lacks intrinsic nature, and thus he pivots between two meanings of "mere": from "a *mere* self (without any ontological commitment about it) to "a *mere* self" (with the ontological commitment that it has no intrinsic nature).[46] This is similar to a slide from conventional to ultimate truth, as we see with a Mind-Only doctrine of mind that slides from ordinary self-awareness to ultimate self-awareness, or from epistemic idealism to absolute idealism.

For instance, Śākya Chokden claimed that conventional self-awareness shares the same features (e.g., pre-reflective, inward looking, subjective) with ultimate gnosis, and that only the latter is real. Tsongkhapa, too, claims that an unreflective stance on reality shares some of the same features with conventional truth, and it is the latter that for him is what is real *conventionally*—the only way he affirms something to be real. Thus, in a way that mirrors the way that Śākya Chokden flirts with subjective idealism, Tsongkhapa flirts with naïve realism.

In Tsongkhapa's interpretation of Prāsaṅgika, a conventional self exists as much as any other conventionally existent phenomenon. That is, the conventional self is irreducible, and its (conventional) existence, as a *mere* existent thing, is shielded from the brunt of ultimate analysis. That is to say, it still exists despite not being found by a rational consciousness that seeks it out. We find a parallel feature of a non-reductionist view in Śakya Chokden's absolute idealism, which claims an "irreducible" gnosis that, similar to Tsongkhapa's *mere* self, is shielded from the brunt of ultimate analysis.

45. Tsongkhapa, *Ocean of Reason* 22: *tha snyad kyi dbang gis bzhag pa rtsam zhes pa'i rtsam gyi sgras kyang don rang gi ngo bor yod pa bcod kyi/ tshad mas grub pa mi bcod do*. English trans. in Jay Garfield and Ngawang Samten, *Ocean of Reasoning* (Oxford, England: Oxford University Press, 2006), 39.

46. For more of Tsongkhapa's discussion of "mere," see Tsongkhapa, *Ocean of Reason*, 22–23; English trans. in Garfield and Samten, *Ocean of Reasoning*, 39.

For Tsongkhapa, perceptions for ordinary beings are always already conceptual, or theory-laden. There is nothing behind theory-laden constructions; there is only conception, nothing more, so seeing absence is thus seeing emptiness, the ultimate truth. This is a reason why Tsongkhapa claims that in terms of the object observed, emptiness conceived is the same as emptiness perceived.[47] Immediate perceptions like self-awareness do not play an epistemological role in his tradition. Acknowledging the conventions renowned in the world, without looking for anything special to ground these conventions above or beyond the mundane world, is an important feature of his Prāsaṅgika interpretation. This kind of "nonreductionist" view of conventional truths like the self, that does not reduce the conventions to something they are not, is a central aspect of this view.[48]

In Tsongkhapa's pre-theoretical (or rather, post-theoretical) stance, we are always already embedded in a world, in a socio-linguistic context. We find a likeness here with Heidegger's embedded, *enworlded* structure of experience, where the world we encounter is always already "ready-to-hand" (*Zuhanden*)—a distinction he makes between abstract, decontextualized objects that are "present-at-hand" (*Vorhanden*) and those that are pre-theoretically "ready-to-hand." That is, we interact with the environment that is "ready-to-hand," like a doorknob or a desktop, the things in our world that we are (pre-theoretically) already doing things with. Yet for Heidegger, we do not get at the world better by stepping back from this world, as in Husserl's *epoché*, for Heidegger says:

> When we merely stare at something, our just-having-it-before-us lies before us *as a failure to understand it any more*. This grasping which is free of the 'as,' is a privation of the kind of seeing in which one *merely* understands. It is not more primordial than that kind of seeing, but is derived from it.[49]

That is, by these lights Husserl's phenomenological bracketing does not get us closer to the way things are, but just offers another lens on the

---

47. See Tsongkhapa, *Middling Stages of the Path*, 358; English trans. in Hopkins, *Tsong-kha-pa's Final Exposition of Wisdom*, 142–143; see also Jinpa, *Self, Reality and Reason in Tibetan Philosophy*, 202–203n71.

48. See Jinpa, *Self, Reality and Reason in Tibetan Philosophy*, 110.

49. Heidegger, *Being and Time*, translated by John Macquarrie and Edward Robinson (Oxford: Blackwell, 2001 [1962]),190 [149].

world, a lens that is inherently no more primordial, privileged, or foundational than any other. Similarly, for Tsongkhapa we need not superimpose something else that goes above, beyond, or below the conventional truth of "medium-sized dry goods."[50] That is, for Tsongkhapa neither atoms, sense-data, a dependent nature, a basic consciousness, nor a nondual mind is needed to ground the world. In fact, these foundationalist accounts stray from the world by superimposing another layer of construction, a philosophically concocted imputation piled on top of another conceptual construction. He emphasizes the way that there is only construction, all the way down, so there is no need to revise it with a convoluted philosophical theory that takes us further away from the reality of the world than we already are.

Of course for Tsongkhapa, what obscures the truth is not limited to the gross conceptual superimpositions of bad philosophy; obscuration is also innate and embodied.[51] It is harder to overcome these innate obscurations, as they are embedded more deeply in the body-mind complex of karma and habit-memory. While imputed obscurations of bad philosophy can be overcome with clear-headed reason, innate obscurations require a reprogramming or deprogramming (a.k.a. meditation) to be overcome.

Yet how can a conceptual understanding of emptiness (*via* reason) transform into a direct perception (*via* meditation)? In other words, how can a conceptual apprehension of emptiness become a perceptual one? While it is not so hard to see how one could overcome a reified misconception of something, how can one move from a mediated, conceptual knowledge of emptiness to an immediate, nonconceptual perception?

The shift from conception to perception can be seen in parallel with the process of acquiring a skill. Learning a skill can be deliberate and conceptual in the beginning—as when learning to ride a bike, for instance. First you have to focus intently on the complex process of pushing your legs down on one pedal at a time, while simultaneously adjusting your arms on the handlebars to maintain balance. Over time, this process becomes a skill through training; it becomes second nature, natural, and "nonconceptual" in a sense. Skill-development is a model for cultivation, and meditative skill is actualized in yogic perception.

---

50. I borrow this turn of phrase from J. L. Austin.

51. See Tsongkhapa, *Middling Stages of the Path*, 300; English trans. in Hopkins, *Tsong-kha-pa's Final Exposition of Wisdom*, 46. See also translations from Tsongkhapa's *Essence of Eloquence*, in Jinpa, *Self, Reality, and Reason in Tibetan Philosophy*, 62.

Cultivation

Yogic perception (*yogipratyakṣa*) is a perceptual source of knowledge for Dharmakīrti, a fourth type in addition to sense perception, mental perception, and self-awareness. Dharmakīrti had depicted yogic perception as the internalization of good inference,[52] as a way to cultivate a knowledge, such as the four noble truths, to heightened clarity. In later interpretations, however, rather than simply a clarity that is developed as a direct product of conceptual engineering, yogic perception as nonconceptual gnosis comes to the fore.

In his commentary on Dharmakīrti's *Drop of Reason*, Vinītadeva described yogic perception as the highest phase of conceptual ascertainment, at the stage of the supreme quality (*chos mchog*) on the path of joining (*sbyor lam*),[53] before arriving at a direct (nonconceptual) realization of the way things are on the path of seeing (*mthong lam*). Yogic perception thus functions as a bridge between a conceptual knowledge and a nonconceptual, unmediated access to reality.

As mentioned previously, skill development is one way to frame the path of cultivation, which is quite different from a path framed as innatist, such that we simply uncover what had been there from the start, as in uncovering one's primordial gnosis or innate buddha-nature, or as in Plato's description of learning as recollection. The contrast between yogic perception as a gradual model of development versus an innatist model of discovery or "re-cognition" marks a distinction between two trajectories, or two aspects, of contemplative practice in Tibet.

This shift from a development model of yogic perception to a discovery model of innate yogic perception mirrors a shift in the way that "knowledge" is characterized: from a (conventional) determinate judgment to an (ultimate) ineffable knowledge. This distinction is clearly reflected in the Tibetan terms for two types of cognition: consciousness (*rnam shes, vijñāna*) and gnosis (*ye shes, jñāna*). As opposed to consciousness, it is only gnosis that is really nonconceptual (as even sense-perceptions are conceptual in some sense in the former, as we saw above), so this gnosis is held to

52. See John Dunne, "Realizing the Unreal: Dharmakīrti's Theory of Yogic Perception," *Journal of Indian Philosophy* 34 (2006), 499–500.

53. Vinītadeva, *Commentary on "[Dharmakīrti's] Drop of Reason"* (*Nyāyabinduṭīkā*) (D. 4230), 6b. See also Theodore Stcherbasky, *Buddhist Logic* (New York: Dover Publications, 1962 [1930]), vol. 2, 31–32n2.

be the only reliable source of knowledge in Mahāmudrā traditions like the one represented by the twelfth-century Drikung Kagyü forefather, Jikten Sumgön (1142–1217).[54] We have seen how the Jonang tradition similarly delineates between consciousness (*rnam shes*), the relative truth, and gnosis (*ye shes*), the ultimate truth.

We have also seen how the nonconceptual "content" of self-awareness is a kind of *knowledge by acquaintance* rather than a form of *knowledge about* something. Moreover, in the case of knowledge *by identity*,[55] self-awareness is not governed by an intentional (dualistic) structure. There is supposedly no judgment in this kind of perception; nevertheless, nonjudgmental awareness is attributed with soteriological efficacy. Yet the soteriological role of self-awareness is that of ultimate gnosis (*ye shes*), not self-awareness that is a dualistic consciousness (*rnam shes*). Gnosis is "knowledge" without determinacy; it is a bare "knowing" in contrast to a cognitive judgment, like "this is that" or the Upaniṣadic "I am that," which is arguably conceptual and premised on duality.

Mind-Only and Yogācāra-inspired Tibetan traditions, including Mahāmudrā and the Great Perfection, describe a form of self-awareness as gnosis, which takes on a role with soteriological efficacy in Tibetan tantric traditions. Śakya Chokden also explicitly described yogic perception in terms of self-awareness.[56] Other representatives from tantric traditions, such as the Drikung Kagyü scholar, Chennga Dorjé Sherap (1187–1241), described yogic perception as Mahāmudrā.[57] We will discuss the theory and practice of Mahāmudrā and the Great Perfection in the next chapter.

---

54. Jikten Sumgön said, "The source of knowledge (*tshad ma, pramāṇa*) is the wisdom of Buddha's gnosis." In Chennga Dorjé Sherap, *Single Viewpoint Great Commentary (dgongs gcig 'grel chen snang mdzad ye shes sgron me)*, vol. 1 (Hong Kong: shang kang then mā dpe skrun khang, 2006), 254; English trans. in Peter Alan Roberts, *Mahāmudrā and Related Instructions: Core Teachings of the Kagyü School* (Boston: Wisdom Publications, 2011), 375.

55. On this distinction, see, for instance, Robert Forman, "Mystical Knowledge by Identity," *Journal of the American Academy of Religion* 61, no. 4 (1993), 705–738.

56. Śakya Chokden, *Ornament of the "Treasury of Epistemology"* (*tshad ma rigs gter gyi dgong rgyan rigs pa'i 'khor los lugs ngan pham byed*), *Śākya Chokden's Collected Works* vol. 10, 20.2: "This selflessness is as if the appearing object of yogic perception; selflessness is the self-illuminating, self-awareness empty of the twofold self." (*bdag med de rnal dbyor mngon gsum gi snang yul yin pa lta bu'o/ 'dir bdag med ces pa bdag gnyis kyis stong pa'i rang rig rang gsal lo*).

57. Chennga Dorjé Sherap, *Single Viewpoint Commentary* (*dgongs gcig 'grel chen snang mdzad ye shes sgron me*), vol. 1, 259. See also Leonard van der Kuijp, "An Early Tibetan View of the Soteriology of Epistemology: The Case of 'Bri-gung dJig-ldan mGon-po," *Journal of Indian Philosophy* 15 (1987), 63. Along with the new registers of meaning for self-awareness and yogic

In contrast to the central place of self-awareness in these traditions, Tsongkhapa emphasizes conceptual analysis. For him, the role of inference is important due to the fact that ordinary perceptions are always distorted. That is, if everything that appears to an ordinary being is false, not as it seems, then the deconstructive arguments of Madhyamaka have the final word on reality because self-awareness, and our deepest intuitions about the world, are all false. Thus, the only infallible truth is a lack of real truth. Yet if there is an indubitable foundation for knowledge that goes beyond conceptual constructions (i.e., nonconceptual awareness), then that would surely be the most fundamental nature of mind, reality, and ourselves. To see things as they are would then be to go around, through, or beyond concepts to the nonconceptual, pre-reflective, "primordial" gnosis (*ye shes*).

Furthermore, knowledge of emptiness is for Tsongkhapa the ultimate source of knowledge (*pramāṇa*). Even though Tsongkhapa claims that nonconceptual gnosis perceives emptiness, the emptiness known inferentially is effectively the same as this for him;[58] thus for an ordinary being, inference takes precedent over perception because nothing appears the way it is for an ordinary being. With this kind of error-theory of experience, ordinary perceptions and phenomenology are unreliable. If an ordinary being's perception is not given any real currency in Tsongkhapa's Madhyamaka tradition, one might think that inference is the primary means of knowledge in his depiction of Madhyamaka, given the fact that emptiness alone is the undistorted ultimate truth for an ordinary being. Yet emptiness *qua* absence is a derivative notion, for lacking intrinsic nature presumes an intrinsic nature that is absent. As Nāgārjuna said:

> If there were something non-empty, then there would be something empty.
> Since there is nothing that is non-empty, how can there be something empty?[59]

---

perception, "mindfulness" (*smṛti*) also takes on a new meaning in late Indian and Tibetan Buddhist traditions. See Dunne, "Toward and Understanding of Nondual Mindfulness," *Contemporary Buddhism* 12, no.1 (2011), 72–88. Thus, we find in tantra what is said to be "similar words with exalted values" (*sgra mthun don 'phags*).

58. See Tsongkhapa, *Middling Stages of the Path* (Byllakuppe: Sera Je, 2005), 358; English trans. in Hopkins, *Tsong-kha-pa's Final Exposition of Wisdom*, 142; see also Jinpa, *Self, Reality, and Reason in Tibetan Philosophy*, 61; 202–203n71.

59. Nāgārjuna, *Fundamental Verses of the Middle Way*, XIII.7.

An important part of understanding the nature of things is to circumvent the reality of constructions, even constructions such as "emptiness." This is where the performative function of emptiness comes into play. Emptiness must be perceived nonconceptually to be fully known, so an experiential orientation toward emptiness must follow an ontological analysis. Indeed, liberation involves a perceptual, not merely a conceptual, encounter with the nature of reality, and this is the case in both Madhyamaka and Mind-Only traditions.

In his *Dispelling Disputes*, Nāgārjuna argued that a genuine means of knowledge (*pramāṇa*) is dependent upon warranted objects of knowledge (*prameya*) and that the validity of those objects are, in turn, confirmed by the validity of the means. Thus, the status of a subject (as veridical or not) is determined by the status of the object, and *vice versa*. The validity of what is perceived and the means of perception mutually rise and fall together. For instance, the perception of smoke is confirmed by clear eyesight, but clear eyesight, in turn, is confirmed by smoke being seen; they are mutually confirming. Thus, other than an appeal to consensus (or to another source of knowledge, and yet another to validate that, *ad infinitum*), there is no way out of the circularity without affirming a foundational truth, a God's eye view (outside the relational structure), and/or a self-validating cognition (which is independent and foundational, like self-awareness). As Nāgārjuna states:

> If for you the establishment of warranted objects is by means of a reliable source of knowledge and the establishment of a reliable source of knowledge is by means of warranted objects, neither is established for you.[60]

The twentieth-century Tibetan iconoclast, Gendün Chöpel (1903–1951), elaborated on the implications here with regards to the relationship between inference and perception:

> The object of inferential cognition comes from a perceptual cognition, and
> Perception is discerned by inference as veridical or defective.
> This makes the son the father's witness . . .

---

60. Nāgārjuna, *Dispelling Disputes*, v. 46.

I am uncomfortable with asserting conventional reality as validly established.[61]

Gendün Chöpel argued here that inference and perception are on equal grounds, that neither perception nor inference is prioritized and neither can provide a solid foundation for knowledge.

The question of whether inference or perception is primary is a key issue for the theory and method of Buddhist contemplative practice. In both Madhyamaka and Mind-Only traditions, we find contexts where one or the other plays the lead role. To accept the ultimacy of a nonconceptual cognition is to maintain the primacy of perception, whereas to deny the reliability of such a perception is to affirm that the contents of perception are nothing but conceptual constructions.

As we have seen, Madhyamaka analyses do not privilege the mind; just as objects are dependent on the mind, the mind is dependent on objects. While a powerful analysis and a tribute to interdependence, subject-object co-dependence not only precludes the possibility of a mind-independent world (subjectless objects), but may also preclude an objectless subject, or contentless awareness (*nirālambana-jñāna*), which plays an important role for Buddhist contemplative traditions. Contentless awareness offers the possibility of perception that is not conceptually enframed, a mode of awareness that is not simply derivative of a conceptual cognition. Seeing emptiness, like seeing space, is a common description of this cognition.[62] Whether or not there is content to a nonconceptual vision of emptiness is a hotly disputed topic. Also, the status of what (if anything) remains in emptiness reveals a sharp contrast between traditions of interpretation and fuels a debate between "self-emptiness" (a.k.a. Madhyamaka) versus "other-emptiness" (a.k.a. Mind-Only) in Tibet.

Appeals to the soteriological efficacy of nonconceptual experience are commonly accompanied by claims that conceptual knowledge does not go far enough. For instance, Kongtrül states that reality cannot be realized by Madhyamaka analysis alone because reality is not the realm of

---

61. Gendün Chöpel, *Ornament of Nāgārjuna's View*, 163; English trans. in Donald Lopez, *The Madman's Middle Way: Reflections on Reality of the Tibetan Monk Gendun Chopel* (Chicago: Chicago University Press, 2006), 62.

62. See, for instance, Kongtrül, *Light of Wisdom* (Kathmandu: Jamgon Kongtrul Labrang, 1999), 133.

study and reflection.[63] Buddhists like Tsongkhapa, in contrast, emphasize that nonconceptual experience does not necessarily go far enough because mere nonconceptuality does not necessarily realize the ultimate truth of emptiness nor eliminate the cause of distortion: the apprehension of intrinsic existence.[64] For his tradition, the view of Prāsaṅgika-Madhyamaka is needed to overcome the false apprehension of self and enable an actual nonconceptual realization of emptiness.

Indeed, different traditions, people, and institutional settings in Tibet have placed varying degrees of emphasis on the respective methods for coming to know the ultimate truth: through conceptual, "analytic meditation" (*dpyad sgom*) as a means for knowing nonconceptual emptiness on the one hand, and through the cultivation of "resting meditation" (*'jog sgom*) as a means for knowing nonconceptual emptiness on the other. Both of these methods, arguably, can be complementary, and the richness of Tibetan Buddhist culture is that there is a healthy supply of each (and both).

Conclusion

We have seen a tension in Buddhist epistemology between a dichotomy of perception and conception. This tension is typically resolved in one of two ways: (1) collapsing conception into perception, as with the role attributed to immediate and irreducible self-awareness, or (2) collapsing perception into conception, when ordinary perceptions are ascribed with conceptuality all the way down. Subtle forms of conceptuality, like dualistic appearances or things held to exist on their own, enframe experience in samsara for Buddhists. In Tibet, nonconceptual realization of emptiness is held to overcome the illusion of the reality of these conceptions, and is cultivated in different ways.

---

63. Kongtrül, *Encyclopedia of Knowledge* (Beijing: Nationalities Press, 2002), 556: (*dbu ma'i bstan bcos rnams las rigs pa'i rnam par dpyad pa ji snyed cig byas pa de dag ni pha rol gyi sgro skur gyi rtog pa zlog pa'i 'bras bu can kho na yin gyi/ sgro skur bsal nas gnas lugs kyi don rtogs pa 'ba' zhig rnam par dpyad pa'i mthu las skye ba ma yin te/ gnas lugs ni thos bsam gyis dpyad pa'i yul ma yin pa'i phyir*).

64. Tsongkhapa, *Great Exposition of the Stages of the Path*, 787–788; English trans. in Cutler (ed.), *The Great Treatise*, 343–344; See also Tsongkhapa, *Middling Stages of the Path* (Byllakuppe: Sera Je, 2005), 295–296; 307–308; English trans. in Hopkins, *Tsong-kha-pa's Final Exposition of Wisdom*, 38; 57.

In Madhyamaka, as exemplified in the interpretation of Tsongkhapa, all knowledge (excepting emptiness) is fundamentally distorted. Conceiving emptiness—that is, the lack of an object's intrinsic existence—is knowledge of the ultimate. Cultivating this knowledge becomes yogic perception by which one can achieve liberation from false ideas of subjectivity and objectivity. In Mind-Only-inflected traditions, except for nondual gnosis, all experiences of subject-object duality are fundamentally distorted. As is the case with cultivating the knowledge of a lack of intrinsic nature, cultivating the presence of nondual gnosis is held to be a means for liberation as well.

When cultivating an awareness of emptiness or the gnosis of self-awareness, one does not identify with the reality of the objects of dualistic experience. That is, cultivating an awareness of emptiness is not to identify with the objects of appearance, for they do not exist the way they appear. Also, cultivating pre-reflective awareness is not to identify with objects or subjectivity, either, for the gnosis to be cultivated is nondual and thus transcends ordinary, dualistic modes of subjective experience. In the next chapter we will discuss contemplative practices that reflect these theories in more detail, and come to see traces of Madhyamaka and Mind-Only in the theory and practice of tantra.

5

Radical Phenomenology

When the dry kindling of cognitive objects is totally consumed, there is peace—the Victorious One's Body of Reality (dharmakāya).

At that time there is no arising and no ceasing—the mind stops, and there is actualization through the body.

—CANDRAKĪRTI, *Introduction to the Middle Way* XI.17

Introduction

We have seen an important facet of Dharmakīrti's epistemology in the way that language functions by distorting reality, yet the creative function of language (as we see in tantra) tends to be downplayed in his system. In Tibet, tantric traditions, including Mahāmudrā and the Great Perfection, filled the void left by Dharmakīrti's epistemology by explicitly articulating the emancipatory role of self-awareness. Tantric traditions also offer an aesthetic and affirming appraisal of nonconceptual gnosis and its domain, as an alternative to what is simply conceptually and linguistically delimited.

In this chapter, we will consider tantra, and the contemplative practices in Tibet informed by Mind-Only and Madhyamaka, where language plays a more explicitly creative and liberating role. Tantric traditions, including the Great Perfection and Mahāmudrā, resonate deeply with Mind-Only. In significant ways, these traditions can even be said to be iterations of Yogācāra, as extensions of its contemplative (*yoga*) practice (*ācāra*). This chapter will discuss the "radical phenomenology" of these traditions, as extensions of Mind-Only. It will address how the guiding principle of emptiness, a Madhyamaka forte, is embedded in these traditions as well. Indeed, the "three greats" of the Great Madhyamaka, the Great Seal (Mahāmudrā), and the Great Perfection explicitly incorporate features of Madhayamaka.

And the Flesh Became Word: On the Inversion and Creation of Values in Tantra

The anti-essentialism we find in Mind-Only and Madhyamaka dissolves the notion that there is an element (subjective or objective) that has a privileged status in the open network of relations, a network with infinite variables, where all meanings are only ever found interactively, in interactions. In other words, everything is dependent or mediated; distinctions (and identities) are arbitrary and contingent. When we look at two figures that shaped two major trajectories of contemporary philosophy, Wittgenstein and Heidegger, we find similar sentiments: in Wittgenstein's critique of private language and Heidegger's notion of being-in-the world, in particular.

Heidegger's notion of being-in-the-world sheds light on the way that the mind (and body) are deeply intertwined in the world. The notion of being-in-the world conveys the subject's relational, enworlded structure, rather than a nugget-like essence encapsulated in isolation within. The work of the later Wittgenstein, too, puts a separate internal mental world on par with a private language; that is, it simply does not exist.[1] Language and mind are extended and embedded; they both encode the world and are encoded by it. Here again we can see a parallel between linguistic theory and ontology: meanings (like the "doors of action" of body, speech, and mind) are neither inside nor outside.

Longchenpa expressed an idea similar to Heidegger's being-in-the-world, which critiques an isolated subject or transcendental ego. When Longchenpa claimed that self-existing gnosis is not like the self-illuminating, self-aware mind of Mind-Only, he said that "since there is no internal or external, [gnosis] is not an internal mind; and since there is no self and other, it is not only self-awareness."[2] He makes here an important point that dissolves the inner/outer dichotomy implicated in the idea of an internal mind standing apart from an external world or an internally delimited self-awareness opposed to an "other" discrete entity. For

1. See Robert Thurman, "Philosophical Nonegocentrism in the Works of Wittgenstein and Candrakīrti," *Philosophy East & West* 30, no. 1 (1980): 321–337; Ludwig Wittgenstein, *Philosophical Investigations*, translated by G. E. M. Anscombe (Malden, MA: Blackwell Publications, 2001 [1953]), I.199–272.

2. Longchenpa, *Treasure Trove of Scriptural Transmission: Autocommentary on the "Precious Treasury of the Basic Field of Reality,"* in *Seven Treasuries* (*mdzod bdun*), vol. 3, ed. Tarthang Tulku (Sichuan, China, 1996), 321.

Longchenpa, the delimited modes of mind (*sems*) are distortions, or rather, *expressions*, of unbounded awareness (*rig pa*).

In contrast to the later Wittgenstein's move to "language-games," which are simply the conventions of transactional usage (analogous to the conventional truth of Prāsaṅgika-Madhyamaka),[3] with (the later) Heidegger, language comes to be not simply about games, but dynamic modes of disclosure.[4] With Heidegger we can see that language is the means through which to aesthetically articulate new modes of subjectivity or new forms of life. Unlike the way that language is often portrayed in Yogācāra as concealing and distorting, here the emphasis is on the way that language is revealing and creative, like magic (*māyā*). And so it is with the magic of *poetic* language and thought that we discover the linguistic affordances of creative evocation: of worlds and modes of being-in-the-world that destabilize and reenact our orientation as subjects within a world. That is, with poetry, the world is not simply confirmed in its pregivenness. Rather, preconceptions of the world are challenged, and ordinary modes of subjectivity are ruptured, as language creatively calls forth new forms of perception, participation, and enaction. Poetry is the paradigmatic case of language as art form—where meaning is expressed through the dynamic relation of receptivity and aesthetic object—as the rich interiors of aesthetic meaning call for participation to be *drawn out*.

It is in poetic and aesthetic theory where I see a resonance with tantra, and a way of theorizing this Buddhist literature and practice in Tibet as an extension of the phenomenological traditions of Mind-Only and Madhyamaka. In tantric practices in Tibet we encounter the acts of body, where the *body-subject* is staged in a highly aestheticized phenomenology of performance, involving the generation of a new identity of felt body image (or body schema)[5] from emptiness, emerging from within

---

3. See Wittgenstein, *Philosophical Investigations*, I.23–43.

4. See, for instance, Heidegger, "What Calls for Thinking?" in *Martin Heidegger: Basic Writings*, ed. David Krell (New York: Harper & Row, 1977), 345–367.

5. Reflecting the distinction between what Tibetan Buddhists refer to as the imputed and innate sense of self (with regard to the body), Gallagher and Zahavi characterize the difference between a *body image* (imputed) and a *body schema* (innate) as follows: "A *body image* is composed of a system of experiences, attitudes, and beliefs where the object of such intentional states is one's own body. . . By contrast the concept of *body schema* includes two aspects: (1) the close-to-automatic system of processes that constantly regulates posture and movement to serve intentional action; and (2) our pre-reflective and non-objectifying body-awareness." Shaun Gallagher and Dan Zahavi, *The Phenomenological Mind* (New York: Routledge, 2008),

an undetermined field (*śūnyatā*). Visualization practices embedded in rituals where meaning is inscribed upon the (enminded) *bodily* processes of birth, death, and sex are central in these contexts. After these body-mind schemas are acted out in a richly symbolic ritual context, all is together dissolved back into emptiness. Since being-in-the-world is a radically contingent affair (that is, it is interdependent and empty), subjective identity is not fixed; one's orientation and comportment toward the world is malleable. Subjectivity is constitutive of the world; and thus a shift here is a shift there (in the world).

Subjectivity can be reified as an insulated, isolated self in the center of experience, and stagnate into a first-personal perspective that is held captive as an immutable substrate (transcendental ego) enclosed within the epidermis or encapsulated within the grey matter of the brain. It can also be inscribed or inhabited in other ways, as a relational polarity intertwined with the world that is a fundamental component in a dynamic structure, part of the horizon within which the world takes place. In the first case, subjectivity is taken to be a singular agent or owner with unique access to a world of objects *out there*, as if staring out of the peephole of the body, as in a "spectatorial epistemology." In the latter case, subjectivity is seen to be an irreducible feature of life in the universe—the eyes of the world. In the words of Lackoff and Johnson in *Philosophy in the Flesh:*

> The environment is not an 'other' to us. It is not a collection of things that we encounter. Rather, it is part of our being. It is the locus of our existence and identity. We cannot and do not exist apart from it.[6]

The inhabited environment is where ontology and phenomenology overlap, where subjectivity is no more (*and no less*) than an index upon the "flesh" of the world. I draw upon Merleau-Ponty here, who took the lead from Heidegger to express the way that phenomenology becomes ontology, to show how appearance and emptiness are a unity as the *flesh* of appearing emptiness. What appears is infused with emptiness and awareness, or in

146. We might say that a goal of visualizing one's body as a deity in deity yoga is to retrain our body schema by reshaping our body image.

6. George Lackoff and Mark Johnson, *Philosophy in the Flesh* (New York: Basic Books, 1999), 566.

Merleau-Ponty's terms, the flesh of the world is the horizon of meaning, and the sensible and the sense compose two sides of this flesh. Merleau-Ponty speaks of this relation as a *chiasm* or *intertwining*,[7] rather than a relation of a subject as a disembodied spectator standing above or outside the world. The important point of this proposal is that the body, like the mind, is both "inside" and "outside" (or rather, it is not either).

With the example of the body as object and the body as subject, Merleau-Ponty conveys the place of this flesh: "Between my body looked at and my body looking, my body touched and my body touching, there is an overlapping or encroachment, so that we must say that the things pass into us as well as we into things."[8] The intertwining of body here is paralleled in Vasubandu's (Yogācāra) theory of mind and language, as neither inside nor outside.[9] One reason Mind-Only is not subjective idealism is because the environment is an immersive structure through which awareness inhabits (and knows) the world; minds are never free-floating or disembodied. Even at the stage of a buddha, the cognitive dimension of gnosis (*jñāna*) occurs with/in the dimension of body (*kāya*). Despite the association of Mind-Only with subjective idealism, Mind-Only is not simply a philosophy of mind, but a philosophy of embodiment, too, or *flesh*. That is, it reflects a philosophy that incorporates mental and bodily comportment, and orientation with/in an environment, as Merleau-Ponty states: "The presence of the world is precisely the presence of its flesh to my flesh."[10]

The intertwining of mind, body, and world occurs through the route of phenomenology, when it reaches its limit and becomes infused with the ontological, as Ted Toadvine says in his book, *Merleau-Ponty's Philosophy of Nature*: "It is by pushing phenomenology to its limit that we can overcome the bifurcation of mind and nature, locating the turning point at which each passes into the other."[11] This reciprocal nature of phenomenology

---

7. See Maurice Merleau-Ponty, *The Visible and the Invisible* (Evanston, Ill: Northwestern University Press, 1968), 130–155.

8. Merleau-Ponty, *The Visible and the Invisible*, 123.

9. See Jonathan Gold, "No Outside, No Inside: Duality, Reality and Vasubandhu's Illusory Elephant," *Asian Philosophy* 16, no. 1 (2006): 1–38.

10. Merleau-Ponty, *The Visible and the Invisible*, 127.

11. Ted Toadvine, *Merleau-Ponty's Philosophy of Nature* (Evanston, Ill: Northwestern University Press, 2009), 118.

and ontology, mind and nature, reflects the relationship between body and mind. It is "flesh" that expresses the unified field of ontology and phenomenology, the nondual truth. David Abram draws out implications of Merleau-Ponty's notion of flesh in his *Spell of the Sensuous:*

> A wholly immaterial mind could neither see things nor touch things—indeed, could not experience anything at all. *We* can experience things—can touch, hear, and taste things—only because, as bodies, we are ourselves included in the sensible field, and have our own textures, sounds, and tastes. We can perceive things at all only because we ourselves are entirely a part of the sensible world that we perceive! We might as well say that we are organs of this world, flesh of its flesh, and that the world is perceiving itself *through* us.[12]

The language of flesh can help us to make sense of Mind-Only, the unity of the two truths in Madhyamaka, and the place of body in the Buddhist practices in Tibet, for the imagery of Buddhist tantra is constituted by a world of flesh, a world composed of empty-appearance. In tantra, the roles of enminded body and embodied mind emerge from the background into the foreground. The move to the body in tantric practices reflects a focal shift from an abstract engagement in the philosophical worlds of Mind-Only and Madhyamaka to one that lives and breathes their insights. Thus, this is not just the "stuff" of metaphysical substance; rather, it is also the "stuff" of phenomenology.[13]

The "stuff" of the world is the phenomenality of emptiness, or appearing emptiness. Emptiness and appearance are inseparable, as are emptiness and awareness. This indivisible "structure," or *textured* flesh, is the ontological ground of tantra. Understood as the unity of phenomenality and emptiness, we can see how this groundless ground also resonates with the insights of Madhyamaka.

---

12. David Abram, *The Spell of the Sensuous* (New York: Pantheon Books, 1996), 68.

13. The physicality of tantra can be theorized (or not) in many other ways; what I offer here is one of many ways to theorize it. Tantra tends to be severely undertheorized in scholarly literature for several reasons, not limited to but including its perceived debauchery, its esoteric nature, its constructed nature (i.e., " 'tantra' as Western invention"), its prominent ritual dimensions, its highly specialized and complex theoretic structures, its perceived lack of having any theoretical structures, a simple lack of interest and/or knowledge.

Thinking of this open horizon of appearing-emptiness with Merleau-Ponty's flesh can help us to see the role of *embodiment* in tantra, and the importance of enaction—where mental images, body schemas, and performed utterances become the means to overcome rigid habits of perception, thought, and action. The body is infused with mind in tantra rather than simply being an afterthought or an expression of mind. The body is also empty, while appearing. The role of body emerges in tantra as a primary locus of meaning in theory and practice.

Language or speech, like body and mind, is also located in/between us: it, too, is neither inside nor outside. Speech mediates body and mind—as body manipulations produce sounds that invoke and evoke meanings in minds. Thus, speech is an important part of tantra (a.k.a. *mantrayāna*—"the vehicle of mantra"). Given that sounds as language are received as meaningful, understanding language is another case of the rupture of the dichotomous split between nonconceptual perception and conception, given that (spoken) language, like the touching/touched body and knowing/known mind, is a paradigm of double duty: language is perceived (in the auditory perceptions of sound) and conceived (words are encoded in sounds). Yet again, another duality collapses, this time the percept-concept dichotomy.

Visualization or mental imagery in the literature and practice of Buddhist tantra can be understood in the context of the confluence of Mind-Only and Madhyamaka as a distinct type of phenomenological intervention that purports to be a contemplative practice to free a person from false consciousness. Like the tools of mereological analysis (i.e., part/whole analyses) and contemplative exercises of habituation to the insight of the lack of real object constancy (i.e., meditation on impermanence), mental imagery of felt shifts in experiential orientation—that are constructed and dissolved—offer a unique entry point to stage our felt bodily presences in new ways, akin to the "interventions" of art and poetry, which can play a role in dismantling our ordinary senses of self and world. These practices also can serve to rupture habitual patterns of identity by recreating them in deliberate and expressive ways. Seen in this light, we find another way to understand Heidegger's move to poetry in his later writings as well as Merleau-Ponty's language "singing the world."

Tantric rituals for generating the appearance of deities commonly begin with the mantra, *oṃ svabhāvaśuddhāḥ sarvadharmāḥ svabhāvasuddho 'haṃ*, which can be translated as: "All phenomena are naturally pure; I am naturally pure."[14] Here we find subjectivity identified with *purity*, and the meaning of "pure" carries the dual connotations of emptiness (pure *of* self-identity) as well as a quality of the purity of appearance (pure *as* divine), the pantheistic ground or flesh within which the universe is enfolded.[15] This purity of appearance in tantra[16] can be seen as an extension of the second of the "three natures" of Yogācāra—the imagined, dependent, and consummate natures—because the fabric of reality (or flesh of the world) gets articulated as *pure* in the "pure dependent nature" (*dag pa'i gzhan dbang*), as distinguished from the "impure dependent nature" (*ma dag pa'i gzhan dbang*), which refers to the causal process of dualistic cognition and hence, suffering.[17] The articulation of a pure dependent nature—or positive flux of enminded, yet empty, appearances—is one way Yogācāra traditions inform tantric theory in Tibet. The pure dependent nature is the *pure appearance* of the world, appearances not encapsulated by conceptual constructions. The pure ground is the dependent nature undifferentiated from the consummate nature (*yongs grub*); it takes on a positive articulation, not simply an absence of conceptual construction. The positive articulation of this ground is also expressed in buddha-nature (*tathāgatagarbha*), which forms the pure basis of lived experience in the world, not simply a world of distortion and suffering to be shunned. It is the positive expression of this ground or "flesh" that characterizes the presence of Mind-Only in the contemplative traditions in Tibet.[18]

In the embrace of appearance, after emptiness has been determined (as indeterminate) in deconstructive ontological analyses, we find the domain of tantra: where appearance becomes the site of transformation, and its

---

14. See, for instance, Getsé Paṇchen, *Husks of Unity*, trans. in *Deity, Mantra, and Wisdom* (Ithaca, NY: Snow Lion Publications, 2006), 113; see also Stephan Beyer, *The Cult of Tara* (Ithaca, NY: Snow Lion Publications, 2006), 143–144.

15. For more on the connections between Buddhism and pantheism, see Douglas Duckworth, "Buddha-Nature and the Logic of Pantheism," in *The Buddhist World*, ed. John Powers (London: Routledge, 2015), 234–247.

16. On the role of "the recollection of purity" (*dag pa dran pa*) in tantric practice, see Getsé Paṇchen, *Husks of Unity*, 132. See also Beyer, *The Cult of Tara*, 80.

17. See, for instance, Longchenpa, *Precious Treasury of Philosophical Systems*, ed. Tarthang Tulku (Sichuan, China, 1996), 746–747.

18. For another discussion of the transformation of a positive ground in Tibet, which I refer to as "the tantric turn," see Duckworth, "Grounds of Buddha-Nature in Tibet," *Critical Review of Buddhist Studies* 21 (2017): 109–136.

expression. Here, language is no longer simply distorting (as emphasized in non-tantric Mahāyāna), but is creative. A similar move from emptiness to presence, or from denial (in modern nihilism) to affirmation of value can be found in the works of Nietzsche and his musings on the creation of values.[19] Value-creation is the affirmation of life; a creative act in response to Nietzsche's portrayal of nihilism (or emptiness) in which the "highest values devalue themselves."[20]

A similar trajectory is exemplified in the literature and practice of tantra, where poetic thought and expressive language therein resonate with creative expression, which we also find in the works of the later Heidegger. Yet while Heidegger did not explicitly theorize the body, that course was picked up in Merleau-Ponty's notion of flesh, which is a notion that can help us to see a development of Mind-Only that parallels the phenomenological tradition running from the early Husserl, through Heidegger, to Merleau-Ponty. Through this lens, tantra can be seen to represent the culmination of Madhyamaka ontology, where the ontology of absence becomes phenomenological—as emptiness must be *known* (and thus is found to be inseparably wed to appearance and awareness). Emptiness here is dramatically embodied, participatory, and performative (not simply propositional). Seen in this way, we find bodily processes emerge in force in the theory and practice of tantra as an extension of the Mind-Only and Madhyamaka theories of the subject's intertwining with the world. Thus, tantra can be understood as the performance of this intertwining upon the groundless ground in which the intertwining of the embodied mind and enminded body is evoked and enacted.

In the Geluk school following Tsongkhapa, there is no difference between the view of sūtra (i.e., Prāsaṅgika-Madhyamaka) and that found in tantra.[21] Since the highest view is Prāsaṅgika-Madhyamaka in this tradition, the associated methods for realizing this view (e.g., critical analysis and debate) are particularly emphasized, as we saw in the last chapter, while tantra is not seen to offer a unique philosophical orientation. Whereas the dominant Geluk tradition makes the tantric distinction based solely on

---

19. See Friedrich Nietzsche, *Beyond Good and Evil*, trans. by Walter Kaufmann (New York: Random House, 1966), 205.

20. Friedrich Nietzsche, *Will to Power*, trans. by Walter Kaufmann and R. J. Hollingdale (New York: Random House, 1967), 8.

21. Tsongkhapa, *The Great Exposition of the Stages of Mantra* (Xining, China: Nationalities Press, 1995), 18.

method, this is not the case for Tibetan traditions that assert what we may call "philosophical tantra" and make an explicit distinction between sūtra and tantra based on a *philosophical* view as well.[22] In these traditions (e.g., Kagyü, Nyingma), we see more of a role for Yogācāra analyses, such as the phenomenological reduction (*snang ba sems su bsgrub*), both in coming to terms with emptiness in Madhyamaka and in the philosophical formulation of tantra.

The practices of Mahāmudrā and the Great Perfection in these Tibetan traditions can also be seen in parallel as taking the "final" step of Madhyamaka and Mind-Only analyses. We see this reflected in the way that emptiness is no longer treated as just an object, as in the beginning of a Madhyamaka ontological analysis, but is lived through—as participatory and performative. Also, these practices can be seen as the culmination of Mind-Only analyses, which moves from the first step of establishing appearances as mind to a view that is compatible with Madhyamaka in articulating the conceptuality of all dualistic appearances. From India to Tibet we can chart an arch of the trajectory of this dialectical tension—from a position that deconstructs concepts to one that enthrones a view of nonconceptual, nondual experience. The tension is enacted in the literature and performance of Mahāmudrā and the Great Perfection, which re-present a fundamental insight into the phenomenal macrostructure of reality within which the whole world takes place. Since this is not the context to discuss elaborate tantric practices and associated theories (for a concise overview, see Appendix C), before concluding I will briefly address two specific traditions of tantric theory and practice in Tibet.

Mahāmudrā Phenomenology

A phenomenological tradition that bears the imprint of the synthesis of Mind-Only and Madhyamaka is Mahāmudrā. Practical instructions for the contemplative practices of Mahāmudrā commonly begin with techniques of calm abiding (*zhi gnas, śamatha*) before moving into meditations on special insight (*lhag mthong, vipaśyanā*). As it is necessary to settle the mind before recognizing its nature according to Mahāmudrā instructions, the instructions begin this way, and are also preceded by preliminaries

22. On "philosophical tantra," see Duckworth, "Tibetan Mahāyāna and Vajrayāna," in *A Companion to Buddhist Philosophy*, ed. Steven Emmanuel (Hoboken, NJ: Wiley-Blackwell, 2013), 99–109

that include fundamental Buddhist contemplative exercises like meditation on impermanence.

In the twelfth century, Gampopa (1079–1153) had described Mahāmudrā as the path of "recognition" as opposed to rejection (in the Perfection Vehicle) or transformation (in the Mantra Vehicle).[23] In contrast to a nihilistic escapism that rejects this world for another one, or an effort to forcibly change the world into something else, he described the path of Mahāmudrā as a cognitive shift, a re-cognition. Gampopa also laid out the three paths as follows: the dialectical vehicle of the perfections, which is "the path of inference," Mahāyāna Mantra, which is "the path of blessings," and the innate luminosity (of Mahāmudrā), which is "the path of perception."[24] Thus, perception is the way of Mahāmudrā, picking up where Yogācāra theorists like Dharmakīrti left off.

Mahāmudrā instruction manuals begin with cultivating attention. The practice of focused attention in calm abiding typically begins with attending to an object, like a stone or stick in front of you, and then moving to objectless meditations. The transition from supported to "signless" (*mtshan med*) meditations is made by first training with an external focus (*rten can*) like a stone, then without a material support (*rten med*), by paying attention to the movement of breath. This is done by turning attention to sensations of inhalation and exhalation rather than to some external form. Observing the breath—which mediates the internal and external worlds, the voluntary and the natural—helps one to achieve a calm focus, among other things.

Attending to an object like the breath is a practice that exercises the quality of attention. Before the focus of observation shifts from *objects* of experience to the structure of experience itself, the object of attention is, for the most part, arbitrary. In the next phase of "objectless" calm abiding meditations, attention is directed toward nothing but the quality of attention itself, as tightly focused or loose. As the practice develops, one is

---

23. Gampopa discusses the three paths of renunciation, transformation, and recognition in *Abundant Qualities*, vol. 1, 527, in *Gampopa's Collected Works*, vol. 1, 505–575 (Kathmandu: Khenpo Tenzin and Lama Namgyal, 2000); see also David Jackson, *Enlightenment by a Single Means* (Vienna: Verlag der Österreichischen Akademie der Wisschenschaften, 1994), 27; Klaus-Dieter Mathes, *A Direct Path to the Buddha Within* (Sommerville, MA: Wisdom Publications, 2008), 40–41.

24. Gampopa, *Response to Düsum Khyenpa's Request*, in *Gampopa's Collected Works*, vol. 1 (Delhi: Shashin, 1976), 438; see also Jackson, *Enlightenment by a Single Means* (Vienna: Verlag der Österreichischen Akademie der Wisschenschaften, 1994), 25.

encouraged to gently balance the attention from being too focused or too lax,[25] like tuning the strings of a guitar. Navigating between agitation and dullness, the two primary forms of distraction, is key to developing meditative stability.

The practice of calm abiding is a preparatory phase for the main part (*dngos gzhi*) of Buddhist meditation. Even while meditations on the breath may calm you down and boost your immune system, this is not the goal of the practice. Honing attention prepares for the phase of special insight, which is the central pillar of Buddhist meditative traditions. Special insight has a central place because it is liberative, not just palliative; that is, it undermines the root cause of suffering, not just the symptoms of dis-ease.

In Mahāmudrā instructions, special insight begins with a contemplation of the nature of mind. The investigation engages questions that probe the mind in terms of its location, shape, and form. What does the mind look like? Is there something that it is like? Does it have a color, form, or shape? Where is the mind? Is it in the body? Is it empty, clear or both? What does that mean? After searching for the nature of mind with these kinds of questions, the practice of special insight proceeds to investigate the mind's "expressions" (*rtsal*), which are thoughts and perceptions. This stage of inquiry examines the nature of thoughts with questions such as: Where are thoughts? Where do thoughts come from and where do they go? It is significant that the contemplative practices here begin with questions, not answers: it is an invitation to a way of thinking and relating to the world. Unlike calculative thinking, it is not aimed toward the manipulation of ready-made facts nor is it simply the internalization of a set of propositions.[26] A question is open-ended, and thus can function to orient or "direct" toward openness. That is, a question can be the answer, or rather, can be even better than an answer: for unlike answers, questions can leave the mind open and undirected (but not aimless).

In his Mahāmudrā instructions, Dakpo Tashi Namgyel (1512/13–1587), a Kagyü teacher, emphasized that it is not enough simply to relate to this practice intellectually, but one has to perform the exercise to really understand it.[27] In other words, the analysis cannot be left as dry words; you have

25. See Dakpo Tashi Namgyel, *Illuminating the Innate Nature*, 4–10.

26. On the distinction between "meditative thinking" and "calculative thinking," see Heidegger, "Memorial Address," in *Discourse on Thinking*, trans. by John Anderson and Hans Freund (New York: Harper & Row, 1969), 43–57.

27. See, for instance, Dakpo Tashi Namgyel, *Illuminating the Innate Nature*; 10–11, 18.

to really engage in it such that you feel it and it impinges on your world. For instance, it is like the difference between learning the skill of bike-riding by reading a manual and by riding a bike. There is a real difference. The difference shows the distinctive role of participatory knowledge in contemplative traditions, and hints at just how different meditative knowledge can be from mere intellectual knowledge. Buddhists have traditionally distinguished knowledge gleaned from studying from a deeper relationship with knowledge gained through contemplation, and still deeper ways of knowledge that come from meditation.

The central place of embodied, personal knowledge here—as an active, living truth—contrasts sharply with the modern ideal of disinterested knowledge, or impersonal, faceless facts. Indeed, for Buddhists, transformative knowledge is the most important kind of knowledge there is. The supposition that valueless, dead ideas—static truths—are the only real truths there are is what Donald Evans has referred to as the dogma of *impersonalism.* He characterized impersonalism as "the dogmatic rejection of any claim that requires personal transformation to be adequately understood and appraised."[28] Moreover, "disinterested" impersonal facts are arguably never completely separate from personal interests and values. An implication of this is that there can be no real distinction between facts and values, nor between the domains of ontology and ethics, and this is as true for the orientations of science as it is for Buddhism.[29]

The next phase in Mahāmudrā instruction manuals is a four-stage process of "cutting through the root."[30] The first step begins by ascertaining that thoughts are mind with questions like: Are thoughts the same or different from the mind? How are they related? In some Mahāmudrā instructions, it is said that thoughts are the nature of mind, or that *the nature of thoughts* is the nature of mind (or *dharmakāya*).[31] That is, other than

---

28. Donald Evans, *Spirituality and Human Nature* (Albany: SUNY Press, 1992), 101. Echoing Quine's two dogmas of empiricism, Evans refers to impersonalism, along with perspectivalism (the Kantian presupposition that all knowledge is mediated), as "the two dogmas regarding skepticism of spiritual reality" (p. 100).

29. The discourses of science reflect the socially constituted values of the culture in which those scientific discourses are embedded, as well as the financial and institutional systems that enable scientific practices. Even the claim that the value of science is "knowledge for knowledge's sake" exemplifies a value embedded within the personal interests of a community. Despite the ideal of impersonal, objective truth, nothing (even science) exists in a vacuum.

30. See Dakpo Tashi Namgyel, *Illuminating the Innate Nature*, 13–18.

31. See, for instance, Dakpo Tashi Namgyel, *Illuminating the Innate Nature*, 21.

thoughts, there is no nature of mind; they are indivisible. The integral relationship between thoughts and mind-nature described in Mahāmudrā texts differs from accounts found in the tradition of the Great Perfection, where the conceptual mind (*sems*) is distinguished from the nature of mind, or awareness (*rig pa*).[32] In both cases of Mahāmudrā and the Great Perfection, however, the relationship between mind and mind-nature is likened to the relationship between ice (thoughts) and water (mind-nature);[33] without water, there is no ice, but the two can be said to be conceptually and phenomenally distinct.

The next step is to come to know appearances as mind. This comes directly out of Mind-Only analysis, from the observation that objects always coincide with a perceiving subject. By reflecting on the nature of experience, one comes to understand that there is nothing that exists without being perceived. This is to acknowledge that "to exist is to be perceived" (*Esse est percipi*), an insight expressed by Bishop Berkeley and Dharmakīrti (*sattvam upalabdhir eva*) over one thousand years earlier.[34]

The third stage is to investigate the mind that is still, without thought, and the mind that is thinking. What is the difference between stillness and thought activity? Is there stillness in the thought activity that recognizes a thinking mind? Is there thought activity when the mind thinks it is still? The practice here is simply to observe the mind, whether thinking or still, and recognize its open and clear nature without fabrication. Dakpo Tashi Namgyel states that it is a mistake to presume that thoughts are bad and that being thoughtless is good, as he probes: "Is calming abiding without thoughts something positive, to be happy about, and having many thoughts bad, and something to be sad about? If you don't recognize this fault, your meditation will be famished . . . Don't be partial to stillness or movement."[35]

The last of the four-stage process of "cutting through the root" culminates with seeing the mind's emptiness. This process is similar to

32. David Higgins helpfully outlines these two contrasting ways in which the relationship between ordinary consciousness and wisdom is portrayed as "differentiation and unity models." See David Higgins, "How Consciousness (*rnam shes*) Is Related to Wisdom (*ye shes*)? The Eighth Karma pa on Buddhist Differentiation and Unity Models," *Studia Religiologica* 48, no. 4 (2015): 341–362.

33. Dakpo Tashi Namgyel, *Illuminating the Innate Nature*, 14–15.

34. See John Dunne, *Foundations of Dharmakīrti's Philosophy* (Boston: Wisdom Publications, 2004), 85n52.

35. Dakpo Tashi Namgyel, *Illuminating the Innate Nature*, 21.

Madhyamaka reasoning, and involves determining the indeterminate (or undetermined) nature of mind. In Madhyamaka, the mind is not found when sought, just as is the case with objects. In the analyses in Mahāmudrā, too, we see a parallel contemplative process of looking for the mind in terms of color, shape, form, location, point of origin, and point of departure. While these forms of inquiry resemble Madhyamaka analyses, they are distinctive in that the analyses here probe subjectivity, not simply the mind as object.[36]

Central practices in Mahāmudrā are also integral to the practices of the Great Perfection. For instance, Longchenpa described an analytic process of "dislodging the mind" (*sems kyi khang bu bshigs pa*), a preliminary practice that begins with analyzing where the mind comes from, remains, and goes.[37] After looking for the mind in this way, the practice proceeds with pointing out the mind as empty, then emptiness as appearing, and finally, appearance and emptiness as nondual.[38]

Following the instructions on calm abiding and special insight, the next phase in Mahāmudrā instruction manuals is the so-called "pointing out" instructions. A danger of pointing out the nature of mind is that the instructions can be misunderstood such that it may be thought that someone else introduces it to you, rather than you introducing it to yourself, or (reflexively) knowing thyself. That is, recognizing the nature of mind is a *reflexive* act (*not reflective* or introspective) whereby the looker looks to itself/oneself. This process entails more than the paradox of self-reference (this statement is a lie) or of emptiness (emptiness itself is empty) because here

36. In a parallel context in the Great Perfection, Longchenpa says: "'Isn't this just repeating the analysis of coming, abiding, and going explained before?' No. Earlier the analysis showed its unreality in terms of its object (*de'i yul*); here, its essence is ascertained through the analysis of subjectivity (*yul can*)." Longchenpa, *Ocean Cloud of the Profound Meaning* (*zab don rgya mtsho phrin*), *snying thig ya bzhi* (*mkha' 'gro yang thig*), In *snying thig ya bzhi* (*mkha' 'gro yang thig*) (Delhi: Sherab Gyaltsen Lama, 1975), vol. 8, 354.

37. See Longchenpa, *Instructions on the Meaning of Breakthrough Meditation* (*khregs chod ye babs so gzhag gi don khrid*), in *snying thig ya bzhi* (*bla ma yang thig*), vol. 1 (Delhi: Sherab Gyaltsen Lama, 1975), 371.

38. This is part of an analysis of mind developed from Pema Ledrelsel, *Instructions on the Meaning of Liberation Through Wearing* (*btags grol don khrid*), in *Snying thig ya bzhi* (*mkha' 'gro snying thig*), vol. 10 (Delhi: Sherab Gyaltsen Lama, 1975), 88. See also Ngedön Tenzin Zangpo, the Third Dzokchen Rinpoché, *Excellent Chariot* (*rdzogs pa chen po mkha' 'gro snying thig gi khrid yig thar lam bgrod byed shing rta bzang po*) (Chengdu: Nationalities Press, 1997), 305–309.

it is not just propositional theory, but participatory enaction—a dynamic, living reality.

Another problem with understanding instructions that point out the nature of mind is that they can create a sense that mind-nature is something that is to be grasped onto and held, or that the instruction will point out a determinate *thing*—an essence to be identified. This is a problem analogous to the reification of emptiness. The nature of mind is not determinate, so the mind cannot be known like an object, by positively identifying or determining it. In terms of seeing the nature of mind, determinative cognition is only present to the extent that its indeterminacy is determined, as in the meaning of "seeing" emptiness described in the tenth-century Nup Sangyé Yeshé's *Lamp of Meditation*: "Since in all phenomena there is no self or other, knower or known, seeing nothing whatsoever is imputed with the name "seeing," but there is certainly nothing separate seen."[39] The eleventh-century Nyingma scholar, Rongzom, also glossed the meaning of "seeing the truth" as not seeing anything at all.[40] These authors put forward that the only way that the nature of mind is "determined" is in the sense that it is indeterminate or undetermined;[41] this is the "certainty" of the view. On this kind of "certainty," Klein and Wangyel remarked, "Ontological undecidability does not preclude epistemological certainty. Indeed, one provokes the other, since the clearer one is about the open, unfettered, and indefinable nature of reality, the more confidence one has in it."[42] In other words, the more you understand the lack of any determinate essence in things, the more confidence you have in this indeterminacy.

The pointing out instructions in Mahāmudrā include a threefold "co-emergence" that recognizes: mind-nature as co-emergent, the nature of thoughts as co-emergent, and appearances as co-emergent. "Co-emergent" can mean that samsara is co-emergent with nirvana, or that nondual

---

39. Nup Sangyé Yeshé, *Lamp for the Eye of Meditation* (*bsam gtan mig sgron*), 307. Cited in Karmay, *The Great Perfection*, 111.

40. Rongzom, *Entering the Way of the Mahāyāna* (*theg chen tshul 'jug*), cited in Karmay, *The Great Perfection* (Leiden: E. J. Brill, 1988), 111n26.

41. On a subtle but important difference between "indeterminate" and "undetermined," see Jorge Ferrer, "Spiritual Knowing as Participatory Enaction," in *The Participatory Turn: Spirituality, Mysticism, Religious Studies*, ed. Jorge Ferrer and Jacob Sherman (Albany, NY: SUNY Press, 2008), 168n63.

42. Anne Klein and Tenzin Wangyel, *Unbounded Wholeness: Dzogchen, Bon, and the Logic of the Nonconceptual* (New York: Oxford University Press, 2006), 72.

gnosis is co-emergent with a deluded, dualistic mind. This co-emergence entails that nondual gnosis is always present, that nonduality envelops duality as the infinite incorporates the finite within it, as a condition for its possibility. Accordingly, nirvana is always accessible because it is always there in some sense; despite the fact that it may not be noticed, the unconditioned realm of nirvana is never beyond reach.

The first co-emergence is that of mind-nature with existence or reality. Mind-nature is the nature of reality. The practice in this phase is simply to let the mind be without distraction; there is nothing that need be added or removed. In this there is the unity of calm abiding and special insight, which in reality are not separate,[43] like appearance and emptiness, stillness and movement. Here again duality collapses, as every other practice is positioned as either a tool for understanding this, peripheral to this, an expression of this understanding, or is misguided.

Thoughts are co-emergent with mind-nature, too, because they are not separate from mind. There is no separate gnosis apart from the mind in Mahāmudrā, either, in contrast to the way that nonconceptual awareness is distinguished from conceptual mind in some other contexts, such as what we find in the Great Perfection. Here, the practice is to experience the empty clarity of thoughts without trying to stop them or focus on them. Mind and gnosis are nondual, too.

Appearances are also co-emergent with mind-nature. Appearances are the nature of mind, as we saw in Mind-Only's analysis of the co-dependence of perceiver and perceived. The practice in Mahāmudrā is to recognize the unity of appearance, mind, and emptiness. Whereas Madhyamaka's ontological analyses expose how objects are products of conceptual discrimination, in Mahāmudrā, by contrast, the focus shifts to the quality of the subject (as in Mind-Only) and then goes beyond subjectivity. In the section on the co-emergence of appearance in his chapter on Mahāmudrā, the Drikung Kagyü master, Rikzin Chödrak (1595–1659), states as follows (for a complete translation of his instructions in the Mahāmudrā chapter, see Appendix D):

> When you look directly at something in front of you like a pillar or pot, its appearance as something truly real with genuine characteristics is the *imagined nature* because it is imputed by the deluded

43. Dakpo Tashi Namgyel, *Illuminating the Innate Nature*, 19.

> mind. It is produced by other conditions; hence, it is the *dependent nature*. When its essence is examined and scrutinized, the *consummate nature* is the realization that it is essentially not established other than being a mere name, a mere sign, and a mere designation. As illustrated by this, all appearances—such as forms, sounds, scents, tastes, and textures—have these three natures.[44]

Here we clearly see the presence of Mind-Only in Mahāmudrā instructions, in addition to Madhyamaka. Moreover, we have further evidence here that Mind-Only is not subjective idealism, because *all appearances* have three natures. There is the imposition of true reality on appearances (the imagined nature), the conditioned and relational process of their arising (the dependent nature), and the absence of any essence of an appearance beyond being a conceptual designation (the consummate nature).

One of the earliest sūtras that shaped Mind-Only uses the example of the appearance of a crystal to show how these three natures function together.[45] The crystal (the dependent nature) reflects its background. That is, it appears blue when placed on blue fabric, red against a red backdrop, or green while lying against something green. The colors of the crystal's background (the imagined nature) do not inhere in the crystal; in other words, colors do not exist in the crystal (the consummate nature). An important feature of this example is that an appearing crystal is *always embedded against a background*. The idea of a crystal alone, floating in the void without a background to reflect, is a fiction. As is the case with the color of a crystal, the three natures are intermingled in any appearance. An implication of this interpretation of the three natures is that a colorless crystal is a normative ideal, but never a real appearance. Accordingly, such an ideal of purity, as if chasing after a pure vacuum, devoid of even an observer (a novice scientist's fetish) or a nonconceptual experience devoid of any object (a novice meditator's fetish) is, in practice, only theory. Yet the unconditioned nonduality (of subjects and objects) is always the background of the conditioned duality of a foreground.

---

44. Rikzin Chödrak, *Words of Dharmakīrti*, in *phyag chen lnga ldan byin rlabs dpal 'bar sogs* (Delhi: Tenzin Chodak, 1975), 147–148.

45. This example is taken from the *Sūtra Explaining the Intent*, chapter VI. See Tibetan edition and English translation in John Powers, *Wisdom of Buddha: The Saṃdhinirmocana Mahāyāna Sūtra* (Berkeley: Dharma Publishing, 1995), 84–87.

The mind and the appearing world are dependently interconnected, like the backdrop of a crystal is integral to its appearance. Yet a number of questions remain in this account: can a crystal (or mind) remain in a pure, colorless glory, independent of a backdrop of an environment to reflect? Or do cognitions, like crystals, always only subsist as long as they are embedded in a world of appearances? And if so, are appearances necessarily illusory, fueled solely by distorting habits? Or can there be pure appearances, arising as pure expressions of gnosis? The different answers given to these questions reflect different interpretations of Yogācāra (e.g., the so-called "stained" and "stainless" views of the proponents of false representations), and mark a "tantric turn" in the interpretation of Yogācāra: from phenomenal appearance interpreted as mere distortions that come to a close in liberation to phenomenal appearance interpreted as the creative dynamics of gnosis.

The kind of entanglement of things like crystals, which are always situated in relationships among subjects and things (relationships that do not implicate real differences, nor sameness, neither plurality nor singularity), is expressed as "unity." Within unity, there is no real separation between subject and object, nor is there a real distinction between appearance and emptiness. This unity distinguishes Buddhist phenomenological traditions like Mahāmudrā and the Great Perfection from ordinary Madhyamaka, which speaks of two *separate* truths.[46] Unity is beyond subjectivity (and objectivity); it is the place where ordinary (ontological)

---

46. Mipam claimed that the unique object of negation of the Prāsaṅgika is the perception of the two truths as distinct, and that there is nothing more to be developed in Prāsaṅgika beyond that: "In this way, one should know that the Prāsaṅgika's unique object of negation is the aspect of apprehending the two truths as distinct because if the Svātantrikas were free from this object of negation of conceiving the two truths as distinct, then other than that view, there would not be the slightest thing to develop for even the Prāsaṅgikas, etc." Mipam, *Words that Delight Guru Mañjughoṣa* (Sichuan: Nationalities Press, 1990), 97. In his *Beacon of Certainty*, Mipam made a distinction between a lesser and great middle way: "The distinction I make differentiate between two: the Middle Way of the path and the Middle Way of meditative equipoise, the main part (*dngos gzhi*)—the gross and subtle, or the causal and resultant. The distinction is made between the lesser and great Middle Ways which are the contexts of consciousness or gnosis." Mipam, *Beacon of Certainty* (Sichuan: Nationalities Press, 1997), 42–43. He states that the lesser Middle Way, together with assertions and the two truths distinct, is designated as the "Middle Way" due to it being the cause of the Middle Way: "Therefore, the Middle Way together with assertions of the respective two truths is the lesser Middle Way of alternation, which is the designation of a cause with the name of the result." Ibid., 47.

Madhyamaka analyses end, or where "Great Madhyamaka" begins (as radical phenomenology).

Mahāmudrā moves the focus of inquiry squarely into the presence of experiential reality, or the unity of appearance and emptiness. As an object of mind, the unity of appearance and emptiness can be interpreted (monistically) as a unified field or (pluralistically) as a matrix of interrelations. Yet both of these interpretations of an undetermined field are object-oriented, and thus metaphysical. Unity is an irreducibly experiential reality and cannot be adequately described in any way. Mahāmudrā instructions emphasize this point where representation fails and participatory, evocative language comes to the fore.

Since unity is an inherently *dynamic* field or matrix of experience, the practice of Mahāmudrā evokes an acute awareness of the role of the living subject (or awareness), a role that does not translate into another theory, and consistently defies the gaze of a metaphysical orientation. That is to say, Mahāmudrā contemplation probes the dynamics of living nature and challenges claims to truth and understanding that are only observed from a safe distance, abstracted from living reality. Mahāmudrā is foremost a practice, not (merely) a theory. In fact, theorizing is said to be a sidetrack for the main part of Mahāmudrā practice.

An important element of Mahāmudrā practice is the identification of misunderstandings, which are called "faults" or "sidetracks" (see Appendix D). These are commonly enumerated in four ways, as the sidetracks of: the basic nature of knowledge, the remedy, the path, and stamping with the seal.[47] The first sidetrack is to hold on to an idea of emptiness by conceiving emptiness as an absence. The fact that this is a sidetrack in Mahāmudrā reveals Mahāmudrā's affinity with Madhyamaka's ontological analyses, and shows how its inquiry extends from Madhyamaka. Emptiness understood as unity is something more (and less) than just an absence. It is more because it is a dynamic, living reality, not just an abstract thought of negation. It is less because it is not defined or confined by language and the dichotomous structures of affirmation and negation. This is why Mahāmudrā goes further than a Madhyamaka ontological analysis that stops with emptiness understood as simply a lack of intrinsic nature, which is a derivative and dichotomously framed idea.

47. On these four sidetracks, see Dakpo Tashi Namgyel, *Illuminating the Innate Nature*, 31–32; Thrangu Rinpoché, *An Ocean of the Ultimate Meaning*, trans. by Peter Alan Roberts (Boston: Shambhala Publications, 2004), 133–136.

The second sidetrack also involves a misunderstanding of emptiness, where emptiness is again related to as an object. In this case, a sidetrack is flagged in which emptiness becomes object-ified as a *remedy* for the afflictions. Indeed, authentic realization of emptiness is what overcomes the afflictions, and thus there is a context in which an insight into emptiness can (and should) be understood as a remedy, in the sense that knowing emptiness is what brings freedom from afflictions. But in the context of meditative equipoise (the practical orientation of Mahāmudrā), to see emptiness as destroying afflictions is to objectify emptiness (as well as the afflictions). This is because *any* conception of emptiness presumes a duality of emptiness on the one hand and a substratum of emptiness (e.g., an affliction) on the other. This kind of notion of emptiness—as a discrete entity tied to a dichotomous structure—is not the genuine meaning of emptiness (unity), which is not separate from the afflictions (nor any other thing). By acknowledging this integral emptiness (unified with appearance and awareness) according to Mahāmudrā, its lived understanding undermines the afflictive power of reactive and reifying habits.

The third sidetrack pertains to another mistaken concept, the notion of a "path." This sidetrack involves a distorted view of time. That is, it involves a misconception that holds the path to be a temporal process that brings about a result that is qualitatively different from right now. In Mahāmudrā, to denigrate the present reality in this way and superimpose one's own idea of a final, climatic fruition—an otherworldly ideal or heavenly state—is a sidetrack. It is a sidetrack that involves constantly deferring to the future, with paradise forever postponed and the apocalypse (of samsara) always now. This sidetrack of constantly deferring to the future and devaluing the present exemplifies how Nietzsche depicted nihilism,[48] or what the contemporary cultural critic, Wendell Berry, has dubbed the "cult of the future."[49] Awakening, however, always occurs in the present (like everything else).

Furthermore, in this sidetrack of the path we can see the distinctive outlook of tantra, the "resultant vehicle," which takes the result as the

48. Nietzsche said, "A nihilist is a man who judges of the world as it is that it ought *not* to be, and of the world as it ought to be that it does not exist," *The Will to Power*, 318.

49. See Wendell Berry, *The Unsettling of America: Culture and Agriculture* (San Francisco: Sierra Club Books, 1977), 56–59.

path.[50] The "causal vehicle" of sūtra sees the path as a process of development, in which the path serves as the way to a goal in some distant future (always at a later time, never now). In the resultant vehicle, however, not only is the path the goal, but the goal is (always already) the reality that is to be acknowledged as the path. In other words, the path is the goal (or the goal is the path); they are not different. Another duality bites the dust. Longchenpa explains this as follows:

> It is called the 'Causal Vehicle' because of asserting temporal causality—due to accepting that the basic element, the buddha-nature, is merely a seed that is further developed through the conditions of the two accumulations, by which one attains buddhahood; [in contrast,] that essential nature of Mantra exists in all sentient beings—inherently and spontaneously present—complete with vast qualities.[51]

The fourth sidetrack is called "stamping with the seal of emptiness." This sidetrack conveys another misconception of emptiness, another way of relating to emptiness as an object. Here, the sidetrack is taking emptiness to be a quality that entities *have*, as their mark or characteristic. Yet emptiness is not (only) a quality of things, nor is it only something that can be held in mind to demarcate objects with its imprint or seal. Again, we can see a parallel misconception of emptiness from the Madhyamaka tradition, as exemplified in Maja's eleventh-century critique of those who "regard emptiness as a mark" (*stong pa mtshan mar lta ba*)[52] and in Candrakīrti's statement that emptiness is not something that destroys real entities.[53] Since emptiness is the indeterminate nature of all things, it is not to be understood *instrumentally* as a tool like a hammer that demolishes entities. Rather, it is to be understood *integrally* as the (absent) nature of things, or rather, *performatively* as an ongoing process of undermining

50. Longchenpa characterizes the Resultant Vehicle as taking the effect as the path in his *Precious Treasury of Philosophical Systems*, 1032. See also Tsongkhapa, *The Great Exposition of the Stages of Mantra*, 15–16.

51. Longchenpa, *White Lotus: Autocommentary on the "Precious Wish-Fulfilling Treasury,"* in Seven Treasuries, vol. 7, ed. Tarthang Tulku (Sichuan, China, 1996), 1169–1170.

52. See Maja Jangchup Tsöndrü, *Appearance of Reality* (*de kho na nyid snang ba*). Tibetan edition in Thomas Doctor, *Reason and Experience in Tibetan Buddhism*, 130; English translation in 117; see also 56–57.

53. Candrakīrti, *Introduction to the Middle Way*, VI.34.

reification (a process that never ends). In these four sidetracks, we can see how Mahāmudrā is an heir to both Madhyamaka and Mind-Only traditions.

Rikzin Chödrak laid out other sidetracks in his description of the practice of Mahāmudrā:

> To denigrate the causality of karma, resolving that the meaning of emptiness is such that there are no results from good or evil deeds, is to deviate into nihilistic prattle. Furthermore, holding what is to be abandoned, identifying it, and meditating on emptiness as a remedy to it is the root of the sidetracks and deviations. Moreover, it is said that to view all phenomena as relatively existent and ultimately nonexistent, as relatively nonexistent and ultimately existent, as both relatively and ultimately existent, or as nonexistent, is to deviate into holding extremes.[54]

Here we see how these Mahāmudrā instructions undermine theoretical approaches to emptiness understood in two separate truths. In contrast to a descriptive system of two truths (as we saw in the "enframed" interpretation of emptiness in chapter 1), emptiness here is performative, embracing the indeterminacy of all things. This move reflects the radical "unenframed" interpretation of the negation of the four lemmas, the move to step outside the dichotomization (or *tetrato*mization!) of thought rather than enframe emptiness within another theoretical structure (e.g., "emptiness conventionally exists") with tools like parameters (e.g., "it is *ultimately* nonexistent but *conventionally* existent"). While such tools may be helpful to reach a nonconceptual understanding of emptiness or represent it (to others), such conceptual frameworks are seen as obstacles for embodying emptiness in the main part of Mahāmudrā practice.

Other deviations of Mahāmudrā meditation involve confusing a fleeting taste of experience (*nyams*) with the presence of authentic realization (*rtogs*)—such as deviating into feelings of bliss, moments of clarity, or states of nonconceptuality. These three deviations are respectively associated with the desire, form, and formless realms of Buddhist cosmology. They also represent transient psychological states, as symptoms of contemplative practice that do not in themselves carry liberative force. While

54. Rikzin Chödrak, *Words of Dharmakīrti*, 155–156.

they may occur during Mahāmudrā practice, these states are not authentic realization and are not to be confused as such. We can also find these three deviations in Great Perfection instruction manuals, in addition to four sidetracks.[55]

The Great Perfection

As is the case with Mahāmudrā, the confluence of Mind-Only and Madhyamaka can be seen in the literature and practice of the Great Perfection, too. Like Mahāmudrā, the Great Perfection presumes the possibility of a radical shift in experiential orientation from one that is conceptually enframed to one that is not. That is, it is founded upon the potency of reorientation, from a static subjectivity identified with intentional consciousness to the unmediated horizon from within which the play of subject-object-action unfolds. This shift within the matrix of interrelation is not to escape or step out of the relation of experience (as in caricatures of Advaita Vedānta or Husserl's transcendental ego), but is something more akin to not stagnantly reifying anything like a subjective pole or any other object. It is to re-cognize the node of awareness in the phenomenal field and inhabit this space that is intertwined with the world. Recognition is not a directed awareness or a focus on awareness, but is prompted by something like releasement (*Gelassenheit*), by letting go of the dualistic structure of representation by releasing into "the basic field of reality" (*chos kyi dbyings, dharmadhātu*). The Great Perfection exemplifies a move to avoid philosophical stagnation in abstract thought that remains within the presumptions of either subjective idealism (the bane of Mind-Only) or objective realism (the bane of Madhyamaka).

The perspectival shift embraced in the Great Perfection is non-ideational and non-representational. It is not object-oriented, as ontological projects presume or those who insist upon playing by the rules of ontologized language-games demand, but rather is better expressed as an *attunement* to the nature of pure phenomenality.[56] As a knowledge *by*

---

55. See, for instance, instructions of Jikmé Lingpa (1729–1798), translated in van Shaik, *Approaching the Great Perfection* (Boston: Wisdom Publications, 2004), 229–230.

56. David Higgins describes this kind of attunement as "intransitive, non-ideational meditation" as opposed to concept-directed meditations: "Non-ideational meditations are . . . intransitive and likewise devoted to leaving the mind denuded of its familiar objects, activities and points of reference." Higgins, "A Reply to Questions Concerning Mind and Primordial Knowing," *Journal of the International Association of Buddhist Studies* 34 (2011): 53. He

acquaintance (or identity) rather than a knowledge *about*, attunement is not a propositional attitude, nor is thematized in any way as an object-oriented or directed consciousness. Rather, it is a way of acknowledging the world in a participatory way, attending to the sheer open horizon of experience. This gnosis is "knowledge" without determinacy in contrast to a cognitive judgment, like "A is B," which is necessarily conceptual and premised on duality. As a nondual cognition, this awareness cannot be represented as an object or even a subject, and is often evoked by poetic metaphor rather than propositional prose.

As with Mahāmudrā, awareness (or gnosis) in the Great Perfection does not have an intentional structure in an ordinary sense; it is not *objective* because it is not *about* anything. There is also no *for me* structure in a first-person perspective because the experience is not *subjective* either. Rather, as simply the open horizon within which the duality of subjects and objects arises, it is pre-subjective (or *super*jective rather than *sub*jective). That is, it is more primordial than first-personal; it is *zero-personal* (empty) or *fourth-personal* (the holistic ground of unity). The phenomenal play or display unfolds within this pre-personal or *suprapersonal* horizon of being, which is not to be confused with a distorted baseline of the basic consciousness (*ālayavijñāna*), which is the basis of a Mind-Only phenomenology, for it is explicitly distinguished from this as the *dharmakāya*—"the body of reality," which is "space-like awareness untouched by samsara."[57]

The basic consciousness, like self-awareness (conventional or ultimate), takes on different meanings here. First, Longchenpa distinguishes the basic consciousness from the Truth Body, saying that "the basic consciousness (*kun gzhi*) is the root of samsara, for it is like the reservoir (*rten*

---

furthermore describes the structural distinction between ideational and non-ideational cognition in the (attunement) practice of the Great Perfection: "These teachings often take the form of personal instructions advising the practitioner to discern within the flux of adventitious thoughts and sensations that characterize dualistic mind (*sems*) an invariant prerepresentational structure of awareness known as primordial knowing (*ye shes*), open awareness (*rig pa*) or the nature of Mind (*sems nyid*), from which the turmoil arises. The idea is to directly recognize (*ngo sprod*) and become increasingly familiar with this abiding condition without confusing it with any of its derivative and distortive aspects." Higgins, "An Introduction to the Tibetan Dzogchen (Great Perfection) Philosophy of Mind," *Religion Compass* 6, no. 10 (2012): 442.

57. Longchenpa, *Precious Treasury of Words and Meanings*, in *Seven Treasuries* (*mdzod bdun*), ed. Tarthang Tulku (Sichuan, China, 1996), 929–938. For more on the distinction between the basic consciousness (*kun gzhi, ālaya*) and the Truth Body (*chos sku, dharmakāya*), see, for instance, Longchenpa, *Treasure Trove of Scriptural Transmission*, 500–506, and *Precious Treasury of the Supreme Vehicle*, vol. 1, ed. Tarthang Tulku. (Sichuan, China, 1996), 1020–1027.

rdzing) of all predispositions; the Truth Body (*chos sku, dharmakāya*) is the root of nirvana because it is free from all predispositions."[58] Moreover, in contrast to the Truth Body, "which is empty essence, abiding as the Truth Body; natural clarity, abiding as the Enjoyment Body; and unobstructed expressions of compassion, abiding as the Emanation Body," Longchenpa explains the basic consciousness as follows:

> The essence of the basic consciousness is neutral nonconceptuality, dull like a consciousness of the Formless Realm; its nature is the basis for the arising of the sense consciousnesses, which are the aspects of the basic consciousness; its expression, instead of compassion, is fixation upon the objects of the six consciousnesses.[59]

Longchenpa characterizes the basic consciousness as an uninterrupted, momentary continuum in the context of explaining the philosophy of Mind-Only. He says it takes as an observed object an unclear, vast world of environment and inhabitants and is divided into two: (1) the aspect of maturation, and (2) the aspect of potentiality.[60] A few pages later, Longchenpa systematically refutes the reality of the basic consciousness as he characterized it: he critiques the notion of the basic consciousness as a momentary continuum with a critique of causality, and he critiques its dual properties of predisposition and maturation with a part/whole analysis.[61] Thus, he parts ways with the appeal to the basic consciousness as a real basis by drawing upon familiar Madhyamaka arguments.

Longchenpa distinguishes his tradition of the Great Perfection from Mind-Only, stating that some people think that the self-illuminating, self-awareness without duality in the Great Perfection is the same as that in the

---

58. Longchenpa, *Treasury of Words and Meanings*, in *Seven Treasuries* (*mdzod bdun*), ed. Tarthang Tulku (Sichuan, China, 1996), 926–927.

59. Longchenpa, *Treasure Trove of Scriptural Transmission*, 501–502. Mipam also distinguishes awareness (*rig pa*) and the basic consciousness by stating that awareness is lacking the conditioned mental states of identification, feeling, etc. See Mipam, *Precious Vajra Garland*, in *Mipam's Collected Works*, vol. 24, 724.

60. See Longchenpa, *White Lotus: Autocommentary on the "Precious Wish-Fulfilling Treasury,"* in *Seven Treasuries* (*mdzod bdun*), vol. 7, ed. Tarthang Tulku (Sichuan, China, 1996), 1065–1066. Mipam also defines the basic consciousness in the same way in *Words that Delight Guru Mañjughoṣa*, 265.

61. See Longchenpa, *White Lotus*, 1090–1092.

Mind-Only, and thinking thus, those with little intelligence boast that they have realized this.[62] However, he affirms that

> The approach (*'jal tshul*) of the natural Great Perfection is mostly similar to Prāsaṅgika-Madhyamaka in understanding what is free from extremes, etc. Mādhyamikas consider space-like emptiness as the basis, whereas the space-like approach here takes merely the undetermined, unobstructed, primordially pure naked awareness as basis, and whatever arises within that state of awareness is free from extremes, understood like space.[63]

We can see that Madhyamaka and emptiness play a role in the Great Perfection, as does gnosis. Distinguishing concepts like the basic consciousness from the Truth Body is a crucial way a distinction is made between the disembodied realism that we see in caricatures of Mind-Only (as subjective idealism) and the embodied realism of the Great Perfection. Yet the realism of the Great Perfection is tempered by embodied *anti*realism, too, which—*contra* Madhyamaka ontology—breathes life into emptiness rather than treating emptiness as an object. That is, emptiness, while unconditioned, is not separate from awareness—the body-subject, as the organ of the universe that fully pervades the nature of all things. As a Great Perfection text states: "The essence of awareness is emptiness; awareness and emptiness are indivisible."[64] In what may be called a "radical phenomenology," the practice of the Great Perfection sustains depth (or interiority) and appearance (or surface), holding this dynamic tension in place, as the line between two truths, appearance/emptiness or dual/nondual is erased (and so is the difference between meditation and postmeditation, buddhas and sentient beings). We see a similar collapse of duality in the case of "non-meditation" at the summit of Mahāmudrā's four yogas (see Appendix D).

In contrast to Mahāmudrā's highlighting the inseparability of mind and mind-nature, the Great Perfection marks a clear distinction between conceptual mind and nonconceptual gnosis. Longchenpa often describes

---

62. Longchenpa, *Treasure Trove of Scriptural Transmission*, 322.

63. Longchenpa, *Treasure Trove of Scriptural Transmission*, 322–323.

64. *Subsequent Tantra of the Quintessential Instructions of the Great Perfection* (*man ngag rdzogs pa chen po'i rgyud phyi ma*), 100. See critical edition in van Schaik, *Approaching the Great Perfection* (Boston: Wisdom Publications, 2004), 252.

the mind (*sems*) in distinction to gnosis in a way that parallels the distinction he makes between the Truth Body and the basic consciousness.[65] He characterizes the mind as "dualistic cognition, the thoroughgoing conceptuality within the three realms,"[66] and, "the essence of mind is perception from the thoroughly conceptual apprehension of subject and object together with self-apprehension."[67] Longchenpa describes the mind as conditioned and prompted by habitual reactions of confusion in contrast to gnosis. He describes gnosis as "luminous and clear awareness, the buddha-nature."[68] Gnosis is pre-reflective and nonconceptual; the primacy of gnosis is shown in its etymology, which Longchenpa conveys as follows: "It is gnosis (*ye shes*) because it is the primordially (*ye*) abiding sacred awareness (*shes*)."[69] In another text, he gives this etymology: "It is gnosis because it is awareness that remains primordially as the Truth Body."[70] Thus, he delineates mind and gnosis into two domains (*yul*):

> The domain of mind (*sems kyi yul*) is the deluded appearances of samsara—forms, sounds, scents, tastes, textures, and mental objects—appearing due to predispositions, like a hallucination of falling hairs . . . the domain of gnosis (*ye shes kyi yul*) is the pure basic nature, like space, and the vast appearances of luminous clarity—embodiments of buddhahood and field of gnosis (*ye shes kyi zhing*).[71]

---

65. For Longchenpa's distinctions between mind and awareness/gnosis, see Longchenpa, *Most Profound Essence*, vol. 1, 449; *Most Profound Essence* vol. 2, 280; 292; *Treasure Trove of Scriptural Transmission*, 231–234; 506–509; *Precious Treasury of Philosophical Systems*, 1201; *Precious Treasury of the Supreme Vehicle*, vol. 1, 1037–1050; *Treasury of Words and Meanings*, 940–947.

66. Longchenpa, *Treasury of Words and Meanings*, 953. Longchenpa also states that "the mind observes an apprehended object" since (1) the object-mind (*yul gyi sems*) apprehends objective appearances through signs, words, and universals, and (2) the subject-mind (*lit.* "object-possessing-mind," *yul can gyi sems*) apprehends by discriminating and examining those objects. See Longchenpa, *Precious Treasury of the Supreme Vehicle*, vol. 1, 1040.

67. Longchenpa, *Treasury of Words and Meanings*, 950.

68. Longchenpa, *Treasury of Words and Meanings*, 956: *ye shes kyi ngo bo 'od gsal ba'i rig pa bde bar gshegs pa'i snying po ste.*

69. Longchenpa, *Treasury of Words and Meanings*, 956: *nges tshig ni ye nas gnas pa'i shes pa dam pa yin pas ye shes te.*

70. Longchenpa, *Treasure Trove of Scriptural Transmission*, 506: *nges tshig ye nas de ltar chos sku la gnas pa'i shes pa yin pas ye shes.*

71. Longchenpa, *Treasury of Words and Meanings*, 940.

He summarizes the difference by stating that "the abode of mind (*sems kyi gnas*) is the basic consciousness; the abode of gnosis (*ye shes kyi gnas*) is the Truth Body."[72]

Despite his critiques of the basic consciousness, a universal ground (*kun gzhi*) is also sometimes cast in a positive light in the context of the Great Perfection. At least two distinct meanings of the universal ground can be found in Longchenpa's *Wish-Fulfilling Treasury*,[73] where he divides the universal ground into (1) "the universal ground of various predispositions" (*bag chags sna tshogs pa'i kun gzhi*), which is the basis of all cyclic existence, and (2) "the ultimate universal ground" (*don gyi kun gzhi*), which is the basic element (*khams*) that is naturally pure nirvana together with unconditioned qualities.[74] In the context of the Great Perfection, the universal ground or foundational cognition (as gnosis) becomes a positive ground of being rather than simply the structure by which distortion is perpetuated.

In a positive portrayal, Longchenpa describes the ultimate universal ground as the support for both samsara and nirvana, and as a synonym for buddha-nature.[75] He says that the ultimate universal ground is unconditioned and resides as great primordial purity. Longchenpa also calls the ground of both samsara and nirvana "the general ground" (*spyi gzhi*).[76] Since this ground is a basis for both samsara and nirvana, he refers to an "ultimate universal ground of union," designated in this way due to

---

72. Longchenpa, *Treasury of Words and Meanings*, 948: *sems kyi gnas kun gzhi ye shes kyi gnas chos sku*.

73. Longchenpa also renders a fourfold depiction of the universal ground: two that concern the ultimate: "the universal ground of the primordial ultimate" (*ye don gyi kun gzhi*) and "the ultimate universal ground of union" (*sbyor ba don gyi kun gzhi*); and two that concern propensities: "the universal ground of various propensities" (*bags chags sna tshogs pa'i kun gzhi*), and "the universal ground of propensities for embodiment" (*bag chags lus kyi kun gzhi*). He states that the four types of universal ground are actually the same and only conceptually distinct; thus, in reality there is only one universal ground. Longchenpa, *Treasury of the Supreme Vehicle*, vol. 1, 1028–1029: (*don shes pa gcig gi cha la ldog pa bzhir dbyer yod pa la btags pa yin no*); *Treasury of Words and Meanings*, 933.

74. See Longchenpa, *White Lotus*, 1066–1067. Sam van Schaik discusses the basic consciousness, albeit exclusively in its negative depictions as distinct from the Truth Body, in *Approaching the Great Perfection*, 56–60.

75. Longchenpa, *Precious Wish-Fulfilling Treasury*, 151–152.

76. Khenpo Pema Sherap (*pad ma shes rab*, b. 1936) described the "general ground" as the aspect of the basic nature (*chos nyid kyi cha*). He also explained that the general ground and the ground of the primordial ultimate (*ye don gyi gzhi*) are not the basic consciousness (*kun gzhi*) that is to be distinguished from the Truth Body (*chos sku*). Personal communication, December 2007.

the aspect of it being that which unites with nirvana when aware, and that which unites with samsara when unaware.[77] In this way, the universal ground is sometimes cast in a positive light, as the reality of buddha-nature, or as the Great Perfection to be realized; and sometimes negatively, as the basic consciousness in Mind-Only; and alternatively, it is represented as neutral, as a ground for both.[78]

The Ground as Fruition

Depictions of a positive ground are not developed in early Yogācāra texts. In fact, the primary function of the basic consciousness in most Yogācāra texts is the perpetuation of confused experience in samsara. The positive cast to the basic consciousness we find in Tibet, however, gives a foundation for the possibility of a positive, creative existence, not just an existence that must be denied to be true.[79]

In the shift from Yogācāra to tantra, we can see how the basic consciousness and self-awareness function as the grounds for liberation rather than simply as grounds for suffering.[80] This shift resonates with a parallel shift elsewhere in Mahāyāna thought. From its early formulations of nirvana, Mahāyāna distinguished itself from the sterile version of "nirvana without remainder" (*nirupadhiśeṣanirvāṇa*) of the "Hīnayāna" by evoking a more vibrant mode of enlightened, *engaged* existence in "unlocated nirvana" (*apratiṣṭhitanirvāṇa*), a dynamic mode of being that neither dwells in samsara (due to wisdom) nor nirvana (due to compassion). Such a notion is also latent in the Yogācāra notion of the transformation of the ground (*āśrayaparivṛtti*), which led Paramārtha to posit a ninth-consciousness, the stainless consciousness (*nirmalavijñāna*), upon the eight consciousnesses to account for the transformed gnosis. This positive ground is also

---

77. Longchenpa, *Precious Treasury of the Supreme Vehicle*, vol. 1, 1028.

78. For further discussion of the difference between discourses of "the ground" in Yogācāra and the Great Perfection, see David Higgins, *The Philosophical Foundations of Classical Rdzogs Chen in Tibet* (Wien: Arbeitskreis für Tibetische und Buddhistische Studien, 2013), 140–182.

79. A similar trajectory can be seen in developments of Buddhism in China. See for instance Ph.D. dissertation by Robert Gimello, "Chi-yen (602–668) and the Foundations of Hua-Yen Buddhism," (Columbia University, 1976), 426.

80. See, for instance, the *Victorious Arising of the Peak* (*rtse mo byung rgyal*), one of the eighteen Mind-Series (*sems sde*) texts of the Great Perfection: "The basic consciousness is the basic field of reality from the beginning" (*kun gzhi rnam par shes pa ye nas chos kyi dbyings*), in *Collected Nyingma Tantras* (*mtshams brag* ed.), vol. 1, 612.

reflected in the shift from the impure dependent nature to the *pure dependent nature* (*dag pa'i gzhan dbang*) among the three natures of Yogācāra.

A positive ground is a prominent theme in Buddhist tantras like the *Wheel of Time* (*Kālacakra*) *Tantra*, where emptiness is interpreted differently than a simple lack of intrinsic nature (as we see in portrayals of Madhyamaka *qua* abstract philosophy). The *Wheel of Time Tantra* speaks of "empty forms" or "reflections of emptiness" (*śūnyatā-bimba*) in terms of a sentient emptiness (*ajaḍā-śūnyatā*) with a cognitive dimension as opposed to an inert void.[81] This sentient quality of emptiness, inseparable from the living dynamics of subjectivity—appearing and aware—is a positive ground of emptiness that has played a dominant role in Mind-Only and Yogācāra-inflected traditions in Tibet, in what comes to be called "other-emptiness" (*gzhan stong*) Madhyamaka,[82] an interpretative strand of Madhyamaka that takes a Mind-Only trajectory to articulate "what remains in emptiness."[83]

Along with the dynamic emptiness of "other"—the diaphanous third category of the *Wheel of Time* beyond the dichotomous "inner" and "outer"—the tantra also affirms that the engine of existence is not karma, but the gnosis of the Ādibuddha, the original Buddha. The Ādibuddha is the supreme deity in the *Wheel of Time Tantra*, and is understood as the nature of mind.[84] As the primordial basis of awakening, it has a prominent place in the old schools of Tibetan tantric traditions as well. We see this in

81. See *Wheel of Time Tantra*, ch. II, v. 161. Trans. in Vesna Wallace, *The Kālacakratantra: The Chapter on the Individual Together with the Vimalaprabhā* (New York: Columbia University Press, 2004), 219. Kalki Puṇḍarīka's commentary, the *Vimalaprabhā*, glosses the sentient emptiness as that which has all supreme aspects, like a divination mirror, a metaphor often associated with Tibetan depictions of "other-emptiness" (*gzhan stong*).

82. The issue at stake in the competing interpretations of emptiness resonates with Paul Ricoeur's statement that: "The question remains open for every man whether the destruction of idols is without remainder." Paul Ricoeur, *Freud and Philosophy: An Essay on Interpretation*, trans. by Denis Savage (New Haven: Yale University Press, 1970), 235.

83. Gadjin Nagao, "What Remains in Śūnyatā: A Yogācāra Interpretation of Emptiness," in *Mādhyamika and Yogācāra* (Albany: SUNY Press, 1991), 51–60.

84. See *Wheel of Time Tantra*, ch. II, v. 92 with *Vimalaprabhā* commentary. English trans. in Wallace, *The Kālacakratantra: The Chapter on the Individual Together with the Vimalaprabhā*, 140–141. The notion of the Ādibuddha has a precedent in the doctrine of buddha-nature, as an intrinsically pure reality that is to be discovered (recognized) rather than developed through transformation on a path. *Wheel of Time Tantra*, ch. V, v. 66: "Sentient beings are buddhas. There are no other great buddhas here in this world." *sattvā buddhā na buddhas tv apara iha mahān vidyate lokadhātau*. Sanskrit cited from Vesna Wallace, *Inner Kālacakra* (Oxford: Oxford University Press, 2001), 239n12. Similar statements are found in other *anuttarayogatantras*, such as the *Hevajra Tantra*: "Sentient beings are the buddha as such, yet obscured by adventitious defilements." Part II, IV.69; Tibetan ed. in David Snellgrove, *The Hevajratantra: A Critical Study* (Oxford: Oxford University Press, 1959), vol. 2, 71. See

the role of the a-temporal ground (*gzhi*),[85] which forms the basis of the narrative of the primordial Buddha Samantabhadra's liberation through *recognition* (*ngo shes*) in the Nyingma exegetical traditions of the *Secret Essence* (*Guhyagarbha*) *Tantra*, a tantra that is central to the Nyingma tradition in Tibet.[86]

The twelfth-century Nyingma scholar, Dampa Deshek, stated in his *Overall Structure of the Vehicles* that "everything is the magical display of awareness (*rig pa*); the unceasing play of Samantabhadra."[87] In the works of another Nyingma scholar, Rongzom (fl. 11th c.), we see a similar gesture in his *Entering the Way of the Mahāyāna*, when he asserts "seeing all distorted appearances as the play of Samantabhadra" and "seeing everything as the self-appearance of self-arising gnosis."[88] In Rongzom's influential work, *Establishing Appearances as Divine*, he further demonstrates how a shift is made in tantra in terms of relating to the nature of appearance not simply as illusions, but as divine. Divine pride (*lha'i nga rgyal*), identifying with the deity, is the distinctive subjectivity taken up in tantra. Along with the objective aspect of appearance shifting from illusion to divine manifestation, we see a parallel shift in the nature of subjectivity. That is, in contrast to subjectivity based in distortion (as in the case with the basic consciousness of early Yogācāra), the nature of subjectivity in Buddhist tantra is gnosis.[89]

---

also *Reverberation of Sound* (*sgra thal 'gyur*), in *The Seventeen Tantras of the Nyingma* (*snying ma'i rgyud bcu bdun*), vol. 1 (New Delhi, India: Sangye Dorje, 1973–1977), 137–138, the root text of the seventeen Dzokchen tantras of the Quintessential Instructions Series (*man ngag sde*): "Sentient beings are buddhas."

85. See, for instance, *Reverberation of Sound*, 107–108; see also Longchenpa, *Treasury of Words and Meanings*, ch. I.

86. The relationship between the Great Perfection and tantra is complex. The *Guhyagarbha Tantra* is interpreted both as a Mahāyoga tantra and as teaching the Great Perfection. Mipam referred to Rongzom and Longchenpa's interpretation of the text in accord with the Great Perfection as the "Rong-Long" tradition in contrast to the Zur tradition, which interprets it in light of Mahāyoga. Mipam, *Overview: Essential Nature of Luminous Clarity*, 388; English trans. in Dharmachakra Translation Committee, *Luminous Essence*, 5.

87. Dampa Deshek, *Overall Structure of the Vehicles (theg pa spyi bcings)*, 23: *thams cad rig pa'i chos 'phrul las/ kun bzang rol pa 'gags pa med.*

88. Rongzom, *Entering the Way of the Mahāyāna* (*theg chen tshul 'jug*), in *Rongzom's Collected Works*, vol. 1 (Sichuan, China: Nationalities Press, 1999), 492–493.

89. In his commentary on the *Secret Essence Tantra*, Mipam described arguments for establishing appearances as divine to be for those who accept an external world, and arguments that establish the subject as gnosis for those who do not accept the existence of commonly appearing external objects. Mipam, *Overview: Essential Nature of Luminous Clarity*,

In his commentary on the *Secret Essence Tantra*, Rongzom presents the unique setting of the tantra in terms of fivefold perfections: (1) teacher, (2) place, (3) retinue, (4) time, and (5) tantra (teaching). According to his commentary, the perfect teacher is not a "trained individual" but is rather the primordial Buddha Samantabhadra, the primordial nature of reality. The perfect place is not a specific location, like Deer Park or Vulture Peak, but lacks spatial dimensions with center and periphery. The perfect retinue is not a gathering of exclusively bodhisattvas, but the retinue is the buddha's own expression. The perfect time is also not a certain time, but is the "fourth time," a timeless time—not past, present, or future. And the perfect tantra, or teaching, proclaims that all phenomena are the buddha from the beginning.[90] It is significant that each of the Great Perfection texts in the set of seventeen Seminal Heart (*snying thig*) tantras begins with this kind of uncommon setting (*mthun mong ma yin pa'i gleng gzhi*), along with a common one (*mthun mong gi gleng gzhi*). The uncommon one sets a scene of a reflexive, gnostic cosmogony.

We see this gnostic cosmogony across the Great Perfection literature. For instance, *The Self-Arising of Awareness*, one of the seventeen Seminal Heart tantras of the Great Perfection, states: "Everything arises from self-awareness, the unchanging spirit of awakening (*bodhicitta*)."[91] This is also proclaimed throughout the *All-Creating King*, a Great Perfection text that is the main tantra of the "eighteen Mind Series (*sems sde*) texts," and the first text in the *Collected Tantras of the Nyingma*: "Listen great Vajrasattva,

---

443; 450; English trans. in Dharmachakra Translation Committee, *Luminous Essence*, 45–46; 50. See also, Duckworth, "From Yogācāra to Philosophical Tantra in Kashmir and Tibet," *Sophia* (2017).

90. See Rongzom, *Commentary on "Secret Essence Tantra"* (*rgyud rgyal gsang ba'i snying po dkon cog 'grel*), in *Rongzom's Collected Works*, vol. 1 (Sichuan: Nationalities Press, 1999), 60–62. The *Hevajra Tantra* also expresses this: "I am the speaker; I am the teaching; I am the listener with good retinue. I am what is to be accomplished; I am the teacher of the world. I am the world and beyond the world." *Hevajra Tantra* 2.ii.39. Translation from the Tibetan (edition in Snellgrove, *The Hevajratantra*, 49–50). For variant Sanskrit reading, see Ronald Davidson, "Reflections on the Maheśvara Subjugation Myth: Indic Materials, Sa-skya-pa Apologetics, and the Birth of Heruka," *Journal of the International Association of Buddhist Studies* 14, no. 2 (1991), 217.

91. *Self-Arising Awareness* (*rig pa rang shar*), 471: *rang gi rig pa 'gyur med byang chub sems las thams cad byung*, in *The Seventeen Tantras of the Nyingma* (*snying ma'i rgyud bcu bdun*), vol. 1 (New Delhi, India: Sangye Dorje, 1973–1977).

I am the primordial, all-creating king. I created the teacher, the teaching, the retinue, and the time."[92] The role of gnosis as agent is central in the *All-Creating King*: "Since objects are gnosis from the beginning, I do not teach gnosis and objects as distinct. Thus, objects too are said to be self-existing gnosis; there is nothing besides the single self-existing gnosis."[93] And, "From the nature of me, the all-creating king, everything that appears and exists, the environment and its inhabitants, all were created by me, and since they arise from me, there is not a single phenomena that is not contained within me."[94] This sentiment is also found in Bön texts, like *The Source of Knowledge That is Awareness,* which cites a Bön title that says, "Nothing, not even one thing, does not arise from me. Nothing, not even one thing, dwells not in me. Everything emanates from me; thus am I only one."[95]

In this sampling of early Tibetan texts we can clearly see a transformation of Mind-Only and Madhyamaka in what may be called a "tantric turn." In this turn we see a shift from a cognitive process that is driven by fundamental distortion, or error theory, to an absolute idealism that is driven by the creative expression (*rtsal*) of a divine spirit or gnosis. With the unfolding of absolute gnosis, the story of samsara is rewritten by replacing the antagonist—karmic creation—with gnostic creativity in the lead role.

Conclusion

In Tibetan tantric traditions including Mahāmudrā and the Great Perfection, the structure of the world unfolds in a narrative of gnosis. Indeed, a new articulation of awareness, as the positive ground and flesh of the world, plays a major role in tantric literature and practice. The fact that this awareness is important to tantric traditions in Tibet reflects the

---

92. *All-Creating King* (*kun byed rgyal po'i rgyud*), in *Collected Tantras of the Nyingma* (*rnying ma'i rgyud 'bum*) (Thimphu, Bhutan: National Library, Royal Bhutan, 1982), ch. 16, pp. 76–77.

93. Ibid., ch. 50, p. 170.

94. Ibid., ch. 1, p. 56.

95. The *Secret Scripture* (*mdo lung gsang ba*) is cited in Lishu Takring, *The Source of Knowledge That Is Awareness* (*gtan tshig gal mdo rig pa'i tshad ma*), 52: *nga las ma byung gcig kyang med/ nga las mi gnas gcig kyang med/ kun kyang nga las sprul pa'i phyir/ des na nga rang nyag gcig go.* Translation adapted from Klein and Wangyal, *Unbounded Wholeness,* 229.

legacy of Mind-Only, yet the fact that the primordiality of a kind of pre-reflective self-awareness is not (only) internal, nor is it described in terms of a "self" in contrast to an "other," reflects the legacy of Madhyamaka, too. Thus, we can see how both Mind-Only and Madhyamaka are interpreted through, and framed by, tantric traditions, the main contemplative practices of Tibet.

Conclusion

WE BEGAN BY looking at two trajectories of interpretation of Mahāyāna Buddhism that stem from India: Madhyamaka and Yogācāra. These trajectories of thought were transposed in Tibet as the two "great chariot traditions" of Madhyamaka and Mind-Only. A distinct contribution of Madhyamaka is its critical ontological analysis and formulation of two truths, the ultimate and the conventional. A distinctive contribution of Mind-Only is a phenomenological analysis oriented toward subjectivity and the lived dimensions of knowledge. These competing and complementary approaches have shaped the face of Buddhist theory and practice in Tibet.

The relationship between Madhyamaka and Mind-Only is configured in different ways among Tibetan traditions, and how their relationship is configured informs the shape of the distinct contemplative practices there. I have described the interplay of these two traditions in conversation with the discourses of ontology and phenomenology with the aim to clarify some of the issues at stake in Tibetan thought and connect them to contemporary issues, in order to enrich a more global philosophical conversation. Like Mind-Only and Madhyamaka, ontology and phenomenology represent divergent modes of thought and practice that can be seen to offer unique lenses on the world, yet they can also be seen to overlap, or even mutually entail each other.

The story of Tibetan philosophy I seek to convey is one of interconnectivity, intertwining, and entanglement. We can see this not only in the relationships between theory and practice, ontology and phenomenology, or Madhyamaka and Mind-Only, but also in how each of the three "doors of action"—body, speech, and mind—is entangled with the others; and how neither body, speech, or mind are what they seem. The body is not inside nor is it outside. Speech, or language, is not a private affair either. It is not only physical or simply mental—neither inside nor outside. Mind, too, is not inside. It is not outside either. With nothing inside or outside, the only place left is in/between (and without boundaries, no-thing is really in/between, either).

This book is my attempt to probe this in/between space in dichotomies like Mind-Only and Madhyamaka to highlight the hybrid nature of Tibetan Buddhist philosophy—an array of interpretations held together loosely by a collective challenge to rigid dichotomies like subject-object, appearance-emptiness, mind-matter, self-other, inside-outside, and so on. Tibetan Buddhist philosophy is not monolithic or static; nevertheless, it can be characterized as a set of concerns that shapes and transgresses borders and boundaries, boundaries of the unconditioned and the contingent, the one and many, the nonconceptual and the conceptual, the real and the constructed. A central theme here is the entangled nature of (false) dichotomies, and the creative freedom within and without them.

Appendices

In the Appendices are four excerpted translations that demonstrate to some extent the wide range of Buddhist philosophical writings across different Tibetan traditions. Each translation stands alone, and highlights something unique about the particular tradition that its author represents.

Appendix A is an excerpt from *Roar of the Fearless Lion* by Khenpo Lodrö Drakpa, a twentieth-century Jonang scholar. The text describes the Jonang tradition's unique interpretation of "other-emptiness" as a positive ground of being. This text also shows the hermeneutical dimension of Buddhist philosophy, a deep involvement with issues of interpretation and a commitment to the project of organizing into a singular whole a large canon of Buddhist texts that contain many different messages.

Appendix B is an excerpt from an overview of the "Wisdom Chapter" of Śāntideva's celebrated *Way of the Bodhisattva* by Künzang Sönam. Künzang Sönam formulates his discussion around Tsongkhapa's eight unique features of Prāsaṅgika-Madhyamaka. This excerpt comes to quite opposite conclusions about the nature of emptiness and Madhyamaka as the Jonang text translated in Appendix A. This excerpt illustrates the distinct object of negation in Prāsaṅgika, in contrast to Svātantrika, as it is represented in Tsongkhapa's tradition. The Svātantrika-Prāsaṅgika distinction is a widely disputed topic in Tibetan philosophical literature, and Tsongkhapa's Prāsaṅgika represents the culmination of a particular style of ontological analysis for which Tibet stands out as unique in the world of Buddhist philosophy.

Appendix C is a translation of another late nineteenth-century text, *Concise Summary of the Philosophical Systems from the "Wish-Fulfilling Treasury"* by Mipam. It is also exegetical in that it describes a hierarchy of Buddhist philosophical systems as outlined by the fourteenth-century visionary of the Nyingma tradition, Longchenpa. The excerpt from this text illustrates the complexity and diversity of Buddhist philosophical traditions, and demonstrates the way that different views are organized into a systematic structure or philosophical school (typically four) in this genre. We often see philosophical schools placed within a hierarchical structure, yet this text shows how systems of tantra are also included in this hierarchy, with distinct philosophical views placed at the top of a hierarchy that culminates with the Great Perfection. Extending the fourfold structure of philosophical schools to include tantras is a unique feature of the way philosophical systems are presented in the Nyingma tradition.

Appendix D is a chapter from a seventeenth-century Drikung Kagyü text, *Words of Dharmakīrti* by Rikzin Chödrak. This excerpt shows the distinctive contemplative practice of Mahāmudrā in this tradition. Mahāmudrā is a meditative practice that can be seen to blend elements of Madhyamaka (e.g., critical ontology) and Mind-Only (e.g., phenomenological orientation). The practice of Mahāmudrā is the culmination of the Kagyü tradition and exemplifies the way that Buddhist philosophy informs contemplative practice.

APPENDIX A

Prologue to Roar of the Fearless Lion

Introduction

Roar of the Fearless Lion, also known as *The Great Other-Emptiness,* is an exegesis on the distinctive Jonang doctrine of other-emptiness. It was composed by Khenpo Lodrö Drakpa (1920–1975), a scholar from Dzamtang (*'dzam thang*) in Eastern Tibet, where a prominent Jonang monastery has remained active to the present day. The text is organized around a presentation of the ground, path, and fruition—following a similar structure as Dölpopa's classic, *Ocean of Definitive Meaning.*

Below we will see how the Jonang tradition interprets the "three wheels" of Buddhist sūtras. Here, the emptiness understood as the mere lack of intrinsic nature in phenomena, a prominent subject matter of the middle wheel (e.g., in the Perfection of Wisdom Sūtras), is not held to be the complete teaching of the ultimate truth. Rather, it is the positive attributes of the buddha-nature, which are most clearly articulated in the last wheel of the sūtras, that they hold to be definitive in meaning. Their interpretation contrasts with the interpretation of emptiness, and the relationship between the middle and last wheels of sūtra, found in the Geluk school. This difference reveals not only a bit of the diversity of Buddhist interpretations of Madhyamaka in Tibet, but the diversity of the messages found in Buddhist sūtras as well.

The translated excerpt shows how the Jonang tradition supports their interpretation of "other-emptiness" in the interpretation of Buddhist sūtras. In contrast to the meaning of self-emptiness, other-emptiness does not refer to a phenomenon's emptiness of its own essence. Rather, it refers to ultimate reality's emptiness of all that it is not. This text supports a view of other-emptiness through an appeal to Buddhist scriptures, and by appealing to the principle that "Buddha knows best" about subjects that are inconceivable (e.g., buddha-nature, karma). Indeed, Buddhist hermeneutics is a complex topic; the different models and strategies of interpretation that are employed by different schools play a major role in shaping the way that a particular philosophical stance is taken up.

The claims made in this text to the existence of buddha-nature at the ground of reality are based on descriptions of experience and in authoritative statements across the Buddhist canon. Yet unless the experiences are one's own, they remain theoretical assertions, metaphysical or even theological claims (assertions of faith). The *modus operandi* of this view of other-emptiness can be formulated as "faith seeking understanding," to borrow Anselm's apt phrase, which may help bring to light the soteriological dimensions at play in this Buddhist philosophy, and Buddhist philosophy in general, in which faith and reason play complementary roles. Further, along with the exegetical project to put forward a unified message in Buddhist texts, the soteriological orientation of Buddhist traditions are important to keep in mind as a background for understanding these texts.

Prologue to Roar of the Fearless Lion

Prologue to Roar of the Fearless Lion

By Khenpo Lodrö Drakpa

All that was spoken by our teacher, the eighty-four thousand sections of doctrine, are included within two: the Causal Perfection Vehicle and the Resultant Vehicle. The profound point of these, the paramount, definitively secret essence, falls upon only one viewpoint (*dgongs pa*). How this is so is in dependence upon the individual constituents and faculties of each disciple: there arose distinct ways in which the status of the three vehicles is realized by means of various practices for different contexts. Also, many various philosophies progressively split. The presentation of the four philosophies in our system flourished in the Noble Land [of India]. From there, in Tibet as well, due to the various essential instructions as to the way of realizing the mode of reality of the Mahāyāna's Madhyamaka philosophy, there came to be distinctive views and philosophies of Madhyamaka, Mahāmudrā, and the Great Perfection. From among these, the great lord Jonangpa [Dölpopa] thoroughly opened the way for the chariot tradition in the exceptional way that is definitive in meaning—the Great Madhyamaka. The essential points of the profound meaning of other-emptiness Madhyamaka in Sūtra and Mantra will be progressively disclosed based on this tradition.

This has two parts: (1) the subject of the extensive discussion here, an explanation of the progression of profound points of the ground, path, and fruition of the Sūtra Perfection Vehicle, and (2) an appended brief disclosure of the profound points of the ground, path, and fruition of the Vajrayāna of Mantra [the latter topic is not included in this translation].

1. The Subject of the Extensive Discussion Here, an Explanation of the Progression of Profound Points of the Ground, Path, and Fruition of the Sūtra Perfection Vehicle

This section has three parts: (1) the way of the teaching of the profound mode of reality of the Perfection Vehicle that is definitive in meaning, (2) the subject of the teaching, which is the actual profound mode of reality of the ground, path, and fruition, and (3) the way that the explanation is beneficial [the latter two topics are not included in this translation].

1. The Way of the Teaching of the Profound Mode of Reality of the Perfection Vehicle that is Definitive in Meaning

This section has two parts: (1) the progression of the wheels of doctrine that are the means of teaching the mode of reality that is definitive in meaning, and (2) the way that these commentaries on the Buddha's viewpoint are supreme.

I. The Progression of the Wheels of Doctrine that are the Means of Teaching the Mode of Reality that is Definitive in Meaning

This has three parts: (1) the wheels of doctrine indicated in the *Sūtra Explaining the Intent* (*Saṃdhinirmocanasūtra*), (2) the wheels of doctrine indicated in the *Inquiry of King Dhāraṇīśvara Sūtra* (*Dhāraṇīśvararājaparipṛcchāsūtra*), and (3) in accord with that, the way they are indicated in the *Nirvāṇa Sūtra* and so forth.

1. *The Wheels of Doctrine Indicated in the* Sūtra Explaining the Intent

This section has two parts: (1) presenting scripture and (2) establishing the reason for that being the way it is.

1. PRESENTING SCRIPTURE

In general, with respect to the supreme teacher's first Word ("the wheel of doctrine of the four truths"), stemming from the topic of the four truths, for those disciples of dull faculties who had not trained in the Mahāyāna and were to engage in the vehicle of the Disciples, he mainly taught relative phenomena in the manner of their existence as real entities. Concerning the Middle Word ("the wheel of doctrine of the absence of attributes"), for disciples of not very mature faculties, who although had not trained in many stages of the vehicle of the Mahāyāna, were in general to engage in the Mahāyāna, he mainly taught all phenomena, from form to omniscience, in the manner of their lacking true nature. In the last Word ("the wheel of doctrine of the thorough differentiation of the ultimate"), for disciples of sharp and extremely mature faculties, who had trained their mental continua through all the vehicles, he mainly taught, through elegantly differentiating: (1) the ultimate truth itself as truly existing, meaning that it is permanent, steadfast, and eternal in the perspective of the gnosis of sublime beings because it is the primordially unchanging essence of the indivisible basic field and awareness (*dbyings rig dbyer med*) and (2) relative phenomena comprising the perceiving subjects and perceived objects as not truly existing, meaning that they are primordially non-arising like reflections in a mirror—merely expressions (*rnam 'gyur*) of the ultimate.

Therefore, he progressively taught the disciples of the three wheels according to their respective mental abilities—being of dull, mediocre, or sharp faculties—in order that they progressively reach the consummate mode of reality of phenomena. In the first wheel, he taught relative phenomena in the manner of their existing as real entities. That is to say, he taught that the incontrovertible functionings of conventional phenomena are truths only relatively, in accordance with their appearance; they were not taught to exist as truly established in the context of analyzing the mode of reality. In the middle wheel is the teaching that all phenomena of samsara and nirvana lack true nature. That is to say, he taught that in the context of analyzing the mode of reality, the signs of the self of phenomena to be refuted do not exist in the way that one clings to them through the reification of signs (*mtshan 'dzin*). However, it was not taught that these illusory relative phenomena are not suitable to exist in general. Moreover, the basic field of profound gnosis, the mode of reality beyond the domain of reified signs, was known to temporarily not be the subject of this teaching based on the mental capacities of the disciples of that occasion. Other than not teaching it to either exist or not exist, there was no teaching upon having resolved that this kind of profound basic field is completely unreal—a lie.

Consequently, the consummate viewpoint of all three wheels, directly and indirectly, is one: the buddha-nature itself—the ground-field (*gzhi dbyings*), the ultimate self-existing gnosis that is free from all signs, the luminous clarity, the empty-ground, the totality of all aspects. However, due to the context, that is to say, due to the disciples: (1) first the relative was taught in the manner of the ordinary four truths; (2) in the middle, the basic field free from the constructs of all signs was taught, merely half of what is definitive in meaning; and (3) finally, what is ultimately definitive in meaning was taught, the nonconceptual ground-field, the great gnosis. Aside from merely distinctive teachings emphasized in accordance with necessity, the three wheels are in fact definitively one in the end. Therefore, the prior great chariots—the ornaments of this continent—the sublime and honorable Nāgārjuna, Asaṅga and brother [Vasubandhu], with minds in harmony established the three wheels as having one viewpoint. So it is also in our tradition of the scriptural viewpoint of the lord, the great Jonangpa, as well as the gentle protector Künga Nyingpo,[1] the master bearing his lineage.

Moreover, with regard to such a progression of the three wheels of the Word, the clear distinction of the temporal (*gnas skabs*) and the consummate (*mthar thug*) is elegantly pronounced in the way of the supreme teacher's own definitive elucidation of the viewpoint. That is to say, the status of being surpassable or unsurpassable is determined by way of it being provisional or definitive in meaning:

> Thereupon, the bodhisattva Paramārthasamudgata said to the Blessed One, "Initially, the Blessed One at Ṛṣivadana in Deer Park, in the region of Vārāṇasī, taught the four noble truths to the ones who fully engage in the vehicle of the Disciples. He fully turned the miraculous and amazing wheel of doctrine in a way unlike anything that had been turned in this world before by anyone, human or deity. Furthermore, this wheel of doctrine that the Blessed One turned is surpassed, affords an occasion of refutation, is provisional in meaning, and is subject to dispute.
>
> Based on the essencelessness of phenomena, and based on non-arising, unceasing, primordial peace, and naturally complete nirvana, the Blessed One turned the greatly miraculous and amazing second wheel of doctrine

1. Kunga Nyingpo (*kun dga' snying po*) is another name for Tāranātha.

> with the feature of the discourse of emptiness, for those who fully engage in the Mahāyāna. Furthermore, this wheel of doctrine that the Blessed One turned is surpassed, affords an occasion of refutation, is provisional in meaning, and is subject to dispute.
>
> However, based on the essencelessness of phenomena, and based on non-arising, unceasing, primordial peace, and naturally complete nirvana, for those who fully engage in all of the vehicles, the Blessed One taught the completely amazing and miraculous third wheel endowed with the excellent differentiation. This wheel of doctrine turned by the Blessed One is unsurpassed, affords no occasion of refutation, is definitive in meaning, and is not subject to dispute.[2]

The disciples for which the turning of the first wheel is concerned are those of the Hīnayāna. These are the dull faculty-types, those who are obscured as to the way of the causality of thorough affliction and complete purification in general, and in particular, are obscured about the selflessness of persons. Therefore, since on this occasion merely that system was taught in accordance with their faculties and constituents, at the appropriate time the teacher indicated to those disciples the style of doctrine mainly in accord with that. Hence, in general, compared with the consummate viewpoint of the teacher, there is a viewpoint higher than the main explicit meaning of the topic of this wheel, and there is still another occasion that is the domain of what is definitive in meaning. If the mere explicit meaning of this wheel is held to be the consummate viewpoint, since there is something that one needs to be directed to other than that, the reality of what is definitive in meaning, the first wheel is subject to dispute in the sequence of inferior and superior vehicles. Hence, it is not the consummate viewpoint.

The disciples for which the turning of the middle wheel is concerned are those of the Mahāyāna. These are the mediocre-types, those who engage the appearances of constructed signs as real entities when analyzing the character of phenomena. Therefore, in order to purge their conceptualities that reify signs, he mainly taught, by merely eliminating the object of negation, an extensive presentation of emptiness free from constructs according to their constituents and faculties. Consequently, compared with the more grand consummate viewpoint of the Great Madhyamaka that is definitive in meaning, the viewpoint of the main explicit meaning of what is taught in this wheel is surpassed and affords an occasion of refutation. Furthermore, this is provisional in meaning and a domain that is subject to dispute; hence, it is not the consummate viewpoint.

The disciples for which the turning of the last wheel is concerned are those of the Mahāyāna. These are the ones with extremely sharp faculties, who, through

---

2. Tibetan and English editions of this passage are found in Powers, *Wisdom of the Buddha*, 138–141.

their greatly distinctive power of mind, are the type that can splendidly engage in the mode of reality of the Great Madhyamaka—the unity of the emptiness of signs and the non-emptiness of natural reality—in the way of the essential point of what is definitive in meaning: the basic field free from all constructs of relative phenomena, the totality of ultimate aspects, the greatly wondrous array of environment and inhabitants, teacher and retinue as the self-appearance of luminous clarity, and the perpetually unceasing expansive appearance of gnosis completely encompassing the parameters of thoroughly impartial space. Therefore, the supreme teacher indicated to the disciples of this occasion the profound and secret essential point of what is consummately definitive in meaning just the way it is, the Causal Perfection Vehicle according to the disciples' constituents and faculties. For this reason, on the side of Sūtra, there is nothing more consummate than this. Hence, the topic of this last wheel is the consummate viewpoint, not surpassed nor affording an occasion of refutation, what is definitive in meaning, and not subject to dispute.

2. ESTABLISHING THE REASON FOR THAT BEING THE WAY IT IS

In general, the three vehicles are not definitely posited in terms of being earlier, in the middle, or later. This is because there exists an indeterminate and varied sequence of sūtras of the three wheels without being limited to such an order. For instance:

- Some sūtras of the first wheel that teach impermanence, etc., were taught when the Victorious One was on the verge of death (*parinirvāṇa*),
- Most of the chapters of the *Flower Garland Sūtra* (*Avataṃsakasūtra*) of the last wheel were spoken before the turning of the wheel of the four truths, for instance, at the *vajra* seat, immediately after the Buddha's enlightenment in the abode of the ruler king of the gods, and
- The *Nirvāṇa Sūtra* was taught at the time when the Buddha was on the verge of death (*parinirvāṇa*).

Therefore, here the three wheels are clearly understood through the levels of meanings of their topics. The first Word teaches the status of the four truths principally in the way of the selflessness of persons. The middle Word extensively teaches mainly the freedom from constructs, all relative phenomena's emptiness of true existence, which is the selflessness of phenomena, as well as the vast activities of the Mahāyāna. The last Word clearly teaches the difference between the real and unreal, having excellently distinguished as separate:

- The way of relative phenomena that are empty of their own essences, and
- The way of the ultimate ground-field that is the totality of all aspects—because of being true in the mode of reality of that basic nature, not empty of its own essence

> nor nothing at all—existing primordially unchanging, while certainly never at any time tainted by the signs that are the constructed masses of other relative phenomena.

This way of understanding the meaning of the three wheels of doctrine, based on the fact of there being a different series of topics by way of those teachings, is the unsurpassed excellent tradition because it is done in accord with the Victorious One's viewpoint as he himself explains it.

Some people think: "The first Word teaches all phenomena as self-subsistent (*tshugs thub pa*) and the middle Word teaches all phenomena as not truly existent. Therefore, according to the first, not only the ground-field, but all phenomena are truly established; and according to the middle Word, all phenomena comprising the two truths including the ground-field are just not real. Hence, even the statements in the last Word that teach the lack of true existence of relative phenomena and the true existence of the ultimate directly contradict both the first and middle Words."

I will explain. In the first Word, as described earlier, due to the faculties of the disciples, relative phenomena, considered merely in the way they appear, are taught in the manner of their existing as real entities. Other than that, the actual reality of phenomena remains as taught in the last wheel. Consequently, even though it was not the appropriate time to teach that actual reality, in order to progressively guide them, initially he taught merely the mode of doctrine that fits in the minds of these disciples. However, the consummate meaning, the mode of the ascertainment of Madhyamaka relinquishing the two extremes, was in fact taught. If one does not progressively realize the mode of reality of Madhyamaka of the categorized and uncategorized free from the ordinary and extraordinary extremes of eternalism and nihilism, then one will not be freed from the coarse and subtle samsara. This is taught in accord with the position of the sublime Nāgārjuna in the *Sūtra of the Instructions to Kātyāyana*:

> Kātyāyana, in this world, because of grasping to existence and nonexistence, one will not be completely free from birth, old age, sickness, death, sorrow, lamentation, suffering, unhappiness, and distress. One will not be liberated from the five migrations of samsara.[3]

Therefore, the consummate viewpoint of the first wheel is not suitable to be anything other than the totality of aspects, the basic field free from constructs which itself is the viewpoint of the middle and last Word. Also, it is said that everything exists in the explicit teachings; however, it is taught in that way with respect to mere relative appearances out of necessity, but as for the actual reality, it does not contradict the

3. I did not locate this passage in an extant sūtra, but this passage is cited by Candrakīrti in *Clear Words* (*Prasannapadā*), (D. 3860, vol. 102), 91a.

viewpoint of the last Word. Also, in the middle Word it is stated that everything does not exist—real entities are negated with regard to all phenomena comprising the relative. Nevertheless, there is also the fact that the ultimate ground-field itself, real as the natural state (*gshis lugs*), is not negated in the chapter of Maitreya's Inquiry:

> The Blessed One spoke to the bodhisattva Maitreya, "Maitreya, completely imagined forms should be viewed as insubstantial. Imagined forms should be viewed as substantially existent since conceptuality is substantially existent, not because they exist under their own power. Basic nature form should be viewed as neither insubstantial nor substantially existent, but as distinguished by ultimacy."[4]

The three natures are variously delineated earlier and later in the Maitreya Chapter. It describes the imagined nature of form and so forth as insubstantial, conceptual imputation. It describes the dependent nature as efficacious phenomena, which are the mere appearances of the relative. It describes the mode of reality of the basic nature, which is the consummate nature, as the reality of the ultimate that is definitive in meaning, free from all constructs of the relative. Consequently, that reality of the ground-field, without being refuted, is established. Therefore, the main topic extensively shows all relative phenomena to lack true existence and to be free from constructs from the mere perspective of the disciples on that occasion. Nevertheless, this middle Word also definitely contains the consummate viewpoint—the empty-ground of the mode of reality, in the way of being endowed with all aspects, and not being merely a voidness that is a non-implicative negation that negates true existence. Further, apart from the middle wheel's merely being taught from the aspect of a freedom from constructs out of necessity, the actual viewpoint in fact is not distinct from the viewpoint of the last wheel. Hence, even the viewpoints of the middle and last wheels do not contradict. For these reasons, it is not our tradition that the topic of the first wheel is only true establishment and the topic of the middle wheel is only a lack of true existence; consequently, there is no fault of contradiction between the first and middle wheels and this last wheel.

Also, other people claim this: "Since the disciples of the first Word are exclusively Hīnayānists, the disciples of the middle Word are exclusively Mahāyānists, and the disciples of the last Word are of a variety of vehicles, the middle teaching is definitive in meaning and the first and last teachings are provisional in meaning. Therefore, it is not reasonable that the last wheel is definitive in meaning."

Regarding this, generally there are many ways in which what is provisional and definitive in meaning is set forth due to philosophies, but our tradition is as follows. The *Sūtra Instructing Akṣayamati* (*Akṣayamatinirdeśasūtra*) says:

---

4. *Perfection of Wisdom in Twenty-Five Thousand Stanzas* (*Pañcaviṃśatisāhasrikāprajñāpāramitā*), (H. 10, vol. 28), 493b.

> Those sūtras that teach the establishment of the relative are called "provisional in meaning." Those sūtras that teach the establishment of the ultimate are called "definitive in meaning."[5]

As is said, that which teaches the relative truth as a support for the path that leads to the supreme reality is "provisional in meaning," and that which teaches the reality of the ultimate truth is called "definitive in meaning." Although that is said in general, in particular, the *Nirvāṇa Sūtra* states:

> That which expresses "the Tathāgata is impermanent, mutable, and changing," is the meaning that guides. That which expresses "the Tathāgata is permanent, immutable, and unchanging," is called "definitive in meaning."[6]

The ultimate Tathāgata, that permanent mode of the indivisible ground and fruition just as it is, is said to be definitive in meaning, and those impermanent and changing phenomena other than that are said to be provisional in meaning. Accordingly, the ultimate buddha of the ground-field endowed with all aspects is definitive in meaning, and all the other ephemeral appearances of the relative are provisional in meaning. Therefore, the topics in accord with that are:

- The mode of the relative, taken as what is principally the topic of the first wheel,
- The mode of the categorized ultimate, taken as what is principally the topic of the middle wheel, and
- The consummate uncategorized that is definitive in meaning, taken as what is clearly and principally the topic of the last wheel.

Hence, the sūtras that are provisional and definitive in meaning are posited in that way in consideration of the topic in the sequence of the three wheels in general, from the aspect of taking what is provisional in meaning, what is temporarily definitive in meaning, and what is consummately definitive in meaning as what is principally the topic. However, it is not appropriate for the consummate meaning of the topic to be provisional in meaning, nor is it good pedagogy that after a disciple has been instructed in what is definitive in meaning, to again be instructed in what is provisional in meaning. Therefore, the way of taking the first and last wheels as provisional in meaning and the middle wheel as definitive in meaning is not asserted in our tradition. Moreover, the *Descent to Laṅka Sūtra* (*Laṅkāvatāra Sūtra*) states:

> "If it were conceptualized as a self, it would not be proper." Thus, I do not teach this to immature beings.

---

5. *Sūtra Instructing Akṣayamati* (H. 176, vol. 60), 231a–231b.

6. *Mahāparinirvāṇa Sūtra* (H. 368, vol. 77), 154b.

It is said that if the ultimate basic field were taught to be real to those whose minds have not been trained by the middle wheel, there is a danger that the view of a self will arise; therefore, they are not suitable recipients for that teaching. Hence, the profound, paramount topic difficult to realize is established to be the teaching of only the last wheel. Therefore, the statement in the *Sūtra Explaining the Intent* that the disciples of the last wheel are those "who fully engage in all of the vehicles" moreover should be understood as extremely mature bodhisattvas with sharp faculties whose minds have been trained through engagement in all the vehicles. In this way, even though the consummate viewpoint of the three wheels, as explained before, comes down to just one, nevertheless, the way of what is principally taught in each wheel is distinct. Moreover, from a certain perspective there are greater and lesser degrees of accordance because, from a particular perspective, (1) there is great accordance between the first and middle wheels, and (2) there is a vast difference, without such great accordance, between the first and last wheels. This follows because:

(1) There is great accordance between the first and middle wheels due to such factors as:
   - both of the first two wheels do not teach appearances to be mind,
   - nor mention the eightfold collection of consciousness,
   - presentations of the five principles, three natures, and so forth are not mentioned at all in the first wheel, nor even in the middle wheel did they appear extensively, and
   - such a teaching of the last wheel as the gnosis without duality of subject and object was not explained in either of the other two wheels.

(2) However, there is a great difference between the first and last wheels because in the last wheel:
   - appearances are taught to be mind,
   - there are extensive teachings of the eightfold collection of consciousness, five principles, and three natures,
   - external objects as asserted by the Disciples are taught to be nonexistent, and
   - there are teachings of nondual gnosis, not at all asserted by the Disciples, as truly established.

Through this, the first and last wheels can also be known to be discordant with respect to being provisional in meaning. Also, in considering from a certain perspective the topic in the three wheels, there is a way of understanding the first and middle wheels as provisional in meaning and the last wheel as definitive in meaning because, from the aspect of just the topic:

- the first is the perspective of the relative, the four [noble] truths,
- the middle is the perspective of a mere emptiness that is included in the relative, and
- the last is the perspective of ultimate reality;

The first and the second are asserted as provisional in meaning and the last as definitive in meaning. However, there is no conflict in meaning.

Moreover, some people claim: "The last wheel in general and also the *Sūtra Explaining the Intent* in particular, other than being mere Mind-Only Sūtras, are not reasonable to be Madhyamaka Sūtras. This is because the [Buddha-]Nature Sūtras and so forth of the last Word generally teach that the nondual gnosis is truly established, and the *Sūtra Explaining the Intent* delineates all phenomena by the three natures."

Regarding this, it does not follow that the supreme sūtras of the last Word, such as the [Buddha-]Nature Sūtras, become the tradition of the Mind-Only Realists through the mere teaching that generally the nondual gnosis is truly established. This is because there is a great difference in the utterly dissimilar ways of establishing as true (1) the truly established gnosis that is the subject of the teaching of the last wheel and (2) the truly established dependent and consummate natures in the tradition of the Mind-Only Realists. This is so because (1) the gnosis that is the subject of the last teaching is truly established due to its being true in the mode of reality of the basic nature as the domain of ultimate self-awareness free from constructs; and (2) since the truly established dependent and consummate natures in the Mind-Only tradition are posited from a philosophy that is not beyond the appearance factor of consciousness, from the aspect of their observing signs as real entities, which is an object of negation—there is a great difference, as will be explained below.

In particular, through having an extensive presentation of the three natures, the *Sūtra Explaining the Intent* does not become the tradition of the Mind-Only Realists because if it did:

- the chapter of Maitreya's Inquiry in the *Perfection of Wisdom* (*Prajñāpāramitā*) and the *Perfection of Wisdom in Five-Hundred Stanzas* also extensively teach the three natures
- and thus even these two sūtras would have to be asserted as sūtras of the Mind-Only Realists.

This would be unreasonable. The first point is established because:

(1) the three natures are delineated in the chapter of Maitreya's Inquiry by way of an extensive statement:

> Maitreya, it should be known that the bodhisattvas engaged in the perfection of wisdom and abiding in the skill of completely discerning phenomena designate classifications of form through three types. It should be known that the designated classifications encompass from feeling, identification, formation, and consciousness up until the attributes of a buddha: In this way, this is completely imagined form, this is imagined form, this is basic nature form. In this way, this is completely imagined feeling, this is imagined feeling, this is basic nature feeling. In this way, this is completely imagined identification, this is imagined

identification, this is basic nature identification. In this way, this is completely imagined formation, this is imagined formation, this is basic nature formation. In this way, this is completely imagined consciousness, this is imagined consciousness, this is basic nature consciousness . . . In this way, this is a completely imagined buddha attribute, this is an imagined buddha attribute, this is a basic nature buddha attribute.[7]

(2) the three natures are clearly taught in the *Perfection of Wisdom in Five-Hundred Stanzas* through its extensive statement:

> Subhūti, form is a nonexistent entity, an inferior entity, and an existent entity . . . mental-consciousness [is a nonexistent entity, an inferior entity, and an existent entity] . . . Since immature ordinary beings, not knowing form as three types, do not know the authentic as it is, they grasp at form, establish it, and obscure it. Since through grasping at and establishing form they obscure it, if their deliverance does not even occur by means of the vehicle of the Disciples or the vehicle of the Self-Realized Ones, then it is needless to mention that it does not occur by means of the Mahāyāna.[8]

The second point [that it is unreasonable to assert that the chapter of Maitreya's Inquiry in the *Perfection of Wisdom* and the *Perfection of Wisdom in Five-Hundred Stanzas* are sūtras of the Mind-Only Realists] is established because these two sūtras are great scriptures of the *Perfection of Wisdom*, the scriptural tradition of Madhyamaka that vastly teaches profound emptiness.

Therefore, it follows that the sūtras of the last wheel of the Word are the extraordinary, supreme sūtras of the tradition of Madhyamaka that are definitive in meaning because these scriptures are unexcelled scriptures that signify well the basic nature, the mode of reality that relinquishes the two extremes. In particular, it follows that the *Sūtra Explaining the Intent* is not a scripture of the Mind-Only Realists because it teaches the mode of reality of Madhyamaka. This follows because this sūtra teaches that adventitious phenomena of relative truth are non-arising, unceasing, and primordial peace; and that the empty-ground, which is the ultimate truth itself, is supreme as naturally nirvana.

Moreover, the last Word is not Mind-Only scripture because the Victorious One himself says that it transcends Mind-Only in the *Descent to Laṅka Sūtra*:

> Relying on mind-only,
> One does not imagine external objects.

---

7. *Perfection of Wisdom in Eighteen Thousand Stanzas* (*Aṣṭādaśasāhasrikā-prajñāpāramitā*), (H. 12, vol. 32), 245b–246a.

8. *Perfection of Wisdom in Five-Hundred Stanzas* (*Pañcaśatika-prajñāpāramitā*), (H. 16, vol. 34), 163a; see also Edward Conze, *Perfect Wisdom: the Short Prajñaparamitā Texts* (London: Luzac and Co. Ltd., 1973), 108.

Relying on non-appearance,
One passes beyond mind-only.
Relying on authentic observation,
One passes beyond non-appearance.
Yogis who dwell in non-appearance,
Do not see the Great Vehicle.[9]

Therefore, the foremost king of the three realms, the second Victorious One, the great Jonangpa himself, with this in mind also spoke these words:

> If it is said, "Since the middle wheel is Madhyamaka and the last wheel Mind-Only, the fact that the middle wheel is definitive in meaning and the last wheel is provisional in meaning invalidates your position." This is extremely unreasonable because there is neither scripture nor reasoning whatsoever that the last wheel is Mind-Only scripture and because the last wheel teaches what is beyond Mind-Only, teaches the meaning of the consummate Great Madhyamaka, and teaches in accord with the meaning of the consummate Vajrayāna.

2. *The Wheels of Doctrine Indicated in the* Inquiry of King Dhāraṇīśvara Sūtra

This section has two parts: (1) presenting scripture and (2) establishing the reason for that being the way it is.

1. PRESENTING SCRIPTURE

Initially, the teacher himself, by means of the three wheels according with the respective disciples of the occasion, elegantly turned the three progressive wheels of doctrine. He did so in order for disciples to progressively purify—through practicing the meaning expressed in the respective teaching of the doctrine—the coarse and subtle defilements that obscure the vision of the buddha-nature, the basic nature that resides in each of their mental continua. Furthermore, the *Inquiry of King Dhāraṇīśvara Sūtra* states:

> Noble child, consider this: a person skilled in gemstones, for instance, knowing well the manner of refining gems, takes a thoroughly impure gemstone from the class of valuable gemstones, and after leaving it in astringent salt water, thoroughly washes it with a haircloth to refine it. However, he does not cease his efforts with just this; after that, he leaves it in an astringent fluid and washes it with a woolen cloth to refine it. However, he does not cease his efforts with just this; after that he leaves it in a great medicinal serum

9. *Descent to Laṅkā Sūtra* X.256–257 (H. 111, vol. 51), 270a.

> and then washes it with a fine cloth to refine it. Thoroughly refined and free from defilements, it is called "the great class of *vaiḍūrya*" (star-gem). Noble child, just so a Tathāgata as well, knowing the constituents of thoroughly impure sentient beings, by means of the disquieting discourse of impermanence, suffering, selflessness, and impurity, makes sentient beings who delight in samsara give rise to disillusionment, causing them to enter into the disciplinary doctrine of sublime beings. However, a Tathāgata does not cease his efforts by just this; after that, by means of the discourse of emptiness, signlessness, and wishlessness, he causes them to realize the way of the Tathāgatas. However, a Tathāgata does not cease his efforts by just this; after that, by means of the discourse on the wheel of the irreversible doctrine—the discourse on the complete lack of the threefold conceptualization—he causes those sentient beings who are the results of various natures to enter the realm of the Tathāgatas. Engaging and realizing the basic nature of the Tathāgata, they are called "the unexcelled place of offering."[10]

As discussed previously, the wheels of doctrine indicated in the *Sūtra Explaining the Intent*—through distinguishing what is definitive and provisional in meaning from the aspect of the meaning of the topic—mainly teach in accordance with the needs of the disciples. Here is the elegant teaching in the *Dhāraṇīśvara Sūtra* illustrating, through the aspect of partial concordance with the exemplified meaning, the method for cleaning the defilements in three stages through the example of cleaning the impurities of a jewel, upon having taken the defilements of the mental continuum endowed with the [buddha-]nature as defilements of the essential nature. In this system, there is the example of someone skilled with gemstones bringing out the natural luster of a gem through cleaning well the three—coarse, subtle, and extremely subtle—defilements of the gem in progression through three separate methods, and thereby accomplishing the benefit of whatever is desired. Similarly, the Victorious One, skilled in the constituents of the disciples, purifies in stages the three defilements in the mental continua of the disciples, which are the adventitious defilements arising due to the power of beginningless habituation to the defilements in the mental continua of the ones to be trained—obscuring the proper vision of the primordial Buddha. He teaches:

- the view of the transitory collection, thoroughly imagining a self of person and so forth, which are the coarse defilements included within what is to be removed on the path of seeing,

---

10. This passage can be found in the *Tathāgatamahākaruṇānirdeśasūtra* (*de bzhin gshegs pa'i snying rje chen po nges par bstan pa'i mdo*) P. 814, vol. 32, p. 300, 176b–177a.

- in general, the mere apprehension of an I or self and so on, which are the subtle defilements included within what is to be removed on the path of meditation up to the seven impure grounds, and
- the subtle threefold conceptualization and so forth, which are the extremely subtle defilements included within what is to be removed on the path of meditation on the three pure grounds.

He does this by means of excellently teaching the methods of thorough purification, discerning the distinctive sections of the path of skillful means in accord with the propensities of the disciples. Namely, the numerous types of paths are mainly three:

- the selflessness of persons,
- the selflessness of phenomena—a mere freedom from constructs, and
- the luminously clear nature, the view of the unity of appearance and emptiness.

Moreover:

(1) The first wheel clearly teaches the mode of impermanence, suffering, selflessness, and so forth. The disciples of this occasion, by means of practicing in such a way, relinquish what is to be removed on the path of seeing. Thereby, they are made to directly see the truth of the doctrine of sublime beings—they are made to enter the discipline.
(2) The middle wheel clearly teaches the mode of the three gates of liberation and so forth. The disciples of this occasion, by means of practicing in such a way, are made to authentically ascertain the aspect of the empty property of reality. Thereby, the realization of the mode of the Tathāgata—the profound basic nature free from constructs—is made more intense than before through eliminating the defilements that are to be removed on the seven impure grounds.
(3) The last wheel excellently teaches the irreversible, the consummate ground empty of the constructs of the relative, the luminously clear buddha-nature with all the ultimate aspects, distinguishing separately the modes of (1) the nonexistence of the adventitious constructs in the basic nature and (2) the primordial existence of the natural reality. Thereby, the disciples of this occasion, the results of an abundance of types of realization of all the vehicles, are made to enter the ever-immutable, consummate suchness that is the reality of the basic nature—the realm of the Tathāgatas empty of all the aspects of the relative and certainly not empty of the nature of the great treasury of the expansive attributes of the three mysteries of the ultimate, primordial Buddha.

In this way, since the defilements of the disciples are progressively purified by the three wheels, the ground-field —the buddha-nature as such—is progressively actualized due to temporarily being seen in different ways. It is initially seen as merely the mode of reality of common truths; then it is seen as the quality of emptiness, the nature free from constructs; then the mode of reality of the ultimate buddha-nature is seen as it is. Hence, according to the way it is, even though it is nothing other than the sole ground-field itself, the different ways of seeing arise due to the power of meditators on the path. This can be known through the Buddha's teaching by way of the example of a jewel.

2. ESTABLISHING THE REASON FOR THAT BEING THE WAY IT IS

Since the nature of the mode of reality demonstrated by the three wheels on this occasion is also elegantly taught by means of the later wheels clarifying much more than the previous ones, the supreme among the three wheels is firmly established as the last Word, which itself distinguishes the ultimate. This is so because the three-stage wheels are the scriptures of the lesser, middling, and greater scriptural collections demonstrating the progressively more excellent meaning indicated by means of the mode of reality demonstrated being a more profound meaning indicated in the later wheels than that indicated in the previous ones. This being the case, it is necessarily that the first wheel teaching of the mere common mode of reality is exceeded by the middle wheel teaching of Madhyamaka, the nature free from constructs; and yet more supreme than that is the last wheel clearly teaching the freedom from constructs from the aspect of the totality of aspects.

The disciples of this teaching as well, according to the *Sūtra Explaining the Intent*, proceed by way of the transformation of their mental continua—a progression of the lowest, higher, and paramount faculties—because the mental continua of the disciples of the middle occasion are more excellent than the mental continua of the disciples of the first occasion, and the mental continua of the disciples of the occasion of the last phase are even more excellent and mature than those.

Regarding this, some people say: "If the way of purifying the defilements of disciples by the wheel of doctrine of this last occasion is like that, then it absurdly follows that whoever are the disciples of this last wheel exclusively possess an undetermined heritage. This is because whoever is a disciple of this last wheel necessarily engages in the three vehicles progressively, and as such they are exclusively those who progressively engage with an undetermined heritage, lacking a determined heritage for a distinctive vehicle."

Here in our tradition of Madhyamaka that is definitive in meaning, we assert that even if heritage is determined for the distinctive temporary vehicles, since there is not a single being who does not possess the essential nature of the buddha, in the end—at the time when each of them connects with the fortune of meditating on the Mahāyāna path—there is not anyone who does not actualize unexcelled awakening. Therefore, in our tradition, since we do not accept the endowment of determined heritages for three distinct consummate vehicles, distinctive, merely temporary heritages are necessary. Temporarily, due to the influence of that heritage, disciples are varied. For instance, there are disciples exclusively of the first wheel, disciples of just the first and second, and disciples of all three wheels. Hence, it also does not necessarily follow that whoever is a disciple of the last wheel is exclusively undetermined. In the end, at the time of possessing the fortune of the Mahāyāna, it is also suitable to progressively actualize the meaning of the mode of reality according to the meanings indicated in the three wheels.

Also, some people say: "It is not reasonable that the continua of disciples are necessarily purified progressively by the three wheels in this way because, in contrast to such a progression, the first wheel is intended for the Disciples, the second as Mahāyāna's Madhyamaka, and the last as Mind-Only. Therefore, the progression of purifying defilements also is not consistent with such a sequence."

In the tradition of the Victorious One, the regent [Maitreya] and his followers, the progression of the intended meaning taught in the wheels of doctrine is the excellent path itself that is uncorrupted as to the sequence of the method for progressively actualizing the mode of reality as it is. It is needless to say that after the mode of reality is seen, the way of a corrupt, crooked sequence of obscuring gibberish could never be the way it is. So what inconsistency from any perspective is there in that sequence as mentioned previously? There certainly is none.

Further, some people also say: "The wheels are like this: through the first wheel, the disciples enter the realization of the selflessness of persons; thus becoming mature, they enter the path of discipline. Through the middle wheel, by means of entering the realization of the selflessness of phenomena exceeding that realization of the first wheel, they are caused to be liberated. Through the last wheel they are caused to enter the gate of practice together with the vast path of the characteristics of the relative exceeding that of the middle wheel. This gift of greater liberation is the intended meaning of this last wheel of doctrine."

In our tradition, in the way explained above, if the primordially residing buddha-nature in the continua of disciples is progressively actualized like a jewel, in that way, there is no contradiction in whichever way it is explained. Yet once one considers the Truth Body to be only a new production of what did not exist previously, as soon as that tradition is taken up it becomes adverse to our tradition of Madhyamaka that is definitive in meaning. Therefore, the great lord Jonangpa said:

> Through practicing the meaning of the three wheels, one accords with the purifying of the coarse, subtle, and extremely subtle defilements of the buddha-nature, which is like a wish-fulfilling jewel. Moreover, the first wheel is also a preliminary for, and follows in accord with, meditation on the profound Mahāyāna that is definitive in meaning. The second wheel also accords with the practice of the exceptional meditative stabilization of resting in equipoise on the profound meaning. The third wheel points out in accord with the profound Secret Mantra by distinguishing well what exists and what does not exist when an exceptional meditative stabilization arises.

This is the way of our tradition.

3. In Accord with That, the Way They Are Indicated in the Nirvāṇa Sūtra *and So Forth*

This section has three parts: (1) presenting scripture, (2) establishing through reasoning that being the way it is, and (3) an appended identification of the scriptural collections that are definitive in meaning.

1. PRESENTING SCRIPTURE

This section has two parts: (1) presenting scripture from the *Nirvāṇa Sūtra* and (2) presenting scripture from the *Aṅgulimāla Sūtra* (*Aṅgulimālīyasūtra*).

1. Presenting Scripture from the *Nirvāṇa Sūtra*

In general, there is no difference with respect to what is mainly indicated by the last Word—the basic nature, the ground-field, self-existing gnosis, buddha-nature, the totality of ultimate aspects. Therefore, it is the general way that these are the consummate of all the scriptures of the Perfection Vehicle, among all the sūtra collections, from the aspect of making what is definitive in meaning principally the topic. In particular, there is also a way in which this *Mahāparinirvāṇa Sūtra*, of the category of the last Word, is the supreme paramount essence of all the scriptural collections on the side of sūtra. The *Mahāparinirvāṇa Sūtra* itself states:

> From the twelve-branched sūtra collections, the [Mahāyāna] sūtra collection emerged; from the [Mahāyāna] sūtra collection, the extremely expansive collection emerged; from the extremely expansive sūtra collection, the *Perfection of Wisdom* emerged; from the *Perfection of Wisdom*, the *Mahāparinirvāṇa* completely emerged, like the butter-essence. "Butter-essence" is an example for the nature of the buddha, "the nature of the buddha" is the Tathāgata.[11]

As is said, the supreme essence that emerged from the twelve-branched scriptures is the Mahāyāna Sūtras; and more essential yet is the extremely expansive collection. From such Mahāyāna Sūtras, the supreme essence—the *Perfection of Wisdom Sūtras* emerged; and yet more consummately essential than these *Perfection of Wisdom Sūtras* is said to be this *Mahāparinirvāṇa Sūtra* itself that teaches the buddha-nature that is definitive in meaning, like the butter-essence. Moreover, this sūtra is said to be paramount among all scriptures because the teacher, having finished teaching the meaning of the nine-branched scriptures, taught the consummate profound meaning that is definitive in meaning, calling it "the tantra teaching the essential nature," here understood as a sūtra:

11. *Mahāparinirvāṇa Sūtra* (H. 368, vol. 77), 343a–343b.

> Since the Tathāgata had completed the teaching activity of the meaning within the nine-branched scriptures, he taught "the permanent buddha-nature" from the culminant tantra of buddha-nature to the monks.[12]

Thus, culminant sūtras such as this are said to be paramount. Moreover, the *Mahāparinirvāṇa Sūtra* itself says:

> "A"[13] is the culminant tantra; this sūtra teaches the culmination of the culminant meaning of all the sūtras. I taught the single letter or the single sphere that was previously unheard of by any of the Disciples and Self-Realized Ones. This great sūtra is supremely sacred because, for example, in the way the beings of the northern continent of Kurava are endowed with merit, those who listen to this great sūtra are transcendent—it should be known that they are bodhisattvas, great beings. Therefore, "greater" is the meaning of "culminant tantra."[14]

Since the profound meaning of the viewpoint of the culminant sūtras is not the domain of the Hīnayāna, it is said to be the way of the unexcelled, most secret, supreme meaning. Furthermore, the *Mahāparinirvāṇa Sūtra* clearly states that the reason this is so is the elegant teaching of the ultimate essential nature itself. In this way, since that *Mahāparinirvāṇa Sūtra* teaches buddha-nature, it is boundless.

The way this supreme sūtra is the supreme essence of all sūtras is in the realization of the audience retinue of great beings. After the Buddha spoke the sūtra, the audience in a respectful manner made a firm pledge to uphold, propagate, and act according to the sūtra. It is as the *Mahāparinirvāṇa Sūtra* says:

> Then, the bodhisattva Kāśyapa said this to the Blessed One: "Blessed One, as the Tathāgatas taught, the *Mahāparinirvāṇa Sūtra*, like the butter-essence, is supreme—is paramount! For whoever drinks it, the various illnesses will be purified, it also becomes 'a medicinal elixir!' Having heard it, I think that those who do not listen to nor want this sūtra are extremely foolish; they do not enact a virtuous mind. Blessed One, I will peel my skin to use it as a foundation to write letters on, draw my blood to use it as ink, extract my marrow to use it as water, and crack my bones for a pen—I will endure writing this *Mahāparinirvāṇa Sūtra*! Having written it, I will also endure reading, reciting, understanding, teaching, and expounding it extensively to others."[15]

---

12. I did not find this passage in a sūtra.

13. This is the short vowel *a* in Sanskrit, the first letter of the Sanskrit alphabet.

14. I did not find this passage in the *Mahāparinirvāṇa Sūtra*.

15. *Mahāparinirvāṇa Sūtra* (H. 368, vol. 77), 343b.

2. Presenting Scripture from the *Aṅgulimāla Sūtra*

Aṅgulimāla, an emanation of the Tathāgata, and the sublime Pūrṇa, the son of Maitrāyaṇī hold a dialogue. Trying to settle whether the consummate reality is either selflessness (the meaning of the two initial Words) or the ground-field of self-existing gnosis (the meaning of the last Word), they discuss by way of questions and answers about this topic. In the end, the sublime Aṅgulimāla extensively explains the essential viewpoint of the Sugatas and their heirs of the three times, the mode of the essential nature that is definitive in meaning. Here it is stated extensively in the *Aṅgulimāla Sūtra*:

Then Aṅgulimāla addressed Pūrṇa, the son of Maitrāyaṇī:

> "That which every buddha and Disciple never finds,
> Having fully become buddha, that doctrine
> Will be taught to all living beings.
> What is the meaning of these words?"

Pūrṇa replied:

> "The buddhas and the Blessed Ones of the past, not finding the element of a sentient being, a self, a soul, a person, a human, a human being, even though they searched all phenomena with extreme persistence, passed away thinking, 'selflessness is the word of the Buddha.' Similarly applied, the buddhas and Blessed Ones of the present and future also do not find nor will find it. Having stated that it applies in the same way to all the Disciples and Self-Realized Ones, in this way, the soul, the person, the being, the human, the sentient being, the element of self are taught not to exist; thus, selflessness is taught. In that way, emptiness is taught—the discourse of such a doctrine is taught."

Aṅgulimāla again addressed Pūrṇa, the son of Maitrāyaṇī, saying:

> "Alas! You, noble Pūrṇa, acting the behavior of a bee, do not know how to indicate the discourse of doctrine! Bees also know how to produce a buzzing sound, you, stupid like a bee, do not say anything! Pūrṇa, since you do not know the covert speech (*ldem po'i ngag*) of the Tathāgata, thinking that selflessness is the doctrine is falling like a moth into the flames of deluded doctrine. 'That which the buddhas do not find': the buddhas and Blessed Ones of the past passed away without finding in any sentient being a lack of buddha-nature. The buddhas and Blessed Ones of the present also do not find any sentient being lacking the element of self. The buddhas and Blessed Ones of the future as well will not find any sentient being lacking the element of sentient being. Also, the Self-Realized Ones and the Disciples in the three times

have not, do not, nor will find any sentient being without buddha-nature. This is the meaning of that verse."[16]

The meaning of the scriptural words of Aṅgulimāla is this: in response to a question to Pūrṇa, Pūrṇa explains the mode of reality according to the explicit teaching of the first and middle Words—the meaning of the twofold selflessness—as the viewpoint of the buddhas and their heirs. Aṅgulimāla extensively speaks of the mode of reality of the explicit teaching of the last Word that exceeds that—the essential nature of the Victorious Ones, the ground-field that is all-pervasive, permanent, the perfection of the sacred self, the mode of the consummate grand viewpoint of the buddhas and their heirs. Thereby, he elegantly establishes the intended meaning of the last wheel as the consummate mode of reality.

2. ESTABLISHING THROUGH REASONING THAT BEING THE WAY IT IS

Generally, according to the spoken words of the omniscient Victorious One himself, who has thoroughly actualized the consummate mode of reality and thus possesses the unexcelled supreme knowledge in which all delusion is exhausted, the last wheel in general, and the supreme sūtra of the *Mahāparinirvāṇa* in particular, is the essence of all the sections of scripture from the aspect of the meaning of its topic. It is the unexcelled Word that is definitive in meaning, teaching the consummate mode of reality of phenomena. This is because of the fact that, for instance, the glorious melody of the Victorious One himself teaches that the scripture of the *Mahāparinirvāṇa* is the essence of all sūtras, like the butter-extract—the essential topic of all scriptures. Hence, through the impact of statements over and over as to this culminant sūtra itself teaching the consummate mode of reality that is definitive in meaning, endowed with limitless good qualities, by means of that, other similar sūtras of the last Word can be understood to be sūtras that are definitive in meaning.

Moreover, it follows that this sūtra that teaches what is definitive in meaning, rare like an *udumbāra* flower, excellently distinguishes the differences between the three sequential wheels of the Word through its way of teaching. This is because this sūtra, in excellently distinguishing the way of the profound mode of reality, certainly engenders a greatly distinctive and glorious quality of causing those fortunate disciples who are close to activating the power of the heritage of the supreme vehicle to quickly reach the inner basic field—the mode of reality that is definitive in meaning—and actualize it as it is. This is done by means of excellently gaining certainty, extensively and in detail, as to the state of the intrinsic basic nature that is the suchness of all phenomena. This is not merely reduced to a non-implicative negation, emptiness that is nothing whatsoever, a mere negation of the constructs that are the objects of negation—but in the way of the great self-existing gnosis that is the immutable

16. *Aṅgulimāla Sūtra* (H. 214, vol. 62), 232b–233a; P. 879, vol. 34, p. 317, 157b–158b.

essence of the reality of the basic nature, the sole ground-field empty of all relative constructs, the totality of aspects naturally luminous and clear that innately exists primordially, thoroughly luminous like a *vaiḍūrya* (star-gem). That reason entails [excellently distinguishing the differences between the three sequential wheels of the Word through its way of teaching] because

(1) on the occasion of explaining the mode of reality in the way of the basic nature, the sūtra excellently distinguishes as separate the modes of:
- the categorized mode of reality, the lack of constructs that is a mere non-implicative negation, and
- the consummate mode of reality, the luminous clarity that is the totality of aspects; and

(2) scriptures that clearly teach this mode of reality in stages are certainly like the progression as was explained before according to the way of the three-stage wheel of the Word.

Some people say: "Isn't the *Mahāparinivāṇa Sūtra* a sūtra of the Mind-Only Realist's tradition?"

It is not because

(1) the mode of reality of the Mind-Only Realist's tradition does not transcend the mere appearance factor of consciousness, and
(2) the mode of reality that is explicitly taught by this sūtra is the self-existing gnosis, the totality of aspects free from constructs, which transcends consciousness.

Hence, there is no ground of likeness with the Mind-Only Realist traditions' assertions.

If it is said, "Well, isn't this sūtra renowned as a Mind-Only Sūtra?"

Even though it is renowned as such a sūtra, aside from being renowned as that by later proponents of Mind-Only just taking the viewpoint of the sūtra as their own tradition, actually that sūtra is unmistakably certain to be a scriptural source of what is definitive in meaning, the Great Madhyamaka.

If it is thought, "According to this Great Madhyamaka tradition, wouldn't there be no difference between the sūtras of both Mind-Only and Madhyamaka?"

There is no difference between the sūtras of those two because, aside from the mere distinction between better and worse ways of explaining the viewpoint of one sūtra, actually there are no sūtras to be distinctly posited. For example, although the Vaibhāṣikas and the Sautrāntikas do not have different sūtras, the difference is merely in how they adopt a viewpoint (*dgongs pa len lugs*).

Again, someone might say, "The words of Aṅgulimāla are not suitable to be the source of what is definitive in meaning because he was a great evil-doer."

It is not appropriate to entertain doubts in this way because the sublime Aṅgulimāla was an emanation of the Buddha. Moreover, this is because the *Aṅgulimāla Sūtra* itself says that to the south of this land, beyond as many buddha-fields as grains of sand in sixty-two Ganges rivers, in the pure realm called "Adorned With All Precious Gems" there resided a Buddha called "Sarvalokapriyadarśanābhyudgatamahābhiyukta" and he emanated as Aṅgulimāla.

In this way, the purpose of these supreme sūtras is to elegantly establish the last Word as consummately definitive in meaning by means of the way that the three wheels are progressively more excellently supreme. Moreover, in general, the teacher extensively taught the selflessness of persons in the first Word in order to destroy the view of a self of worldly people, causing disciples to enter the gate of the doctrine. In the middle wheel, to the disciples who were able to comprehend the basic field of the selflessness of phenomena even more free from constructs than that selflessness of persons in the first wheel, by teaching this type of emptiness he caused the disciples to strive in training and endeavoring in that way. From then, having seen the degeneration of some fools with faulty views of emptiness, and to turn them away from wrong views in order to at some point guide them on the authentic path after their faculties have progressively matured—and in particular, since the time had also come to teach what is consummately definitive in meaning to the mature disciples of the last wheel with extremely sharp faculties, he elegantly distinguished the ultimate in the last Word for the sake of that tradition accomplishing vast benefit. The Victorious One himself said in the *Great Drum Sūtra* (*Mahābherīsūtra*):

> In order to destroy the "self of worldly people," selflessness was taught. If the demonstrated teaching was spoken otherwise, would it not merely have referred to death? It is renowned that the Buddha, the Blessed One, taught selflessness, evoking astonishment. After that, one is caused to enter the teaching by means of causes and hundreds of thousands of reasonings. Through being caused to enter that way, at some point when faith in the most high is born and enters, one is caused to train, persevere, and strive in the doctrine of emptiness. After that, seeing a view that squanders liberation, fools teach emptiness and selflessness from among all the Buddha's teachings. Fools who do not know the meaning of emptiness and selflessness will degenerate.[17]

And,

> If the discourse of the buddha-nature is not taught, since the essential nature is denigrated, the discourse of the permanent buddha itself is rejected; due to that, the person will not pass beyond sorrow.[18]

17. *Great Drum Sūtra* (H. 223, vol. 63), 178a–178b; P. 888, vol. 35, p. 91, 113a–113b.

18. *Great Drum Sūtra* (H. 223, vol. 63), 200b.

This has a purpose and was excellently spoken from the Buddha's own mouth. Since there is no one in this world more greatly learned than the Victorious One himself, and other than he himself, there is no one who knows all phenomena without exception, disrupting the viewpoint of the exceptional sūtra collections destroys the way of the Capable One's doctrine (*thub pa'i chos*) and is therefore inappropriate. Who can have faculties superior to the Victorious One himself? Since the source of the doctrinal tradition comes to only the Buddha, he should be held as the source of knowledge (*tshad ma*); thinking this, the words of the undefeated victorious regent [Maitreya] say:

> There is not a single person in this world more greatly learned than the Victorious One.
> Since there is no other who knows properly everything without exception and supreme thusness by means of omniscience,
> Therefore, do not disrupt whichever sūtra collections the Sage himself set forth
> Because this destroys the way of the Capable One and also causes harm to the sacred doctrine.[19]

And in the words of the sublime Nāgārjuna:

> Regarding this meaning,
> Who has faculties superior to the Victorious One?[20]

And so on.

Consequently, this last wheel of the Word—having elegantly distinguished the way that the natural basic nature (the ultimate) exists and is not empty, and the way that adventitious fabrication (the relative) does not exist and is empty and so forth—teaches by way of pointing out in accordance with the way it actually is. Since the indicated meaning of the three wheels is as such, confidence is excellently brought forth for the disciples of this occasion. The way things are in the consummate mode of reality—not being reduced to the non-establishment of everything or simply a mere emptiness that is nonexistence—is the primordially residing ultimate basic nature of luminous clarity, an implicative negation, within the ground of the emptiness of all relative constructs, a non-implicative negation. Therefore, since the ultimate totality of aspects, the luminous great gnosis completely free from constructs, is changeless in the manner of inclusion (*yongs gcod*) within the ground of elimination through the exclusion (*rnam par bcad*) of the relative, within that basic nature are the

19. Maitreya, *Sublime Continuum* V.20 (D. 4024, vol. 123), 72b; English trans. in Fuchs, *Buddha Nature*, 75.

20. Nāgārjuna, *Precious Garland* (*Ratnāvalī*) v. 391 (D. 4158, vol. 172), 121b.

spontaneously present, primordial qualities, exceeding the number of grains of sand on the Ganges, of the self-existing ultimate buddha who has never been stained by any negative fault. This is so because it was spoken with that intention in the words of the great lord Jonangpa:

> In this way, when there arises the meditative stabilization of the unity of calm abiding and special insight through the engagement in the yoga of the perfection of wisdom, there needs to be the pointing out of the way it is according to the way things abide, teaching through distinguishing the existent and the nonexistent, the empty and not empty, etc. because everything does not abide as nonexistent and not established and so forth. This is because, within the ground of a non-implicative negation—nonexistence, emptiness, and the grounds of those, etc.—there is an implicative negation; and inclusion resides within the ground of elimination by exclusion; and within the ground that naturally relinquishes all faults resides the spontaneously present realization complete with all consummate qualities. Therefore, the third wheel is called "that endowed with excellent differentiation."

3. AN APPENDED IDENTIFICATION OF THE SCRIPTURAL COLLECTIONS THAT ARE DEFINITIVE IN MEANING

Thus, appended to the explanation of the wheels of doctrine, a concise summary is set forth here according to what was said in the words of the foremost lama, the gentle protector Künga Nyingpo. Through mainly a rough sketch, scriptures will be identified from which arose the Great Madhyamaka of the Causal Vehicle that is definitive in meaning. This supreme mode of other-emptiness Madhyamaka is the consummate viewpoint of all three wheels, yet the sūtras mainly relied upon are: the Maitreya Chapter of the *Perfection of Wisdom in Twenty-Five Thousand Stanzas*, the *Perfection of Wisdom in Five-Hundred Stanzas*, the *Sūtra Explaining the Intent*, the *Descent to Laṅka Sūtra*, the *Densely Arrayed* (*Gaṇḍavyūha*), the common and concordant explanations in the *Flower Garland*, the *Buddha-Nature Sūtra* (*Tathāgathagarbhasūtra*), some sections of the *Great Heap of Jewels* (*Mahāratnakūta*) such as the *Lion's Roar of Śrīmālādevī* (*Śrīmālādevīsiṃhanādasūtra*) and so forth, the *Dhāraṇī for Entering the Nonconceptual* (*Nirvikalpapraveśadhāraṇī*), the *Golden Light* (*Suvarṃaprabhā*), the *Inquiry of King Dhāraṇīśvara Sūtra*, *Entering Inconceivable Qualities and Wisdom* (*Tathāgataguṇajñānācintyaviṣayāvatāra*), the *Aṅgulimāla Sūtra*, the *Great Clouds* (*Mahāmegha*), the *Cloud of Jewels* (*Ratnamegha*), the *Great Drum Sūtra*, the *Mahāparinirvāṇa*, the *Sūtra on the Meditative Stablization Ascertaining Great Peace* (*Praśantaviniścayasamādhisūtra*), and so forth, in addition to relying upon most of the tantras that teach very clearly the extraordinary meaning.

The explicit teaching of the middle wheel for the most part mainly applies to meditative equipoise—being situated at the time of resting in equanimity on the profound basic field without any reference. The teachings by means of delineating objects of knowledge are explained as other-emptiness according to how the teacher himself explained in the Maitreya Chapter and the *Perfection of Wisdom in Five-Hundred Stanzas*. There are mistaken assumptions that some sūtras such as the *Jewel Lamp* (*Ratnolkā*) teach self-emptiness; nevertheless, while the *Way of the Bodhisattva* (*Bodhicaryāvatāra*) and a plethora of sūtras that mainly teach a presentation of the path and fruition are connected with both [self-emptiness and other-emptiness], it is said that there are many in accord with this tradition of Madhyamaka in most of those remaining, the *Stage of the Buddha* (*Buddhabhūmi*), the *Compendium of Dharma* (*Dharmasaṃgīti*), and so forth.

2. The Way that These Commentaries on the Buddha's Viewpoint Are Supreme

In general, that which is the supreme doctrine of Madhyamaka that is definitive in meaning, the profound essential point of the Victorious One's consummate viewpoint, is the distinctive Kṛtayuga[21] doctrine excluding the threefold debasements. Moreover, there are two "Kṛtayuga" in terms of time: the great four times and the lesser four times. The great four times are posited based on the quality of the time of the aeon: a quarter of the 4,320,000 years of that being made into four segments [1,080,000 years], when these four are totally complete it is the Kṛtayuga; and similarly, the first, second, and third segments are progressively posited as the Tretayuga, the Dvāparayuga, and the Kaliyuga. The four lesser times are posited by means of the quality of the teaching; a quarter of the span of 21,600 human years [5,400 years] of that being made into the length of the respective four times: flawless, complete with good qualities is the Kṛtayuga doctrine; similarly, the degeneration of a quarter is the former Tretayuga, the degeneration of nearly half is the latter Tretayuga, the remainder of the degeneration of three-quarters is the Dvāparayuga, and when there does not exist even a quarter it is posited as the Kaliyuga.

Therefore, if treated in terms of the context of the flawless teaching, the teaching, as if undiluted on the occasion when the Buddha was residing, in general is the Kṛtayuga doctrine of such an occasion. From among the teachings as well, there is a reason for calling the sūtras of the last Word the Kṛtayuga doctrine because they are called such since the ultimate mode of reality of the basic field of phenomena is thoroughly and completely taught. Compared with that, the other scriptures, from

21. The Kṛtayuga is the "golden age," and is one of four "ages" (*yuga*)—the others being the Tretayuga, the Dvāparayuga, and the Kaliyuga—the later three being ages of increasing degeneration. Drawing from the commentarial tradition of the *Wheel of Time* (*Kālacakra*), particularly the *Stainless Light* (*Vimālaprabhā*), Dölpopa refers to these four ages in terms of time as well as to the quality of the Buddhist teaching. See Stearns, *The Buddha from Dolpo*, 80.

the aspect of teaching a little bit variously, without teaching thoroughly and completely the factor of the basic field of reality, could be posited as Tretayuga and so forth. However, the actual threefold debasements came later. They are the scriptural traditions explaining everything to be exclusively self-empty that are unable to reach the consummate viewpoint of the Victorious One.

I have previously addressed solely sūtras in the progression of the Word that is the supreme excellent teaching of the Kṛtayuga doctrine transcending such threefold debasements. Also, the progression of treatises, composed by many great masters and accomplished beings, provide commentary on the viewpoint of the sūtras that are definitive in meaning. There are extremely many exceptional commentaries on the Buddha's viewpoint variously present or absent from the Tibetan region; there are the works of the regent Maitreya:

- the *Ornament of Manifest Realization* (*Abhisamayālaṃkāra*), a commentary on the Buddha's viewpoint of the middle wheel of the Word,
- the *Ornament of Mahāyāna Sūtras* (*Mahāyanāsūtrālaṃkāra*), a commentary on the Buddha's viewpoint of the Mahāyāna Sūtras in general,
- *Distinguishing Phenomena and the Basic Nature* (*Dharmadharmatāvibhāga*) and *Distinguishing the Middle and the Extremes* (*Madhyāntavibhāga*), commentaries on the Buddha's viewpoint of the Mahāyāna in general, principally explaining the viewpoint of the last Word, and
- the *Sublime Continuum* (*Uttaratantra*), a commentary on the Buddha's viewpoint of the distinctive last Word.

Maitreya's exceptional five, supreme vehicle commentaries on the Buddha's viewpoint, first opening the way of the chariot tradition of Madhyamaka that is definitive in meaning, are the consummate treatises that are the doctrinal source of the Great Madhyamaka. There are commentaries on the viewpoint of the Doctrines of Maitreya composed by the sublime Asaṅga, praised by the scriptures as supreme in distinguishing the definitive and provisional sūtras by the Victorious One himself, who having met the supreme regent and obtained well the instructions on those profound doctrines, excellently opened the way in this world for the chariot tradition of the Great Madhyamaka, the supreme Kṛtayuga doctrine. Also, there are commentaries on the viewpoint composed by Vasubandhu, the brother of the great master; and the followers of these two, progressively, masters Sthiramati, Dignāga, Dharmakīrti, and later arrivals, the honorable Ratnākaraśānti, as well as Vinītadeva, Guṇaprabha, Candragomin, Līlāvajra, Ānandagarbha, Buddhajñāna, Buddhaguhya, the sovereign Maitrīpāda, and so forth.

In general, the scriptural traditions of the Doctrines of Maitreya, Asaṅga, and his brother [Vasubandhu] teach through integrating the consummate viewpoint of all three wheels. Also in accord with these, the sublime Nāgārjuna, who came before them, stated in the *Fundamental Verses of the Middle Way* (*Mūlamadhyamakakārikā*):

The Blessed One,
Knowing entities and nonentities,
Refuted existence and nonexistence
In the *Instructions to Kātyāyana*.[22]

He establishes that the first wheel also teaches Madhyamaka free from the two extremes. Also, since he states, "Nirvāṇa, being the sole truth . . .,"[23] the consummate viewpoint of the middle wheel as well is excellently taught as other-emptiness Madhyamaka, definitive in meaning. This sublime master himself in the commentaries on the viewpoint of the last Word, the Collection of Praises—the *Praise to the Basic Field of Reality* (*Dharmadhātustotra*), *Praise to the Ultimate* (*Paramārthastotra*), *Praise to the Incomparable* (*Nirupamastotra*), *Praise to the Transcendent* (*Lokātītastotra*), and so forth—and also through some scriptures of Mantra, indisputably explains well, certainly in accord with the viewpoint of the profound essential point of the supreme Kṛtayuga doctrine, as well as the Doctrines of Maitreya and its followers. Due to this, among the gathering of disciples of this master, such as master Nāgāhvaya, many came who were great developers of the tradition of the essential nature that is definitive in meaning. From them, the followers of that lineage as well, by means of upholding and developing the Kṛtayuga doctrine, the viewpoint of the last wheel, there were many who contributed various short works that engage the Great Madhyamaka that is definitive in meaning—the consummate viewpoint.

In this way, in the Noble Land [of India], while the viewpoints of the two chariots, Nāgārjuna and Asaṅga, are not in conflict, there were many followers of these two also, who in certain respects were greatly in accord with Madhyamaka that is definitive in meaning; and in the time before master Buddhapālita came, there was nothing other than the single Great Madhyamaka, the viewpoint of both Nāgārjuna and Asaṅga.

If it is thought, "Then what is to be identified as the treatises of the Realist Mind-Only tradition?"

Previously, before Nāgārjuna, and after the five hundred Yogācāra masters who were proponents of the Mahāyāna (such as the great venerable Apitarka), it is reasonable that some from among them produced some scattered treatises of the Realist Mind-Only tradition; however, like the treatises of the eighteen sects, they were not translated into Tibetan. Later, Asaṅga and his brother [Vasubandhu] were merely renowned as such later, after Buddhapālita and others came, although these two together with their followers were not at all Mind-Only Realists.

22. Nāgārjuna, *Fundamental Verses of the Middle Way* XV.7.

23. Nāgārjuna, *Reason in Sixty Verses* (*Yuktiṣaṣṭikā*) v. 35 (D. 3825 vol. 68), 21b.5; see also Christian Lindtner, *Master of Wisdom* (Berkeley: Dharma Publishing, 1997 [1986]), 84.

Here in the land of snow, there were many upholders of the way of our tradition of the Kṛtayoga doctrine of the regent [Maitreya] and his followers. Among them, the greatly exceptional one who opened the way of the chariot tradition is the foremost, second Victorious One, the ruler of the authentic and profound wheel of doctrine in the three realms, endowed with the heritage, the great Emanation Body, the omniscient Jonangpa. He is the sole, unsurpassed supreme guide of what is definitive in meaning, "the one with the four reliances,"[24] whose supreme deeds are certainly meaningful. Also, there was the thoroughly perfect sovereign of the definitive meaning teaching of this supreme guide, the lord of doctrine, the foremost Tāranātha, who is the bearer of the treasury of the profound great secret. Concerning the elegant opening of the way of the supreme Kṛtayuga doctrine—the excellent tradition of the essential nature—in the cool land [of Tibet], these two, who are the peerless lords of the teaching that is definitive in meaning, explained the basic nature of the profound mode of reality in accord with the viewpoint of the Victorious One, the regent [Maitreya], and their followers.

These words follow them as much as my mind can fathom, through previous karma this fortune of the doctrine—the descent of the divine flower[25]—has befallen me at this time, as such here it is. This completes the brief progression of the wheels of doctrine.

> Since the Victorious One himself explained his own viewpoint—
> The dew-like nectar of the viewpoint of the All-Seeing Guide
> In the way of the miraculous last wheel excellently distinguishing the ultimate—
> It is reasonable that there is no one more learned on this subject.

This is a stanza at the interlude.

---

24. This is an epithet for Dölpopa. The four reliances are reliance on the doctrine, not individuals; reliance on the meaning, not words; reliance on what is definitive in meaning, not provisional in meaning; reliance on gnosis, not consciousness.

25. This is in reference to throwing a flower into the mandala during initiation.

APPENDIX B

Excerpt from A Lamp Completely Illuminating the Profound Reality of Interdependence

Introduction

The translation that follows is from Künzang Sönam's overview of the ninth chapter of Śāntideva's *Way of the Bodhisattva* on wisdom, entitled *A Lamp Completely Illuminating the Profound Reality of Interdependence*. Künzang Sönam lived in Eastern Tibet in the nineteenth century, was a student of the famed Patrül Rinpoché, and wrote an extensive, three-part commentary on the *Way of the Bodhisattva*. In his commentary, he illustrates the unique view of Prāsaṅgika-Madhyamaka through the lens of Tsongkhapa's characterization of this view. Künzang Sönam's integration of Geluk-inspired Madhyamaka and his Nyingma lineage exemplifies the dynamic synergy that characterizes the "Gemang movement."

After laying out the two truths, the conventional and ultimate, according to the Madhyamaka tradition, Künzang Sönam argues that there is a radical difference between the respective Svātantrika and Prāsaṅgika interpretations of Madhyamaka. He says that the main difference is that Svātantrikas accept something that exists on its own (*rang mtshan kyis grub pa*), while nothing exists this way, even conventionally, for Prāsaṅgikas. His characterization of the highest view of Madhyamaka, and how the three wheels of doctrine are interpreted, contrasts sharply with what we see in the Jonang tradition. The contrast between the excerpt translated here and what we see in Khenpo Lodrö Drakpa's text translated in Appendix A provides a sample of the wide spectrum of Buddhist interpretations in Tibet.

A Lamp Completely Illuminating the Profound Reality of Interdependence

Excerpt from A Lamp Completely Illuminating the Profound Reality of Interdependence

By Künzang Sönam

I will explain the identification of the object of negation here in two parts: (1) a brief demonstration of the necessity of identifying the object of negation and enumerating the objects of negation, and (2) an extensive explanation of the ways the objects of negation are respectively identified by Prāsaṅgikas and Svātantrikas.

1. Brief Demonstration of the Necessity of Identifying the Object of Negation and Enumerating the Objects of Negation

In order to generate the pure view of Madhyamaka within your continuum, it is first necessary to identify the subtle object of negation through reasoning investigating the ultimate in the Madhyamaka system. This is because, before the concept of true existence (the object to be negated) appears to cognition, emptiness (which is a non-implicative negation negating that object) does not appear to cognition. For instance, it is just like how one is unable to ascertain by a source of knowledge the lack of a vase in a certain place without first having an appearance to cognition of the concept of vase, the object to be negated. In this way, this [*Way of the Bodhisattva*] text says:

> Without contacting an imputed entity,
> One cannot apprehend the lack of this entity.[1]

Moreover, it is not sufficient merely to identify the appearance of the concept of true existence that has been imputed by a philosophical system. Since an innate apprehension of true existence is engaged from beginningless time in everyone, regardless of whether one has been influenced or not by philosophies, it is necessary for this apprehension and its apprehended concept of true existence to appear clearly to cognition.

If this criterion for the object of negation is not properly understood, then either the object of negation identified is over-extended—and what need not be negated is negated—causing one to fall into the extreme of denigration; or, the object of negation identified is not extensive enough, and something that needs to be negated is not negated fully. Thereby, one falls into the extreme of superimposition with something extra remaining.

In general, the object of negation is twofold: (1) the objects of negation by the path and (2) the objects of negation by reason. The former are, for instance, the two obscurations. These are existent objects of knowledge; if they did not exist, all beings would automatically be liberated and striving to cultivate the path would be pointless. How to negate these is to stop them in a way that they can never arise again in one's continuum, but their existence as objects of knowledge is not negated. As for objects of negation by reason, they are identified here as what is negated by reasoning investigating the ultimate; their status as objects of negation by reasoning investigating the conventional will not be described here.

Objects of negation by reasoning are twofold: (1) misconceptions that superimpose distortions onto reality and (2) the objects of these kinds of apprehension. The former is an existent object of knowledge, like the apprehension of true existence. The latter is not existent as an object of knowledge, like true existence. Among these two, the main object of negation is the latter. This is because, if it is not seen that what a misconception takes to exist is undermined by reason, then there is no other way for that misconception to be negated. When it is seen that what a misconception takes to exist is undermined by reason, then through this one can ascertain that things do not exist in the way they are apprehended. Based on this, one can uproot the seeds of misconception.

---

1. Śāntideva, *Way of the Bodhisattva* IX.139ab.

2. Extensive Explanation of the Ways the Objects of Negation are Respectively Identified by Prāsaṅgikas and Svātantrikas

If the distinctive criteria for the objects of negation of the Prāsaṅgikas and Svātantrikas are not known, then the distinction of their views will not be known. Therefore, one should ascertain the distinct criteria for these two systems' objects of negation. This section has two parts: (1) how Svātantrikas identify the object of negation and (2) how Prāsaṅgikas identify the object of negation.

1. *How Svātantrikas Identify the Object of Negation*

This section has two parts: (1) identifying true existence and the apprehension of true existence and (2) the example of an illusion to make it easy to understand.

1. IDENTIFYING TRUE EXISTENCE AND THE APPREHENSION OF TRUE EXISTENCE

I will explain in brief here the essential points stated in the *Light of the Middle Way* (*Madhyamakāloka*) in detail, which are cited in texts like Tsongkhapa's explanation of the *Introduction to the Middle Way* (*Madhyamakāvatāra*). Phenomena such as forms that are posited through the force of a cognition not impaired by a temporary cause of distortion are said to be conventionally existent phenomena. The opposite of these, namely, what is not posited by the force of an appearance to an unimpaired mind, but exists objectively from its own unique mode of being (*yul rang gi mthun mong ma yin pa'i sdod lugs kyi ngos nas*), is said to truly exist, ultimately exist, correctly exist, and exist in reality. These are the consummate objects of negation by reasoning investigating the ultimate, which do not exist even conventionally.

A cognition that apprehends these to exist, without relying upon analysis by reason, is said to be the "innate apprehension of true existence." The negation of its conceived object should be held to be the ultimate truth. In this Svātantrika system here, there is no such thing as this kind of truly existent phenomenon. Nevertheless, they do not accept that what objectively exists, naturally exists, exists on its own, and substantially exists are objects of negation for reason investigating the ultimate. This is because they assert that phenomena must exist in these three ways (e.g., objectively) and that to be an entity is necessarily to substantially exist. Thus, although they claim that phenomena are mentally imputed and conceptually designated, they hold that the essence of those mentally imputed and conceptually designated phenomena objectively exists first.

One might wonder: "The *Light of the Middle Way* states, "The claim, 'they do not ultimately arise' is explained to mean that they do not arise to an accurate cognition."[2]

2. Kamalaśīla, *Light of the Middle Way* (D. 3887), 229b.

Arising, and so forth, not existing in the perspective of an intelligent cognition (*rigs shes*) is explicitly shown to be the meaning of not ultimately existing. This shows implicitly that if arising and so forth were to exist in that perspective, then it would mean that they would ultimately exist. This conflicts with the previous criterion given for what constitutes ultimate existence."

There is no problem because there are two ways of understanding the ultimate when qualifying the object of negation with "ultimately." It is important to know the difference between these two when coming to ascertain the views of both Prāsaṅgika and Svātantrika, so I will describe it briefly.

One way is to claim that the meaning of not ultimately existing refers to what is considered ultimate and does not exist in the perspective of an investigation into reality by an intelligent cognition by means of study, contemplation, and meditation. Another way is to claim that the meaning of not ultimately existing refers to what is not posited through the force of its appearance to an unimpaired cognition, and what does not exist objectively from its own mode of being. These are the dividing lines. In this context, what we really need for identifying the object of negation is the latter.

The ultimate in the former sense and the reality that is ascertained in the perspective of an intelligent cognition's ascertainment both exist. This is because an intelligent cognition investigating reality, and what exists in its perspective, both exist. What exists in the perspective of that intelligent cognition exists because emptiness exists in the perspective of this kind of intelligent cognition's ascertainment of reality. The ultimate in the latter way of understanding does not exist, nor is there something that exists there. If there were something that existed there, then it would follow that this would truly exist and be an object of negation. Therefore, there is nothing that can be ultimately existent in the latter way of understanding. If there could be something truly existent there, it would necessarily have to be ultimate in the former sense as well because that kind of intelligent cognition is what investigates whether something is existent or not.

If these points are understood, then so is the essential point of why there is no conflict between the statement that the basic nature—the way things are—is the ultimate truth and the statement that the basic nature is established as the way things are, yet does not ultimately exist. The basic nature is the object warranted by an intelligent cognition investigating the ultimate and is the object it finds; nevertheless, it need not withstand analysis by that intelligent cognition. These distinctions are to be clearly differentiated. Due to not differentiating these, it is said that there come to be claims such that the ultimate truth truly exists and withstands analysis or that the ultimate truth is not an object of cognition.

2. THE EXAMPLE OF AN ILLUSION TO MAKE IT EASY TO UNDERSTAND

An example of the way an illusion appears is used here to illustrate whether or not phenomena are considered to be posited through the force of cognition and whether or not there is appearance and conception. When a magician conjures a horse and ox from a pebble and stick, for the audience whose eyes have been influenced by the mantra substance, the pebble and stick appear as a horse and an ox, and they conceive them that way. Similarly, for ordinary beings who have not realized emptiness, phenomena appear to exist objectively by their own power without being posited through the force of cognition's appearance, and they conceive them that way. For the magician, however, the horse and ox merely appear, but are not conceived to exist that way. Similarly, for ordinary beings who have realized emptiness, phenomena appear as if they objectively existed by their own power without being posited through the force of cognition's appearance. Even so, they do not apprehend them to exist this way because they have realized that phenomena are merely posited through the force of their appearance to cognition.

Those in the audience whose eyes were not influenced by the mantra substance do not have either the appearance of the pebble and stick as a horse and ox nor do they conceive them that way. Likewise, in the perspective of the gnosis of a sublime being's meditative equipoise that directly realizes emptiness, since there is no such appearance as before of what is truly existent, then it is needless to mention that they are not conceived that way. This is because this kind of gnosis is free from the influences of predispositions for ignorance.

In brief, in this Svātantrika system it is accepted that from the side of appearance, phenomena must be both merely projected (*phar bzhag*) by the power of appearing to an unimpaired cognition and be established out there (*tshur grub*) in an objective way. This is because an entity like a sprout must be both posited by an unimpaired cognition and be established objectively by the sprout's own mode of being. The former is necessary because otherwise, a sprout would have to be established as a sprout even in the perspective of someone who did not know the designation "sprout," but this is not the case. The latter is necessary because otherwise, everything would be like a nominally designated space-flower and a conceptually apprehended space-flower.

For example, when a pebble and stick are conjured as a horse and ox by a magician, the appearance of the horse and ox in the pebble and stick is projected by the force of the cognition of those whose eyes were infected by the mantra substance. Also, objectively from the pebble and stick, the horse and ox appear out there. Both must be in conjunction. The first is necessary because otherwise, those in the audience whose eyes were not infected by the mantra substance would also have to see the appearance of the horse and ox in the pebble and stick; but this is not the case. The second is necessary because otherwise, on a basis where there is no pebble or stick, this kind of appearance of a horse and ox would also have to arise; but this is not the case.

From the side of emptiness, an object must be empty of being established from its own mode of being, objectively without being posited by the force of an unimpaired cognition. If it were not empty, it would be established in that way. If it were established in that way, it would have to be established in the consummate reality. If it were established in that way, it would have to be realized by the perception of a sublime being's gnosis; but it is not. As for cognition, in the claim that phenomena are posited through the force of cognition, there are two types: conceptual and nonconceptual.

It is not that everything that is posited by just any cognition is accepted as conventionally existent; rather, the understanding cognition must be an unimpaired cognition. The meaning of being unimpaired is that it is not influenced by temporary causes of distortion; that which is understood by such a cognition is said to be undistorted. As for the meaning of being undistorted, it is asserted as that which can be warranted by a cognition in the way that the object objectively exists in its own mode of being. It is not that the understanding mind must be unaffected by *fundamental* causes of distortion because the appearance of phenomena existing on their own is an appearance that is influenced by the causes of distortion. This is because it is influenced by the innate apprehension of true existence.

One might wonder what the term "merely" excludes in the phrase "merely posited by the force of appearing to an unimpaired cognition." It does not exclude objective existence that is posited by cognition, which is accepted. Rather, it excludes what is objectively existent from its own mode of being that is not posited through the force of cognition.

2. *How Prāsaṅgikas Identify the Object of Negation*

This section has three parts: (1) the way of conceptually posited phenomena, (2) demonstrating the opposite apprehension—how things are apprehended as truly existent, and (3) showing how everything functions while merely nominally designated.

1. THE WAY OF CONCEPTUALLY POSITED PHENOMENA

In the Prāsaṅgika system here, nothing at all is accepted as an objective object; all phenomena are said to be merely conceptual designations and mere nominal designations. The meaning here is the viewpoint of numerous scriptures that are definitive in meaning and their commentaries. The *Inquiry of Upāli* (*Upālipariprcchā*) states:

> I taught the mind's fear in hell, and
> That thousands of beings are made miserable;
> Yet there never existed one
> Who went to the lower realms after dying.
> There are no harmful
> Razors, big spears, and weapons;
> Through the force of conceptuality they are seen to fall upon the body in the lower realms,
> But there are no weapons there.

The various things that bring joy to the mind,
Flowers in bloom, glorious mansions of gold,
These are not made this way at all;
They are posited through the force of conceptuality.
The world is imputed by the force of conceptuality;
Immature beings discriminate by holding onto identifications.
There is no arising of apprehension nor lack of apprehension;
They are completely conceptual, like an illusion and a dream.[3]

This shows that everything in the world of the lower realms and higher realms is simply a conceptual designation. Another sūtra says:

This teaching has shown before that there is no self and no sentient being,
Yet they are not extinguished.
They are said to be imputed, mere designations.[4]

And,

That which is peaceful, and the completely peaceful contemplation of phenomena,
Is contemplation that never arises.
All constructions are mental concepts;
Therefore, know this to be contemplation of phenomena.[5]

Also, the *Perfection of Wisdom* states extensively:

> "Bodhisattva" is merely a name. Likewise, "transcendent perfection of wisdom" is just a name. Form, feeling, identification, formation, and consciousness are just names. Form is like an illusion. Feeling, identification, formation, and consciousness are like an illusion. Illusion, too, is just a name. It does not abide anywhere or in any place.[6]

The *Reason in Sixty Verses* (*Yuktiṣaṣṭikā*) says that the whole world is merely conceptual imputation:

3. *Inquiry of Upāli* (H. 68, vol. 39), 243b.

4. *King of Meditative Stabilizations Sūtra* (*Samādhirājasūtra*) (H. 129, vol. 55), 231b.

5. *Inquiry of Upāli* (H. 68, vol. 39), 242b.

6. Similar passages are found, in various places, throughout the *Perfection of Wisdom in One Hundred Thousand Verses*.

Since the perfect Buddha taught that
The world is conditioned by ignorance,
How is it unreasonable that
This world is a conception?[7]

Also, the *Precious Garland* (*Ratnāvalī*) states:

The entities of form are mere names;
Space is also merely a name.
Without elements, how could form exist?
Therefore, even name-only does not exist.[8]

Thus, ultimately even name-only does not exist. Also, the same text says that there is nothing at all besides what is conventionally designated by a name:

Other than conventional designation,
What is this world
That really exists or does not exist?[9]

2. DEMONSTRATING THE OPPOSITE APPREHENSION—HOW THINGS ARE APPREHENDED AS TRULY EXISTENT

To apprehend the existence of phenomena in a way that they are not merely posited by names and concepts, as explained above, is the innate apprehension of true existence. If things are established as truly existent in the way they are apprehended, they are said to truly exist, ultimately exist, correctly exist, exist in reality, intrinsically exist, objectively exist, exist on their own, and substantially exist. All these here are, without distinction, objects of negation for reason investigating the ultimate; they do not exist even conventionally. The apprehension of these objects of negation to exist with respect to persons and phenomena is the twofold apprehension of self. The objects of these two modes of apprehension is the twofold self. This will be explained extensively below.

Since Svātantrikas believe that to exist on its own is not necessarily to truly exist, the difference between the degree of subtlety of the object of negation for Prāsaṅgikas and Svātantrikas is enormous. For this reason, as will be explained below, there are many differences between Prāsaṅgikas and Svātantrikas, such as whether or not intrinsic production and production from other are accepted. Thus, in Svātantrika texts, claims such as "not intrinsically existing" or "lacking essence"

7. Nāgārjuna, *Reason in Sixty Verses* v. 37 (D.3825, vol. 96), 21b.

8. Nāgārjuna, *Precious Garland*, v. 99.

9. Nāgārjuna, *Precious Garland*, v. 114.

are not explained to mean not intrinsically existing and not existing on its own even conventionally. Rather, they are necessarily understood to mean *ultimately* lacking intrinsic nature or lacking a truly existent intrinsic nature.

In the context of Prāsaṅgika, every time it is said that all phenomena lack intrinsic nature even conventionally, it is not to be understood as meaning that even conventionally there are no intrinsic natures, like heat being the intrinsic nature of fire and so on. Rather, it is stated in this way to indicate that nothing exists on its own or has an objectively existent intrinsic nature *even conventionally*. For this reason, these two traditions have distinct criteria for positing conventional existence. In the system of Svātantrika, a conventionally existent object, like a sprout, is understood to exist by the force of its appearance to cognition in accord with its own mode of being (*rang gi sdod lugs ltar*). Moreover, prior to cognition's ascription, the cognized sprout is held to first exist with an objective mode of being (*rang ngos kyi sdod lugs*). Due to this essential point, the existence of intrinsically existent sprouts, etc. is asserted.

While Prāsaṅgikas also posit things like sprouts by the force of their appearing to cognition, the conventional existence of things like sprouts is understood to be merely a nominal and conceptual designation. Apart from this, no objects designated by words like "sprout" are accepted whatsoever to exist objectively, from their own side. Merely this is not enough for Svātantrikas to account for existence. There is a big difference in the meaning of "cognition," too, in the phrase "posited through the force of cognition": Svātantrikas accept that conventional existence must be understood exclusively by an unimpaired cognition that is not mistaken regarding the mode of being of a thing like a sprout. Prāsaṅgikas, however, accept that the conventional existence of things like sprouts can be understood even by a cognition that is mistaken with regard to the object's mode of being.

Likewise, even though both traditions are similar in just accepting the necessity of positing all warranted objects by their respective sources of knowledge, there is also a great difference here. What the term "mere" is interpreted to exclude in statements in texts such as the Perfection of Wisdom Sūtras that "all phenomena are *mere* names and *mere* designations" is also different. Svātantrikas interpret "mere" to exclude phenomena's ultimate existence, not their objective existence, whereas Prāsaṅgikas accept that all phenomena are mere names and mere designations, so the "mere" is interpreted to exclude not just true existence, but objective existence as well.

Due to the two systems of Svātantrikas and Prāsaṅgikas identifying the object of negation differently, they also have different criteria for examining reality. Svātantrikas are not satisfied with simply words and conventions that "a sprout comes from a seed." They investigate whether or not there is the arising of a sprout from a seed objectively, and the process of arising. But this does not involve ultimate analysis; it is just conventional analysis. If anything is found by such an analysis it is said to be a conventionally existent thing and something that is established unreflectively without analysis. Ultimate analysis is held to be an analysis of the status of the arising of a sprout from a seed not held to be posited by the force of cognition—an analysis of the production from a seed as the objective way of a sprout's own mode of being; they accept that no phenomenon withstands this type of analysis.

Since it involves a search for a designated object, Prāsaṅgikas also assert the former kind of analysis to be an ultimate analysis. Thus, the line between Prāsaṅgikas and Svātantrikas is also drawn in terms of the way of understanding conventional existence to the same extent as the way of understanding ultimate analysis or a search for a designated object. Nevertheless, in both systems there is no difference in reason's subtle object of negation being accepted as that which is found when a designated object is sought out according to their own respective assertions. This is because phenomena undeniably exist when they are not analyzed in both systems, and it is similarly accepted that when examined with ultimate analysis, a phenomenon withstanding this analysis is impossible, like a rabbit horn.

3. SHOWING HOW EVERYTHING FUNCTIONS WHILE MERELY NOMINALLY DESIGNATED

How all frameworks are understood based on all phenomena being merely conceptually and nominally designated is explained as follows. Through accepting and rejecting based merely on designating conventions such as "this is a form; this is feeling," "arising, ceasing," "coming, going," and so forth, purposes are accomplished. All things are possible—such as existence and nonexistence, being and not being—based on mere names. Without being satisfied with just this, when the object designated by something like "form" is sought out—in terms of its shape, color, or parts, and so on—nothing is ever found and nothing is feasible.

Therefore, there is nothing more than mere nominal designation; it is like imputing a snake onto a colored rope or a person onto a heap of stones. Nevertheless, the meanings of these examples are not the same in terms of the status of conventional existence because there is a difference as to whether an affirmed designation is undermined or not by a conventional source of knowledge. Thus, it is said that since the difference in the status of the existence of these two cannot be distinguished from the side of the object itself, one must draw a fine line by means of differentiating whether or not it is undermined by another conventional cognition. This has been said again and again to be a consummate essential point of the Prāsaṅgika view that is difficult to understand.

In this way, an unexcelled feature of this system is that while things are merely nominally designated, all activities—such as cause and effect, arising and ceasing, coming and going—can be posited with respect to them. The consummate viewpoint of master Nāgārjuna, father and son [Āryadeva], was explained with many stainless scriptures and reasonings by the genuinely great chariots—master Buddhapālita, glorious Candrakīrti, and the Victor's child, Śāntideva—with one intent and one voice.

In master Buddhapālita's commentary on the *Fundamental Verses of the Middle Way* (*Mūlamadhyamakakārikā*), based on the *Jewel Heap* (*Ratnakūṭasūtra*) he used the example of two villagers who visit a temple. They argue about whether a painting is the body of Īśvara or Visṇu, with an arbitrator making the distinction between what is true and what is false. Since no phenomenon exists objectively, nothing is found when a designated object is sought out. Nevertheless, all things can function based on merely mundane names.

The glorious Candrakīrti used the example of a chariot based on a Hīnayāna text:

> In dependence upon a collection of parts
> A chariot is designated;
> Likewise, based on the aggregates
> Conventionally, sentient beings are acknowledged.[10]

Even though phenomena like persons are not found when analyzed, he showed that without analysis, based on merely their bases of designation, all things function while just being posited with mere designations.

Also, in accord with the intended meaning of the *Sūtra on the Meeting of the Father and Son* (*Pitāputrasamāgamasūtra*), the Victor's child, Śāntideva, showed that based on the six elements that are the basis of designation for a being, a being does not exist other than as a mere imputation; it is like an illusion. Even so, he claims that conventionally, there is a difference in the status of a mind's existence in an actual being and an illusory being, and also a difference in the status of the evil deed's existence for killing one of them. In our [*Way of the Bodhisattva*] text here, it is shown many times that everything is merely a nominal designation, like an illusion, such as: "The illusory Victors. . ."[11] "If beings are like illusions . . .,"[12] and, "In killing an illusory being . . ."[13] Nevertheless, he shows that everything can be distinguished, such as the difference between having a mind or not. In this one should know the essential point of there being no contradiction between the claim made above—that there is no division between a correct and incorrect conventional truth in this Madhyamaka system—and the explanation in our Prāsaṅgika system that we can understand the difference between such things as what is true and false in regard to claims about a god's body and between an illusory being and an actual being having a mind or not.

---

10. Candrakīrti, *Autocommentary on the "Introduction to the Middle Way"* (*Madhyamakāvatārabhāṣya*), (D. 3862, vol. 102), 299b; these verses are also cited in Vasubandhu, *Autocommentary on the "Treasury of Metaphysics"* (*Abhidharmakośabhāṣya*), (D. 4090, vol. 141), 86a.

11. Śāntideva, *Way of the Bodhisattva* IX.9a.

12. Śāntideva, *Way of the Bodhisattva* IX.9c.

13. Śāntideva, *Way of the Bodhisattva* IX.11a.

As for the meaning of nominal existence, in name only: "name only" eliminates the extreme of existence or permanence; "nominal existence" eliminates the extreme of nonexistence or annihilation. If it is merely a nominal designation, it need not exist, but if it nominally exists, in name only, it must exist. This is because here (1) existence and (2) nominal existence, in name only, mean the same thing.

Next, as it is said: "For the purpose of guiding the world."[14] The intent of the scriptures that are spoken for the purpose of guiding disciples to the subtle selflessness is described here in two parts: (1) explaining the explicit teaching of our [*Way of the Bodhisattva*] text here, showing sūtras teaching impermanence and so on to be provisional in meaning, and (2) explaining its implicit teaching, the way of classifying sūtras of the three wheels as provisional or definitive.

1. Showing Sūtras that are Provisional in Meaning

In general, there are many descriptions in the Hīnayāna canon of the coarse view of the four noble truths, including the sixteen aspects such as impermanence,[15] which are traversed until the stage of an Arhat. The Mahāyāna also describes both the sixteen aspects such as impermanence, the coarse view, as well as the way of traversing the path of realizing the lack of intrinsic nature. Other masters accept the commentaries on their viewpoints and explain them that way. However, in this Prāsaṅgika system, the actual path of liberation is exclusively the path of realizing the lack of intrinsic nature in phenomena; other than this there is no second gateway to peace, as it is said in the *Four Hundred Verses* (*Catuḥśataka*): "There is no second gateway to peace."[16] Therefore, we assert that merely the path that realizes the coarse view of the sixteen aspects such as impermanence is not able to achieve even a sublime path within any of the three vehicles. This will be explained extensively below.

One might wonder, "If the sixteen aspects such as impermanence are not the actual path of liberation, then why were they taught?" These are paths that purify the continua; by just this they are the actual path of liberation for suitable receptacles. Yet for dull Hīnayāna types who are not yet suitable receptacles, they are taught for the purpose of progressively guiding to the subtle selflessness. It is said in the *Reason in Sixty Verses:*

---

14. Śāntideva, *Way of the Bodhisattva* IX.7.

15. The sixteen aspects of the four truths are as follows: for the truth of suffering, there are the four aspects of (1) impermanence, (2) suffering, (3) emptiness, and (4) selflessness; for the truth of origin, there are the four aspects of (5) cause, (6) origin, (7) complete production, and (8) condition; for the truth of cessation, there are the four aspects of (9) cessation, (10) peace, (11) perfection, and (12) definite emergence; and for the truth of the path, there are the four aspects of (13) path, (14) suitability, (15) accomplishment, and (16) deliverance.

16. Āryadeva, *Four Hundred Verses* XII.13a (D. 3846, vol. 97), 13b; English trans. in Sonam, *Āryadeva's Four Hundred Stanzas on the Middle Way*, 245.

The path of arising and decay
Is taught with a purpose.
By understanding arising, decay is understood;
Through understanding decay, impermanence is understood.
By applying the understanding of impermanence,
One will understand the sublime doctrine.
Those who know
Dependent arising
Abandon arising and decay;
They cross over the ocean of beliefs.[17]

Here is what this means: By holding onto permanence and happiness, and being completely attached in one's mind to what is conditioned, there will be no wish for liberation. As a remedy to this, impermanence and suffering are taught. Based on understanding the arising of the conditioned, conditioned phenomena are understood to be impermanent. Based on this understanding, one becomes averse to existence. Then one understands the endeavor, the wish to dispel it and achieve liberation. Based on this, one directly realizes the path of liberation, the actual sacred doctrine of interdependence, which is free from the nature of arising and decay. Thereby, one crosses over the ocean of existence generated by wrong views.

Also, the *Praise to the Basic Field of Reality* (*Dharmadhātustotra*) states:
Impermanence, suffering, and emptiness -
These three purify the mind.
That which supremely purifies the mind
Is the doctrine of the lack of intrinsic nature.[18]

One might wonder, "Does this not conflict with statements that claim that seeing impermanence and so forth is seeing reality?" Candrakīrti said this in his commentary on the *Reason in Sixty Verses:* "Distortion is the apprehension of things like happiness, because things with this nature do not even conventionally exist. The lack of distortion is to apprehend things like suffering because things with this nature do exist conventionally."[19] The meaning intended here is that objects apprehended that do not even conventionally exist, like permanent aggregates, and objects apprehended that do conventionally exist, like impermanent aggregates, can be distinguished in terms of being distorted or undistorted *conventionally*. Yet in terms of reality, based on

17. Nāgārjuna, *Reason in Sixty Verses* vv. 21cd–23 (D. 3825), 21a.

18. Nāgārjuna, *Praise to the Basic Field of Reality* (D. 1118, vol. 1), 64b.

19. Candrakīrti, *Commentary on "Reason in Sixty Verses"* (*Yuktiṣaṣṭikāvṛtti*) (D. 3864, vol. 103), 7b.

things like forms not existing as either permanent or impermanent, the distinction between being distorted and undistorted cannot be made. Intending this, the *Mother Sūtras* say that whoever regards forms and the like as permanent or impermanent, happiness or suffering, self or no-self, empty or non-empty is coursing in signs.[20]

The selflessness and emptiness realized in the context of the sixteen aspects is a realization of merely the lack of a self that is imputed by non-Buddhists. This is not sufficient to be the remedy to the innate apprehension of self that apprehends an intrinsically existent person. Therefore, the remedy to this is necessarily to realize the lack of intrinsic nature of persons (the selflessness of persons) in the way that the aggregates and so on lack intrinsic existence (the selflessness of phenomena). Without this understanding, as long as form is apprehended to be truly existent, the apprehension of the person as truly existent will persist as well. As long as that persists, there is no removal of the afflictions, so it is impossible to be liberated from existence. It is stated in the *Introduction to the Middle Way*:

> Your contemplative practice (*rnal 'byor, yoga*) that sees selflessness
> Does not realize the reality of forms and so on;
> Since it persists when forms are perceived
> Attachment and the like arise, there being no realization of their nature.[21]

And, "When you realize no-self, the permanent self is relinquished . . . "[22]

2. The Way of Classifying Sūtras as Provisional or Definitive

Here is a brief exposition of the three wheels, and ways of classifying the provisional and definitive. Among the four philosophical systems, the Vaibhāṣikas do not accept the wheel of dharma of scripture; they claim that a wheel of dharma is necessarily the wheel of dharma of realization, and for that to be exclusively the path of seeing. The Sautrāntikas accept both wheels of dharma of scripture and realization. Within the wheel of dharma of scripture, they assert nothing more than simply the words of sūtras that express the four truths. For the most part, both Vaibhāṣikas and Sautrāntikas claim that the Buddha's Word is necessarily definitive in meaning. There are also those who accept it to include both meanings that are provisional and definitive, as is said in the *Blaze of Reasoning* (*Tarkajvāla*).

Proponents of Mind-Only follow the division of the three wheels into provisional and definitive from the *Sūtra Explaining the Intent*. The first two wheels are accepted

20. For instance, *The Condensed Perfection of Wisdom* says: "Even if bodhisattvas conceive 'this aggregate is empty,' they are coursing in signs and do not have faith in the domain of the unborn." *Prajñāpāramitā-sañcayagāthā*, H. 17, vol. 34, 189b–190a.

21. Candrakīrti, *Introduction to the Middle Way* VI.131.

22. Candrakīrti, *Introduction to the Middle Way* VI.130.

as provisional, and the last is accepted as definitive. The reason for this is that the distinctions among the three wheels are posited based on the subject matter. In terms of the subject matter—by way of mainly teaching selflessness—the first wheel teaches merely the selflessness of persons, while phenomena's true existence is not negated. In the middle wheel, the selflessness of phenomena is taught having negated the true existence of all phenomena without a clear differentiation. In the last wheel, the three natures are taught according to Mind-Only, and the selflessness of phenomena is taught having differentiated clearly between what is truly existent and what is not. From among the three cycles teaching selflessness, they accept that the explicit teaching of the first and second wheel is provisional in meaning because it is not suitable to be accepted literally. The explicit teaching of the last wheel is suitable to be accepted literally, and for this reason is accepted as definitive in meaning.

In the Madhyamaka system, it is said in texts such as the *Clear Words* and the *Light of the Middle Way* that one must make the division between the provisional and the definitive following the *Sūtra Instructing Akṣayamati*. As for this way, it is said in the sūtra itself:

> What is a sūtra of definitive meaning and what is a sūtra of provisional meaning? Sūtras that teach the existence of conventional truth are called "provisional in meaning." Sūtras that teach the existence of ultimate truth are called "definitive in meaning."[23]

This means that the distinction between the provisional and definitive is made based on the subject matter. Those sūtras that mainly teach a conventional truth, like phenomena or persons, are provisional in meaning. Those sūtras that mainly teach the ultimate truth, like the lack of self in phenomena and persons, are definitive in meaning. This is the concise explanation of the way of classifying them. At the end of this passage it also clearly states the way of teaching the two truths by identifying sūtras that teach the two truths and the distinct ways of teaching them.

Also, the *King of Meditative Stabilizations Sūtra* (*Samādhirājasūtra*) states:

> Emptiness, as the Sugatas explained—
> Know to be a quality of sūtras that are definitive in meaning.
> All the doctrines that teach sentient beings, persons, and individuals—
> Know to be provisional in meaning.[24]

This meaning is just like the previous sūtra, as is stated in the *Clear Words*.

---

23. *Sūtra Instructing Akṣayamati* (H. 176, vol. 60), 231a–231b.

24. *King of Meditative Stabilizations Sūtra* (H. 129, vol. 55), 33b.

The criteria for what is provisional in meaning are this: In general a provisional meaning sūtra guides disciples. Yet it is not simply by guiding that it is provisional in meaning; here, the meaning of the sūtra must guide elsewhere. Also, from among two ways of guiding, there is one in which the explicit teaching is not suitable to be apprehended literally; its explicit teaching needs to lead elsewhere, as in, "Your mother and father are to be killed."[25] This should be explained as referring to karmic existence and craving. Furthermore, in the statement, "all conditioned phenomena are impermanent," its explicit teaching can be accepted literally, yet mere impermanence is not the consummate reality of conditioned phenomena. It must guide to another reality; it still needs to guide elsewhere, to the meaning of their reality—the emptiness of true reality.

The criteria for what is definitive in meaning are this: a teaching that cuts through constructs, such as the statement, "phenomena do not truly arise," having an explicit teaching of the consummate ultimate reality. Thus, it does not guide anyone anywhere else. It is classified as definitive in meaning if it also has a source of knowledge that establishes it in accord with the meaning that is taught. The *Light of the Middle Way* states: "If one wonders, 'What is definitive in meaning?' It is a statement oriented to the ultimate with the support of a source of knowledge because it cannot be guided anywhere else by another."[26] In this way, from the aforementioned two ways of guiding, since it cannot be guided elsewhere, it is called "the certain meaning" or "definitive in meaning." The *Introduction to the Middle Way* states:

> A sūtra that has a meaning that is not reality
> Is said to be provisional in meaning; when understood, it is what guides.
> Know that what has the meaning of emptiness is definitive in meaning.[27]

In terms of just this way of classifying what is provisional and definitive in meaning, there is no difference between Svātantrika and Prāsaṅgika. Nevertheless, according to the Svātantrika system, not only must a sūtra that is definitive in meaning mainly teach the ultimate truth, but it also must be accepted as the literal truth. For this reason, in the *Hundred Thousand Verse Mother*, for instance, when it says that "this is conventionally a truth for the world, but not ultimately,"[28] there are some times when the qualifier *ultimately* is explicitly applied to the object of negation and these are classified as sūtras that are definitive in meaning. Even though the *Heart Sūtra* mainly teaches the ultimate truth, it does not clearly apply the qualifier *ultimately* to

25. *Tantra Explaining the Four Seats* (*Caturpīṭha-vikhyāta-tantrarāja*) (H. 406, vol. 82), 219b.

26. Kamalaśīla, *Light of the Middle Way* (D. 3887), 148b.

27. Candrakīrti, *Introduction to the Middle Way* VI.97bcd.

28. This passage is not found in the *Śatasāhasrikā-prajñāpāramitāsūtra*.

the object of negation, so it cannot be held to be literal; thus, it is classified as provisional in meaning.

The reason for this is that in the Svātantrika system it is not possible for any phenomenon to ultimately exist. If something did exist in this way, it would have to intrinsically exist; how they assert was explained above. Yet the *Heart Sūtra* says, "The five aggregates are empty of intrinsic existence";[29] since this cannot be taken literally, it is classified as provisional in meaning. If it were said that the five aggregates were ultimately empty of intrinsic existence, applying the qualifier *ultimately*, then it would be classified as definitive in meaning because it could be taken literally.

In the Prāsaṅgika system, there is no difference in whether qualifiers like *ultimately* or *intrinsically existent* are applied to the objects of negation. Thus, in the Svātantrika system, the first wheel is provisional in meaning and the second wheel has two aspects of definitive and provisional: the extensive, middling, and condensed [Perfection of Wisdom] are definitive in meaning, whereas something like the *Heart Sūtra* is held to be provisional in meaning. They accept that the last teaching, the wheel of doctrine of clear differentiation, is provisional in meaning in terms of the framework of the three natures according to the proponents of Mind-Only's assertions. However, there are many ways of explaining their way of understanding what is provisional and definitive in meaning in the last wheel; it is a difficult point in this context here. I will also not mention here the way of explaining what is provisional and definitive in meaning based on the three criteria of having a basis in another intention, and so forth.[30]

In the Prāsaṅgika system, the first wheel spoken of in the *Sūtra Explaining the Intent* must be provisional in meaning; yet in general, the first wheel has aspects of both what is provisional and definitive in meaning. The first wheel teachings of the lack of intrinsic nature in persons and phenomena is definitive in meaning. The first wheel's teachings of merely the coarse selflessness of persons—a person being empty of existence as a self-subsisting substance (*rang skya thub pa'i rdzas yod*)—and the teaching of forms and so on existing on their own are provisional in meaning.

These are explained as provisional in meaning due to having a basis in another intention, having a purpose, and explicit invalidation of the literal meaning. The basis in another intention is its intending merely the conventional existence of forms and so on. The purpose is to teach merely a coarse selflessness of persons to progressively train the minds of those who are, for the time being, not suitable receptacles for the teaching of the subtle selflessness. Thereby, they are progressively led to the subtle selflessness. Explicit invalidation of the literal meaning is found in arguments negating anything existing on its own. The middle wheel asserts that phenomena

29. *Heart Sūtra* (*Bhagavatīprajñāpāramitāhṛdaya*) (H. 499, vol. 88), 45a.

30. Along with having a basis in another intention (*dgongs gzhi*), the other two criteria are having a purpose (*dgos pa*) and explicit invalidation (*dngos la gnod*).

are merely conventionally existent, having refuted any phenomenon that exists on its own. This is the consummate definitive meaning taught to those of extremely sharp faculties, those disciples with the heritage of the Mahāyāna who can understand the meaning of emptiness as dependent arising.

In the Prāsaṅgika system, the literal statements in texts like the *Hundred Thousand Verse Mother*, which explicitly apply the qualifier *ultimately* to the object of negation, are definitive in meaning. Moreover, even when the words of a qualifier *ultimately* are not applied to the object of negation, as in the *Heart Sūtra*, it should be understood in these concise demonstrations as it is in the contexts of the extensive explanations, where *intrinsically* is also applied to the object of negation. Even when this is not applied, as in "no form, no feeling . . . ,"[31] there is no difference in the fact that all the sūtras that teach emptiness are definitive in meaning. This is because when a qualifier is applied in one context, as in the *Hundred Thousand Verses*, all the other sūtras with its shared subject matter also are understood perforce to make this qualification. Therefore, when a *Mother Sūtra* states, "no form, no feeling . . . ," it is not teaching that form and feeling do not exist. Rather, it is teaching that they do not *intrinsically* exist; there is a big difference.

In the last wheel, it is taught that the imagined nature (*kun btags*) does not exist on its own, and that the dependent (*gzhan dbang*) and consummate natures (*yongs grub*) exist on their own. This is provisional in meaning. The basis in another intention is that it intends the mere conventional existence of the distinction between what is posited by nominal designation and what is not, in accord with the assertions of the three natures according to proponents of Mind-Only. The purpose is to prevent disciples who, even though they have the Mahāyāna heritage, would develop a view of annihilation—that holds that karmic causality, bondage, and liberation do not exist—if they were taught from the beginning the subtle selflessness of phenomena that negates phenomena's existence on their own. By training their continua through teaching the coarse selflessness of phenomena, such as the emptiness of a separate substance of the apprehended and the apprehender, later they are led to the subtle selflessness of phenomena, such as is taught in the middle wheel. Therefore, there is a difference between the disciples of the middle and last wheels in terms of the sharpness of their faculties.

As for explicit invalidation of the literal meaning, no functionality can be posited whatsoever in the position of those who assert that phenomena exist on their own. Yet the functioning of everything is suitable in the position of those who assert emptiness; the reasons for this are shown in texts like the *Fundamental Verses of the Middle Way*. In general, a sūtra that is provisional in meaning need not be provisional with another intention, but what is provisional in meaning with another intention necessarily has the threefold criteria of having a basis in another intention, etc.

---

31. *Heart Sūtra* (H. 499, vol. 88), 45b.

Moreover, it says in the *Inquiry of King Dhāraṇīśvara Sūtra*, "Noble child, a skilled jeweler knows well how to clean gems . . . ,"[32] using the example of a jeweler cleaning a jewel with a threefold wash and threefold rub. This shows how the Victorious One, knowing the constituents of sentient beings, teaches in three stages to guide disciples. First, he brings them to enter the disciplinary doctrine through generating aversion for cyclic existence by means of the discourse on impermanence, suffering, and no-self. Later, through the discourse on emptiness and signlessness, he brings them to understand the way of the Tathāgatas. Then, he brings these sentient beings to the domain of the buddha through the discourse of the irreversible wheel. In this way, the three wheels have different meanings; the three wheels are based upon differences among the continua of the disciples of Mahāyāna and Hīnayāna. This is the way of guiding a single individual through the stages of the path. Thereby, this sūtra shows both the ways of guiding on the path those who at that time possess a Hīnayāna heritage, and the stages of the path for those who from the beginning are determined to have the Mahāyāna heritage.

One might think, "According to how proponents of Mind-Only explain, the dependent and consummate natures both truly exist; and according to Madhyamaka, they are both empty of true existence. If both of these positions must be posited as the meaning of this sūtra, then one meaning of the sūtra would negate the other, and there would be an internal contradiction on the part of the author."

This is not a problem. In relation to the mind of a disciple who is a proponent of Mind-Only, the meaning of the last wheel sūtras is that the dependent and consummate natures truly exist. In relation to the mind of a Mādhyamika, these two lacking true existence is the meaning of the middle wheel. They are taught this way based on the minds of the disciples, so there is no negation of the sūtra's meaning, nor is there an internal contradiction on the part of the author. Furthermore, even though the meaning of the subject matter in the *Sūtra Explaining the Intent* teaches that the dependent nature and consummate nature truly exist, this is not the viewpoint of the author's own system; no truly existent phenomenon can be posited there in any time, place, or philosophical system. As it is said in the *Introduction to the Middle Way*: "The buddhas never taught the existence of entities."[33] No buddhas taught in any scripture the true existence of entities as their own system. The *Descent to Laṅkā Sūtra* is cited to establish this in the autocommentary:

> The three existences are mere imputation,
> Essentially without entity.[34]

---

32. See the *Inquiry of King Dhāraṇīśvara Sūtra* (*Tathāgatamahākaruṇānirdeśasūtra, de bzhin gshegs pa'i snying rje chen po nges par bstan pa'i mdo*) P. 814, vol. 32, p. 300, 176b.4–177a.3.

33. Candrakīrti, *Introduction to the Middle Way* VI.68.

34. *Descent to Laṅka Sūtra* (H. 110, vol. 51), 259b. Candrakīrti, *Autocommentary on the "Introduction to the Middle Way"* (D. 3862, vol. 102), 270a.

Likewise, the *Sūtra Explaining the Intent* says that if the dependent nature is apprehended as not truly existent, then all three natures are denigrated. Even so, this is taught from the perspective of those disciples who cannot understand the meaning of emptiness as dependent arising even though they have the Mahāyāna heritage. From the perspective of disciples with supreme intelligence who can understand this, realizing the dependent nature as not truly existent is a supreme method for negating the view of denigration.

Furthermore, the middle wheel is definitive in meaning and the last wheel is provisional in meaning, but this does not contradict the fact that in the perspective of some disciples, the last wheel is definitive in meaning and the middle wheel is provisional in meaning. The *Four Hundred Verses* says:

> For those who are not sublime, apprehending a self is supreme;
> They should not be taught selflessness.[35]

It says that from among the two teachings of self and selflessness, the former is supreme for some disciples. Therefore, until one is able to understand emptiness and interdependence without contradiction, the division is made between some phenomena being truly existent and some that are not. Thereby, disciples are progressively guided through teaching selflessness partially, as was cited earlier in the verses from the *Reason in Sixty Verses* and the *Precious Garland*.[36]

One might wonder, "If the framework of the three natures as presented by proponents of Mind-Only is described as provisional in meaning, then how do Prāsaṅgikas understand the three natures in their own system?"

This is explained as follows. Phenomena such as forms are the dependent nature. Their intrinsic existence is the imagined nature. Their emptiness of intrinsic existence is the consummate nature. This framework for the three natures is reasonable because, for instance, a multicolored rope that is the basis of designation is posited as the dependent nature; the snake designated with respect to that while not existing is posited as the imagined nature; and the genuine reality with respect to the actual snake is posited as the consummate nature. This is stated in the autocommentary on the *Introduction to the Middle Way*: "The snake is designated upon the dependently arisen assemblage of the rope."[37] And later in that text, "The viewpoint of the sūtras

35. Āryadeva, *Four Hundred Verses* XII.12ab (D. 3846, vol. 97), 13b; English trans. in Sonam, *Āryadeva's Four Hundred Stanzas on the Middle Way*, 244.

36. The passages cited earlier in the text were Nāgārjuna, *Reason in Sixty Verses* v. 30 and *Precious Garland* vv. 394–396.

37. Candrakīrti, *Autocommentary on the "Introduction to the Middle Way"* (D. 3862, vol. 102), 282b.

is explained after understanding the framework of the three natures."[38] Based on this explanation, the chapter of Maitreya's Inquiry in the *Mother* is shown to be definitive in meaning and the chapter of Maitreya's Inquiry in the *Sūtra Explaining the Intent* is shown to be provisional in meaning.

To summarize the meaning of the chapter of Maitreya's Inquiry in the *Mother*, the teaching of the subtle emptiness should be applied to each part by understanding the basis of designation for a phenomenon such as a form, which is the aspect of the dependent nature; the designated phenomenon, which is the aspect of the imagined nature; and its emptiness of that, the aspect of the consummate nature. To illustrate this with a form, the form is the *designated form* (*rnam btags kyi gzugs*); the intrinsically existent form is the *imagined form* (*kun btags kyi gzugs*); and the emptiness that is the form's emptiness of intrinsic existence is the *basic nature form* (*chos nyid kyi gzugs*). The first one is a genuine form; the latter two are nominal forms. It is said to apply to other phenomena in the same way.

Therefore, in the Madhyamaka's own system, all three natures are equally without true existence, and equally conventionally existent. If you know this well, then it is easy to establish as provisional in meaning the teaching of the dependent and consummate natures truly existing in the chapter of Maitreya's Inquiry from the *Sūtra Explaining the Intent*. An elaborate treatment of this should be known from texts like the *Essence of Eloquence* that distinguish between the definitive and provisional meanings.

Next, it is said: One might say, 'There is a contradiction [if impermanence] is conventional . . .'[39] What follows here is the way to understand the path to realize the subtle and coarse four truths and their sixteen aspects, such as impermanence. There are two paths: one is the path to realize the coarse sixteen aspects such as impermanence explained in the two Abhidharma texts according to the lower philosophical systems; the other is the path to realize the subtle sixteen aspects according to Prāsaṅgika. The Svātantrikas and below accept that one can be liberated from existence even by just the former path.

Also, they accept that after directly realizing the selflessness (among the sixteen aspects) that is the emptiness of a person existing as a self-subsisting substance, one must apply a method to cultivate a path that produces the actual path that brings liberation and other features. The *Compendium of Metaphysics* (*Abhidharmasamuccaya*) says that the mental engagement of selflessness eliminates the afflictions, and the rest of the features are methods for this complete purification.[40] The *Commentary on Epistemology* (*Pramāṇavarttika*) also says this: "The view of emptiness liberates; other

---

38. Candrakīrti, *Autocommentary on the "Introduction to the Middle Way"* (D. 3862, vol. 102), 283a.

39. Śāntideva, *Way of the Bodhisattva* IX.7cd.

40. See Asaṅga, *Compendium of Metaphysics* (*Abhidharmasamuccaya*, D. 4049), 85a.

meditations are for this purpose."[41] "Emptiness" here refers to the selflessness that is the emptiness of the existence of a self-subsisting substance. Svātantrikas and below do not understand the selflessness of persons as the emptiness of existing on its own; they also do not understand that to apprehend a person existing on its own is to apprehend the self of persons. This is due to the fact that they maintain that these things do exist on their own.

Prāsaṅgikas accept that to realize the subtle selflessness of persons, it is necessary to realize the emptiness of a person's intrinsic existence. Also, Prāsaṅgikas accept that the truth of the path is the realization of this kind of subtle selflessness, and due to this, that the truth of cessation is the elimination of those potentials (*sa bon*) to be relinquished. It is through cultivation, having realized the sixteen subtle aspects with these kinds of features, that it is held to be necessary to become liberated from cyclic existence. Here, the emptiness of a person existing on its own is understood as the selflessness of persons, and apprehending a person existing on its own is understood as apprehending the self of persons. This is due to the fact that nothing is accepted to exist on its own, even conventionally. One should know that this is the meaning of the response below to disputations such as, "By seeing the [four] truths one is liberated . . . "[42]

One might wonder, "How are each of the sixteen aspects such as impermanence divided into two?"

The coarse truth of suffering is the contaminated aggregates produced by the apprehension of self that apprehends the person to exist as a self-subsisting substance. The karma and afflictions that are brought about by this apprehension of self is the coarse truth of origin. The coarse cessation is the relinquishment of manifest afflictions explained in the two Abhidharma texts, those that are temporarily relinquished based on cultivation after directly realizing the selflessness that is the emptiness of the existence of a self-subsisting substance. The path to the direct realization of this kind of selflessness is the coarse truth of the path. The qualities of impermanence, suffering, and so on that characterize this kind of four truths are the sixteen coarse aspects. Furthermore, one should know the subtle truth of suffering as the contaminated aggregates produced by the apprehension of a self of persons that is the apprehension of a person existing on its own. Their qualities, along with the division within sixteen subtle aspects such as impermanence, should be understood to apply like before.

Yet this kind of division made in terms of subtle and coarse is only made upon a qualified basis, like the truth of suffering; one cannot make the division between subtle and coarse in terms of qualities like impermanence and suffering on their own (*rang ngos nas*). This is because, as some intellectuals claim, the former and

41. Dharmakīrti, *Commentary on Epistemology* II.255 (D. 4210), 117a.

42. Śāntideva, *Way of the Bodhisattva* IX.40.

latter types of impermanence are both subtle impermanence. The coarse truth of cessation, as is explained in the two Abhidharma texts, is posited from the aspect of merely relinquishing manifest afflictions temporarily. While this is the truth of cessation explained in the Abhidharma, since it is not based on the elimination of any potentials to be relinquished, this is not posited as the genuine truth of cessation. It is just as it is in the case of an Arhat as explained in the two Abhidharma texts.

This Prāsaṅgika system accepts that it is suitable to have yogic perception that directly realizes the coarse sixteen aspects such as impermanence in the continuum of an ordinary being prior to the attainment of the path of seeing that realizes the subtle selflessness. It is clearly said that they have it: "There is no problem; [impermanence] is conventional for yogis; yet for the world, seen to be ultimate."[43] This system is not like that of the Sautrāntika, Mind-Only, and Svātantrika because they claim that yogic perception is necessarily a sublime being's gnosis.

Next, "If ultimately there is nirvana . . . "[44] Here is a brief explanation of the framework for cyclic existence and nirvana. "Liberation" and "nirvana" have the same meaning. One might think, "What is this cyclic existence that is to be liberated from?"

The aspect of continuously taking birth, or being born due to the force of karma and afflictions, is the actual cyclic existence. Nāgārjuna said: "The suffering in this life is called 'existence.'"[45] Also, the *Succession of Lives* says: "Liberation, with little difficulty, from the fortress of birth . . . " Further, to put forth separately the agent, action, and object in relation to cyclic existence: the ones that cycle are the sentient beings who take birth powerlessly; the place of cycling is in the appropriating aggregates; the way of cycling is to cycle without the slightest interruption—from the summit of existence to the hell of utter torment. The conditions for cycling are the forces of karma and the afflictions.

Furthermore, the cycle in the lower realms is due to the forces of actions that are unmeritorious and their afflictions. There is no effort needed for this; it proceeds naturally. The cycle in the realms of happiness is through the forces of merit, unwavering actions (*mi g.yo ba'i las*), and their afflictions; these are difficult because there is great effort necessary to accomplish their causes. A Vinaya text states that those who go to the lower realms from the higher and lower realms are as numerous as specks of dust on the great earth, whereas those who go to the higher realms from those two realms are like the dust collected on a fingernail.[46] The commentary on *Reason in Sixty Verses* says: "The essence of cyclic existence is the five appropriating

---

43. Śāntideva, *Way of the Bodhisattva* IX.8ab.

44. Śāntideva, *Way of the Bodhisattva* IX.13.

45. Nāgārjuna, *Letter to a Friend* (*Suhṛllekha*) (D. 4182, vol. 173), 46a.

46. See *Foundation of the Vinaya* (*Vinayavastu*) (H. 1, vol. 1), 122a–124b.

aggregates."[47] The *Commentary on Epistemology* says: "The aggregates of cyclic existence are suffering . . . "[48] These texts mainly teach the appropriating aggregates that take birth and cycle through the forces of karma and afflictions to be the truth of suffering; the actual cyclic existence was explained above.

To describe again the way of cycling and its domain, the *Anthology of Training* (*Śikṣāsamuccaya*) cites the *Vast Display* (*Lalitavistara*):

> The three realms are ablaze with the sufferings of aging and sickness;
> This is the blazing fire of death without a protector.
> Beings are constantly bewildered about the way out of existence,
> Like a bee circling around inside a jar.[49]

And,

> Through the force of ignorance, craving existence,
> The unwise constantly cycle in the five classes of beings,
> Taking the three paths of humans, god realms, and lower realms.
> They spin like a potter's wheel.[50]

It is said that beings cycle within five continua like a bee in a jar and like a potter's wheel. In the autocommentary on the *Madhyamakāvatāra*, the way that beings powerlessly circle within cyclic existence through the force of the view of the transitory collective (*'jig lta*) that apprehends me and mine is said to be like the mechanism of a pulley. There are said to be six qualities of similarity between them: As a pulley is tied with a rope, sentient beings are bound by karma and afflictions. As it depends on something to turn it, sentient beings in cyclic existence depend on a restless and untrained consciousness. As it circles all around from the top to the bottom of a well, beings circle from the summit of existence to the hell of utter torment. As it goes down naturally, but takes great effort to pull it up, beings naturally go to the lower realms, but need great effort to go to the higher realms. As it is difficult to determine the sequence of progression when it is spinning, it is difficult to determine the sequence of progression of the twelve links of dependent arising when beings cycle through existence. As it turns, there is pressure pushing on all sides; similarly, when beings cycle in existence, they are constantly afflicted by the three sufferings.

---

47. Candrakīrti, *Commentary on "Reason in Sixty Verses"* (D. 3864, vol. 103), 6a.

48. Dharmakīrti, *Commentary on Epistemology* II.147 (D. 4210), 113a.

49. *Vast Display* (H. 96, vol. 48), 142b; cited in Śāntideva, *Anthology of Training* (D. 3940, vol. 111), 114b; English trans. in Goodman, *The Training Anthology of Śāntideva*, 201.

50. *Vast Display* (H. 96, vol. 48), 142b; cited in Śāntideva, *Anthology of Training* (D. 3940, vol. 111), 114b; English trans. in Goodman, *The Training Anthology of Śāntideva*, 201.

As for nirvana, the liberation from cyclic existence, Nāgārjuna said, "The cessation of this is liberation . . . "[51] The analytical cessation that has relinquished all afflictive obscurations without exception is liberation. Further, the Vaibhāṣikas consider the essence of nirvana to be an unconditioned, permanent entity and an implicative negation. The Sautrāntikas and above consider it to be unconditioned and a non-implicative negation. Svātantrikas assert that nirvana has aspects of both of the two truths, while Prāsaṅgikas accept it to be ultimate truth exclusively.

To divide nirvana in terms of its modes of expression (*sgra brjod rigs*), there is natural nirvana, non-abiding nirvana, nirvana with remainder, and nirvana without remainder. The emptiness that is phenomena's emptiness of true existence is natural nirvana. This and the ultimate truth have the same meaning. In the Prāsaṅgika system, it is not necessarily that natural nirvana is not nirvana, because there is a common ground of the truth of cessation and the ultimate truth. The analytical cessation that has relinquished the two obscurations without exception is the non-abiding nirvana. This and Mahāyāna nirvana, as well as consummate nirvana, have the same meaning.

There are several ways of explaining the difference between nirvana with remainder and nirvana without remainder, and whether or not these are accepted as exclusively Hīnayāna nirvanas. Here, to merely give a rough sketch in the system of Madhyamaka in general, nirvana with remainder is an analytical cessation that has completely relinquished afflictive obscurations and has aggregates of suffering impelled by previous karma and afflictions. Nirvana without remainder is understood as an analytical cessation that has completely relinquished afflictive obscurations and is free from aggregates of suffering impelled by previous karma and afflictions.

Most Vaibhāṣikas and Sautrāntikas, as well as the proponents of Mind-Only following scripture, accept that the engagement with conditioned phenomena ceases at the time of no remainder. The proponents of Mind-Only following reasoning accept no such cessation, since awareness has no beginning or end. Mādhyamikas do not accept that matter or awareness cease at the time of nirvana without remainder. This is because it is held that when it occurs, one is incited by light rays of the Tathāgata's speech, and is thereby brought to enter the Mahāyāna path.

In the *Golden Light* (*Suvarṇaprabhā*) and the *Gateway to the Three Embodiments of Buddhahood* (*Kāyatrayāvatāramukha*) it is said that the two Form Bodies are the nirvana with remainder and the Truth Body (*chos sku*) is the nirvana without remainder.[52] It is nirvana from the aspect of being free from the suffering of the two obscurations; it is said to be with or without remainder from the aspect of whether

51. Nāgārjuna, *Letter to a Friend* (D. 4182, vol. 173), 46a.

52. See *Golden Light* (H. 514, vol. 89), 238b. Nāgamitra's *Gateway to the Three Embodiments of Buddhahood* does not explicitly mention nirvana without remainder but does describe the Truth Body as unconditioned. See Nāgamitra, *Gateway to the Three Embodiments of Buddhahood* (D. 3890), 4a.

or not there is a remainder of manifest appearance for disciples. Yet this is not an actual nirvana because an actual nirvana must be the unconditioned truth of cessation, and the two Form Bodies are not this. Even the Truth Body is not necessarily the truth of cessation. The *Fundamental Verses of the Middle Way* says: "Nirvana is unconditioned,"[53] and the *Treasury of Metaphysics* says: "There are three types of unconditioned phenomena: space and the two cessations."[54]

The unique way of presenting the two nirvanas with and without remainder in the Prāsaṅgika system is as follows. The nirvana without the remainder of appearances as true is the nirvana without remainder from the perspective of a meditative equipoise that manifests the complete cessation of the nature of the aggregates from the beginning in a Hīnayāna Arhat who has relinquished all the afflictions. From the perspective of a postmeditation that has arisen from meditative equipoise, the nirvana that has the remainder of appearances as true is understood as the nirvana with remainder. In this way, the sequence for actualizing these two nirvanas is different from others because first one actualizes the nirvana without remainder in meditative equipoise, and then one actualizes the nirvana with remainder in the context of postmeditation.

---

53. Nāgārjuna, *Fundamental Verses of the Middle Way* XXV.13c.

54. Vasubandhu, *Treasury of Metaphysics* I.5 (D. 4089, vol. 140), 2a.

APPENDIX C

The Buddhist Philosophies Section from the Concise Summary of the Philosophies of the "Wish-Fulfilling Treasury"

Introduction

Concise Summary of Philosophies from the "Wish-Fulfilling Treasury" by Mipam outlines a distinctive presentation of philosophical systems according to the Nyingma school, and Longchenpa in particular. This genre of presenting a hierarchy of philosophical systems is a common way Tibetans have organized the diversity of Buddhist traditions inherited from India. These hierarchical schemes are attempts to make them all hang together. One of the benefits of this genre is that it serves pedagogical purposes for understanding the depth and complexity of Buddhism. In the hierarchy of philosophical systems, each level of Buddhist philosophy can be seen to convey an important message on its own terms, offering real insight into understanding the nature of the world. Yet on a higher level, the problems of a lower level are exposed and resolved within a new system. Thus, each higher level, to a certain extent, transcends and includes the lower ones. This is because not everything is thrown out from the systems of the lower philosophies; some elements in the lower systems are instrumental to reaching a higher understanding. Thus, the structure functions something like a ladder through which one can progressively ascend to a more comprehensive understanding of the Buddhist message.

The translation that follows is an excerpt from Mipam's presentation of the Buddhist philosophical schools that summarizes Longchenpa's discussion in his

Wish-Fulfilling Treasury.[1] What is unique about the framework of philosophies in this Nyingma tradition is that, in addition to presenting a hierarchy of ascending views of the philosophical systems within Sūtra (Vaibhāṣika, Sautrāntika, Mind-Only, and Madhyamaka), the views continue to ascend into tantra, culminating with the Great Perfection. The systems of tantra are complex, and in them we can find the influence of insights from Mind-Only and Madhyamaka, as well as their culmination.

The Buddhist Philosophies Section from the Concise Summary of the Philosophies of the "Wish-Fulfilling Treasury"

1. Another translation of this text can be found interspersed in the pages of Herbert Guenther, *Buddhist Philosophy in Theory and Practice* (Berkeley: Shambhala Publications, 1971).

The Buddhist Philosophies Section from the Concise Summary of the Philosophies of the "Wish-Fulfilling Treasury"

By Mipam

Within the Buddhist philosophies to be accepted, there are two: (1) the Hīnayāna and (2) the Mahāyāna.

1. Hīnayāna

Due to a progression of capacities, there are two vehicles within the Hīnayāna as well: (1) the Disciples and (2) the Self-Realized Ones.

1. *Disciples*

Regarding the Disciples, there is a threefold presentation of (1) schools, (2) nature, and (3) philosophy.

1. SCHOOLS

There are eighteen schools: initially, there were two main schools—the Mahāsāṅghikas and the Sthāviras. The Mahāsāṅghikas split into eight schools: the subsect of the Mahāsāṅghikas, the Ekavyahārikas, the Lokottaravādins, the Bahuśrutīyas, the Nityavādins, the Caityakas, the Pūrvaśailas, and the Uttaraparaśailas. The Sthāviras split into ten schools: the Haimavatas, the Sarvāstivādins, the Hetuvādins, the Vātsīputrīyas, the Dharmottaras, the Bhadrayānikas, the Saṃmitīyas, the Bahudeśakas, the Dharmadeśakas, and the Bhadravarṣikas.[2]

Each of these has distinct claims. These, and the way they are refuted, should be known from the *Precious Wish-Fulfilling Treasury*.

2. NATURE

Disciples abide in pure discipline as the foundation, and on the basis of the aggregates (*phung*), constituents (*khams*), and sense-fields (*skye mched*), which are the objects of knowledge, they study and contemplate the unerring manner of the process and counter-process of the four truths. Thus having eliminated superimpositions, they engage in the path through upholding the four disciplines of virtuous practice: not returning abuse with abuse, not returning hatred with hatred, not returning beating with beating, and not returning insult with insult.

Furthermore, by remaining with few desires and with contentment, they take up the twelve practices of training,[3] eat in moderation, and strive not to sleep in the first and last parts of the night. They train on the five paths and thirty-seven factors of awakening;[4] they meditate on repulsiveness, etc. as antidotes to the three poisons, and meditate properly on the meanings of the four truths and dependent arising. By this, they attain the fruition of liberation from the three realms. Since their path and liberation is authentic, it is not to be negated. Also, since their path and liberation must be integrated within the Mahāyāna as well, the common elements are not refuted.

However, the faults of a mind limited to one's own benefit, and the problems of a philosophy that holds as real the aspects of ground, path, and fruition, should be refuted in this context.

---

2. For more on the eighteen schools, see Jeffrey Hopkins *Meditation on Emptiness* (Boston: Wisdom Publications, 1983), 340; 713–719; and Jeffrey Hopkins (trans.), *Maps of the Profound*, 210–218.

3. On the twelve practices of training, see Yisun Zhang, ed., *The Great Tibetan-Chinese Dictionary (bod rgya tshig mdzod chen mo)*, 2023.

4. The thirty-seven factors are (1–4) the four close applications of mindfulness, (5–8) the four correct exertions, (9–12) the four bases of miraculous power, (13–17) the five powers, (18–22) the five strengths, (23–29) the seven branches of awakening, and (30–37) the noble eightfold path.

3. PHILOSOPHY

There is a twofold division of their philosophy: (1) common assertions and (2) distinctive assertions.

1. Common Assertions

There are seven common assertions amongst the Disciples. Since inferior paths need to be refuted, they should be known here in the context of the Mahāyāna since they are said to be paths transcended through knowing and seeing. Regarding this, the seven assertions are (1) objective four truths, (2) the components as ultimate, (3) the Arhat as the consummate nirvana, (4) the denial of the basic consciousness (*kun gzhi*), (5) the denial of the Mahāyāna, (6) the denial of the ten grounds, and (7) the Buddha as an individual.

1. The Assertion of Objective Four Truths

The four truths are the truth of suffering, the truth of origin, the truth of cessation, and the truth of the path. The first is the aspect of the contaminated fruitional aggregates: the sentient beings who are born into the six classes of beings together with their abodes of birth, which is the world of the outer environment. These are the essence of suffering and the abode, or foundation, of suffering because they are connected with the various kinds of the three sufferings.[5]

The origin is the aspect of the cause of that suffering; it is both karma and afflictions. There is karma that is intent, which is mental karma, and there is karma that is intended, which are physical and verbal actions. For each of these there is virtue, vice, and neutral karma. Afflictions are attachment and so forth.

Cessation is the utter pacification of suffering together with its causes. In this, there is cessation with remainder and without remainder. The path is reliance on the five paths within one's continuum—having acknowledged suffering and abandoning its cause, the origin, for the sake of actualizing its cessation.

2. The Assertion of Components as Ultimate

They claim, "The consummate foundational component of macro-forms is the indivisible particle, and the indivisible moment is the foundational component of consciousness. These two exist ultimately; they compose macro-phenomena (*rags pa*)."

3. The Assertion of the Arhat as the Consummate Nirvana

They claim, "Arhats who pass into nirvana without remainder do not fall into samsara because the causes for being born in the three realms have been exhausted.

5. The three sufferings are the suffering of suffering, the suffering of change, and the all-pervasive suffering of conditioned existence.

Also, they do not become buddhas because they have the determined heritage of an Arhat; like a butter-lamp that has run out of oil, they certainly pass into nirvana."

4. The Denial of the Basic Consciousness

They claim, "Other than the existence of a series of the sixfold collection of cognition, there is no basic consciousness because it is not observed. The existence of a foundational mind that is the ground of all is not reasonable because it would be a self of persons."

5. The Denial of Mahāyāna

Although they claim that the Hīnayāna Word (such as the four sections of the Vinaya)[6] are the Buddha's speech, they say that texts like the Perfection of Wisdom in a hundred thousand verses are not the speech of the Buddha. They claim that these Mahāyāna texts ruin the teachings and are the work of demons and extremists because they appear to contradict the three baskets and the four seals."[7]

6. The Denial of Ten Grounds

They claim, "Having seen the truth, it is not possible to remain in samsara for many aeons because only the best beings who are able to gather the accumulations as an ordinary being for three incalculable aeons can become buddhas. Yet nirvana is actualized upon certain discernment in the span of one night, on one seat."

7. The Assertion of the Buddha as an Individual

They say, "Only the best beings, those who can forebear samsara for countless aeons through training in the Disciple's path and gathering accumulations for many aeons, become buddhas. Other ordinary beings cannot because suffering in samsara is great and they are not able to perform the benefit of unruly sentient beings. Therefore, 'the Buddha' is a sublime person, an individual. However, he is not an Emanation Body because there is a remainder—the aspect of maturation such as him bleeding and hurting his back. The Buddha is not constantly in meditative equipoise either because he gets up from meditative concentration and goes on alms rounds, as is said in the scriptures. After passing into nirvana, his benefit to beings ceases."

---

6. The four sections of the Vinaya are the *Vinayavibhaṅga* (*'dul ba rnam 'byed*), the *Vinayavastu* (*'dul ba lung gzhi*), the *Vinayakṣudraka* (*'dul ba phran tshegs*), and the *Vinayauttaragrantha* (*'dul ba gzhung dam pa*). See Yisun Zhang, ed., *The Great Tibetan-Chinese Dictionary*, 1406.

7. The three "baskets" are the three sections of the Buddhist cannon: Sūtra, Vinaya, and Abhidharma. The four "seals" are (1) all conditioned things are impermanent, (2) all contaminated things are suffering, (3) all phenomena are selfless, and (4) nirvana is peace.

2. Refuting Those Assertions

1. Refuting the Objective Four Truths

The four truths are not ultimately established because the foundation—all of the aggregates and constituents, the environment and inhabitants—is not established at all upon analysis. Also, all that is abandoned, remedied, freed, and attained is merely an imputation; it is not established in reality.

2. Refuting the Components as Ultimate

There are no minute material particles that comprise macro-objects because, in the composition of a macro-object, particles would either have to contact on one side or entirely contact. However, if they were to contact on one side, then it would follow that they had parts. And if they were to entirely contact, then it would follow that even a great mass would be merely a minute particle. Hence, it is not possible for composition through contact.

Also, if they were composed without making contact, then in between there would be room for other particles of light and darkness to exist, and in between those particles there would be room for others as well. Therefore, it would follow that within a mustard seed there would be room for the billionfold universe, etc.; reason invalidates this. Furthermore, upon analysis of the positions of sunlight and shade, long and short, and the movement of an arrow, etc., fundamental particles are not found to be truly established.

Temporal moments also do no truly exist because, if they did, a middle moment would either have to contact the preceding and following moments or not. If it did contact, then it would have to happen progressively or all at once. In the former case, it would follow that a moment had parts; and in the latter case, it would follow that an aeon would be one moment. And if there were no contact, then it would follow that there would be another interval of time in between. Furthermore, that moment in the middle would either intervene or not between an initial and final moment. If it did not intervene, there would be no duration through a succession of many moments, yet if it did intervene, since it abides in between, it would follow that it would have two parts—an earlier and later segment.

3. Refuting the Arhat as Consummate

The Arhat is not the consummate nirvana because it is established that

- what is to be abandoned, the entirety of obscurations of heritage, has not been exhausted;
- they possess the heritage of the nature of buddha, which is the luminous and clear nature of mind;
- the defilements are adventitious;

- it is impossible for the continuity of mind to cease while the entirety of defilements has not been exhausted because the causes are complete for a mental body, etc. to be propelled; and
- they need to train from the beginning in the two accumulations to complete abandonment and realization.

4. Refuting the Denial of the Basic Consciousness

The nonexistence of the basic consciousness also is untenable because there would be no continuous process if there were no basic consciousness, which is the support. Taking a body in samsara or averting samsara would not be possible because there would be no support for predispositions, etc. Also, it would not be reasonable for the mind to arise again after a cessation of the sixfold collection of consciousness in which the mind is absent because the continuity would cease and there would be no perpetuating cause. Furthermore, all appearances are established as mind through reasoning by the power of fact, and a limited cognition is not possible to act as the support for predispositions. Hence, it should be known that there is a common foundation, which is the basic consciousness.

5. Refuting the Denial of the Mahāyāna

The nonexistence of the Mahāyāna is also untenable because not only does it not contradict the meaning of the three baskets and the four seals, etc., but it is established as superior to the expressed meaning of the lower vehicles. The Hīnayāna does not have the complete features of the path to become a buddha, whereas in the Mahāyāna, they are complete. The Mahāyāna exists because it is established by reasoning to be the supreme path and fruition.

6. Refuting the Denial of Ten Grounds

There are ten grounds because one is unable to complete all the accumulations without attaining the powers on the ground of an ordinary being, and there are many obstacles on the path due to having many afflictions. Therefore, even after the sublime path has been attained, it is reasonable that there are accumulations to be gathered. Also, there is a means of establishment; this does not contradict the progressive arising of the remedies for the ten obscurations to be eliminated (which are the wisdoms of the ten grounds).

7. Refuting the Buddha as an Individual

If the Buddha were an individual person with the maturation of karma, then the Buddha would not have eliminated obscurations and ignorance. Also, if the benefit of beings ceased upon attaining nirvana, then it would not be reasonable for such a limited individual, without compassion, etc., to be omniscient. When the essence of luminous clarity free from all defilements is actualized at the time of a buddha, there are various appearances in a magical manifestation of emanations due to the influence of disciples to be trained. However, this is not established in the way of an ordinary individual.

2. Distinctive Assertions

This section has two parts: (1) the assertions of the Vaibhāṣika and (2) the assertions of the Sautrāntika.

1. The Assertions of the Vaibhāṣika

To state merely the main Vaibhāṣika assertions, there are seven: (1) five bases of knowledge, (2) disintegration as extrinsic, (3) the three times as substantially established, (4) acceptance of an inexpressible self, (5) cognition as not aware of itself or objects, (6) a property and what it characterizes as distinct, and (7) the non-perishing substance. Although these are a means to know, or understand, the meaning of the scriptures, they are not correct because they are mixed with various adulterations of philosophical positions.

1. The Assertion of Five Bases of Knowledge

(1) The basis of material form is the four causal forms, which are the elements: earth, water, fire, wind; and the eleven resultant forms, which are the five faculties: eye, ear, nose, tongue, body; the five objects: visible form, sound, scent, taste, texture; and the imperceptible forms.
(2) The basis of the main mind (*gtso bo sems*) is the awareness of mere objects—the six consciousnesses such as the visual consciousness. They are believed to directly apprehend their respective objects.
(3) The basis of the accompanying mental states (*sems byung*) is the apprehension of objects' distinguishing features. When divided, there are fifty-one. There are five omnipresent factors: contact, mental engagement, feeling, identification, intention; and there are five ascertaining factors: aspiration, interest, mindfulness, concentration, insight. Since these occur in all minds, they are called "the ten great grounds of mind."

Due to accompanying all virtuous minds, there are eleven virtuous mental states: faith, conscientiousness, pliancy, equanimity, shame, embarrassment, non-attachment, non-aggression, non-stupidity, non-harmfulness, and diligence. There are six root afflictions: attachment, anger, pride, ignorance, afflicted view, and doubt. There are twenty subsidiary afflictions: belligerence, spite, concealment, resentment, jealousy, miserliness, deceit, trickery, haughtiness, aggression, non-shame, non-embarrassment, lethargy, excitement, non-faith, laziness, non-conscientiousness, forgetfulness, distraction, and non-mindfulness. There are four variables: sleep, remorse, determination, and discernment. Thus, there are fifty-one mental states. The main mind and mental states also operate concurrently by means of the five concurrences: support, percept, character, time, and substance.

(4) The basis of the non-associated formations (*ldan min 'du byed*) are the twenty-three that are substantially different from matter and mind: acquisition, cessation of absorption, non-perceptual absorption, non-perception, the life-force, similar type, birth, aging, abiding, impermanence, words, phrases, letters, ordinary person, engagement, relationship, distinctive ascertainment, speed, sequence, time, place, number, and collection.[8]

(5) The basis of the unconditioned are the three that do not arise from causes and conditions: space, analytical cessation, and non-analytical cessation.

2. The Assertion of Disintegration as Extrinsic

Four properties characterize a conditioned phenomenon such as a pot: arising, aging, abiding, and disintegrating. These four characterize conditioned phenomena by means of four further characterizing properties: the arising of arising, the abiding of abiding, the aging of aging, and the disintegrating of disintegrating. The arising of arising is the production of the original arising; through an original arising, there are the seven other qualities—an eightfold production. With abiding, etc., it should be known that each of the other properties are likewise applied as eightfold. Moreover, they assert that (1) what is characterized and (2) its property are different—like a house that is characterized by [the presence of] a crow.

3. The Assertion of the Three Times as Substantially Established[9]

They assert that the past and the future exist on their own, so all three times substantially exist in the present. When it is said, "As such, it would follow that the past and future would be seen," they respond that the past and future are not seen because they are concealed by having ceased and having not arisen [respectively]. They claim that this is not like the Sāṃkhya assertion because of being a continuum with a momentary nature.

4. The Assertion of an Inexpressible Self[10]

They assert, "A single self who is the performer of actions and the experiencer of their results needs to be asserted because a causal relationship is untenable otherwise.

---

8. Asaṅga's *Compendium of Metaphysics* (*Abhidharmasamuccaya*) enumerates twenty-four, including "non-attainment." See Asaṅga, *Compendium of Metaphysics* (D. 4049), 52a; see also Mipam, *Gateway of Scholarship*, 113–114.

9. This is an assertion of the Sarvāstivāda.

10. This is an assertion of the Pudgalavāda.

Therefore, we assert that the self is neither the same as the aggregates nor different from the aggregates; it is also inexpressible as either permanent or impermanent." The assertion of this inexpressible self is a claim of the Vātsīputrīyas, etc., and is not held by all the Vaibhāṣika schools. It is set forth here because it is claimed by a specific faction within the Vaibhāṣikas, among the Vaibhāṣikas and the Sautrāntikas.

5. *The Assertion of Cognition as Not Aware of Itself or Objects*

They assert, "It is not suitable for cognition to be self-aware because cognition cannot be something known and a means of knowledge. Also, cognitive faculties are aware of objects directly. However, in cognition there are no representations (*rnam pa*), like in a crystal ball. Hence, an object is simply known.

6. *The Assertion of a Property and What it Characterizes as Distinct*

They claim, "In the case a bovine, the dewlap characterizes the cow. These three [what is characterized, property, and instantiation] exist as substantially different. If they were substantially the same, then object and agent would be the same and this is untenable."

7. *The Assertion of the Non-Perishing Substance*

They assert, "Acquisition (*thob pa*), which is a specific non-associated formation, is performed karma called "the non-perishing" (*chud mi za ba*). It is like a loan document. Its essence is neutral and through its force the continuity of karma does not cease."

Investing Those Assertions

1. *Investigating the Five Bases of Knowledge*

(1.1) All the causal and resultant forms are refuted by the refutation of minute particles. Also, imperceptible forms are not genuine forms; they are not established in reality other than as imputations upon the mere formations that impel a continuity of karma, such as virtuous action in dependence upon body and speech.

(1.2) The main mind and (1.3) mental states also have a manifold and momentary nature; they are not established in indivisible moments, nor found anywhere internally or externally. Since what is known is not a means of knowledge, self-awareness is also not ultimately established, nor is awareness of what is other, because no relationship is established between awareness and an object other than awareness, and because awareness is not established simultaneously with an object nor at another time.

(1.4) Non-associated formations are not substantially established because they are merely imputed upon the states of material forms and minds; they are neither the same nor different from them. (1.5) Unconditioned phenomena also are not at all substantially established; they are nothing but mere imputations designating the aspect of a negated object's absence.

2. Investigating Disintegration as Extrinsic

"Disintegration" refers to a conditioned phenomenon like a pot that does not remain for a second instant from the time it was established. The specific properties of a conditioned phenomenon abide like the wetness of water. However, if there were disintegration separate from that entity, then the entity itself would not disintegrate and disintegration would be causeless. This follows because an entity that is separate from disintegration would not be disintegrating, and disintegration would remain independently, apart from entities. If there were disintegration apart from entities, of what would the disintegration be? What would be designated as the cause for its disintegrating? If an entity and its disintegration are simultaneous, then an entity does not disintegrate by that cause; if they occur at different times, then disintegration is meaningless.

3. Investigating the Three Times as Substantially Established

The three times are not substantially established because everything would be the present if entities, which ceased in the past and have not yet arisen in the future, were to presently exist. If it is said, "The past exists merely as the property of what has ceased and is past," we respond that this is merely imputation. It is not substantially established in reality. "Time" is merely a convention applied in dependence upon entities; it does not exist to the slightest degree as an autonomous substance.

4. Investigating the Inexpressible Self

The inexpressible self does not exist because there is no third alternative within a direct contradiction of being the same or different from the aggregates, or being permanent or impermanent. Therefore, it should be known that since it cannot be expressed as one of four alternatives, the self is not an entity.

5. Investigating Cognition as Not Aware of Itself or Objects

It is untenable that cognition is not aware of itself because "self-awareness" expresses, merely conventionally, the clear experience in one's continuum of pleasure, and so forth, without relying on anything else. If this did not exist, all the conventions of perception would not makes sense. Hence, it would follow that all presentations of conventional confined perception (*tshur mthong*) would vanish.

The faculties, which are material, do not have the capacity to cognize objects. If cognition did not have various representations of appearing objects, absurd consequences would follow, such as objects not appearing. Thus, their position is refuted.

6. *Investigating a Property and What is Characterized as Distinct*

Other than just being selected out of what is mutually dependent, a property and what is characterized by it are not separate in reality. This follows because, if fire were different from heat, it would follow that fire could be cold. Since fireless heat is not found anywhere, fire and heat are not different.

7. *Investigating the Non-Perishing Substance*

"The non-perishing substance" is nothing other than the production of the effects of an action because an action and its effects are just mutually dependent. There is no means of establishing the existence of an entity called "non-perishing substance" that is separate from material form and mind. Also, "acquisition" is refuted in general, and specifically, such a substance is untenable and invalidated by reasoning, there being no purpose or power in it and so forth.

2. The Assertions of the Sautrāntika

Distinct from the concordant philosophical tenets shared between Vaibhāṣikas and Sautrāntikas, there are seven unique assertions of the Sautrāntika: (1) four conditions of production, (2) appearance as mind, (3) objects as remote phenomena, (4) no gap between particles, (5) the faculties having capacity, (6) non-associated formations as imputations, and (7) nirvana as a non-entity. The claims of these seven philosophical tenets are also not the correct view because they carry the problems of realism.

1. *The Assertion of the Four Conditions of Production*

They claim, "The causal condition (*rgyu rkyen*) is the essential producer—the mere propensity to assist in the production of an effect. The dominant condition (*bdag rkyen*) is the producer of the distinctive features of an effect that is the mere non-obstruction of its arising. The percept condition (*dmigs rkyen*) is whatever is the object of a cognition. The concordant immediately preceding condition (*mtshungs pa de ma thag rkyen*) is the producer of a later cognition of similar type, immediately following the cessation of a previous cognition.

"Regarding this, five types of causes are subsumed within the causal condition: the concordant cause, the omnipresent cause, the cause of equal fortune, the productive cause, and the co-emergent cause. Also, the mind and mental states arise from the four conditions. The two perceptionless absorptions arise from three conditions, excluding the percept condition. The others, all non-associated formations and material forms, arise from two conditions—the causal condition and the dominant condition."

2. *The Assertion of Appearance as Mind*

They assert that all appearances—such as universals (*don spyi*), clear appearances of absence, and objects that are particulars—are actually one's mind. This assertion accords with the claim of the proponents of true representations.

3. *The Assertion of Objects as Remote Phenomena*

They claim, "In the appearances of universals and clear appearances of absence, there are no objects that are particulars other than the mere appearance. Objects that are particulars seem to be directly perceived, yet the external object transmits to the cognition a representation that is similar to itself. The cognition's representation resembles the object, but the object (like a pot) is never directly seen. The appearing pot and its location are inseparable in perception, yet the object is remote. In the first moment, the representation of the external object—which is the result of the assemblage of the three conditions of object, faculty, and cognition—appears like an image in a mirror. Since it is experienced as a semblance of the object, there is the convention of saying, 'Cognition experiences the object.'"

4. *The Assertion of No Gaps Between Particles*

They assert, "When macro-objects are composed, it is not reasonable for minute particles to either have gaps in between them or not. Therefore, while there are no gaps, they are also not joined. Hence, they contact without joining. Or, since there are no gaps, they join without any surface contact. This is called 'joining without contact.'"

5. *The Assertion of the Faculties Having Capacity*

They claim, "The substance of a faculty is not remote. Rather, it is the capacity to produce its respective cognition, such as a visual cognition. Furthermore, the faculty arises from the power of the previous cognition, and the visual cognition, etc. arise in dependence on the faculty. Therefore, it is established through an invariant process."

6. *The Assertion of Non-Associated Formations as Imputations*

They claim, "Non-associated formations such as birth and decay are not established as either the same or different from a material form and a mind and mental state. Therefore, they are imputations; they are mere names—like 'rabbit horn.'"

7. *The Assertion of Nirvana as a Non-Entity*

They assert that nirvana in the three vehicles is merely the cessation of objects, indivisible with the basic field of reality, having stopped the continuity of aggregates together with their latencies—like a cloud dissolving into space. The assertion of nirvana as nothing whatsoever accords with the Vaibhāṣika assertion; however, the Sautrāntikas do not claim the existence of a separate substance that is freedom.

Investigating the Way of Those Assertions

1. *Investigating the Four Conditions of Production*

Arising through conditions is not ultimately established, when arising is analyzed as to

- whether or not a cause and effect meet,
- whether or not a cause and effect occur at the same time or at a different time,
- whether an effect is the production of an existent or nonexistent thing, and
- whether something arises from itself, etc.—in any of the four alternatives of production.

2/3. Investigating Appearance as Mind and Objects as Remote Phenomena

If appearances are mind and objects are remote, then it is difficult to reasonably maintain the categories of evident and remote phenomena for warranted objects. Also, since remote objects are suitable to appear even while not existing, external objects are not established as truly existent.

4. Investigating No Gaps Between Particles

Furthermore, it would follow that minute particles would become one if they had no gaps between them. And if they did not contact, or join, then it would follow that they have gaps between them; there is no third alternative.

5. Investigating the Faculties Having Capacity

The capacity of faculties is also refuted because faculties are ultimately refuted. Conventionally, since it is sufficient that the faculty itself generates cognition, there is not much purpose in attributing *capacity* to faculties.

6. Investigating Non-Associated Formations as Imputations

If non-associated formations were exclusively imputations, then impermanence [which is one of the non-associated formations] would not be an object of knowledge; therefore, it would follow that this would be a philosophical tenet of the Guhyakas, the proponents of permanence.

7. Investigating Nirvana as a Non-Entity

Nirvana is not merely the non-entity that is a ceased continuity because the Hīnayāna nirvana is not final since the obscurations have not been exhausted. Also, the buddha is not a ceased continuity because the benefit of beings has not been completed, nor is there a cause for the cessation of wisdom.

2. *Self-Realized Ones*

People with the heritage of a Self-Realized One are those of mediocre capacity. Through the power of previous training, at the time of their last existence they observe the authentic meaning by means of meditating on dependent arising itself. Through this, they realize the selflessness of persons, and half of the selflessness of phenomena because they know that perceived objects do not intrinsically exist. They attain the fruition of a Self-Realized Arhat; even so, this is understood to be inferior to that of the Mahāyāna, which is different.

Moreover, all inner and outer phenomena arise by means of dependent origination: outwardly, in dependence upon a seed, a sprout arises, etc., and internally, due to ignorance, there arises old age and death. Regarding this, in a former life, due to the existence of *ignorance*—not knowing the authentic meaning—one accumulates karma that establishes this life, which is *formation*. Due to this, *consciousness*—the cause that propels existence and the propelled effect—is established. Due to consciousness, the fourfold *name and form*, which comprise the aggregates, the fetal mass (*mer mer po*), etc., is established.

From this, the six *sense-fields*, such as the eyes, are established. From the sense-fields occurs *contact*, which is the coming together of object, faculty, and cognition. Due to this there is *feeling*; and from feeling there is *craving* for taking in or rejecting objects. Due to craving, there is *grasping* that takes hold of objects. From this there is the accumulation of karma that accomplishes existence called *existence*. From existence there is *birth* in the six classes of beings; from birth, there is *old age and death*.

Among these twelve, three are afflictions: ignorance, craving, and grasping; two are karma: formations and existence; and the remaining seven are the heap of suffering. In this way, from afflictions there is karma, from karma there is suffering, and afflictions and karma arise again from the basis of suffering. Thereby, until ignorance has been averted, the cycle of dependent arising goes on continuously.

The way that Self-Realized Ones meditate is like this: They look at the bones in a cemetery and acknowledge that this arises from death and that death in turn arises from birth, up through to ignorance. By understanding that ignorance is what is to be eliminated through the insight that realizes selflessness, they rely on the path in their own continua. In this way, through reflecting on the stages of arising, "Since old age and death are the essence of suffering and they arise from birth . . .," they realize the truth of suffering. Through reflecting on the stages of cessation, "Through birth ceasing, old age and death cease . . .," they engage the truth of cessation. Through reflecting on the stages of arising, "Since ignorance is the root of origin, formation arises from it," they realize the truth of origin. Through reflecting on the stages of cessation . . ., "Through ignorance ceasing, formation ceases . . .," they understand the nature of the truth of the path, such as the cultivation of selflessness that is the antidote to the origin of suffering. In this way, the assembled and Rhinoceros-like Self-Realized Ones actualize their fruition on one seat.

INVESTIGATING THE WAY OF SELF-REALIZED ONES

The heritage of the Self-Realized One is not definitively fixed because it is determined that there is one consummate heritage. It is an inferior path, not the consummate fruition. This is because dependent origination too lacks intrinsic existence because production is not established through mutual connections. Also, if perceived objects do not exist, in the same way perceiving subjects do not truly exist either. Further, delighting in isolation in solitude is not the supreme conduct because ultimately there is neither solitary place nor a non-solitary place, and a mind attached to the tranquility of being alone is not the way of the sacred ones.

2. Mahāyāna

"Ocean" is a name for the vastly immeasurable. The name for what is even more greatly immeasurable than that is called "the immense ocean." The immense ocean-like qualities—limitlessly vast and profound—of the Buddha's Mahāyāna is superior in seven ways (such as in the great armor of diligence):

1. Through great diligence, the Mahāyāna has the armor that delights in the benefit of beings for incalculable aeons; the Hīnayāna lacks this. Likewise,
2. the great observation is the observation of the space-like basic nature;
3. the great practice is the practice that benefits both oneself and others;
4. the great wisdom is the wisdom that is the unity of compassion and the basic nature that is empty of the twofold self;
5. the great skillful means is not to abide in existence or peace;
6. the great accomplishment is the limitless qualities of a buddha, such as the powers; and
7. the great enlightened activity is the spontaneous presence of benefit for others as long as samsara remains.

Since the Hīnayāna does not have these and the Mahāyāna does, the Mahāyāna is superior.

In this way, although the nature of the supreme, sublime vehicle is not different, there are dissimilar ways of explaining the viewpoint of the Mahāyāna Word. Due to this, there arose three dissimilar views guided by the initial chariots. These are renowned as "Mind-Only," "Svātantrika," and "Prāsaṅgika."

1. *Mind-Only*

Proponents of Mind-Only assert that all phenomena are comprised within the mind and that the consciousness that is empty of perceiver-perceived duality is ultimate. Regarding this, there are (1) general assertions of Mind-Only and (2) particular assertions in the ways of the proponents of true representations and the proponents of false representations.

1. GENERAL ASSERTIONS OF MIND-ONLY

They assert as ultimate the self-aware, self-luminous cognition that lacks the aspects of perceiver-perceived duality. They posit a philosophy that structures all phenomena within a framework of three natures: the imagined nature, the dependent nature, and the consummate nature. Also, to summarize their philosophy, there is: (1) the observed object, (2) the mode of conduct, and (3) the accomplished fruition.

1. The Observed Object

This section has three parts: (1) heritage, which is the basis of one's fortune, (2) the view of the five bases, which is the basis of observation, and (3) the twofold selflessness, which is the basis of observation in meditation.

1. Heritage, Which Is the Basis of One's Fortune

They assert five heritages: three heritages of the three vehicles [Disciples, Self-Realized Ones, and bodhisattvas], the undetermined heritage, and the outcaste.

2. The Five Bases, Which Are the Basis of Observation in the View

Although there are no actual material objects that are external, external forms appear due to the power of predispositions for appearing objects ripening within the basic consciousness; they assert *material form* as a horse or ox in a dream. The *mind* is eightfold: the six engaged cognitions, the afflicted mind, and the basic consciousness.

Regarding this, the basic consciousness is the ground of predispositions. It is aware of a sheer domain of objects and is a stable continuum of many continuous moments. When divided, it has a twofold nature of effect and cause: the aspect of maturation and the aspect of predispositions. Its essence is obscured and neutral; it is accompanied by the five omnipresent factors such as contact. Its observation is unclear; it observes the greatly vast environment and inhabitants. By this, the seven collections of consciousness do not arise from their own continua. Rather, predispositions that establish a later similar type are infused in the basic consciousness and they arise in each instant of the basic consciousness, like a shadow of a pot. Thereby, it is called the "universal ground (*kun gzhi*) of various predispositions" because it acts as the support for the formations of samsara, the conditioned phenomena that are virtuous, unvirtuous, and neutral, as well as the collections of consciousness.

The basic element, which is the natural purity of buddha-nature, is called the "ultimate basic consciousness" because it is essentially not separate from the unconditioned qualities of nirvana. However, in this context, it is held to be the universal ground of predispositions that is the support of samsara.

The afflicted mind apprehends a self upon observing the basic consciousness; it has nine associated factors such as the view of self. It exists in every state of being except a sublime being's meditative equipoise and the absorption of cessation.

The sixfold collection of consciousness are as they are widely known. The accompanying *mental states* are the fifty-one states, as was explained. The twenty-three *non-associated formations* merely exist as imputations, which are provisional designations; they are not held to be substantially established. In addition to the three *unconditioned phenomena*, there is "the basic nature of selflessness," which is not produced by causes and conditions. Within the basic nature, "unwavering cessation" refers to the condition in which phenomena of the desire realm do not arise. "The cessation of perception and feeling" refers to the condition in which the seven collections of consciousness do not arise in the basic nature. Through this, there are six cessations; they are divided due to there being no separate object of negation in the basic nature, the basis of negation of the other five.

Within all these bases of properties (*mtshan gzhi*), there are three natures: the imagined nature, which is mere imputation that does not exist with instrinsic characteristics. It is the conceived object that dualistically appears; it is that which is expressed by a name. The dependent nature is that which arises in dependence upon causes and conditions. It is the arising of various impure and pure appearances through the force of the various predispositions in cognition itself. The consummate nature is what is positively determined to exist in the dependent nature's lack of the imagined nature. It abides with the nature that is empty of the twofold self.

There are two types of imagined nature: (1) the imagined nature with nonexistent characteristics—mental imputation that is impossible in reality, such as the self of persons and phenomena, and (2) the imagined nature which are categories—that which appears to the mind while not existent, like the appearance of two moons, etc. All that appears while not existent—forms, universals, and nominal imputations—are its nature.

There are two types of dependent nature: (1) the impure dependent nature—mind and mental states together with their objects, and (2) the pure dependent nature—the mind and mental states in a postmeditation of a transcendent mind, like the array of a buddha-field, etc. There are also two types of consummate nature: (1) the immutable consummate nature is the objective basic nature and (2) the undistorted consummate nature is the subjective wisdom.

Regarding this, material form, the twenty-three mental states such as contact, and the basic nature are substantially existent. The twenty-nine mental states such as conscientiousness, all the non-associated formations, space, and the five cessations are nominally existent. Moreover, the dependent nature is asserted as the phenomenal-ultimate (*chos can don dam*) and the consummate nature is the basic nature-ultimate (*chos nyid don dam*), while the imagined nature is asserted as the relative truth. Thus, all the statements in the sūtras that say that all phenomena lack intrinsic nature are intended for the lack of perceiver-perceived duality that is the domain of the imagined nature. They are intended for each of the three natures: the imagined nature lacking the essence of characteristics, the dependent nature lacking the essence of arising from itself, and the consummate nature lacking the essence of an entity. However, the mere self-luminous cognition is the ground of samsara and nirvana; hence, it is not negated. Therefore, they accept no other consummate viewpoint of the Victorious One other than the way of this mind-only.

3. The Twofold Selflessness, Which Is the Basis of Observation in Meditation

The basis of meditation is to rest the mind in the non-referential nature that is free from the perceiver-perceived duality that comprises the self of persons and phenomena.

2. The Mode of Conduct

The mode of conduct is to practice the six transcendent perfections for three incalculable aeons, etc., observing immeasurable beings, who are each imputed as a sentient being upon a mere succession of mental moments.

3. The Accomplished Fruition

The accomplished fruition is the inconceivable transformation of wisdom—acting beautifully through limitless ways in fields, bodies, and activities.

INVESTIGATING THESE PHILOSOPHICAL TENETS

External objects are not established as truly existent; however, internal cognition is not established as truly existent either. Therefore, conventionally they remain as equally existent from the aspect of appearance, and equally nonexistent in the ultimate mode of reality. Hence, there is no cognition established without an external object.

Heritage does not intrinsically exist because cognition does not intrinsically exist. The outcaste heritage also does not exist because: the acuity of faculties is variable, changing with conditions; the mind is naturally luminous and clear, whereas the adventitious defilements are suitable to be removed; and [the luminous and clear nature of mind] is not lost in the slightest—it is the antidote that exhausts the defilements and supports the three jewels.

Also, the dependent nature does not truly exist because it arises from conditions. The basic consciousness, as a stable continuum of a momentary continuity, is not established in reality, either. It is not in the slightest established essentially because all its observations, latencies, and maturations are manifold. Likewise, the afflicted mind, the sixfold collection of consciousness, and all the cessations are also just the nature of dependent arisings; hence, they are not at all established in reality.

2. PARTICULAR ASSERTIONS OF MIND-ONLY

Two distinctive assertions are known to be those of (1) the proponents of true representations (*rnam bden pa*), who assert that appearing objects truly exist as internal cognitions, and (2) the proponents of false representations (*rnam mrdzun pa*), who do not. However, neither is correct because they claim that the self-luminous consciousness is truly established, but this is merely a product of their own thoroughgoing conceptuality.

1. Proponents of True Representations

Regarding this, the brahmin Śaṅkarānanda and others asserted that in perception, the appearance of the perceived aspect is merely the essence of the perceiving cognition because it is clear and knowing, like an experience of pleasure or pain. This tradition also has three divisions, those who assert (1) cognition and representation as distinct, (2) an equal number of representations and cognitions, and (3) a variety of appearances as nondual with a single cognition.

1. Cognition and Representation as Distinct

They assert, "Appearing objects such as mountains are cognitions; however, the appearance of the perceived aspect and the cognition appearing as the perceiver aspect are distinct. Like the separate existence of an egg-white and the yolk of a hard-boiled egg, there is a true apprehension of two discrete aspects—a blue appearance perceived and a blue-perceiving cognition." Due to this, they are also called "Half-Eggists."

2. An Equal Number of Representations and Cognitions

They claim, "To the extent that representations can be divided, so can cognitions. Therefore, the substance of a cognition of five fingers is true as fivefold; it is not true as one. Hence, it is impossible for two representations to appear to a single cognition."

3. A Variety of Appearances as Nondual with a Single Cognition

They assert, "A variety of appearances, such as blue and gold, appear to a single cognition, they are true as the nature of a single cognition."

Investigating the Proponents of True Representations

When external objects are established as cognition by the reason that they are clear and aware, the fact that they are cognized entities and that they are merely cognized also applies to external objects; hence, there is uncertainty [about their status of being cognition]. Also, being clear and aware is not established because that is what is to be established. If the knower and the known occur simultaneously, then their relationship is annulled. Also, if they occur at different times then their relationship is similarly annulled.

If one says, "[Appearing objects] are established as cognition's clarity and awareness." By this, external objects are established as unreal, but it does not establish that they are the same as a truly existent cognition; it is like the fact that a reflection being a face may be negated, but it is not established that the reflection is the mirror.

1. Investigating Cognition and Representation as Distinct

Moreover, as for the Half-Eggists, if external objects are unreal, then it follows that cognition, which is the same as those, is also unreal. If external objects truly existed, then it would follow that they are also established the way they appear in reality. Also, if a cognition appearing as an external object were separate from the internal perceiving cognition, then this would be invalidated by absurd consequences; it would follow that: consciousness would be propelled out from the body, mind would have color, etc., objects like mountains would know things, and it would be possible for one continuum to have as many cognitions as there are varieties of appearances at the same time. For a truly existent consciousness, there would be a distinct cognition of each appearing object.

2. Investigating the Equal Number of Representations and Cognitions

If it were the case that the number of perceived representations was equal to that of the perceivers, it would follow that the simultaneous appearance of variegated macro-objects, such as the sight of something multi-colored, would cease because each cognition would likewise be distinct and truly established that way. Since there would be nothing other than essentially separate cognitions, it would be like a thought in the continua of a group of many people. Therefore, although a cognition that appears as a manifold is not singular, it is not truly established as a separate manifold either. Due to this essential point, cognition can have the appearance of a simultaneous manifold.

3. Investigating the Variety of Appearances as Nondual with a Single Cognition

As for the variety of appearances as nondual with a single true cognition, if an appearance of a manifold is said to be singular, it would absurdly follow that the conventions of there being a manifold would cease, such as there being five colors, etc. This is because there is no way to understand a manifold other than through an appearance of a manifold. Therefore, as a mere convention it is appropriate to speak of the visual cognition that perceives a variegated object as a single cognition. However, this is due to the essential point that it is not truly existent as singular because it is imputed upon a manifold.

Thus, conventions are used according to the way things appear; otherwise, presentations would have additional problems: it would follow that buddhas and sentient beings would have a single continuum because the mental continua of beings clearly appear to buddhas; and if what appears to be separate were truly separate, then it would follow that anything could become anything—a blazing fire would be true as water, etc.—it would be extremely absurd!

Therefore, due to the essential point that neither an object nor a cognition is truly established when its reality is analyzed, objects and cognitions are suitable to appear variously as the same or different. However, it should be known that they are not established the way they appear in reality—this is the essential point.

2. Proponents of False Representations

The masters who are proponents of false representations, such as Dharmottara and others, assert, "All the appearances of objects are neither objects nor cognitions. Due to the distorting power of ignorance, they are merely a clear appearance of absence, like a floating hair in space. Cognition is without representation, like a clear crystal ball."

1. Proponents of the Stained

Regarding this, "the proponents of the stained" (*dri bcas su smra ba*) assert, "At the time of the mind, the eight consciousnesses are ultimately existent. Also, at the stage of a buddha, although representations are not within the fundamental nature, they do not recede because the environment and inhabitants clearly appear."

2. Proponents of the Stainless

"The proponents of the stainless" (*dri med pa*), or purity, claim, "At the time of the mind, the adventitious cognitions, which are the condition of the sevenfold collection of consciousness, are relative phenomena. Since the basic consciousness has no increase or decrease, nor disparate mode of apprehension, its consummate nature is called 'the innate mind,' which is ultimate. Since predispositions are exhausted at the stage of a buddha, it is like dream appearances ceasing upon waking up. Nothing else appears other than the mind, and the nonconceptual experience free from all representations abides as a mere self-aware, self-luminosity; this is the Truth Body. From the blessing of this, in the perspective of those to be trained, there is the complete knowledge of all environments and inhabitants, and the Form Bodies appear to speak the doctrine and perform the benefit of beings, even though there are no such entities."

Investigating the Proponents of False Representations

Regarding this, it is reasonable that they say that appearing objects are not at all truly existent. However, it is not reasonable to claim that consciousness is truly established because subjective cognitions appear in the way that objects appear in a deluded perspective. When analyzed, subjective cognitions are not established in the same way that objects are not established.

Also, self-awareness is not ultimately established. If cognition were established by its own experience, then objects would also be established by experience. In the way that the imagined nature is not established, the dependent nature—mind and mental states—also is not found when sought after. In the way that the conditions of the sevenfold collection of consciousness are not found when analyzed, neither is the basic consciousness. The basic consciousness is posited as the ground of the various appearances, such as the sevenfold collection of consciousness; yet when these various entities do not exist, neither does their ground—like a forest does not exist when each of its trees has been removed.

2. *Svātantrika*

The Svātantrika school describes all phenomena by means of a division of two truths; they fully negate both fabrications—that phenomena really exist, and that they do not exist conventionally. In particular, they make a detailed presentation of appearances as they are evaluated conventionally. Even so, in both the higher and lower philosophies that emerged, they parted from the meaning of the innate basic nature due to a strong fixation upon a web of constructs.

1. LOWER SVĀTANTRIKA

This section has two parts: (1) proponents of reason-established illusion and (2) proponents of appearance and emptiness as separate.

1. Proponents of Reason-Established Illusion

The master Samudramegha and others claim that all phenomena abide within both of the two truths: they are not established essentially and have an illusory nature. The appearances of the relative do not truly exist—they are illusory; and the ultimate emptiness also is the incessant appearance of dependent arising. Thus, through accumulating the illusory two accumulations, an illusory fruition is attained. Then, while in constant meditative equipoise on the nature of illusion, the illusory benefit of sentient beings is performed through illusory enlightened activities. Thereby, all appearances are illusory through the force of the dependent arising of causes and conditions. Distorted appearances are illusory; and even though the constructed objects appearing to undistorted wisdom have been pacified, there are clear and unimpeded appearances, like an illusion. In short, the ground, path, and fruition are like an illusion.

Investigating the Proponents of Reason-Established Illusion

When analyzed, this is not the Buddha's consummate viewpoint because it does not go beyond the net of constructs with absurd consequences such as: it would follow that the ultimate would arise and disintegrate just like an illusion, and it would follow that illusion would sustain analysis.

2. Proponents of Appearance and Emptiness as Separate

Master Śrīgupta and others assert as follows: "Since the ultimate is not established whatsoever, "illusion" is not observed. Conventionally, relative truths such as pots are not ultimate because they appear as efficacious and are true. They are empty because nothing at all is found upon ultimate analysis. Therefore, the ultimate withstands analysis and the relative does not withstand analysis. These two, the relative and the ultimate, are phenomena (*chos can*) and the basic nature (*chos nyid*)—they do not inhere within a single locus because, if they did, it would absurdly follow that the ultimate would be impermanent like the relative, and that the relative would not arise or cease like the ultimate. Hence, appearance is the relative, the phenomena, and emptiness is the ultimate, the basic nature; they are just established in mutual dependence." Also, they make a division of the relative into the correct and incorrect, like the Higher Svātantrikas.

Investigating the Proponents of Appearance and Emptiness as Separate

When analyzed, something empty that does not appear is not possible in either of the two truths. If it does not appear to anyone, then its character is utterly nonexistent; hence, it does not exist even conventionally, like the horn of a rabbit. Also, an appearance that is not empty is not found because whatever appears is not established when analyzed. If the ultimate were not an appearing object of investigation, then it would also not be an object that is suitable to be realized. This is because its features must appear to be evaluated by a means of knowledge and expression; otherwise, it is not suitable to be realized. What is nonconceptual (*spros bral*) is not like this because it is beyond the partiality of appearance and emptiness.

If the emptiness of something is necessarily observed in a lack of appearance, then it is not appropriate; there is no path of meditation on an emptiness that is apart from appearance because that would not eliminate obscurations nor would it be feasible as an antidote for what is to be abandoned. For example, it does not help to know the emptiness of space when becoming angry with an enemy. "Emptiness" is not found by any means because any object of a spatio-temporal cognition has a form that appears.

2. HIGHER SVĀTANTRIKA

The masters Jñānagarbha, Śāntarakṣita, and Kamalaśīla assert as follows: "Since ultimately neither illusion nor emptiness on its own can withstand analysis, the meaning of the consummate mode of reality is beyond all constructs. However, for the time being conventional entities of the relative truth incontrovertibly uphold their intrinsic characteristics. When they are analyzed by reason, they are also equally established to be empty, or the categorized ultimate (*don dam rnam grangs pa*); nothing in the slightest is truly established." Hence, they have assertions. Also, all the establishments of their own position and refutations of other's systems are done by means of autonomous arguments.

Along with the Buddhist philosophies up to here, they too assert production from other. Also, they have two relative truths: (1) the correct relative that functions as it appears, like the moon in the sky, and (2) the incorrect relative that does not function as it appears, like a double-moon. Furthermore, mistaken relative phenomena do not cease until one attains the pure bodhisattva grounds; appearances in a sublime being's postmeditation are called "the pure world." In this way, through knowing the two truths as non-contradictory, one gathers the two accumulations and attains the two embodiments of buddhahood.

INVESTIGATING THE HIGHER SVĀTANTRIKA

When analyzed, in the authentic meaning the correct and incorrect relative are equal because both arise from causes and conditions, and both are appearing objects that are similarly not established when analyzed. Also, entities "established by their intrinsic characteristics" are not established at all when analyzed; they are just zealous imputations by those who delight in constructs.

Also, production from other is like production from self; when analyzed, production is not found at all. One might say, "This is not the same. Production from other is merely conventional." When analyzing the manner of production of a conventionally appearing entity like a seed or sprout, it is not found anywhere from self or from another—there is no other ultimate production from other to be posited.

If one says, "Well, how does a sprout conventionally arise from a seed?" The appearance of causes (such as seeds) incontrovertibly producing results (such as sprouts) is asserted to be dependent arising, but should not be an assertion of the four extremes. There is no assertion of the four extremes. In this way, these appearing entities, which are dependent arisings, are not in the slightest bit established by their intrinsic characteristics even conventionally. Therefore, the whole net of constructs, such as arising or not arising from self or other, is overturned. Due to this, there are also no assertions.

Furthermore, the ultimate that is the non-establishment of all these appearances when investigated does not exist either because appearances themselves do not exist, so their emptiness is also not established; both appearance and emptiness are equally not established other than as mere imputation. The division of two truths remains in the perspective of the mind, yet is not established in reality as two. Hence, this is a philosophically constructed posit of those who make a detailed presentation of appearances; it is also a cause for not averting subtle constructs. Therefore, from the beginning one should engage the meaning of primordial purity—the Great Middle Way—which is the liberation of all appearances as they are, in the way that the meaning of equality is primordially unaffected by intellectual distortions.

3. Prāsaṅgika

The summit of the Vehicle of Characteristics is the Prāsaṅgika-Madhyamaka, which is the essential meaning of the consummate view of the Victorious Ones. It negates all constructs and objective reference (*dmigs pa*) concerning existence, nonexistence, being, non-being, etc. It establishes the great indivisible truth beyond mind by means of primordial purity—the mode of reality that is the fundamental nature not established as anything whatsoever. Thus, due to having no asserted claims in one's own system (*rang lugs*), all reified claims are destroyed through drawing out the absurd consequences within others' assertions.

In this way, all phenomena of appearance and existence are just dependent arisings: existent entities are dependent productions and non-entities are dependent imputations. Thus, all phenomena comprised by dependent arising lack intrinsic natures because if they had intrinsic natures, their arising dependently would not make sense. Since they are dependent arisings, they are not established in the least by means of the four alternatives of production, or as essentially singular or plural. Hence, they are not truly existent—like an illusion. Through being free from the subtle extremes of eternalism and nihilism, the phenomena of the temporary path and the consummate fruition are perfected.

Furthermore, there are five arguments that ascertain the meaning of "not intrinsically established": (1) free from being singular or plural, (2) the diamond shards, (3) free from producing an existent or nonexistent thing, (4) refuting the performance of a function, and (5) the great interdependence.

1. FREE FROM BEING SINGULAR OR PLURAL

It follows that all appearing objects are not established at all as entities or non-entities because they are free from being singular or plural—like the moon reflected in water.

2. THE DIAMOND SHARDS

It follows that the appearance of an object lacks essence because it does not arise from (1) itself, (2) another, (3) both, or (4) causelessly—like a dream:

(1) If it were to arise from itself, then it would absurdly follow that production would be pointless and endless;
(2) If it were to arise from another, then it would absurdly follow that anything could arise from anything;
(3) If it were to arise from both, then the expressed problems of both self-production and other-production would follow;
(4) If it were to arise without cause, then it would absurdly follow that nothing would appear, or that efforts to produce an effect would cease.

Therefore, the production of a sprout from a seed also appears as just a dependent arising; however, since a seed and a sprout cannot be found as either the same or different in reality, there is no objective referent (*dmigs pa*).

3. FREE FROM PRODUCING AN EXISTENT OR NONEXISTENT THING

It follows that this manifold appearance of entities lacks intrinsic nature because there is no arising of an existent or a nonexistent entity. Moreover, an existent thing has already arisen; hence, its arising does not make sense. A nonexistent thing contradicts what is existent; hence, it does not make sense for a nonexistent thing to become existent.

4. REFUTING THE PERFORMANCE OF A FUNCTION

It follows that objects of knowledge are not established as entities because they cannot perform functions. This follows because what is momentary cannot perform a function because it ceases when a performance of a function is initiated. Also, it is not done progressively because continuity is negated with momentariness.

5. GREAT INTERDEPENDENCE

It follows that mere appearances are not established as entities because they arise dependently—like a reflection. Moreover, if an entity were intrinsically established, it would not arise dependently because it would already be established as an entity. Whatever arises dependently is necessarily just empty: from the time illusory horses and oxen appear, they are empty; while empty, they are not established at all, coarsely or subtly. While not established at all, they incontrovertibly appear due to a mere assemblage of causes and conditions. This appearance also is empty while appearing; when analyzed, it is not established at all and no grounds of assertion are found.

There are three further arguments: (1) the argument of lacking permanence or disintegration, (2) the argument of neither changing nor not changing, and (3) the argument refuting the four properties.

1. Argument of Lacking Permanence or Disintegration

Consider a mere appearance. It does not exist as entities because of neither disintegrating nor not disintegrating. This follows because if a pot were to disintegrate, it must disintegrate either when it exists or when it does not exist. It does not disintegrate when it exists because existence is the opposite of disintegration; and when nonexistent, there is nothing to disintegrate. It is also not permanent, without disintegration, because its nature is momentary.

2. Argument of Neither Changing Nor Not Changing

Consider a mere appearance. It does not exist as entities because of neither changing nor not changing. Moreover, if an entity changes its condition, then it would absurdly follow that an old person also could change into a youth. When considering the mode of existence of change itself, as either permanent or impermanent, or considering its parts, it is not established. If there were no change, then it would absurdly follow that it would be impossible for a youth to become old.

3. Argument Refuting the Four Properties

If arising, abiding, aging, and disintegration arose in progression, then they would not be complete in one moment; if they were simultaneous, then birth and death as well as old age and youth would occur simultaneously. As was explained in the context of the Disciples, this is undermined by an influx of these kinds of contradictions.

In this way, in all endeavors, the mind with certainty that all phenomena lack intrinsic existence cuts through all the constructs that reify the signs of what is observed, bringing composure in equanimity. Even while things are this way, the mode of appearance is not blocked conventionally. There is acceptance of (1) the Middle Way of the ground, which is the unity of the two truths, (2) the Middle Way of the path, which is the unity of the two accumulations, and (3) the Middle Way of the fruition, which is the unity of the two embodiments of buddhahood.

1. THE MIDDLE WAY OF THE GROUND

The relative is the realm of mind; the ultimate is the domain of individual self-awareness free from mind. Also, both simply lack an established intrinsic nature. The etymology of the relative is: that which appears while lacking intrinsic nature; and what is infallible in a deluded perspective. The etymology of the ultimate is: that which is the object (*don*) sought; and what is true because it is infallible as the quality of the path and fruition.

The defining character of the relative is: phenomena that do not transcend the domain of mind and do not withstand analysis. The defining character of the ultimate is: the basic nature that transcends the domain of mind and is the complete pacification of referent objects. It is not reasonable for either to withstand analysis; this has previously been refuted. Both of these, ultimate and relative, also are not established separately in reality because they abide as phenomena and the basic nature, purity and equality—the essence that transcends constructs, devoid of mind and signs.

When divided, they are posited as the two truths of the relative and the ultimate. Within the relative also, in terms of what accords with mundane convention, that which appears as the objects of the six unimpaired faculties (such as material forms) is "the correct relative," and that which appears to the impaired six faculties (such as floating hairs) is "the incorrect relative."

2. THE MIDDLE WAY OF THE PATH

The Middle Way of the path is the cultivation of the unity of the relative practice of the six transcendent perfections and the ultimate wisdom—free from constructs and luminously clear. Regarding this, how to settle in the contexts of practicing meditative equipoise is this: Sit cross-legged on a comfortable seat. Having gone for refuge and generated the spirit of awakening, relax the mind completely. In an utterly nonconceptual state, be lucidly clear without thinking of anything at all, in accord with the settled view. Rest without distraction in that, without being diffused or withdrawn. Thus, without the duality of an outer object and an inner mind, the mind in meditation is not rejecting or accepting, so all objective reference is pacified.

Awareness within a freedom from constructs—when the operation of mind and mental states has been pacified—is meditation on the meaning of luminous clarity, the individual, self-aware wisdom. In postmeditation, one should dedicate for the benefit of sentient beings in an illusion-like state; and engage in virtuous actions without attachment or fixation.

3. THE MIDDLE WAY OF THE FRUITION

At the end of the continuum of the tenth ground, the cause of samsara—the mind and mental states together with their predispositions—is pacified, dissolved into the basic field of reality. Then the way of the Truth Body—the nonduality of the basic field and gnosis—and the two Form Bodies that arise from that Truth Body, are spontaneously present; bringing benefit and happiness for as long as samsara remains.

In this context here, it is not reasonable that the Prāsaṅgikas either (1) never have assertions or (2) always have assertions. Hence, there are no assertions in terms of the mode of reality, the way of evaluation that is free from constructs in meditative equipoise. There are assertions in terms of the mode of appearance, the distinctions made in postmeditation. Know these two divisions as they are clearly taught in the *Treasury of Reason* (*rigs mdzod*).

THE RESULTANT VEHICLE OF VAJRAYĀNA

Having explained the Causal Vehicle of Characteristics from the Mahāyāna, now is the explanation of the Resultant Vehicle of Secret Mantra, the Vajrayāna itself. Firstly, there are many ways through which its many distinguishing qualities are superior to the doctrines of the Causal Vehicle. But in short, in the Causal Vehicle temporal causality is asserted because of accepting the existence of buddha-nature as a seed that is further developed through the conditions of the two accumulations, by which after a long time one accomplishes the fruition of buddhahood. In the Vajrayāna, the essential nature—like space itself—which is the nature of luminous clarity abiding with spontaneously present qualities, is taken to be the basis of purification. Within that, the nature of samsara—like clouds—which is the eightfold collection of consciousness together with their appearing objects, is what is purified. The means of purification—like the wind that quickly dispels [the cloud-like nature of samsara]—are the profound methods of empowerment, and the generation and completion stages. The result of purification is the ultimate universal ground—the actualization of the buddha as such—which is accomplished in a short time; in reality, the philosophy of the indivisible cause and fruition is asserted.

Therefore, although it has the same purpose—to accomplish the result of a buddha—there is a difference in the way of accomplishment. The Vehicle of Characteristics has an aspect of obscurity regarding the fact that the appearance of samsara itself is the divine mandala that is infinite natural purity, and regarding the meaning of great equality that is the indivisible nature. Due to this, it is a view that accepts and rejects. In Mantra, everything is acknowledged as the indivisible truth of purity and equality; hence, there is the power to act without accepting or rejecting. Consequently, the view is not obscured.

In the Vehicle of Characteristics, due to observing in terms of accepting and rejecting, one cannot bring everything to accompany the path. In Mantra, since there are more kinds of methods, accomplishing the fruition is more deeply profound. Due to this, in Mantra there are no difficulties in accomplishing the path, unlike in the Vehicle of Characteristics. Also, Mantra is superior due to the support of the individual, being suited for only those of sharp capacity.

Moreover, the actual indivisibility of the cause and the effect is clear in Highest Yoga Tantra, and is completed in the Great Perfection free from effort. However, compared to Sūtra, there are also distinctive qualities of Action Tantra not being obscured, etc. Further, concerning the six tantra sets, each of the higher tantras is superior to the ones below due to not being obscured, etc. Therefore, the path of Sūtra is called the "Causal Vehicle" because the effect is newly accomplished by practicing the path that is a cause to become a buddha. In Mantra, by means of the supreme method right now, the fruition itself is actualized in a short time through the fruitional three embodiments of buddhahood taken as the path; therefore, it is called the "Resultant Vehicle."

Within this distinctive Secret Mantra, too, there are four tantras with supremely great qualities. There are said to be four tantras (such as Action Tantra) based upon the four castes, the progression of capacities, the magnitude of afflictions, etc.

1. *Action Tantra*

In Action Tantra, the main emphasis is on behavior; there is great exertion in the actions of body and speech, such as external bathing and cleanliness. The deity, the wisdom-being (*ye shes pa*), is regarded as a lord, the bestower of accomplishments; oneself, the pledge-being (*dam tshig pa*), is regarded as a servant, the receiver of accomplishments. Through this, one aspires to attain the temporal and consummate accomplishments.

Furthermore, there is (1) view, (2) meditation, (3) action, and (4) fruition.

1. VIEW

Everything is ultimately equal as the nature of the indivisible truth of appearance and emptiness. Nevertheless, conventionally, just the exalted deity—the body of wisdom, which is the actualized nature of the luminous and clear basic field, the identity of all faults exhausted and all qualities perfected—is the bestower of temporal and consummate accomplishments. Therefore, the deity is like a lord; and oneself, the one who receives the deity's blessings, is like a servant. One relies upon a deity due to having obscurations and having not completed one's own benefit. Through this, by means of the ultimate equality and the relative infallibility of dependent arising, one has a view of certainty that—through remaining in apprehension of the attributes of the deity's body, speech, and mind—one will in time accomplish infinite activities and consummately accomplish the essence of the deity.

2. MEDITATION

Action Tantra is renowned to have the sixfold deity. In short, within a state of single-pointed observation of the body mudra, the speech-syllable, the mind-implement, the palace, and the radiation and retraction of light rays, etc.; one invokes again and again the deity's mental continuum through reciting the essence-mantra in the manner of stopping the vitality (*srog 'gog pa*), etc. Consequently, one invokes in oneself the blessings of the deity, like putting an alchemical potion on iron.

3. ACTION

The recitations of secret mantra are accomplished without neglecting the elements of ritual; otherwise, an effect is not produced, as is the case with crops that lack something like seeds or manure. Therefore, one earnestly strives in accordance with what is explained in the tantras regarding physical and verbal actions—such as bathing three times a day, changing clothes three times,[11] worshiping, and performing fire-offerings.

4. FRUITION

Through striving in this way, in time, one attains many common accomplishments such as the body of an awareness-holder equal in fortune to the gods of the Form Realm and Desire Realm; in sixteen lifetimes, one attains the essence of the deities of the three families—the consummate fruition.

2. *Performance Tantra*

In Performance Tantra, there is an equal emphasis on external bathing and cleanliness and internal meditative stabilization. One regards oneself and the deity as friends, through which one aspires to attain the accomplishments. This also has (1) view, (2) meditation, (3) action, and (4) fruition.

1. VIEW

Due to the essential point of having much more certainty in equality than in Action Tantra, oneself and the deity are regarded as friends. Due to the unobstructed appearing aspect of dependent arising, the temporal and consummate objectives are

---

11. *The Great Tibetan-Chinese Dictionary* describes "changing the three clothes" (*gos gsum brje ba*) as the activity of Action Tantra: (1) wearing new outer clothes, (2) guarding the inner clothes of the vows, and (3) meditating on the deity, the secret clothes. See Yisun Zhang, ed., *The Great Tibetan-Chinese Dictionary*, 379.

attained in dependence upon the deity according to the way one observes. Hence, one has a view that is confident in the way of the profound two truths.

2. MEDITATION

One visualizes the deity, which is the wisdom-being, in front of oneself, the pledge-being. Then one performs recitations observing the mantra garland circling back and forth, etc., as well as radiating and retracting. Through this, in the end the wisdom-being leaves and one meditates on the ultimate, free from constructs.

3. ACTION

One exerts oneself in whatever behaviors are appropriate, such as bathing and cleanliness.

4. FRUITION

In time, one accomplishes infinite activities, and in seven lifetimes, the stage of a *vajra*-holder of the four families—the consummate fruition. Also, this is called the Vehicle of Dual Tantra (*gnyis ka'i rgyud, ubhayatantra*) because its internal meditative stabilization enacts the way of Yoga Tantra, and its external activities enact the way of Action Tantra. In fact, it is more profound than Action Tantra by means of the view, etc.; hence, the accomplishment of the fruition is faster.

3. *Yoga Tantra*

Yoga Tantra has two divisions: (1) outer Yoga Tantra and (2) inner Highest Yoga Tantra. In the former, for the continuum of the outer yoga practitioner, cleanliness, etc., is observed merely to assist the accomplishment of the path; however, meditation on the inner mind is the main emphasis. One proceeds by means of the four mudras[12] and the five manifest awakenings;[13] and while meditating on oneself as the pledge-being, one invites a separate wisdom deity from a pure buddha-field. Then, dissolving the deity into oneself, one aspires to attain the accomplishments through meditating on the nonduality of oneself and the deity. This also has (1) view, (2) meditation, (3) action, and (4) fruition.

---

12. The four mudras (*phyag rgya bzhi*) of Yoga Tantra meditation are (1) the action-seal (*las kyi phyag rgya, karmamudrā*), (2) the pledge-seal (*dam tshig gi phyag rgya, samayamudrā*), (3) the doctrine-seal (*chos kyi phyag rgya, dharmamudrā*), and the great seal (*phyag rgya chen po, mahāmudrā*).

13. The five manifest awakenings (*mngon byang rnam pa lnga*) is a manner of cultivating a deity in the generation stage. The five manifest awakenings are (1) awakening from the moon (*lza ba las byang chub pa*), (2) awakening from the sun (*nyi ma las byang chub pa*), (3) awakening from the seed (*sa bon las byang chub pa*), (4) awakening from the implement (*phyag mtshan las byang chub pa*), and (5) awakening from the complete body (*sku rdzogs pa las byang chub pa*). However, Mipam lists a slightly different enumeration in this text, in accord with Longchenpa's explanation in the *White Lotus*.

1. VIEW

The view of equality is superior to the former two (Action Tantra and Performance Tantra). By this, due to the certainty that sees oneself and the deity as equal in reality, conventionally these are also seen as equal, like water in water; thus one meditates. Since all phenomena are merely appearances of one's mind, the deity is actually accomplished in the way that it is observed through the transformative power of meditative stabilization. One has the distinctive view and certainty that the essence of the deity is accomplished through diligently practicing the essence of the four mudras, which is the identity of the deity's body, speech, mind, and activity.

2. MEDITATION

Having gone for refuge and generated the spirit of awakening, one generates the five manifest awakenings within a state of emptiness:

1. Manifest awakening from the seat of the lotus and moon, which is the cause for accomplishing the realm of the perfect place,
2. Manifest awakening from the syllables of speech, which is the cause for the arising of the perfect doctrine,
3. Manifest awakening from the attribute of mind, which is the cause for abiding in the perfect time—inconceivable eternity,
4. Manifest awakening from the completely perfect body along with the mandala circle, which is the cause for the perfect teacher and the perfect retinue, and
5. Manifest awakening from the deity—the wisdom being—which is the cause for the essence of the body, or perfect wisdom.

Also, one meditates through sealing one's three doors of body, speech, and mind, together with their functions, with the essence of the deity's body, speech, mind, and activity by means of:

- The great seal, which is the aspect of body,
- The doctrine-seal, which is the aspect of speech,
- The pledge-seal, which is the aspect of mind, and
- The action-seal, which accomplishes activity through radiating and retracting light rays, etc.

Also, in such a ritual, through the stages of accomplishing the ground, the supreme king of mandalas (*gzhi dkyil 'khor rgyal mchog*), and the supreme king of activity (*las rgyal mchog*) based on that, one practices yoga in meditative stabilizations until the desired accomplishments are achieved.

3. ACTION

There are various practices taken up, such a cleanliness, in accord with the situation; however, it is mainly in accord with the experience of internal yoga and is more open in behavior than in the previous tantras.

4. FRUITION

In time, one increases the qualities of experience and realization further and further. In three lifetimes, one accomplishes the consummate fruition. Having purified the five aggregates, five faculties, and five afflictions, the buddhas of the five families, which are the identity of the five wisdoms, are accomplished.

In this way, all of these three tantra sets hold the two truths in alternation. They mainly meditate on the relative nature of phenomenal appearances as the deity, and subsequently dissolve those appearances of the deity and then meditate without referent object on the ultimate, free from constructs.

4. *Highest Yoga Tantra*

For its distinctive qualities, one should know the distinctions between outer and inner Secret Mantra by means of distinctions pertaining to the ground, path, and fruition. First, for the ground at the time of the ripening empowerment: the vase empowerment is more important for the outer-tantras; and the higher three empowerments are more important for the inner-tantras. Second, for the path, meditation in inner-tantras is the unity of the generation stage and completion stage without alternation due to the view of purity and equality without accepting or rejecting; the outer-tantras are not able to do this. Consequently, the outer-tantras maintain actions of accepting and rejecting—actions of purity with regards to things like place, food, and clothes; and the inner-tantras act in equality. The fruition has the distinction of the time of liberation: in inner-tantras one becomes a buddha in this life; in outer-tantras one becomes a buddha in another life.

The general assertions of these great inner yogas of the distinctive Secret Mantra are as follows: All phenomena comprised within appearance and existence, samsara and nirvana, abide within the state of the great indivisible equality. Moreover, there is the purity of equal taste as the Great Middle Way free from all constructs of the four extremes; it is profound. Due to this, there is the distinctive aspect of appearance: everything subsumed within the aggregates, elements, and sense-fields are acknowledged as the single great mandala of purity—such as the five buddha families. Through meditating in this way, it is vast.

By this, through the king-like, supreme method of self-liberation—without at all abandoning appearances—appearances are transformed to assist the path. Thus, in all activities one meditates on the great self-existing gnosis itself, which is the indivisible truth—the meaning of the primordial unity of the vast generation stage and the profound completion stage, neither conjoined nor separable. Through this, it is accepted that in this life there is attainment of the supreme accomplishment of Mahāmudrā—the stage of the unified Vajradhāra.

Regarding its specific divisions, based upon the antidotes to the three poisons, and the progression of capacities, etc., there are (1) Father Tantras, (2) Mother Tantras, and (3) Nondual Tantras. Highest Yoga Tantras that are "Father Tantras" mainly emphasize the way of accomplishing the generation stage and its various subsidiary activities; the method of the illusory body, which is appearing wisdom; the completion stage winds; and wrathful activity. They are taught as a method to tame angry disciples, and those who are attached to external constructs.

Next, "Mother Yoga Tantras" are those tantras that mainly emphasize the completion stage, from among the two stages of generation and completion; the wisdom of emptiness, from among the twofold method and wisdom—and its path—which is the yoga of luminous clarity; the path of method, which is the bliss that relies upon the retention and control of the seminal essences; and subjugation among the activities, etc. They are taught as a method to tame desirous disciples, those who can apply the essential points of the inner-body, and those who are disciples of mediocre capacities.

The "Highest Nondual Tantras" of Secret Mantra do not emphasize either side of method or wisdom, generation or completion; they emphasize the single sphere of the great wisdom of purity and equality—the self-awareness that is the great spirit of awakening and the consummate reality of everything. They are taught as a method for taming stupid disciples, and those of the highest capacity who engage without effort.

As for these ways, according to some assertions of the new schools of Secret Mantra, all the Highest Yoga Tantras are alike in ascertaining the meaning of unity; however, Father and Mother Tantras are asserted by means of the way they show an emphasis on the aspect of method or wisdom. The ways of the Father and Mother Tantras are also said to come from the degree of emphasis upon such elements as

- whether or not the deities in the mandala are primarily male or female,
- the positioning of the main male or female deity,
- the ornaments and garb,
- the direction of circling being clockwise or counterclockwise,
- the time of commencing activities being day or night, and
- the manner of correlating purity.

According to the new schools, there is also a threefold division within the inner-tantras of Secret Mantra: (1) Father Tantras, such as the *Secret Assembly* (*Guhyasamāja*), (2) Mother Tantras, such as the *Wheel of Great Bliss* (*Cakrasaṃvara*), and (3) Nondual Tantras, such as the *Wheel of Time* (*Kālacakra*). The wisdom of the fourth empowerment itself, which is hidden in the other tantras, is clearly shown in the *Wheel of Time*. Also, due to not falling to either extreme of method or wisdom, it is called "the androgynous stage of Vajrasattva." Further, since it explains through emphasizing the nondual equality, it is "the open treasure-chest of the buddha"; accordingly, it is praised in scriptures as the pinnacle of all tantras.

According to the old school (Nyingma) of Mantra, the three inner-tantras are widely known as the Father Tantras of Mahāyoga, the Mother Tantras of Anuyoga, and the Nondual Tantras of Atiyoga. As is said,

- Mahāyoga, the generation, is like the ground of all phenomena;
- Anuyoga, the scripture, is like the path of all phenomena;
- Atiyoga, the completion, is like the fruition of all phenomena.

Mahāyoga is like the *ground* of all Mantra; compared to the two latter ones, it is like the *tantra*. Anuyoga is like the *path* of Secret Mantra due to showing with great clarity the profound path of its method—which is applying the essential points of the elements and channels of the inner-body. Compared to the *tantra*, it is like the *scripture* that elucidates the essential points of its viewpoint. The Great Perfection nakedly discloses self-existing gnosis, the fruition, which is the consummate objective of all paths. Therefore, it is like the *fruition*, the path of Secret Mantra's completion. Compared to the former two, it is also said to be tantra's *quintessential instructions*. These are the three great inner-tantras.

1. MAHĀYOGA

From among the three, for Mahāyoga, there is (1) the way the ground is ascertained, (2) the way the path is practiced, and (3) the way the fruition is completed.

1. Ground

The aspect of relative phenomena—all that appears while empty—abides from the beginning as the mandalas of *vajra*-body, *vajra*-speech, and *vajra*-mind. This is the superior relative truth (*lhag pa'i kun rdzob bden pa*). The emptiness that is its nature—not established at all—is neither conjoined with, nor separable from the embodiment of buddhahood and wisdom. This is the superior ultimate truth (*lhag pa'i don dam bden pa*). The indivisibility of these two superior truths abides as the great Truth Body itself. It is ascertained by means of scripture and reasoning, such as the reasons of the four realizations,[14] through objectless self-luminosity that transcends the domain of mind.

14. The reasons of the four realizations are drawn from the *Guhyagarbhatantra* XI.1. See Mipam, *Overview: Essential Nature of Luminous Clarity*, 434; 465–466; English translation in Dharmachakra Translation Group, *Luminous Essence*, 38; 61–62.

2. Path

Having ascertained in this way, the practice of the path is as follows: Based on the stages of great emptiness, illusory compassion, the single seal, the elaborate seal, and the practice in a group gathering (*tshom bu tshogs sgrub*),[15] one enters the progressive stages of the awareness-holder of maturation, the awareness-holder of the power of life, the awareness-holder of the great seal, and the awareness-holder of spontaneously presence.[16]

3. Fruition

Having purified all the defilements of delusion by means of the profound path, one attains the stage of the great Vajradhāra—the identity of the twenty-five qualities of fruition upon the ground of the great gathering wheel of syllables (*yi ge 'khor lo tshogs chen gyi sa*).

2. ANUYOGA

There is also the ground, path, and fruition for Anuyoga.

1. Ground

Whatever ways entities appear are all the nature of Samantabhadra—the spontaneously present mandala (*kun tu bzang po rang bzhin lhun grub gyi dkyil 'khor*). The emptiness that is their nature free from extremes is Samantabhadrī—the primordial mandala as it is (*kun tu bzang mo ye ji bzhin pa'i dkyil 'khor*). Also, both of these abide as an equality—essentially neither conjoined nor separable; all phenomena are ascertained as their "offspring of great bliss," the mandala of the spirit of awakening.

2. Path

These mandalas are primordially inseparable from one's mind; within which all phenomena are incorporated (*'ub chub pa*). Even so, there are appearances and fixations variously accepting and rejecting the good and the bad due to thoroughgoing, conceptual duality's deception, conditioned by the predispositions of the three appearances of transference (*snang ba gsum kyi 'pho ba'i bag chags*). In order to remove these appearances and obscuring fixations, one applies the essential points of channels, winds, and seminal essences as a method for actualizing the wisdom of great bliss. Through training in this, one traverses the stages of the aspiring mind on the path of accumulation, the discernment of great reason on the

---

15. On these five stages, see Mipam, *Overview: Essential Nature of Luminous Clarity*, 415–417; English translation in Dharmachakra Translation Group, *Luminous Essence*, 25.

16. On the four awareness-holders, see Mipam, *Overview: Essential Nature of Luminous Clarity*, 429–430; English translation in Dharmachakra Translation Group, *Luminous Essence*, 34–35.

path of joining, the great assurance on the path of seeing, the great prophesy on the path of meditation, and the perfection of great strength on the path of no more learning.

3. Fruition

One accomplishes the buddha, which is the completion of abandonment and realization and the *vajra*-like body of great bliss, on the ground of the perfect, universal mount (*rdzogs pa spyir chib kyi sa*).

3. ATIYOGA

There is also the ground, path, and fruition for Atiyoga.

1. Ground

All phenomena are ascertained as equality—as the self-existing gnosis primordially abiding within the essence of the single sphere itself. Moreover, all phenomena are merely appearances in one's mind; the nature of appearance is not at all established—it is false. Mind-nature (*sems nyid*) abides from the beginning as the identity of the three embodiments of buddhahood: the empty essence is the Truth Body; the natural clarity is the Enjoyment Body; and the all-pervasive compassionate resonance is the Emanation Body. Within the state of this reality that is the indivisibility of primordial purity and spontaneous presence, all phenomena of samsara and nirvana—without accepting or rejecting—are ascertained as the nature of equality, the great mandala of spontaneous presence.

2. Path

Having realized the ground in this way, one progressively actualizes the meaning of the basic nature as it is through resting without effort—without adding or removing, negating or affirming—within the gnosis of the essential nature that abides within. Moreover, although similar in effortlessly taking self-existing gnosis as the path, one completes the four visions[17] having overturned the ground of distortion by means of the practice of content-free (*rnam med*) primordial purity, such as the four means of resting freely (*cog bzhag bzhi*),[18] and the practice of spontaneous presence with images (*rnam bcas*), such as the three gazes of direct-crossing (*thod rgal*).

---

17. The four visions (*snang ba zhi*) are (1) manifestation of the basic nature (*chos nyid mngon sum*), (2) increased experience (*nyams snang gong 'phel*), (3) culmination of awareness (*rig pa tshad bab*), and (4) exhaustion of the basic nature (*chos nyid zad pa*).

18. The four means of resting freely (*cog bzhag bzhi*) are (1) ocean, (2) awareness, (3) appearance, and (4) mountain. For a description of these, see Longchenpa, *Treasure Trove of Scriptural Transmission*, 422–438; English translation in Richard Barron, trans., *A Treasure Trove of Scriptural Transmission*, 226–235.

3. Fruition

Having completed abandonment and realization through becoming free from all adventitious defilements, on the ground of the wisdom teacher (*ye shes bla ma*), the essence of the self-aware spirit of awakening abides free from increase or decrease—nondual with the pervasive sovereign, the primordial protector, Samantabhadra.

Moreover, within the Great Perfection, there are two sections that mainly emphasize the practice of the meaning of primordial purity:

- The Mind Section (*sems sde*), which mainly teaches the view that ascertains the essence of the self-aware spirit of awakening, and
- The Expanse Section (*klong sde*), which mainly teaches the meditation of unfabricated meditative equipoise by means of the fivefold expanse of gnosis pervading samsara and nirvana.

Mainly emphasizing the practice of spontaneous presence, there is

- The Quintessential Instructions Section (*man ngag sde*), which captures the essential point of the basic nature unerringly, without distortion, through ascertaining with the direct perception of the sense faculties the gnosis of luminous clarity abiding within.

Within each of these, there are several presentations concerning the manner of ascertainment in the internal divisions of the path. These should be known elsewhere, from the tantras and the great treasuries of good explanations by the omniscient Longchenpa.

In this way, although many divisions are made, in meaning it comes down to the same essential point: effortless engagement through naturally ascertaining the self-existing gnosis itself—abiding as the unity of primordial purity and spontaneous presence—which is free from the mind's obscuring covering. In this is the completion of all vehicles and philosophies.

> In this concise teaching of the essential points of scripture
> From the philosophy of the *Precious Wish-Fulfilling Treasury*,
> There is not the slightest quality that was not already there;
> However, it is for beginners—
> The ones who tire in reading the vast *Treasury of Reason*.
> After becoming familiar with this elucidation,
> They should look again to the intended meaning of the scripture
> That opens wide the reasoned path of philosophy.

I wrote this short summary according to the intended meaning of the autocommentary on the *Wish-Fulfilling Treasury*. At times, I also added a bit from the

Treasury of Philosophical Systems. From the pure scriptures of my own tradition, without drawing the discussion upon what other scriptures have said and without any of my own fabrications, Mipam Namgyel is the one who composed this with few words. May this benefit the explanation and study of the scriptures—by this virtue, may everyone be established in the state of the hero Mañjuśrī!

APPENDIX D

"Mahāmudrā Meditation: The Essential Nature of the Completion Stage"

Introduction

This text is a meditation instruction by Rikzin Chödrak, who was the first in the Chungtsang (*'bri gung chung tsang*) incarnation line of the Drikung Kagyü tradition. The translation presented here is a chapter from his *Words of Dharmakīrti* on the fivefold Mahāmudra, which is an instruction manual for a Mahāmudra practice that is distinctive to the Drikung Kagyü tradition. The full practice involves the following five elements: (1) the spirit of awakening (*bodhicitta*), (2) deity yoga, (3) guru yoga, (4) mahāmudrā, and (5) dedication. The excerpt that follows is a translation of the fourth element, Mahāmudrā itself, which is the main part from which the tradition of this practice manual gets its name. We can see in this text how philosophical themes of emptiness and the nature of mind inform this distinctive genre of meditation instructions. The footnotes to the text include translations of interlinear notes on Rikzin Chödrak's text by Könchok Trinlé Namgyel (b. 1624).

"Mahāmudrā Meditation: The Essential Nature of the Completion Stage"

"Mahāmudrā Meditation: The Essential Meaning of the Completion Stage"

By Rikzin Chödrak

The Protector of the World, Jikten Sumgön, said:

> In the vast space of mind-nature
> If the gathered clouds of thought do not disperse
> The stars and planets of the two wisdoms will not shine;
> Therefore, persistently strive in this nonconceptual mind.[1]

This has two parts: (1) stages of instruction and (2) pointing out instruction.

1. Stages of Instruction

The first part is twofold: instruction by means of the transcendent perfections of concentration and wisdom; or, (1) calm abiding and (2) special insight.

1. *Calm Abiding*

In general, "calm abiding" means to abide calmly without the disruption of conceptual constructs in the mind. To practice it, there are two ways: (1) with signs and (2) without signs.

1. WITH SIGNS

This is twofold: (1) with support and (2) without support.

---

1. Jikten Sumgön, *Song of Realization of the Fivefold Mahāmudrā* (*phyag rgya chen po lnga ldan rtogs pa'i mgur*), *Jikten Sumgön's Collected Works*, vol. 10, 97. Könchok Trinlé Namgyel's interlinear commentary adds: "'Space' represents the nature of mind, the Truth Body. 'Gathered clouds' represent the adventitious, co-emergent defilements, or thoughts. The stars and planets shining when the gathered clouds disperse represents the following: when persistently sustaining the fundamental nature of mind, which is primordially unborn, or sustaining the nonconceptual meaning without distraction or grasping, thoughts are recognized and purified in themselves—the qualities that are innately present from the beginning, such as the two wisdoms, are actualized."

1. With Support

Concentrate intensely on a support of observation in front of you, one that is not too bright.[2] Without being distracted, stay steadily focused on it for as long as you can within a state of empty clarity.[3] When the mind does not abide and thoughts suddenly arise, cut through them immediately, as soon as they arise. Stay focused nakedly on that support of observation. Rest naturally, without polluting the mind with thoughts such as "the support of observation has been brought into my mind," "my mind has been carried out to the support of observation," "my mind and the support of observation are the same," or "they or different," and so on. It is also fine to use any other support of observation, such as the body of a Tathāgata.

Or, visualize a *yidam* deity with the path of the generation stage. Within that state, stay as long as is comfortable without being distracted from the clear focus of mind, and without polluting the mind with thoughts such as "the color of the body and implements are like so," "the generation stage is clear," or "it is not clear," etc. If you can maintain your attention well in the generation stage, there are great purposes such as eventually gaining stability, integrating the two stages, and perfecting the viewpoint of the path of liberation.

2. Without Support

This section has two parts: (1) with the breath and (2) without the breath.

1. With the Breath

Direct your attention to the breath coming in, remaining, and going out. While meditating, do not pollute the mind with thoughts such as "now it is coming in, now it is going out . . . " Just use the breath as a *mere* support for your attention.

To summarize, to abide naturally in the natural state without disturbing the mind with distorting conceptuality is the defining characteristic of concentration. Also, the precious protector, Jikten Sumgön, claimed this to be the *vajra*-like meditative stabilization because it destroys the conceptuality that grasps at signs.

2. Without the Breath

Without any basis of support for the mind, rest naturally in the state of just how it is. If empty, let be within emptiness; if clear, let be within clarity—let be without fabrication. If thoughts suddenly arise, directly cut through them as was previously explained.

---

2. Könchok Trinlé Namgyel's interlinear notes add: "It seems that the intent here is that something bright and shiny may harm the eyes; or, it may lead one to err into agitation and dispersion."

3. Könchok Trinlé Namgyel's interlinear notes add: "The mind, eyes, and winds are one essential point; the mind abides when the eyes don't move."

2. WITHOUT SIGNS

This section has two parts: (1) tightened and (2) loosened.

1. Tightened

As was stated by Master Padma, for example:

> At the time of the completion stage,
> Sharpen your awareness,
> Invigorate your senses, and
> Awaken your consciousness.

Enliven your body and gaze. At times, dispel stale winds, sharpen your awareness, and resolve not to entertain any thoughts of the past, present, or future. Cut through all the movements of thought and rest within the state of empty clarity.

2. Loosened

If you become fatigued, or your mind becomes agitated by the previous tightened technique, then let your body and mind relax and rest naturally. Within this state, if coarse thoughts such as afflictions arise, directly cut through them. If there is a subtle movement of thought, let it be without obstructing it. Cut through dispersion by balancing these methods. Do short sessions frequently; this is a quintessential instruction.

If you are tightened too long, there is the problem of becoming agitated. If you are too loose, then you fall under the power of drowsiness, dullness, and sloth. Nevertheless, there are specific techniques according to a person's type and constitution: those who are sluggish, dull, bored, and lack clarity of awareness—having a predominance of the earth element—should mainly use the tightened technique. Those whose minds are like monkeys—the type who are predominantly excited and diffuse—should mainly practice the loosened technique. Those of the type who are dull and excited equally should practice tightened and loosened techniques in alternation. Without knowing this essential point, there is a danger that your meditation will be flawed.

2. *Special Insight*

In the instructions on special insight in the general language of the doctrine, there is meditation on "the selflessness of phenomena" and "the selflessness of persons." In the context of the profound instructions here, they are said to be (1) "ascertaining the various appearances as mind" and (2) "cutting through superimpositions at the root of the ground."

1. ASCERTAINING THE VARIOUS APPEARANCES AS MIND

This section has two parts: (1) ascertaining the nature of mind,[4] and (2) ascertaining thoughts, which are its expression.[5]

1. Ascertaining the Nature of Mind

When the mind abides alertly, look nakedly into its essence. Is this abiding the body or the mind? If it is the mind, it must be some kind of entity. Yet how is it? Does it have form, shape or color? Is its shape like a square, triangular, or round? Is its color white, red, or black? Is it in the body, outside the body, or somewhere in between? When the faculties, the eyes and so forth, see visible forms or hear sounds, does a single mind rotate among each of the faculties or does it pervade them all? As such, where is it? In the five major organs, such as the heart? In the six minor organs, such as the intestines? In the upper or lower part? If you think the mind permeates the entire body, then how does it permeate? If it remains as inseparably wed to the body, then where is the mind when the body becomes a corpse? In this way, examine well the mind's arising, abiding, departing, and so forth.

2. Ascertaining Thoughts, Which Are Its Expression

Have the one examining the mind look nakedly at thoughts. Do they have shape and color, etc.? Where do thoughts begin? When do they arise? Where do they abide now? Where do they go in the end? And so forth—examine in detail. It is extremely important to analyze deeply until you have gained certainty for yourself from within.

2. CUTTING THROUGH SUPERIMPOSITIONS AT THE ROOT OF THE GROUND

This section has four parts: (1) resolving that thoughts are the mind, (2) resolving that appearances are the mind, (3) cutting through the root of the abiding and moving mind, (4) resolving, or conclusively settling, that whatever arises is unborn.

1. Resolving that Thoughts Are the Mind

Within the state of a vividly abiding mind, construct a thought and look nakedly at it. Does this thought come from the mind or not? Is it the same as the mind or different? If it came from the mind, does it arise like light rays from the sun? If so, do thoughts and mind arise together like the simultaneous appearance of the sun and light rays?

Or you might think that thoughts arise upon meeting with conditions, and do not when not meeting with conditions—like smoke arising when incense and fire meet.

---

4. Könchok Trinlé Namgyel's interlinear notes add: "The selflessness of phenomena."

5. Könchok Trinlé Namgyel's interlinear notes add: "The selflessness of persons."

Is it the case that along with the cessation of one of the two, mind and thought, the other also ceases with it—like the smoke ceases along with the cessation of fire and incense?

Or you might think that they are like reflected images in a mirror. Well, does a thought depend upon the condition of an object like a reflected image depends upon the condition of an object? Do thoughts arise in one part of the mind and not another, like reflections shine in one part of a mirror but not in another?

Or you might think that they are like the appearance of the moon in water. Well, as the moon appears simultaneously in as many containers of water as there are, many conflicting thoughts, such as pleasure and pain, would likewise be suitable to simultaneously arise in the mind, but they do not.

Or you might think that they arise like a child from his mother. Well, do thoughts and mind live together as a mother and her child live together? Can the mind die when a thought is born, like a mother dying after giving birth to a child? Can thoughts die and the mind live on, like a mother living after her child has died? Is it that thoughts and mind both die, like the possibility that both the mother and child die? Investigate this in detail and reach a decision.

Moreover, you might think that mind and thoughts are the same. Are they the same in that the mind arises as thought, or are they the same by way of thoughts merging into the mind? If they are not the same, how are they different? In this way, investigate well.

2. Resolving that Appearances Are the Mind

Look directly at something in front of you like a pillar. Does this form arise from the mind or not? Is it the same as the mind or different? If it does not come from the mind, then even when dead, it would be suitable to appear to a corpse, but it does not. If it comes from the mind, then when you leave this place to go somewhere else, it would be suitable that objects like pillars accompany you, but they do not. Investigate in the same way as before with such things as sounds, scents, tastes, and textures.

Again, if the mind and objects are the same, are they the same in that the mind becomes appearances or are they the same by way of appearances merging into the mind? If they are not the same, are appearances and mind such that they are independently self-subsisting? How are they different? Investigate in this way.

3. Cutting Through the Root of the Abiding and Moving Mind

Look nakedly at the essence of the abiding mind at the time of calm abiding. Also, look nakedly at the essence of the moving mind, as when searching for the mind in special insight. Is there a difference between the two or not? If there is difference, what is it like? If not, how is it that the mind both moves and abides?

Further, through discerning examination, thoroughly resolve the presence of subtle movements within an abiding mind, such as the thought "it is still," and the subtle aspect of abiding within the state of a moving mind, such as the thought "it is moving."

4. Resolving, or Conclusively Settling, that Whatever Arises Is Unborn

Without paying attention to thoughts and appearances such as those of the sixfold collection of consciousness, look nakedly at the essence of mind-nature itself. Is it clear? Is it empty? Is it predominantly clear or predominantly empty? Is it indivisible as empty clarity? It is extremely important to investigate thoroughly in this way.[6]

2. Pointing Out Instruction

This section has three parts: (1) the actual pointing out instruction, (2) explanation of the faults of meditation, and (3) the experience of faultless meditation, or the way to sustain the continuity of practice.

1. *Actual Pointing Out Instruction*

From among the three types of co-emergence [co-emergence of thoughts, appearances, and mind-nature], I will first state the pointing out instructions for the co-emergence of thoughts.

1. CO-EMERGENCE OF THOUGHTS

Previously at the time of ascertaining thoughts, and ascertaining thoughts as the mind, if you understood thoughts and mind to be the same or different, then you still have yet to resolve them. In the previous explanation of metaphors, if you understood the relationship between thoughts and mind to be like light rays arising from the sun, it is similar from the aspect that thoughts just arise from the mind. However, in the way that the sun and light rays appear distinctly, it is impossible for two, mind and thoughts, to appear as if together.

If you understand the relationship to be like incense and smoke, it is similar from the aspect of simply arising when meeting with conditions. However, while the smoke is gone when the incense is consumed, it does not make sense that when one of the two, mind and thought, is gone that the other is consumed too.

Or, if you understand the relationship to be like a child born from his mother, it is similar from the aspect that one arises from the other. However, since the mother and child are separate continua, if the mother dies the child can live, or if the child

6. Könchok Trinlé Namgyel's interlinear notes add: "On these points, if you leave it as a mere intellectual understanding, and think 'I have heard this before,' without probing to the depths of analysis, then later you will enter into a web of doubt. Some so-called mature meditators still need to search out the pointing out instructions and the obstacles to be dispelled; this problem is due to their failure to decisively resolve this here."

dies the mother can live, or they can both live or die together, but this is impossible for mind and thought.

Thus, a nearly appropriate metaphor is like gold and tarnish. Mind and thought arise co-emergently. Even though it appears as if thoughts obscure the nature of mind, which is the Truth Body, by recognizing that thoughts themselves are the Truth Body they are self-purified; understand that they are inseparably liberated. They are not the same by such ways as the mind becoming thought or thought merging with the mind. Rather, mind and thought are essentially indivisible; they are only different conceptually, in the way that water and ice appear differently due to the conditions of temperature, but in essence are none other than water. Therefore, when it is realized that they are neither the same nor different, the co-emergence of thoughts is recognized. Furthermore, the sovereign Maitripa said:

> Adventitious thoughts arise from the unborn;
> Thoughts themselves are the essential nature of the basic field.
> From the beginning, these two are not different;
> The equal taste of these two is my teaching.

2. CO-EMERGENCE OF APPEARANCES[7]

When you look directly at something in front of you like a pillar or pot, its appearance as something truly real with genuine characteristics is the *imagined nature* because it is imputed by the deluded mind. It is produced by other conditions; hence, it is the *dependent nature*. When its essence is examined and scrutinized, the *consummate nature* is the realization that it is essentially not established other than being a mere name, a mere sign, and a mere designation. As illustrated by this, all appearances—such as forms, sounds, scents, tastes, and textures—have these three natures.

Not even the Victorious Ones can stop this mere appearance; the mere appearance itself is empty of its own essence. Therefore, appearances and mind are not such that they are independently self-subsisting. Appearances are not left outside and the mind is not left inside; they are essentially indivisible, from either aspect of clarity or emptiness. They are also not the same by way of the mind going out to merge with appearances or appearances coming in to merge with the mind. When appearances and mind are realized to be neither the same nor different in reality, then the co-emergence of appearances is recognized. Furthermore, the *Inconceivable Tantra* states:

> The co-emergent nature of mind is the Truth Body.
> Co-emergent appearances are the radiance of the Truth Body.
> Therefore, indivisible appearances and mind are co-emergent.

---

7. Könchok Trinlé Namgyel's interlinear notes add: "Pointing out that appearances are resolved to be mind."

3. CO-EMERGENCE OF MIND-NATURE[8]

From among the flawless calm abidings in the beginning, middle, and end, in the end, there is calm abiding that is like an ocean undisturbed by waves. All thought-constructs are completely pacified; nevertheless, it is not like a nonconceptual oblivion. The sixfold collections of consciousness are unhindered and lucid, yet the mind does not follow after them, but resolves their essence as indivisible clarity and emptiness. No matter how many waves form on the vast ocean, other than the surface, the depths are not moved. Likewise, even movements within abiding and abiding within movement, etc., are none other than mind-nature's mere aspect of lucidity; when self-liberated as the essence of indivisible emptiness and clarity, the co-emergence of mind-nature is recognized. Furthermore, the Glorious Shawari said:

> Just as all the various rivers, such as the Ganges,
> Are of one taste in the salty ocean,
> Know that the investigating mind and all the various mental states
> Are of one taste in the basic field of reality.

2. *Explanation of the Faults of Meditation*

For an extensive presentation of the faults of meditation, you should know it from the *Vajra Song of the Nonconceptual Ultimate*.[9] What I write here is extracted from that *Vajra Song:*

> For those following the meditation on such a meaning
> The mistakes and faults of meditation are as follows.
> When mainly holding onto the aspect of the abiding mind
> The sixfold collections cease or the mind blocks them.
> Becoming like a lake covered with ice,
> This is abiding in nothing at all.
> It causes the attainment of the three states spoken by the Lord [Sakya] Paṇḍita;
> This is a fault.
> Even when the perceptions of the sixfold collections are not obstructed,
> When they are unclear and hazy
> This is the fault called "foggy meditation."
> When oblivious,
> Without noticing whether or not the sixfold collections are clear,

8. Könchok Trinlé Namgyel's interlinear notes add: "The pointing out instructions on ascertaining the nature of mind, cutting through the root of the abiding and moving mind, and resolving that whatever appears is unborn."

9. Könchok Trinlé Namgyel's interlinear notes add: "This was written by the Lord [Rikzin Chödrak] himself."

This is the fault called "neutrality."
After a previous thought subsides and
Before the next thought arises,
Meditation with an unfocused mind in a blank state
Is faulty because special insight is not involved.
Even if it is embraced by special insight,
Desiring blank meditation
To be the unwavering Mahāmudrā
Has the fault of "famished meditation."
Even when meditating on sheer bliss in the mind,
Since there is no gnosis of special insight
Thoughts and appearances are held as enemies.
This is the fault of holding one as two.
Also, when your mind is utterly empty,
Without engaging in any thoughts of the three times,
Since this also is not embraced by special insight,
It has the fault of blocking the appearing quality.
Meditation with an apprehension of the unreality
Of anything and everything that appears,
With certainty in the emptiness that is provisional and definitive,
Has the fault of holding onto an absence of entities.
Also, thinking meditation to be mindless perception,
Without accepting or rejecting within the sixfold collections,
Has the fault of abiding in indifference.
Also, one may maintain that the nature of mind that is clear and nonconceptual is meditation—
An unidentifiable clarity of awareness
After thoughts have pacified on their own.
While this is similar to the meaning of the mode of reality,
Since the nonconceptual is eagerly held,
This too is an ultimate that is partial.
When the mind and all mental states
Are in a vivid state of empty clarity,
This is similar to meditation; however,
This does not have the natural swells of mindfulness and
The aspect of loose relaxation.
It also is difficult for one who is overly tight and rigid
To realize the mode of reality.
Those who boast the emptiness of all of samsara and nirvana—
Without maintaining the three supreme refuges as refuge and
Without cultivating compassion for the six downtrodden beings—
Act without regard for causality.

This is the nihilistic prattle of voidness.
It may be thought that whether the mind is abiding or moving
One sustains that alone,
Having thrown out the necessary essentials such as faults and qualities,
Dispelling obstacles, and making enhancements.
Like the blind leading the blind,
There are many who say "Mahāmudrā" and
Claim to have realized the ultimate entity of mind.
Yet when afflictive thoughts arise
Immediately they run wild into the coarse five poisons.
When medicine becomes poison there is no cure;
This is the root of all the faults.[10]

Further, here is a presentation of the four sidetracks and three deviations, etc.

1. FOUR SIDETRACKS

There are four sidetracks: (1) sidetrack within the basic nature, (2) sidetrack within the remedy, (3) sidetrack within the path, and (4) sidetrack within stamping a seal. Each of the four has two parts: (1) a fundamental sidetrack and (2) a circumstantial sidetrack.

1. Sidetrack within the Basic Nature

The fundamental sidetrack is to hold on to only the empty aspect, in resolving that all things—from form to omniscience—lack a basic nature from the beginning. The circumstantial sidetrack is to meditate on nonexistence, thinking "nothing is real" at the time of practice.

2. Sidetrack within the Remedy

The fundamental sidetrack is to think that everything in the sūtras and tantras, etc., is only a remedy, and that the afflictions, etc., are only to be rejected. The circumstantial sidetrack is to meditate on Mahāmudrā as a remedy to thoughts and afflictions.

3. Sidetrack within the Path

The fundamental sidetrack is to view the ground as inferior, the path as what is to be abandoned, and the fruition as excellent. The circumstantial sidetrack is to take to the path of Mahāmudrā meditation now, hoping to achieve some other Truth Body in the future.

---

10. Rikzin Chödrak, *Vajra Song of the Nonconceptual Ultimate* (*rtog med don dam rdo rje'i glu*), in *Great Treasury of Drikung Kagyü* (*'bri gung bka' brgyud chos mdzod chen mo*), vol. 101, 542–544.

4. Sidetrack within Stamping a Seal

The fundamental sidetrack is to act as if stamping everything that was previously existent with a seal of primordial nonexistence. The circumstantial sidetrack is to instantly purify real entities into emptiness by means of a mantra with three purities, for instance, as if stamping them with a seal.

2. THREE DEVIATIONS

There are three deviations: (1) deviation into bliss, (2) deviation into clarity, and (3) deviation into non-thought.

1. Deviation into Bliss

Deviation into bliss is clinging to, or falling under the power of, the bliss that arises in the sixfold collections of consciousness or blissful experiences, such as the dripping of milk and blood, without bringing them onto the path. This also includes clinging to happiness resulting from pacifying sickness or alleviating suffering through meditation.

2. Deviation into Clarity

Deviation into clarity is attachment to experiences of clarity, being awe-inspired by the occurrence of paranormal powers such as: seeing what is hidden, like one's body, house, or the universe, etc.; reading someone's mind, or hearing remotely.

3. Deviation into Non-Thought

Deviation into non-thought is to cling to the cessation of thoughts of the sixfold collections of consciousness, the experience of the emptiness of cessation, or a nonconceptual vacuity.

Other than respectively leading to birth in the Desire Realm, the Form Realm, and the Formless Realm, these three deviations do not go on the path of liberation. Also, to denigrate the causality of karma, resolving that the meaning of emptiness is such that there are no results from good or evil deeds, is to deviate into nihilistic prattle. Furthermore, holding what is to be abandoned, identifying it, and meditating on emptiness as a remedy to it is the root of the sidetracks and deviations. Moreover, it is said that to view all phenomena as relatively existent and ultimately nonexistent, as relatively nonexistent and ultimately existent, as both relatively and ultimately existent, or as nonexistent, is to deviate into holding extremes.

After explaining the faults of meditation, now I will describe the experience of faultless meditation.

3. The Experience of Faultless Mediation, or the Way to Sustain the Continuity of Practice

This section has two parts: (1) identifying the fresh, ordinary mind, and (2) the actual way of sustaining the practice.

1. IDENTIFYING THE FRESH, ORDINARY MIND

First of all, it is important to identify the meaning of "ordinary mind." Master Toktsepa taught its meaning in this context of Mahāmudrā as follows:

> Let the guest, the fatigued nature of mind,
> Relax free from constructs.
> Fresh, innate, and natural—
> This is Mahāmudrā beyond the intellect.

The way to let the guest—the nature of mind fatigued by the constructs of perceiver-perceived duality—rest is threefold: (1) fresh, (2) innate, and (3) natural. The past has finished and the future has yet to arise. This present mind is new; this is the meaning of *fresh*. Although the word "fresh" is used, since it is the original or primordial mind itself, it is *innate*. One might think, "Isn't this a mind of the future?" Due to the essential indivisibility of the three times, it is *natural*. Since the meaning is beyond the domain of mind, it is as stated, "This is Mahāmudrā beyond the intellect."

Or, explained in conjunction with the views of the four philosophies,[11] the Protector Maitreya stated:

> Becoming aware that there is nothing apart from the mind,
> They realize that also the mind does not exist at all.
> Having seen that the two do not exist, the intelligent ones abide
> In the basic field of reality, which does not contain that.[12]

All phenomena of samsara and nirvana—the outer and inner environment and inhabitants—are one's mind. The mind too is empty of essence. Even though appearances and mind appear dualistically, they are not taken as referent objects. They are realized as free from the constructs of existence and nonexistence, etc. Or, according to Mantra in the context of the fourth empowerment:

> This gnosis is extremely subtle and
> Like a *vajra* in the center of space.[13]

---

11. Könchok Trinlé Namgyel's interlinear notes add: "Among the four philosophical systems, the Vaibhāṣikas assert perceived objects as minute particles and the perceiving mind as momentary; Sautrāntikas accept appearances as the mind, yet dualistically, with perceiving subjects and perceived objects; proponents of Mind-Only accept self-awareness, without perceiver-perceived duality, as truly real; Mādhyamikas assert all phenomena to be free from constructs."

12. *Ornament of the Great Vehicle Sūtras* (*Mahāyanasutrālaṃkāra*) VII.8 (D. 4020, vol. 123), 6b; English trans. in Dharmachakra Translation Committee, *Ornament of the Great Vehicle Sūtras*, 138.

13. Könchok Trinlé Namgyel's interlinear notes add: "Or 'essence equal to space.'

Immaculate, liberation-bestowing[14] peace;
You are its father, too.

Since the primordial mind from the beginning is not understood by thought constructs, it is *extremely subtle*. It is indestructible by conditions. Samsara is destroyed when it is realized; nirvana is destroyed when it is not realized. Therefore, it is a *vajra*. Since it is the nature of both samsara and nirvana, it is the *essence*; it is *equal to space* due to having a meaning that is like space, beyond color and shape. Or, stated as "like a *vajra* in the center of space," the center is the meaning of the indivisibility of center and periphery in space. Through realizing afflictions themselves as its essence, defilements are purified without being abandoned; therefore, it is *immaculate*. It is the perfection of samsara and reaches the great nirvana; hence, it is *perfection* and peace. Or, because it attains or bestows liberation, it is *liberation-bestowing peace*. This is to be realized for oneself; it cannot be shown by another. Tilopa said,

Know this as presented in self-awareness.[15]

Since this is similar it is said, "You are its father, too." In short, the natural way of mind, the fundamental nature of mind undisturbed by thoughts of the three times, cannot be expressed by words, but it can be experienced. It is not a nonconceptual vacuity nor is it a mind that follows after thoughts; it is the naked and vivid awareness that is the ordinary mind. Furthermore, the *Thoroughly Non-Abiding Thusness Tantra* says:

The nature of the ordinary mind is the supreme fruition.
When let be without fabrication, the fruition of the three embodiments of buddhahood is attained.
When let loose as it is, it is the consummate gnosis.

And Nāgārjuna said:

Don't conceptualize or think of anything at all.
Don't alter; relax naturally.
Without fabrication, be natural and unborn.

14. Könchok Trinlé Namgyel's interlinear notes add: "Or 'perfection.'

15. Rikzin Chödrak cites here a close variant of Tilopa's statement found in Wangchuk Gyeltsen, *Biography of Nāropa* (Bir, India: tsondu senghe yorey tsang, 2006), 96.

And Shawari said:

Do not disturb the innate way of the ordinary mind
With fabricated objects of reference.
You don't need to alter the mind that is naturally pure.
Don't hold it or let it go; let it be just as it is.

And Tilopa said:

Without thinking, pondering, or reflecting, and
Without meditating or analyzing, let be naturally.[16]

Nāropa said:

If you look, look at your mind.
Since the nature of mind is not established at all
It is inexpressible and transcends objects;
Free from constructs; it has the nature of space.

And Maitripa said:

Other than remaining undistracted within this state
There is nothing to do with the body or speech, and nothing to meditate on.

And Lord Marpa said:

It is not to be meditated on nor are you to be distracted;
It is unthinkable and inexpressible.
It cannot be illustrated by anything.
I realized it as such through the kindness of the lama.

And the Venerable [Milarepa] said:

When meditating on Mahāmudrā,
Do not exert yourself in virtuous activities of the body and speech;
There is a danger that nonconceptual gnosis will dissipate.
Rest in the uncontrived, innate state.

16. Wangchuk Gyeltsen, *Biography of Nāropa*, 96.

And Lord Gampopa said:

> Do not alter; loosely relax.
> Do not search; just let be.
> Do not engage the mind; rest without reference.

And Lord Pakmo Drupa said:

> Upon investigation and analysis, there are no real entities.
> That which is beyond shape and color
> Becomes poison if found by the mind.
> So rest naturally without fabrication.[17]

And the Lord [Jikten Sumgön,] Protector of the World said:

> One's own awareness, the uncontrived, ordinary mind,
> Left naturally to itself as it is right now, is called "Mahāmudrā."
> Therefore, mindful of only this, sustain it.[18]

Also, the Lord Yanggönpa said, "In short, the ordinary mind, not created by anyone, is just this; this itself recognizing itself is called 'the birth of Mahāmudrā meditation'."

2. THE ACTUAL WAY OF SUSTAINING THE PRACTICE

This section has four parts: (1) the way of sustaining meditation in general; (2) the ways of sustaining meditation in particular: (a) for beginners, (b) for those with a little familiarity, and (c) for those with a lot of familiarity; (3) the way of bringing onto the path; and (4) the way of realization.

1. The Way of Sustaining Meditation in General

The arising of meditation is not enough; it needs to be sustained well. For this, aversion is the foot, or ruler, of meditation. Therefore, contemplate the sufferings of samsara. Put the impermanence of this life and [samsara's] lack of essence at the forefront of your mind. Give up worldly attachments and cultivate your mind to equalize your life with your practice.

Devotion is the head, or enhancement, of meditation. Therefore, without being apart from the attitude that the lama and Kagyü [masters] are actual buddhas, supplicate them longingly from your heart. Mindfulness is the watchman, or main part, of meditation. Therefore, when not in a session, don't let your mind stray elsewhere. At all times and circumstances, train to not be separate from being mindful of the mode of reality.

---

17. I did not locate this passage among Pakmodru's collected works.

18. I did not locate this passage among Jikten Sumgön's collected works.

The activity of meditation is compassion in action. Cultivate love, compassion, and the spirit of awakening for all sentient beings. Dedicate and make aspirations to protect them. Until you perfect your meditation, teaching others and developing them is a semblance of the welfare of others. It is the obstructing hold of demons, so rely on solitude. The armor of meditation is having a conscience and knowing shame: internally, let your mind be your own witness, and externally, don't shame the lamas, the [three] jewels, and your dharma friends. Meditate earnestly by means of reliable mountain retreats, sealed retreats, and silence, and so on.

Moreover, the essential point of consummate profundity is to rely on uninterrupted, undistracted mindfulness as previously explained. Jikten Sumgön said:

> The highway of the buddhas of the three times
> Is continuous, uninterrupted mindfulness.
> Without knowing constant mindfulness
> There is not much benefit in the deeds of body and speech.[19]

And Lord Pakmo Drupa said:

> Give up hopes for the paranormal and magical powers, etc.;
> Look at your mind.
> When not separate from watching the mind
> It is certain that all the buddha's qualities without exception—
> Such as the ten powers, eighteen unshared qualities, and
> Four fearlessnesses—will come in the first intermediate state (*bar do*).[20]

2. The Way of Sustaining Meditation in Particular

1. For Beginners

As for the way of sustaining meditation for beginners, sustain in the way spoken by Lord Götsangpa:

> Look nakedly at your mind.
> It is not seen by looking; it is not a real entity.
> Relax within the state of absence.
> Rest vividly, without grasping.[21]

---

19. Jikten Sumgön, *Blazing Victory Banner of the Precious Stages of the Bodhisattva Path* (*rgyal sras rnams kyi lam rim rin po che 'bar ba'i rgyal mtshan*), *Jikten Sumgön's Collected Works*, vol. 1, 231.

20. Pakmodru, *Precious Staircase* (*rin po che'i them skas*), *Pakmodru's Collected Works*, vol. 3, 76.

21. Götsangpa, *One Hundred Thousand Songs of Götsangpa* (*dpal mnyam med rgyal ba rgod tshang pa'i mgur 'bum chen mo*), in *Collected Works of Götsangpa Gönpo Dorjé*, vol. 5, 257.

Look nakedly at your mind; no nature of mind is seen whatsoever. Relax into the nature of mind—into the way it is—within the state of experiencing the lack of a real entity. Moreover, without falling into neutrality, and without a referent object, meditate without contrivance within the unborn with a bright and vivid awareness. Without accepting or rejecting, or holding onto the empty or non-empty, rest within an empty and clear state without grasping at anything whatsoever.

2. For Those With a Little Familiarity

Those with a little familiarity just look nakedly at the essence of whatever appears or arises; other than that, they do not need to make deliberate efforts to set the mind.

3. For Those With a Lot of Familiarity

Those with a lot of familiarity do not need the slightest bit of effortful meditation because they are free from clinging to something to be meditated on and a meditator.

> In summary, as was stated by the Lord Atīśa:
> The eighty-four thousand sections of doctrine
> Come down to this basic nature.

The essential meaning of all the topics of the sacred dharma is only this uncontrived, ordinary mind. The great Venerable One [Milarepa] said:

> By sustaining the ordinary mind
> I left ignorance and confusion in the dust.

As for sustaining this practice, it is said that there is nothing better than not clinging to whatever appears. I see this to singularly comprise all the essential points of practice because clinging to self and other is the root of samsara. Even clinging to what is positive—such as the view, meditation, and conduct—obstructs liberation, needless to mention clinging to what is negative such as the three poisons! Thus, all defects and faults are initiated by a clinging mind. Therefore, the supreme path is to rest without clinging to anything whatsoever that appears, no matter what arises—such as appearances of meditative experiences with and without signs or mundane appearances that arise in dependence upon ordinary habits. The matchless Gampopa said:

> Whatever may arise, don't cling to it at all!
> There is nothing that will take you further than this supreme path.

And,

> Without fixation, all is equality.
> When realized as such, meditation is uninterrupted.

And Saraha said:

> Whatever you are attached to, give it up!

These statements have a similar intent.

Further, some other meditators claim to have it sometimes and other times not—depending on such conditions as whether they are in a gathering or in solitude, at ease or busy at work. Although they understand this mode of reality that completely pervades samsara and nirvana on the surface, like the waves on the ocean, they don't realize it from the depths, which is a problem. In reality, if the mind is there, so is Mahāmudrā. If there is no mind, there is no Mahāmudrā.

Therefore, it does not rely at all on good or bad conditions, such as gatherings or solitude, leisure or work. Do not accept or reject, and have no hopes or fears, doubts or worries such as thinking, "Is this Mahāmudrā or not?" "Is this meditation or not?" At all times, no matter what appears, look nakedly[22] at whatever arises, and without fabrication, sustain [Mahāmudrā].

3. The Way of Bringing onto the Path

Moreover, there are many different practices for bringing onto the path, such as the famed "sixfold equal taste" to identify thoughts—along with afflictions, gods and demons, sickness, suffering, and death, etc.—in the different activities of Mahāmudra. Nevertheless, Jikten Sumgön said,

> The arising of an affliction itself is a thought.
> Self-apprehension is also a thought.
> To meditate as a remedy to this is also a thought.
> I do not construct this stack of three thoughts![23]

Since all this is the function of just your mind, the single sufficient way to bring onto the path is to sustain [Mahāmudrā] without clinging to whatever may arise; the remedy and what is to be abandoned are indivisible. To illustrate this with gods and demons, the thought that apprehends them itself is the obstruction or troublemaker. If you know the essential point of resting just as it is, there are no outer

---

22. Könchok Trinlé Namgyel's interlinear notes add: "It was asked whether there was a difference between (1) looking nakedly at whatever arises and (2) relaxing loosely. The response was 'no.' As an implication of this, it has been said that the past masters had no more profound method for sustaining meditation than mindfulness. Among the two types of mindfulness explained—effortful mindfulness and effortless mindfulness—relaxing without clinging to whatever arises is effortless mindfulness. This is taught to be superior to effortful mindfulness."

23. I did not locate this passage among Jikten Sumgön's collected works.

troublemakers at all. For example, the Venerable Milarepa took the Rock Ogress as an enemy. However, just his thought fixating on the Rock Ogress was the enemy. Other than that, there was no harm at all done by the Rock Ogress. Therefore, the meaning of the "single sufficient remedy" taught by the past masters has the intent of not needing to rely on anything else to bring onto the path. If you know the essential point of practice such as this, however coarse your afflictions are, the power of your realization will be that much stronger. Hence, you do not need to see them as faults. Also, a sūtra says,

> The way that afflictions accompany the path of a bodhisattva is as follows:
> In the way that the filthy manure of the center of the city
> Helps the sugarcane in the fields,
> The manure of a bodhisattva's afflictions likewise
> Helps the Victorious Ones and their triumphant qualities.[24]

Just as the filthy manure of the center of the city produces sugarcane, or crops, likewise, when strong afflictions meet with a strong remedy, the fruition is instantly attained. For example, when the Buddha taught the dharma to Midungwa, "the one with the garland of fingers," who was extremely angry, he instantly saw the truth.

Moreover, for those who bring afflictions onto the Secret Mantra path, the potency of the path corresponds with how strong the afflictions are. In this context of Mahāmudrā, not only afflictions, but even love, compassion, the spirit of awakening, and deity meditation, etc.—all positive and negative thoughts—in reality are not different in just being thoughts. They are not to be deliberately abandoned or taken up; the authentic essential point of practice[25] is to sustain [Mahāmudrā] within whatever arises without contrivance.

It is said that due to attaining mastery in the authentic meaning of one's mind, one is called a "realized one" (*rtogs ldan*) because of realizing, or seeing, the essence of yoga and mind. In accord with the aforementioned statements on bringing onto the path, Saraha said:

> Lions, elephants, tigers, black bears, brown bears,
> Fierce wild animals, poisonous snakes, fires, and precipices,
> Punishment by kings, poisons, thunder and lightning;
> Since the essence of all of them is only this, there is no harm.
> By overcoming the great enemy of thought, you overcome all enemies.

---

24. *Sūtra of the Kāśyapa Chapter* (*Kāśyapaparivartasūtra*), (H. 87, vol. 40), 227b-228a.

25. Könchok Trinlé Namgyel's interlinear notes add: "The Protector [Jikten Sumgön] said that the afflictions, etc. are dispelled by the fivefold path; however, this was intended for those who have not yet achieved mastery. The consummate intent is the indivisibility of what is abandoned and the remedy."

By taming the toxic view of self, you tame the entirety of toxins.
Therefore, be the jewel of mind sublime.

And Nāropa said:

All obstacles of sicknesses and demons
Are comprised within thought.
When you're sick, it is thought itself that is sick;
When you are harmed, it is thought itself that is harmed;
When you die, it is thought itself that dies;
When you're born, it is thought itself that is born;
All happiness and suffering, etc. is thought—
There is nothing other than mind.
If you cut through the root basis of thought,
No sickness or demons will come.

To meditate on the meaning of this mode of reality comprises everything within the Sūtra path—the threefold study, contemplation, and meditation, and the six transcendent perfections—as well as the generation stage and the elaborate completion stage in the Mantra path. Saraha said:

It is reading, it is memorization and meditation, too.
It is also holding the treatises in your heart.

The *Vajrasamādhi Sūtra* says:

Not wavering from emptiness
Comprises the six transcendent perfections.

The *Condensed Perfection of Wisdom Sūtra* states:

> Any learned person who wants to perfect all the trainings should train in the buddha's training, this perfection of wisdom.[26]

The *Two Sections [Hevajra Tantra]* says:

Within the nature free from constructs
Mantras and deities authentically dwell.[27]

---

26. *Condensed Perfection of Wisdom Sūtra* (*Prajñāpāramitā-sañcayagāthā*), (H. 17, vol. 34), 209b–210a.

27. *Hevajra Tantra* (H. 378a, vol. 79), 341b.

And,

> It is mantra recitation; it is doing austerities; it is doing burnt offerings;
> It is the lord of the mandala; it is the mandala itself.
> In short, the mind embodies the collective.[28]

Therefore, there is more merit in meditating for a single instant on the meaning of the profound mode of reality than there is in performing conditioned virtues for many aeons. The *Sūtra of Maitreya's Great Lion's Roar* in the *Jewel Heap* (*Ratnakūṭa*) says:

> Someone may fill all the world-realms in the great billionfold universe with *stūpas* made from the seven precious substances and as big as the king of the supreme mountains. Yet there is greater, inconceivable merit in attaining the forbearance of the profound doctrine for the duration of just a finger-snap.[29]

The *Sūtra of the Meeting of the Father and Son* says:

> There is more merit in hearing about thusness than in practicing the five perfections for ten aeons. There is more merit in teaching one sentient being than in listening for ten aeons. O Śāriputra, someone may teach others about thusness for ten aeons, but the merit of one who meditates on the meaning of thusness for the duration of just a finger-snap is greater and increases immeasurably.[30]

By realizing that what is to be abandoned and the remedy are indivisible, all evil deeds, obscurations, and predispositions are purified. Tilopa said:

> For example, in the way that a single torch dispels a mass of darkness
> That was dark for thousands of aeons,
> Likewise, a single instant of a luminous and clear mind
> Dispels the evil deeds, obscurations, and ignorance accumulated for aeons.[31]

---

28. *Hevajra Tantra* (H. 378a, vol. 79), 352b.

29. I did not find this exact passage in the text, but similar passages are found there. See, for instance, *Sūtra of Maitreya's Great Lion's Roar* (*Maitreya-mahāsiṃhanāda-sūtra*) (H. 67, vol. 39), 176b.

30. *Sūtra of the Meeting of the Father and Son* (*Pitāputrasamāgamasūtra*), (H. 60, vol. 38), 357b.

31. Tilopa, *Ganges Mahāmudrā* (*phyag rgya chen po'i man ngag*), v. 17. See Tibetan edition and English translation in Sangye Nyenpa, *Tilopa's Mahamudra Upadesha* (Boston: Snow Lion, 2014), 12–13.

The *Precious Garland* states:

> Those with little merit
> Do not even have doubts about this doctrine.
> Merely having a doubt about it
> Tears existence to shreds.[32]

All the joy and happiness—of this world and that which is transcendent—is brought forth without needing the exertion of effort. The *Condensed Perfection of Wisdom Sūtra* says:

> One should know that all happiness—the happiness that is conditioned and the happiness that is unconditioned—comes from this.[33]

And,

> The buddhas, their [bodhisattva] offspring, Disciples, Self-Realized Ones, the deities, and
> Whatever happiness and joy there is for anyone,
> All comes from the supreme perfection of wisdom.[34]

Along with this, it destroys attachment and aversion to the eight [worldly] concerns, such as gain and loss. The *Way of the Bodhisattva* says:

> In these empty entities
> What is there to gain and what is there to lose?
> Who is there to honor me?
> And who is there to scorn?
> From where does this happiness and suffering come?
> What is there to be happy or sad about?[35]

---

32. Although attributed here to the *Precious Garland*, this passage is from Āryadeva, *Four Hundred Verses* (*Catuḥśataka*) VIII.5 (D. 3846, vol. 97), 9a; English trans. in Ruth Sonam, *Āryadeva's Four Hundred Stanzas on the Middle Way* (Ithaca: Snow Lion Publications, 2008), 188.

33. *Condensed Perfection of Wisdom Sūtra* (*Prajñāpāramitā-sañcayagāthā*), (H. 17, vol. 34), 193a.

34. *Condensed Perfection of Wisdom Sūtra* (*Prajñāpāramitā-sañcayagāthā*), (H. 17, vol. 34), 210a.

35. Śāntideva, *Way of the Bodhisattva* (*Bodhicaryāvatāra*) IX.151–152ab.

Unbearable, great compassion comes about for sentient beings who do not realize this. Nāgārjuna said:

For yogis who have meditated
On emptiness in this way,
There is no doubt that
There is joy in benefiting others.[36]

Through just this realization one traverses the path and quickly actualizes the state of the buddha, without needing to reckon with the stages of the grounds and paths. The *King of Meditative Stabilizations Sūtra* states:

Someone who upholds this supreme meditative stabilization
Attains the ten grounds:
Complete joy, the stainless, illumination,
The radiant, extremely difficult to train, the manifest
Gone afar, unwavering, good mind, and the cloud of dharma.[37]

And from the *Tent* (*gur*):

Through meditating that the mind is just the supreme buddha,
You become a buddha in this life.

And in the *Sun and Moon Accomplishment* (*nyi zla grub pa*):

Yogis of highest capacity
Engage in unwavering concentration
Through relying on the ultimate Mahāmudrā.
By this, in accord with the cause, their meditation is the meditative stabilization of empty bliss.
In three years and one and a half months,
They attain the supreme accomplishment.

4. The Way of Realization

Concerning the way of realization, together with enhancement, there are four yogas: (1) single-pointedness, (2) freedom from constructs, (3) one-taste, and

36. Although attributed to Nāgārjuna, this passage is found in Atiśa's *Open Treasury of Essential Instructions on the Middle Way* (*Ratnakaraṇḍodghāṭa-madhyamakopadeśa*), (D. 3930, vol. 110), 97b.

37. *King of Meditative Stabilizations Sūtra* (*Samādhirājasūtra*), (H. 129, vol. 55), 160a.

(4) non-meditation. It is said that each has a division into lesser, middling, and great, so there are twelve.

1. Four Yogas

1. Single-Pointedness

Lesser single-pointedness is when there is slight difficulty sustaining a meditative stabilization with experiences of bliss, clarity, and non-thought, up until meditation comes whenever one meditates. Middling single-pointedness is when there is meditative stabilization sometimes even when not meditating and there is stability at the times of meditation. Great single-pointedness is when one is utterly immersed within the state of empty clarity continuously, without interruption in sessions or breaks, during the four activities, in the day and night.

2. Freedom from Constructs

Lesser freedom from constructs is when one realizes thoughts and appearances as the essence of mind, free from the constructs of arising and ceasing, yet not free from addiction to the certainty that fixates upon emptiness. Also, one has hopes and fears regarding samsara and nirvana. Middling freedom from constructs is when addiction to the certainty that fixates upon emptiness has dissipated, yet there are hopes and fears regarding appearances as well as superimpositions that have not been cut through. Having become free from holding onto the certainty that fixates on the emptiness of all that appears and exists in samsara and nirvana, great freedom from constructs is when one is free from hopes and fears and has cut through superimpositions.

3. One-Taste

Lesser one-taste is when one realizes that all thoughts and appearances are the one-taste of Mahāmudrā, the nature of mind, yet there is still addiction to the certainty that fixates upon that experience. After the defiling certainty that fixates on the experience of the one-taste of plurality is purified, middling one-taste is when the indivisibility of mind and appearances vividly manifests; appearances are not left outside and the mind is not left inside. Great one-taste is when everything is pacified within the innate state of equality; the one-taste of plurality is realized and one-taste arises in plurality.

4. Non-Meditation

Lesser non-meditation is when there is no need to maintain mindfulness and no need to deliberately rest in meditative equipoise; all appearances arise as meditation. It is lesser non-meditation as long as there arises a slight illusory clinging. Middling non-meditation is when even slight illusory clinging is gone. All night and all day are constant non-meditation, yet there is a subtle aspect of consciousness that arises as self-luminosity in ensuing perceptions. Great non-meditation is when everything is constantly gnosis after that subtle aspect of consciousness has also transformed into gnosis.

Moreover, there are three ways of developing these for individuals who are (1) the instantaneous type (*cig car ba*), (2) the leap-over type (*thod rgal ba*), or (3) the progressive type (*rim gyis pa*). It is also said that there are various, undetermined ways of development due to greater and lesser degrees of mental fortitude within these three types as well. You can see extensive presentations on the stages of four yogas by previous masters, concerning the respective essences of the four yogas being seen or not, having perfected the strength or not, whether or not thoughts dawn as meditation or not, whether qualities arise or not, whether the relative has been mastered or not, and whether the seed of the Form Bodies has been planted or not, etc.

2. Enhancement

The details of enhancements in the respective contexts of the four yogas can be known elsewhere. In general, it is mainly to rely on solitary places and maintain silence; and to let go of the three attachments: attachment to oneself, attachment to enjoyments, and attachment to meditative stabilization. As Jikten Sumgön said, "Method and wisdom mutually aid each other's enhancement."[38] Practice by integrating the precious spirit of awakening, the precious discipline, and the virtuous practices with signs (such as the generation stage) within a state of meditative equipoise. The main enhancement is just devotion to the lama. Jikten Sumgön said,

> The enhancement for Mahāmudrā
> Is devotion to the sacred lama.[39]

The way that the four yogas are conjoined with the grounds and paths is stated in the *Vajra Song of the Nonconceptual Ultimate:*

> The fruition of meditation in this way
> Is aligned with the grounds and paths as follows:
> From entering the path of blessings
> Up until the completion of the yoga of single-pointedness
> Is called the "path of accumulation" for beginners.
> During freedom from constructs, one with aspiring conduct
> Has the essence of the "path of joining."
> From one-taste up to the lesser and middling non-meditations

38. I did not locate this passage among Jikten Sumgön's collected works.

39. I did not locate this passage among Jikten Sumgön's collected works.

> Is the gnosis of the "path of seeing" on the first ground.
> From the second ground to the tenth
> Is called the "path of meditation."
> The ultimate great non-meditation
> Is the "path of perfection," the buddha as such.
> These are the grounds and paths in the Vehicle of Characteristics;
> Although it is difficult to bring it together with scriptures and reasoning,
> It is not mistaken in meaning, so hold it as authoritative.[40]

Regarding this, I asked about the discord between Jikten Sumgön's assertion of the correlation with the pure essences supported within the four *cakras*—the navel, heart, throat, and crown—as stated in the Mantra path, and the four yogas—single-pointedness with the path of joining, freedom from constructs with the path of seeing, one-taste with the path of meditation, and non-meditation with the path of no more learning—as asserted by some of the past Kagyü masters. I was told that it is not a mistake to correlate them in the way of the past masters by means of the aspect of the essence of realization, but in this context it was explained in this way by means of the aspect of quality; hence, there is no contradiction here within these assertions.

---

40. Rikzin Chödrak, *Vajra Song of the Nonconceptual Ultimate*, 552–553.

Bibliography

CANONICAL WORKS

(D.) *sde dge mtshal par bka' 'gyur: a facsimile edition of the 18th century redaction of Situ chos kyi 'byung gnas prepared under the direction of H.H. the 16th rgyal dbang karma pa.* Delhi: Delhi Karmapae Chodhey Gyalwae Sungrab Partun Khang, 1977.

(H.) *lha sa bka' 'gyur.* Lhasa edition of the Translated Word (*bka' 'gyur*). Zhol, 1934.

(P.) Suzuki, Daitetz T., ed. *The Tibetan Tripitika, Peking edition.* Tokyo: Tibetan Tripitika Research Institute, 1957.

All-Creating King Tantra (*kun byed rgyal po'i rgyud*). In *Collected Tantras of the Nyingma* (*rnying ma'i rgyud 'bum*), vol. 1, 2–192. Thimphu, Bhutan: National Library, Royal Bhutan, 1982.

Aṅgulimāla Sūtra (*Aṅgulimālīyasūtra, 'phags pa sor mo'i phreng ba la phan pa zhes bya ba theg pa chen po'i mdo*). H. 214, vol. 62.

Condensed Perfection of Wisdom (*Prajñāpāramitā-sañcayagāthā, 'phags pa shes rab kyi pha rol tu phyin pa sdud pa tshigs su bcad pa*). H. 17, vol. 34.

Descent to Laṅka Sūtra (*Laṅkāvatārasūtra, 'phags pa lang kar gshegs pa'i theg pa chen po'i mdo*). D. 107, vol. 49; H. 110, vol. 51.

Foundation of the Vinaya (*Vinayavastu, 'dul ba gzhi*). H. 1, vols. 1–4.

Golden Light (*Suvarṇaprabhāsūtra, 'phags pa gser 'od dam pa mdo sde'i dbang po'i rgyal po zhes bya ba theg pa chen po'i mdo*). H. 514, vol. 89.

Great Drum Sūtra (*Mahābherīsūtra, 'phags pa rnga po che zhes bya ba theg pa chen po'i mdo*). H. 223, vol. 63; P. 888, vol. 35.

Heart Sūtra (*Bhagavatīprajñāpāramitāhṛdaya, bcom ldan 'das ma shes rab kyi pha rol tu phyin pa'i snying po*). H. 499, vol. 88.

Hevajra Tantra (*kye'i rdo rje rgyud rgyal po*). H. 378, vol. 79.

Inquiry of King Dhāraṇīśvara Sūtra (*Dhāraṇīśvararājasūtra, gzungs kyi dbang phyug rgyal pos zhus pa'i mdo*)/ *Tathāgatamahākaruṇānirdeśasūtra* (*de bzhin gshegs pa'i snying rje chen po nges par bstan pa'i mdo*). P. 814, vol. 32.

Inquiry of Upāli (*Upālipariprcchā, 'phags pa 'dul ba rnam par gtan la dbab pa nye bar 'khor gyis zhus pa zhes bya ba theg pa chen po'i mdo*). H. 68, vol. 39.

King of Meditative Stabilizations Sūtra (*Samādhirājasūtra, 'phags pa chos thams cad kyi rang bzhin mnyam pa nyid rnam par spros pa ting nge 'dzin gyi rgyal po zhes bya ba theg pa chen po'i mdo*). H. 129, vol. 55.

Nirvana Sūtra (*Mahāparinirvāṇa Sūtra, 'phags pa yongs su mya ngan las 'das pa chen po'i mdo*). H. 368, vol. 77.

Perfection of Wisdom in Eighteen Thousand Stanzas (*Aṣṭādaśasāhasrikā-prajñāpāramitā, shes rab kyi pha rol tu phyin pa khri rgyad stong pa*). H. 12, vol. 32.

Perfection of Wisdom in Five-Hundred Stanzas (*Pañcaśatika-prajñāpāramitā, shes rab kyi pha rol tu phyin pa lnga brgya pa*). H. 16, vol. 34.

Perfection of Wisdom in Twenty-Five Thousand Stanzas (*Pañcaviṃśatisāhasrikā-prajñāpāramitā, shes rab kyi pha rol tu phyin pa stong phrag nyi shu lnga pa*). H. 10, vol. 28.

Reverberation of Sound (*sgra thal 'gyur*). In *The Seventeen Tantras of the Nyingma* (*snying ma'i rgyud bcu bdun*), vol. 1, 1–205. New Delhi, India: Sangye Dorje, 1973–1977.

Self-Arising Awareness (*rig pa rang shar*). In *The Seventeen Tantras of the Nyingma* (*snying ma'i rgyud bcu bdun*), vol. 1, 389–855. New Delhi, India: Sangye Dorje, 1973–1977.

Sūtra Explaining the Intent (*Saṃdhinirmocanasūtra, 'phags pa dgongs pa nges par 'grel pa zhes bya ba theg pa chen po'i mdo*). H. 109, vol. 51; Tibetan edition and English trans. in John Powers, *Wisdom of the Buddha: The Saṃdhinirmocana Mahāyāna Sūtra*. Berkeley: Dharma Publishing, 1995.

Sūtra Instructing Akṣayamati (*Akṣayamatisūtra, 'phags pa blo gros mi zad pas bstan pa zhes bya ba theg pa chen po'i mdo*). H. 176, vol. 60; P. 879, vol. 34.

Sūtra of the Kāśyapa Chapter (*Kāśyapaparivarta, 'phags pa 'od srung gi le'u zhes bya ba theg pa chen po'i mdo*). H. 87, vol. 40.

Sūtra of Maitreya's Great Lion's Roar (*Maitreya-mahāsiṃhanāda-sūtra, 'phags pa byams pa'i seng ge'i sgra chen po zhes bya ba theg pa chen po'i mdo*). H. 67, vol. 39.

Sūtra of the Meeting of the Father and Son (*Pitāputrasamāgamasūtra, 'phags pa yab sras dang mjal ba zhes bya ba theg pa chen po'i mdo*). H. 60, vol. 38.

Tantra Explaining the Four Seats (*Caturpīṭha-vikhyāta-tantrarāja* (*dpal gdan bzhi pa'i rnam par bshad pa'i rgyud kyi rgyal po zhes bya ba*). H. 406, vol. 82.

Vast Display (*Lalitavistara, 'phags pa rgya cher rol pa zhes bya ba theg pa chen po'i mdo*). H. 96, vol. 48.

Vimalakīrti Sūtra (*Vimalakīrtinirdeśasūtra, 'phags pa dri ma med par grags pas bstan pa zhes bya ba theg pa chen po'i mdo*). H. 177, vol. 60.

CANONICAL TREATISES

Āryadeva. *Four Hundred Verses* (*Catuḥśataka, bstan bcos bzhi brgya pa zhes bya ba'i tshig le'ur byas pa*). D. 3846, vol. 97; English trans. in Ruth Sonam, *Āryadeva's Four Hundred Stanzas on the Middle Way*. Ithaca: Snow Lion Publications, 2008.

Asaṅga. *Compendium of Determinations* (*Yogācārabhūmi Viniścayasaṃgrahanī, rnal 'byor spyod pa'i sa rnam par gtan la dbab pa bsdu ba*). D. 4038.

Asaṅga. *Compendium of Mahāyāna* (*Mahāyānasaṃgraha, theg pa chen po bsdus pa*). D. 4048.

Asaṅga. *Compendium of Metaphysics* (*Abhidharmasamuccaya, chos mngon pa kun las bdus pa*). D. 4049.

Atīśa. *Open Treasury of Essential Instructions on the Middle Way* (*Ratnakaraṇḍodghāṭa-madhyamakopadeśa, dbu ma'i man ngag rin po che'i za ma tog kha phye ba*). D. 3930, vol. 110.

Buddhapālita. *Buddhapālita's Commentary on the "Fundamental Verses of the Middle Way"* (*Buddhapālitamūlamadhyamakavṛtti, dbu ma rtsa ba'i 'grel pa buddha pā li ta*). D. 3842.

Candrakīrti. *Autocommentary on "Introduction to the Middle Way"* (*Madhyamakāvatārabhāṣya, dbu ma la 'jug pa'i bshad pa zhes bya ba*). D. 3862, vol. 102.

Candrakīrti. *Clear Words* (*Prasannapadā, tshig gsal*). P. 5260, vol. 98; D. 3860, vol. 102.

Candrakīrti. *Commentary on "Reason in Sixty Verses"* (*Yuktiṣaṣṭikāvṛtti, rigs pa drug cu pa'i 'grel pa*). D. 3864, vol. 103.

Candrakīrti. *Introduction to the Middle Way* (*Madhyamakāvatāra, dbu ma la 'jug pa*). D. 3861.

Dharmakīrti. *Ascertaining Sources of Knowledge* (*Pramāṇaviniścaya, tshad ma rnam par nges pa*). D. 4211, vol. 174.

Dharmakīrti. *Commentary on Epistemology* (*Pramāṇavarttika, tshad ma rnam 'grel gyi tshig le'ur byas pa*). D. 4210.

Dharmakīrti. *Drop of Reason* (*Nyāyabindu, rigs pa thigs pa zhes bya ba rab tu byed pa*). P. 5711; D. 4212.

Dharmakīrti. *Investigation of Relation* (*Sambandhaparīkṣā, 'bral ba brtag pa rab tu byed pa*). D. 4214.

Dignāga. *Compendium of Epistemology* (*Pramāṇasamuccaya, tshad ma kun btus*). P. 5700; D. 4203.

Dignāga. *Investigating the Percept* (*Ālambanaparīkṣā, dmigs pa brtag pa*). P. 5703; D. 4205.

Haribhadra. *Clear Meaning* (*Sphuṭārtha, shes rab kyi pha rol tu phyin pa'i man ngag gi bstan bcos mngon par rtogs pa'i rgyan zhes bya ba'i 'grel pa*). D. 3793.

Jñānagarbha. *Distinguishing the Two Truths* (*bden nyis rnam par 'byed pa*). D. 3881, vol. 107.

Kamalaśīla. *Light of the Middle Way* (*Madhyamakāloka, dbu ma snang ba zhes bya ba*). D. 3887.

Maitreya. *Distinguishing Phemomena and the Basic Nature* (*Dharmadharmatāvibhāga, chos dang chos nyid rnam par 'byed pa*). P. 5523, vol. 108; D. 4022.

Maitreya. *Distinguishing the Middle and the Extremes* (*Madhyāntavibhāga, dbus dang mtha' rnam par 'byed pa*). P. 5522, vol. 108; D. 4027; English trans. in

Dharmachakra Translation Group, *Middle Beyond Extremes*. Ithaca: Snow Lion Publications, 2006.

Maitreya. *Ornament of the Great Vehicle Sūtras* (*Mahāyānasūtrālaṃkāra, theg pa chen po mdo sde'i rgyan zhes bya ba'i tshig le'ur byas pa*). D. 4020; English translation in Dharmachakra Translation Committee, *Ornament of the Great Vehicle Sūtras*. Boston: Snow Lion Publications, 2014.

Maitreya. *Sublime Continuum* (*Uttaratantra, theg pa chen po rgyud bla ma'i bstan bcos*). D. 4024, vol. 123; English trans. in Rosemarie Fuchs, *Buddha-Nature: The Mahayana Uttaratantra Shastra with Commentary*. Ithaca: Snow Lion Publications, 2000.

Mokṣākaragupta. *Discourse on Logic* (*Tarkābhāṣa*). Varanasi, India: Central Institute of Higher Tibetan Studies, 2004; English trans. in Kajiyama, Yuichi. *An Introduction to Buddhist Philosophy: An Annotated Translation of the Tarkābhāṣa of Mokṣākaragupta*. Kyoto University: Memoirs of the Faculty of Letters (1966), 10: 1–173.

Nāgamitra. *Gateway to the Three Embodiments of Buddhahood* (*Kāyatrayāvatāramukha, sku gsum la 'jug pa'i sgo*). D. 3890.

Nāgārjuna. *Dispelling Disputes* (*Vigrahavyāvartanī, rtsod pa bzlog pa'i tshig le'ur byas pa*). P. 5228, vol. 95; D. 3828.

Nāgārjuna. *Finely Woven Scripture* (*Vaidalyasūtra, zhib mo rnam par 'thag pa zhes bya ba'i mdo*). D. 3826.

Nāgārjuna. *Fundamental Verses of the Middle Way* (*Mūlamadhyamakakārikā, dbu ma rtsa ba'i shes rab*). P. 5224, vol. 95; D. 3824.

Nāgārjuna. *Letter to a Friend* (*Suhṛllekha, bshes pa'i sbring yig*). D. 4182, vol. 173.

Nāgārjuna. *Praise to the Basic Field of Reality* (*Dharmadhātustotra, chos kyi dbyings su bstod pa*). D. 1118, vol. 1.

Nāgārjuna. *Precious Garland* (*Ratnāvalī, rgyal po la gtam bya ba rin po che'i phreng ba*). D. 4158, vol. 172; English translation in Jeffrey Hopkins, *Nāgārjuna's Precious Garland: Buddhist Advice for Living and Liberation*. Ithaca, NY: Snow Lion Publications, 1998.

Nāgārjuna. *Reason in Sixty Verses* (*Yuktiṣaṣṭikā, rigs pa drug cu pa'i tshig le'ur byas pa zhes bya ba*). D. 3825, vol. 96.

Śāntarakṣita. *Ornament of the Middle Way* (*Madhyamakālaṃkāra, dbu ma rgyan*). P. 5238, vol. 101; D. 3884.

Śāntideva. *Anthology of Training* (*Śikṣāsamuccayakārikā, bslab pa kun las btus pa'i tshig le'ur byas pa*). D. 3939; English trans. in Charles Goodman, *The Training Anthology of Śāntideva*. Oxford: Oxford University Press, 2016.

Śāntideva. *Way of the Bodhisattva* (*Bodhicaryāvatāra, byang chub sems dpa'i spyod pa la 'jug pa*). P. 5272, vol. 99; D. 3871; also in *byang chub sems dpa'i spyod pa la 'jug pa rtsa ba dang 'grel ba*. Sichuan: Nationalities Press, 1990.

Vasubandhu. *Autocommentary on the "Treasury of Metaphysics"* (*Abhidharmakośabhā ṣya*). D. 4090, vol. 141.

Vasubandhu. *Commentary on "Distinguishing Phenomena and the Basic Nature" (Dharmadharmatāvibhāgavṛtti, chos dang chos nyid rnam par 'byed pa'i 'grel pa)*. D. 4028.

Vasubandhu. *Concise Elucidation of the Secret Meaning (Vivṛtagūḍhārthapiṇḍavyākhyā, don gsang ba rnam par phye ba bsdus te bshad pa)*. D. 4052.

Vasubandhu. *Thirty Verses (Triṃśikā, sum cu pa)*. D. 4055.

Vasubandhu. *Treasury of Metaphysics (Abhidharmakośa, chos mngon pa'i mdzod kyi tshig le'ur byas pa)*. D. 4089, vol. 140.

Vasubandhu. *Treatise on the Three Natures (Trisvabhāvanirdeṣa, rang bzhin gsum nges par bstan pa)*. D. 4058.

Vasubandhu. *Twenty Verses (Viṃśatika, nyi shu pa)*. P. 5557; D. 4056.

Vinītadeva. *Commentary on [Dharmakīrti's] "Drop of Reason" (Nyāyabinduṭīkā, rigs pa'i thigs pa'i rgya cher 'grel ba)*. D. 4230.

OTHER WORKS CITED

Abram, David. *The Spell of the Sensuous*. New York: Pantheon Books, 1996.

Armstrong, David. *A Materialist Theory of the Mind*. London: Routledge, 1968.

Arnold, Dan. *Brains, Buddhas, and Belief*. New York: Columbia University Press, 2012.

Arnold, Dan. "Nagarjuna's 'Middle Way': A Non-Eliminative Understanding of Selflessness." *Revue Internationale de Philosophie* 64, no. 253 (3) (2010): 367–395.

Beiser, Fredrick. *German Idealism: The Struggle Against Subjectivism, 1781–1801*. Cambridge: Harvard University Press, 2002.

Berry, Wendell. *The Unsettling of America: Culture and Agriculture*. San Francisco: Sierra Club Books, 1977.

Beyer, Stephan. *The Cult of Tara*. Berkeley: University of California Press, 1978.

Bötrül (*bod sprul mdo sngags bstan pa'i nyi ma*, 1898–1959). *Ornament of Mañjughoṣa's Viewpoint: An Explanation of the Words and Meanings of "Distinguishing the Views and Philosophies: A Lamp of Essential Points" (lta grub shan 'byed gnad kyi sgron me'i tshig don rnam bshad 'jam dbyangs dgongs rgyan)*. *Bötrül's Collected Works*, vol. 1, 53–259; English trans. in Bötrül, *Distinguishing the Views and Philosophies: Illuminating Emptiness in a Twentieth-Century Tibetan Buddhist Classic*, translated, annotated, and introduced by Douglas Duckworth. Albany: SUNY Press, 2011.

Bradley, F. H. *Essays on Truth and Reality*. Cambridge: Cambridge University Press, [1914] 2012.

Bradley, F. H. *The Principles of Logic*, vol. 1. Oxford: Oxford University Press, 1922.

Brentano, Franz. *Psychology from an Empirical Standpoint*. New York: Routledge, 1995 [1874].

Brunnhölzl, Karl. *Center of the Sunlit Sky: Madhyamaka in the Kagyü Tradition*. Ithaca, NY: Snow Lion Publications, 2004.

Brunnhölzl, Karl. *Gone Beyond*, vols. 1–2. Ithaca, NY: Snow Lion Publications, 2011–2012.

Brunnhölzl, Karl. *Straight from the Heart: Buddhist Pith Instructions.* Ithaca: Snow Lion Publications, 2007.

Cabezón, José and Geshe Lobsang Dargyay. *Freedom from Extremes: Gorampa's "Distinguishing the Views" and the Polemics of Emptiness.* Boston: Wisdom Publications, 2007.

Chennga Dorjé Sherap (*spyan snga rdo rje shes rab*, 1187–1241). *Single Viewpoint Commentary: Illuminating Lamp of Gnosis* (*dgongs gcig 'grel chen snang mdzad ye shes sgron me*), vols. 1–3. Hong Kong: shang kang then mā dpe skrun khang, 2006.

Chödrak Gyatso. The Seventh Karmapa (*chos grags rgya mtsho*, 1454–1506). *Ocean of Epistemological Scriptures and Reasoning* (*tshad ma rigs gzhung rgya mtsho*), vols. 1–2. Varanasi: Nithartha International, 1999.

The Cowherds. *Moonshadows: Conventional Truth in Buddhist Philosophy.* Oxford: Oxford University Press, 2011.

Cozort, Dan. *Unique Tenets of the Middle Way Consequence School.* Ithaca: Snow Lion Publications, 1998.

Dakpo Tashi Namgyel (*dwags po bkra shis rnam rgyal*, 1512/13–1587). *Illuminating the Innate Nature* (*gnyug ma'i de nyid gsal ba*); English translation by Erik Pema Kunzang in *Clarifying the Natural State.* Hong Kong: Rangjung Yeshe Publications, 2001.

D'Amato, Mario. *Matreya's Distinguishing the Middle from the Extremes.* New York: Columbia University Press, 2012.

Dampa Deshek (*dam pa bde gshegs, ca.* twelfth c.). *The Overall Structure of the Vehicles* (*theg pa spyi bcings rtsa 'grel*). Chengdu, China: Nationalities Press, 1997.

Davidson, Ronald. "Reflections on the Maheśvara Subjugation Myth: Indic Materials, Sa-skya-pa Apologetics, and the Birth of Heruka." *Journal of the International Association of Buddhist Studies* 14, no. 2 (1991): 197–235.

Dennett, Daniel. *Consciousness Explained.* Boston: Back Bay Books, 1991.

Dölpopa (*dol po pa shes rab rgyal mtshan*, 1292–1361). *The Categories of the Possible and the Impossible* (*srid mi srid kyi rab dbye dbu phyogs legs par bzhugs so*). *Dölpopa's Collected Works* (*'dzam thang* ed.), vol. 6, 305–316.

Dölpopa. *The Great Assessment of the Doctrine Which Has the Significance of the Fourth Council* (*bka' bdus bzhi pa don bstan rtsis chen po*). In *bka' bdus bzhi pa don bstan rtsis rtsa 'grel*, 1–36. Hong Kong: Tupten Ewam Publications, n.d.; English translation in Cyrus Stearns, *The Buddha from Dolpo*, Albany, NY: SUNY Press, 1999.

Dölpopa. *The Mountain Doctrine: Ocean of Definitive Meaning* (*ri chos nges don rgya mtsho*). *Dölpopa's Collected Works* (*'dzam thang* ed.), vol. 3, 189–742; English translation in Jeffrey Hopkins, *Mountain Doctrine: Tibet's Fundamental Treatise on Other-Emptiness and the Buddha Matrix.* Ithaca, NY: Snow Lion Publications, 2006.

Dölpopa. *The Sun Elucidating the Two Truths* (*bden gnyis gsal ba'i nyi ma*). *Dölpopa's Collected Works* (*'dzam thang* ed.), vol. 6, 695–726.

Dreyfus, Georges. *Recognizing Reality: Dharmakīrti's Philosophy and Its Tibetan Interpretations.* Albany, NY: SUNY Press, 1997.

Dreyfus, Georges. “Would the True Prāsaṅgika Please Stand? The Case of ’Ju Mipham.” In *The Svātantrika-Prāsaṅgika Distinction*, edited by Georges Dreyfus and Sara McClintock, 317–347. Boston: Wisdom Publications, 2003.

Duckworth, Douglas. “Buddha-Nature and the Logic of Pantheism.” In *The Buddhist World*, edited by John Powers, 234–247. London: Routledge, 2015.

Duckworth, Douglas. “Echoes of Tsültrim Lodrö: An Indigenous Voice from Contemporary Tibet on the ‘Buddhism and Science Dialogue.’” *Journal of Contemporary Buddhism* 16, no. 2 (2015): 267–277.

Duckworth, Douglas. “From Yogācāra to Philosophical Tantra in Kashmir and Tibet.” *Sophia* (2017). doi:10.1007/s11841-017-0598-5

Duckworth, Douglas. “Grounds of Buddha-Nature in Tibet.” *Critical Review of Buddhist Studies* 21 (2017): 109–136.

Duckworth, Douglas. *Jamgön Mipam: His Life and Teachings*. Boston: Shambhala Publications, 2011.

Duckworth, Douglas. “Madhyamaka in Tibet: Thinking Through the Ultimate Truth.” *Critical Review of Buddhist Studies* 20 (2016): 171–197.

Duckworth, Douglas. *Mipam on Buddha-Nature: The Ground of the Nyingma Tradition*. Albany, NY: SUNY Press, 2008.

Duckworth, Douglas. “Non-Representational Language in Mipam’s Re-Presentation of Other-Emptiness.” *Philosophy East & West* 64, no. 4 (2014): 920–932.

Duckworth, Douglas. “Onto-theology and Emptiness: The Nature of Buddha-Nature.” *Journal of the American Academy of Religion* 82, no. 4 (2014): 1070–1090.

Duckworth, Douglas. “Other-Emptiness in the Jonang: The Theo-logic of Buddhist Dualism.” *Philosophy East & West* 65, no. 2 (2015): 485–497.

Duckworth, Douglas. “The Other Side of Realism: Panpsychism and Yogācāra.” In *Buddhist Philosophy: A Comparative Approach*, edited by Steven Emmanuel, 29–43. Hoboken, N J: Wiley-Blackwell, 2017.

Duckworth, Douglas. “Self-Awareness and the Integration of Pramāṇa and Madhyamaka.” *Asian Philosophy* 25, no. 2 (2015): 207–215.

Duckworth, Douglas. “Tibetan Mahāyāna and Vajrayāna.” In *A Companion to Buddhist Philosophy*, edited by Steven Emmanuel, 99–109. Hoboken, N J: Wiley-Blackwell, 2013.

Duckworth, Douglas. “Two Models of the Two Truths: Ontological and Phenomenological Approaches.” *Journal of Indian Philosophy* 38, no.5 (2010): 519–527.

Duckworth, D., D. Eckel, J. Garfield, J. Powers, Y. Thabkhas, and S. Thakchoe. *Dignāga’s Investigation of the Percept: A Philosophical Legacy in India and Tibet*. Oxford, England: Oxford University Press, 2016.

Dunne, John. *Foundations of Dharmakīrti’s Philosophy*. Boston: Wisdom Publications, 2004.

Dunne, John. “Realizing the Unreal: Dharmakīrti’s Theory of Yogic Perception.” *Journal of Indian Philosophy* 34 (2006), 497–519.

Dunne, John. "Toward and Understanding of Nondual Mindfulness." *Contemporary Buddhism* 12:1 (2011), 71–88.

Evans, Donald. *Spirituality and Human Nature.* Albany: SUNY Press, 1992.

Fasching, Wofgang. "'I am of the Nature of Seeing': Phenomenological Reflections on the Indian Notion of Witness-Consciousness." In *Self, No Self? Perspectives from Analytical, Phenomenological, & Indian Traditions,* edited by Mark Siderits, Evan Thompson, and Dan Zahavi, 193–216.. Oxford: Oxford University Press, 2011.

Ferrer, Jorge. "Spiritual Knowing as Participatory Enaction." In *The Participatory Turn: Spirituality, Mysticism, Religious Studies,* edited by Jorge Ferrer and Jacob Sherman, 135–169. Albany, NY: SUNY Press, 2008.

Forman, Robert. "Mystical Knowledge by Identity." *Journal of the American Academy of Religion* 61, no. 4 (1993), 705–738.

Gallagher, Shaun, and Dan Zahavi. *The Phenomenological Mind.* New York: Routledge, 2008.

Gampopa (*sgam po pa bsod nams rin chen,* 1079–1153). *Abundant Qualities* (*tshogs chos yon tan phun tshogs*). In *Gampopa's Collected Works,* vol. 1, 505–575. Kathmandu: Khenpo Tenzin and Lama Namgyal, 2000.

Gampopa. *Response to Düsum Khyenpa's Request* (*dus gsum mkhyen pa'i zhu lan*). *Gampopa's Collected Works,* vol. 1, 376–469. Delhi: Shashin, 1976.

Garfield, Jay. "The Conventional Status of Reflexive Awareness: What's at Stake in a Tibetan Debate?" *Philosophy East & West* 56, no. 2 (2006): 201–228.

Garfield, Jay, and Graham Priest. "Nāgārjuna and the Limits of Thought." In Graham Priest, *Beyond the Limits of Thought,* 249–270. Oxford: Oxford University Press, 2002.

Gautama. *Nyāya Sūtra.* In *Gautamīyanyāyadarśana with Bhāṣya of Vātsyāyana,* edited by Anantalal Thakur. Delhi: Indian Council of Philosophical Research, 1997.

Gendün Chöpel (*dge 'dun chos 'phel,* 1903–1951). *Ornament of Nāgārjuna's View* (*dbu ma'i zab gnad snying por dril ba'i legs bshad klu sgrub dgongs rgyan*). In *mkhas dbang dge 'dun chos 'phel gyi gsung rtsom phyogs sgrig,* 133–249. Chengdu: Nationalities Press, 1989; English translation in Donald Lopez, *The Madman's Middle Way: Reflections on Reality of the Tibetan Monk Gendun Chopel.* Chicago: Chicago University Press, 2006.

Getsé Paṇchen (*dge rtse paṇ chen, 'gyur med tshe dbang mchog grub,* 1761–1829). *Husks of Unity* (*bskyes pa'i rim pa cho ga dang sbyar ba'i gsal byed zung 'jug snye ma*); English translation in Dharmachakra Translation Committee, *Deity, Mantra, and Wisdom,* 97–151. Ithaca, NY: Snow Lion Publications, 2006.

Gimello, Robert. "Chi-yen (602–668) and the Foundations of Hua-Yen Buddhism." Ph.D. Dissertation, Columbia University, 1976.

Gold, Jonathan. "No Outside, No Inside: Duality, Reality and Vasubandhu's Illusory Elephant." *Asian Philosophy* 16, no. 1 (2006): 1–38.

Gold, Jonathan. *Paving the Great Way: Vasubandhu's Unifying Buddhist Philosophy.* New York: Columbia University Press, 2015.

Gorampa (*go rams pa bsod nams seng ge*, 1429–1489). *Distinguishing the Views* (*lta ba'i shan 'byed*). Sarnath: Sakya Students' Union, 1988.

Gö Lotsāwa (*'gos lo tsā ba gzhon nu dpal*, 1392–1481). *Mirror That Completely Illuminates Reality: A Commentary on the Uttaratantra* (*theg pa chen po rgyud bla ma'i bstan bcos kyi 'grel bshad de kho na nyid rab tu gsal ba'i me long*), edited by Klaus-Dieter Mathes. Nepal Research Centre Publications 24. Stuttgart: Franz Steiner Verlag, 2003.

Götsangpa (*rgod tshang pa mgon po rdo rje*, 1189–1258). *One Hundred Thousand Songs of Götsangpa* (*dpal mnyam med rgyal ba rgod tshang pa'i mgur 'bum chen mo*). *Collected Works of Götsangpa Gönpo Dorjé*, vol. 5, 1–423. Thimphu: Tango monastic community, 1981.

Guenther, Herbert. *Buddhist Philosophy in Theory and Practice*. Berkeley: Shambhala Publications, 1971.

Hackett, Paul. "On the Epistemological Distinction between Sautrāntika and Cittamātra in Tsong-kha-pa's *Legs bshad snying po*." In *Vimalakīrti's House: A Festschrift in Honor of Robert A. F. Thurman on the Occasion of his 70th Birthday*, edited by Christian Wedemeyer et al., 345–377. New York: AIBS, 2015.

Hattori, Masaaki. *Dignāga on Perception*. Cambridge: Harvard University Press, 1968.

Heidegger, Martin. *The Basic Problems of Phenomenology*, translated by Albert Hofstadter. Bloomington: Indiana University Press, 1988 [1982].

Heidegger, Martin. *Being and Time*, translated by John Macquarrie and Edward Robinson. Oxford: Blackwell, 2001 [1962].

Heidegger, Martin. "Memorial Address." In *Discourse on Thinking*, translated by John Anderson and Hans Freund, 43–57. New York: Harper & Row, 1969.

Heidegger, Martin. "What Calls for Thinking?" In *Heidegger: Basic Writings*, edited by David Krell, 345–367. New York: Harper & Row, 1977.

Heidegger, Martin. "What Is Metaphysics?" In *Heidegger: Basic Writings*, edited by David Krell, 92–112. New York: Harper & Row, 1977.

Higgins, David. "How Consciousness (*rnam shes*) Is Related to Wisdom (*ye shes*)? The Eighth Karma pa on Buddhist Differentiation and Unity Models." *Studia Religiologica* 48, no. 4 (2015): 341–362.

Higgins, David. *The Philosophical Foundations of Classical Rdzogs Chen in Tibet*. Wien: Arbeitskreis für Tibetische und Buddhistische Studien, 2013.

Higgins, David. "A Reply to Questions Concerning Mind and Primordial Knowing." *Journal of the International Association of Buddhist Studies* 34 (2011): 31–96.

Hopkins, Jeffrey. *Maps of the Profound*. Ithaca: Snow Lion Publications, 2003.

Hopkins, Jeffrey. *Tsong-kha-pa's Final Exposition of Wisdom*. Ithaca, NY: Snow Lion Publications, 2008.

Houben, Jan E. M., Helārāja, and Bhartṛhari. *The Saṃbandha-Samuddeśa (chapter on relation) and Bhartṛhari's Philosophy of Language: A Study of Bhartṛhari Saṃbandha-Samuddeśa in the Context of the Vākyapadīya, with a translation of Helārāja's Commentary Prakīrṇa-prakāśa*. Groningen: E. Forsten, 1995.

Hugon, Pascale. "Phywa pa chos kyi seng ge's Views on Perception." In *Religion and Logic in Buddhist Philosophical Analysis: Proceedings of the Fourth International Dharmakīrti Conference*, edited by H. Krasser, H. Lasic, E. Franco, B. Kellner, 159–176. Vienna: Verlag der Österreichischen Akademie der Wisschenschaften, 2005.

Husserl, E. *Ideas Pertaining to a Pure Phenomenology and to a Phenomenological Philosophy—First Book: General Introduction to a Pure Phenomenology*, translated by F. Kersten. The Hague: Nijhoff, 1982.

Ichigo, Masamichi. *Madhyamakālaṃkāra of Śāntarakṣita with His Own Commentary or Vṛtti and with the Subcommentary or Pañjikā of Kamalaśīla.* Kyoto: Sangyo University, 1985.

Jackson, David. *Enlightenment by a Single Means: Tibetan Controversies on the Self-Sufficent White Remedy (dkar po chig thub).* Vienna: Verlag der Österreichischen Akademie der Wisschenschaften, 1994.

James, William. *A Pluralistic Universe.* Cambridge: Harvard University Press, 1977.

Jha, Ganganath, trans. *Śābara-bhāṣya*, vol. 1. Baroda: Oriental Institute, 1973.

Jha, Ganganath, trans. *Ślokavārttika.* Calcutta: The Asiatic Society 1985 [1908].

Jikten Sumgön (*'jig rten gsum mgon rin chen dpal*, 1142–1217). *Blazing Victory Banner of the Precious Stages of the Bodhisattva Path* (*rgyal sras rnams kyi lam rim rin po che 'bar ba'i rgyal mtshan*). *Jikten Sumgön's Collected Works*, vol. 1, 226–240. Delhi: Drikung Kagyu Ratna Shri Sungrab Nyamso Khang, 2001.

Jikten Sumgön. *Single Viewpoint* (*dgongs gcig*). In Chennga Dorjé Sherap (*spyan snga rdo rje shes rab*), *Single Viewpoint Commentary* (*dgongs gcig 'grel chen snang mdzad ye shes sgron me*), vols. 1–3. Hong Kong: shang kang then mā dpe skrun khang, 2006.

Jikten Sumgön. *Song of Realization of the Fivefold Mahāmudrā* (*phyag rgya chen po lnga ldan rtogs pa'i mgur*). *Jikten Sumgön's Collected Works*, vol. 10, 96–97. Delhi: Drikung Kagyu Ratna Shri Sungrab Nyamso Khang, 2001.

Jinpa, Thupten. *Self, Reality and Reason in Tibetan Philosophy.* London: RoutledgeCurzon, 2002.

Kapstein, Matthew. "We Are All Gzhan stong pas." *Journal of Buddhist Ethics* 7 (2000): 109–115.

Karmay, Samten. *The Great Perfection (rDzogs Chen): A Philosophical and Meditative Tradition in Tibetan Buddhism.* Leiden: E. J. Brill, 1988.

Kasser, H. "Are Buddhist Pramāṇavādins non-Buddhistic? Dignāga and Dharmakīrti on the Impact of Logic and Epistemology on Emancipation." *Hōrin* 11 (2004), 129–146.

Kassor, Constance. "Gorampa Sonam Senge on the Refutation of the Four Extremes." *Revue d'Etudes Tibétaines* 22 (2011): 121–137.

Keira, Ryusei. *Mādhyamika and Epistemology.* Wien: Arbeitskreis für Tibetische und Buddhistische Studien, 2004.

Khenpo Lodrö Drakpa (*'dzam thang mkhan po blo gros grags pa*, 1920–1975). *Roar of the Fearless Lion* (*rgyu dang 'bras bu'i theg pa mchog gi gnas lugs zab mo'i don *rnam par nges pa rje jo nang pa chen po'i ring lugs 'jigs med gdong lnga'i nga ro*). Dharamsala: Library of Tibetan Works and Archives, 1993.

King, Richard. "*Vijñaptimātratā* and the Abhidharma Context of Early Yogācāra." *Asian Philosophy* 8, no. 1 (1998), 5–17.

Klein, Anne, and Tenzin Wangyal. *Unbounded Wholeness: Dzogchen, Bon, and the Logic of the Nonconceptual*. New York: Oxford University Press, 2006.

Komarovski, Yaroslav. *Visions of Unity*. Albany: SUNY Press, 2011.

Kongtrül (*kong sprul blo gros mtha' yas*, 1813–1899). *Encyclopedia of Knowledge* (*shes bya kun khyab*). Beijing: Nationalities Press, 2002.

Kongtrül. *Light of Wisdom* (*lam rim ye shes snying po'i 'grel pa ye shes snang ba rab tu rgyas ba*). Kathmandu: Jamgon Kongtrul Labrang, 1999.

Künzang Sönam (*kun bzang bsod nams*, 1823–1905). *Overview of the Wisdom Chapter: A Lamp Completely Illuminating the Profound Reality of Interdependence* (*spyod 'jug shes rab le'u'i spyi don rim par phye ba zab mo rten 'byung gi de kho na nyed yang gsal sgron me*). In Tupten Chödrak (*thub bstan chos kyi grags pa*), *spyod 'jug gi 'grel bshad rgyal sras yon tan bum bzang*, 645–829. Beijing, China: China's Tibet Publishing House, 2007 [1993].

Lackoff, George and Mark Johnson. *Philosophy in the Flesh*. New York: Basic Books, 1999.

Lishu Takring (*li shu rtag ring*). *The Source of Knowledge That Is Awareness* (*gtan tshig gal mdo rig pa'i tshad ma*). In *Gal mdo: Texts Concerned with the Logical Establishment of the Authenticity of the rDzog-chen Teachings of Bon*, 47–129. Dolanji, India: Tibetan Bonpo Monastic Centre, 1972.

Longchenpa (*klong chen rab 'byams*, 1308–1364). *Instructions on the Meaning of Breakthrough Meditation* (*khregs chod ye babs so gzhag gi don khrid*). In *snying thig ya bzhi* (*bla ma yang thig*), vol. 1, 371–388. Delhi: Sherab Gyaltsen Lama, 1975.

Longchenpa. *Most Profound Essence* (*zab mo yang thig*), vols. 1–2. In *snying thig ya bzhi*, vols. 12–13. Delhi: Sherab Gyaltsen Lama, 1975.

Longchenpa. *Ocean Cloud of the Profound Meaning* (*zab don rgya mtsho phrin*). In *snying thig ya bzhi* (*mkha' 'gro yang thig*), vol. 8, 1–488. Delhi: Sherab Gyaltsen Lama, 1975.

Longchenpa. *Precious Treasury of Philosophical Systems* (*theg pa mtha' dag gi don gsal bar byed pa grub mtha' rin po che'i mdzod*). In *Seven Treasuries* (*mdzod bdun*), edited by Tarthang Tulku. Sichuan, China, 1996.

Longchenpa. *Precious Treasury of the Supreme Vehicle* (*theg pa'i mchog rin po che'i mdzod*), vols. 1–2, edited by Tarthang Tulku. Sichuan, China, 1996.

Longchenpa. *Precious Treasury of Words and Meanings* (*gsang ba bla na med pa 'od gsal rdo rje snying po'i gnas gsum gsal bar byed pa'i tshig don rin po che'i mdzod*). In *Seven Treasuries* (*mdzod bdun*), edited by Tarthang Tulku. Sichuan, China, 1996.

Longchenpa. *Precious Wish-Fulfilling Treasury* (*yid bzhin rin po che'i mdzod*). In *Seven Treasuries* (*mdzod bdun*), vol. 7, edited by Tarthang Tulku, 1–138. Sichuan, China, 1996.

Longchenpa. *Treasure Trove of Scriptural Transmission: Autocommentary on the "Precious Treasury of the Basic Field of Reality" (chos dbyings rin po che'i mdzod kyi 'grel pa lung gi gter mdzod)*. In *Seven Treasuries* (*mdzod bdun*), vol. 3, edited by Tarthang Tulku, 83–765. Sichuan, China, 1996.

Longchenpa. *White Lotus: Autocommentary on the "Precious Wish-Fulfilling Treasury" (theg pa chen po'i man ngag gi bstan bcos yid bzhin rin po che'i mdzod kyi 'grel pa padma dkar po)*. Published in *Seven Treasuries* (*mdzod bdun*), vol. 7, edited by Tarthang Tulku, 139–1544. Sichuan, China, 1996.

Lutz, A., J. Dunne, and R. Davidson. "Meditation and the Neuroscience of Consciousness: An Introduction." In *Cambridge Handbook of Consciousness*, edited by P. D. Zelazo, Morris Moscovitch and Evan Thompson, 499–551. Cambridge: Cambridge University Press, 2007.

MacKenzie, Matthew. "The Illumination of Consciousness: Approaches to Self-Awareness in the Indian and Western Traditions." *Philosophy East & West* 57 (2007): 40–62.

MacKenzie, Matthew. "Ontological Deflationism in Madhyamaka." *Contemporary Buddhism* 9, no. 2 (2008): 197–207.

Maja Jangchup Tsöndrü (*rma bya byang chub brtson grus, ca.* twelfth c.). *Appearance of Reality* (*de kho na nyid snang ba*), Tibetan edition in Thomas Doctor, *Reason and Experience in Tibetan Buddhism.* New York: Routledge, 2014.

Mathes, Klaus-Dieter. *A Direct Path to the Buddha Within*. Sommerville, MA: Wisdom Publications, 2008.

Mathes, Klaus-Dieter. "Gos Lo tsā ba Gzhon nu dpal's Commentary on the *Dharmatā* Chapter of the *Dharmadharmatāvibhāgakārikās*." *Studies in Indian Philosophy and Buddhism*. Tokyo: University of Tokyo, 2005.

Matilal, Bimal Krishna. "Mysticism and Ineffability: Some Issues of Logic and Language." In Steven Katz (ed.), *Mysticism and Language*, 143–157.Oxford: Oxford University Press, 1992.

McClintock, Sara, and Georges Dreyfus (eds.). *The Svātantrika-Prāsaṅgika Distinction.* Boston: Wisdom Publications, 2003.

Merleau-Ponty, Maurice. *The Visible and the Invisible.* Evanston, Ill: Northwestern University Press, 1968.

Mipam (*'ju mi pham rgya mtsho*, 1846–1912). *Beacon of Certainty* (*nges shes sgron me*). Published in *nges shes sgron me rtsa 'grel*, 1–54. Sichuan: Nationalities Press, 1997.

Mipam. *Concise Summary of the Philosophies from the "Wish-Fulfilling Treasury" (yid bzhin mdzod kyi grub mtha' bsdus pa)*. *Mipam's Collected Works*, vol. 21, 439–500.

Mipam. *Difficult Points of Scriptures in General (dbu ma sogs gzhung spyi'i dka' gnad skor gyi gsung sgros sna tshogs phyogs gcig tu bsdus pa rin po che'i za ma tog)*. *Mipam's Collected Works*, vol. 22, 427–710.

Mipam. *A Feast on the Nectar of the Supreme Vehicle: Commentary on the "Ornament of the Great Vehicle Sūtras" (theg pa chen po mdo sde'i rgyan gyi dgongs don rnam par bshad pa theg mchog bdud rtsi'i dga' ston)*. *Mipam's Collected Works*, vol. 2 (*a*), 1–760;

English translation in Dharmachakra Translation Committee, *Ornament of the Great Vehicle Sūtras*. Boston: Snow Lion Publications, 2014.

Mipam. *Garland of Light Rays: Commentary on "Distinguishing the Middle and the Extremes" (dbu dang mtha' rnam par 'byed pa'i bstan bcos kyi 'grel pa 'od zer phreng ba)*. *Mipam's Collected Works*, vol. 4 (pa), 659–786.

Mipam. *Light of the Sun (brgal lan nyin byed snang ba)*. Published in *spyod 'jug sher 'grel ke ta ka*. Sichuan: Nationalities Press, 1993; English trans. in Padmakara Translation Group, *The Wisdom Chapter*. Boulder: Shambhala Publications, 2017.

Mipam. *Light of Wisdom: Commentary on "Distinguishing Phenomena and the Basic Nature" (chos dang chos nyid rnam 'byed 'grel pa ye shes snang ba)*. *Mipam's Collected Works*, vol. 4 (*pa*), 609–658.

Mipam. *Mipam's Collected Works* (Dilgo Khyentsé's expanded redaction of *sde dge* edition). Kathmandu: Zhechen Monastery, 1987.

Mipam. *Overview: Essential Nature of Luminous Clarity (spyi don 'od gsal snying po)*. Published in *bka' brgyad rnam bshad dang spyi don 'od gsal snying po yang dag grub pa'i tshig 'grel bcas bzhugs*, 381–605. Sichuan: Nationalities Press, 2000; English trans. in Dharmachakra Translation Committee. *Luminous Essence: Guide to the Guhyagarbha Tantra*. Ithaca: Snow Lion Publications, 2009.

Mipam. *Precious Vajra Garland (gnyug sems zur dpyad skor gyi gsung sgros thor bu rnams phyogs gcig tu bsdus pa rdo rje rin po che'i phreng ba)*. *Mipam's Collected Works*, vol. 24, 567–774.

Mipam. *[Commentary on Changkya's] "Song of the View" (lta ba'i mgur ma)*. *Mipam's Collected Works*, vol. 4 (*pa*), 821–867; English trans. in Karl Brunnhözl, *Straight from the Heart: Buddhist Pith Instructions*, 391–428. Ithaca: Snow Lion Publications, 2007.

Mipam. *Shedding Light on Thusness (gzhan gyis brtsad pa'i lan mdor bsdus pa rigs lam rab gsal de nyid snang byed)*. Published in *spyod 'jug sher 'grel ke ta ka*. Sichuan: Nationalities Press, 1993.

Mipam. *Sword of Insight (don rnam par nges pa shes rab ral gri mchan bcas)*. *Mipam's Collected Works*, vol. 4 (*pa*), 787–820.

Mipam. *Words That Delight Guru Mañjughoṣa: Commentary on the "Ornament of the Middle Way" (dbu ma rgyan gyi rnam bshad 'jam byangs bla ma dgyes pa'i zhal lung)*. Published in *dbu ma rgyan rtsa 'grel*. Sichuan: Nationalities Press, 1990.

Naess, Arne. "The Shallow and the Deep, Long-Range Ecology Movement: A Summary." *Inquiry* 16 (1973): 95–100.

Nagao, Gadjin. "What Remains in Śūnyatā: A Yogācāra Interpretation of Emptiness." In Gadjin Nagao, *Mādhyamika and Yogācāra*, 51–60. Albany: SUNY Press, 1991.

Ngedön Tenzin Zangpo, the Third Dzokchen Rinpoché (*nges don bstan 'dzin bzang po*, 1759–1792). *Excellent Chariot (rdzogs pa chen po mkha' 'gro snying thig gi khrid yig thar lam bgrod byed shing rta bzang po)*. Chengdu: Nationalities Press, 1997; English trans. in Cortland Dahl, *Great Perfection*, vols. 1-2. Ithaca, NY: Snow Lion Publications, 2008.

Nietzsche, Friedrich. *Beyond Good and Evil.* Translated by Walter Kaufmann. New York: Random House, 1966.

Nietzsche, Friedrich. *Will to Power.* Translated by Walter Kaufmann and R. J. Hollingdale. New York: Random House, 1967.

Nup Sangyé Yeshé (*gnubs sangs rgyas ye shes, ca.* ninth c.). *Lamp for the Eye of Meditation* (*bsam gtan mig sgron*). Leh: smanrtsis shesrig spendzod, 1974.

Pakmodru (*phag mo gru rdo rje rgyal po,* 1110–1170). *Precious Staircase* (*rin po che'i them skas*). *Pakmodru's Collected Works,* vol. 3, 1–186. Kathmandu: Khenpo Shedrup Tenzin and Lama Thinley Namgyal, 2003.

Pema Ledrelsel (*padma las 'brel rtsal*). *Instructions on the Meaning of Liberation Through Wearing* (*btags grol don khrid*). In *snying thig ya bzhi* (*mkha' 'gro snying thig*), vol. 10, 82–106. Delhi: Sherab Gyaltsen Lama, 1975.

Priest, Graham. *Beyond the Limits of Thought.* Oxford: Oxford University Press, 2002.

Rangjung Dorjé, the Third Karmapa (*rang byung rdo rje,* 1284–1339). *Treatise Distinguishing Consciousness and Gnosis* (*rnam par shes pa dang ye shes 'byed pa'i bstan bcos*). In *dpal spungs dpe rnying gsar bskrun las gzhung lugs phyogs bsgrigs,* vol. 12, 275–326. Palpung Monastery (H.P., India): *spal spung dgon pa'i par khang,* 2006; English trans. in Brunnhölzl, Karl, *Luminous Heart: The Third Karmapa on Consciousness, Wisdom, and Buddha-Nature.* Ithaca, NY: Snow Lion Publications, 2009.

Ricoeur, Paul. *Freud and Philosophy: An Essay on Interpretation.* Translated by Denis Savage. New Haven: Yale University Press, 1970.

Ricoeur, Paul. *Interpretation Theory: Discourse and the Surplus of Meaning.* Fort Worth: Texas University Press, 1976.

Rikzin Chödrak (*rig 'dzin chos kyi grags pa,* 1595–1659). *Vajra Song of the Nonconceptual Ultimate* (*rtog med don dam rdo rje'i glu*). In *Great Treasury of Drikung Kagyü* (*'bri gung bka' brgyud chos mdzod chen mo*), vol. 101, edited by Agon Rinpoche, 539–553. Lhasa: n.p., 2004.

Rikzin Chödrak. *Words of Dharmakīrti* (*phyag rgya chen po lnga ldan gyi khrid kyi zin bris dharma kīrti'i zhal lung*). In *phyag chen lnga ldan byin rlabs dpal 'bar sogs,* 27–207. Delhi: Tenzin Chodak, 1975.

Robert, Peter Alan, trans. *Mahāmudrā and Related Instructions: Core Teachings of the Kagyü Schools.* Boston: Wisdom Publications, 2011.

Rongzom (*rong zom chos kyi bzang po, ca.* eleventh c.). *Commentary on "Secret Essence Tantra"* (*rgyud rgyal gsang ba'i snying po dkon cog 'grel*). *Rongzom's Collected Works,* vol. 1, 33–253. Sichuan: Nationalities Press, 1999.

Rongzom. *Entering the Way of the Mahāyāna* (*theg pa chen po'i tshul la 'jug pa*). *Rongzom's Collected Works,* vol. 1, 415–555. Sichuan, China: Nationalities Press, 1999; English trans. in Dominic Sur, *Entering the Way of the Great Vehicle: Dzokchen as the Culmination of Mahāyāna.* Boulder: Snow Lion Publications, 2017.

Rosenthal, David. *Consciousness and Mind.* Oxford: Oxford University Press, 2005.

Ruegg, David. *Two Prolegomena to Madhyamaka Philosophy*. Wien: Arbeitskreis für Tibetische und Buddhistische Studien, 2002.

Russell, Bertrand. *The Problems of Philosophy*. Oxford: Oxford University Press, 1997 [1912].

Śākya Chokden (*shākya mchog ldan*, 1428–1507). *Enjoyment Ocean of the Seven Treatises: An Explanation of the "Treasury of Epistemology" (tshad ma rigs pa'i gter gyi rnam par bshad pa sde bdun ngag gi rol mtsho)*. *Śākya Chokden's Collected Works*, vol. 19, 447–749. Thimphu, Bhutan: Kunzang Tobgey, 1975.

Śākya Chokden. *Meaningful to Behold (bshes gnyen mus pa rab 'byams pa'i 'dri lan mthong ba don ldan)*. *Śākya Chokden's Collected Works*, vol. 23, 297–418. Thimphu, Bhutan: Kunzang Tobgey, 1975.

Śākya Chokden. *Splendor of the Sun (tshad ma'i bstan bcos kyi shin rta'i srol rnams ji ltar 'byung ba'i tshul gtam du bya ba nyin mor byed pa'i snang bas dpyod ldan mtha' dag dga' bar byed pa)*. *Śākya Chokden's Collected Works*, vol. 19, 1–137. Thimphu, Bhutan: Kunzang Tobgey, 1975.

Śākya Chokden. *The Unprecedented Sun: The Definitive Meaning of the Uttaratantra (rgyud bla ma'i bstan bcos kyi nges don sngon med nyi ma)*. *Śākya Chokden's Collected Works*, vol. 13, 113–124. Thimphu, Bhutan: Kunzang Tobgey, 1975.

Sakya Paṇḍita (*sa skya paṇḍita kun dga' rgyal mtshan*, 1182–1251). *Treasury of Epistemology (tshad ma rigs gter)*. Beijing, China: Nationalities Press, 1989.

Śankara. *Brahmasūtrabhāṣya*; English trans. in George Thibaut, *Vedānta Sūtras*, Part I. *Sacred Books of the East*, vol. 34. Delhi: Motilal Banarsidass, 1998 [1904].

Schmithausen, Lambert. *On the Problem of the External World in the Ch'eng wei shih lun*. Tokyo: The International Institute of Buddhist Studies, 2005, 1–66.

Sellars, Wilfred. *Empiricism and the Philosophy of Mind*. Cambridge: Harvard University, 1997 [1956].

Siderits, Mark. *Buddhism as Philosophy: An Introduction*. Indianapolis: Hackett Publishing Co., 2007.

Siderits, Mark. "Causation and Emptiness in Early Madhyamaka." *Journal of Indian Philosophy* 32, no. 4 (2004): 393–419.

Siderits, Mark, Evan Thompson, and Dan Zahavi (eds.) *Self, No Self? Perspectives from Analytical, Phenomenological, and Indian Traditions*. Oxford: Oxford University Press, 2011.

Siderits, Mark, Tom Tillemans, and Arindam Chakrabarti (eds.) *Apoha: Buddhist Nominalism and Human Cognition*. New York: Columbia University Press, 2011.

Smith, E. Gene. *Among Tibetan Texts*. Boston: Wisdom Publications, 2001.

Snellgrove, David. *The Hevajratantra: A Critical Study*, vols. 1–2. Oxford: Oxford University Press, 1959.

Spinoza, Baruch. *Ethics*. In *Spinoza: Complete Works*, translated by Samuel Shirley, edited by Michael Morgan, 218–383. Indianapolis: Hackett Publishing, 2002.

Stcherbatsky, Theodore. *Buddhist Logic*, vols. 1–2. New York: Dover Publications, 1962 [1930].

Strawson, Galen. "Radical Self-Awareness." In *Self, No Self? Perspectives from Analytical, Phenomenological, & Indian Traditions*, edited by Mark Siderits, Evan Thompson, and Dan Zahavi, 274–307. Oxford: Oxford University Press, 2011.

Subramania Iyer, K. A. *Bhartṛhari: A Study of the Vākyapadīya in the Light of the Ancient Commentaries*. Poona: Deccan College, 1969.

Subramania Iyer, K. A., trans. *The Vākyapadīya of Bhartṛhari with the Vṛtti, Chapter I*. Poona: Deccan College, 1965.

Subramania Iyer, K. A., ed. *The Vākyapadīya of Bhartṛhari with the Vṛtti and the Paddhati of Vṛṣabhadeva*. Kaṇḍa I. Poona: Deccan College Monograph Series 32, 1966.

Subramania Iyer, K. A., trans. *The Vākyapadīya of Bhartṛhari, Kaṇḍa II: English Translation with Exegetical Notes*. Delhi: Motilal Banarsidass, 1977.

Subramania Iyer, K. A., ed. *Vākyapadīya of Bhartṛhari, Containing the Ṭīkā of Puṇyarāja and the Ancient Vṛtti*. Kāṇḍa II. Delhi: Motilal Banarsidass, 1983.

Tāranātha (*jo nang rje btsun tā ra nā tha*, 1575–1634). *Twenty-One Profound Points (zab don nyer gcig pa.)*. *Tāranātha's Collected Works*, vol. 18, 209–222. *'dzam-thang*: Dzamthang Monastery, 199?; English trans. in Klaus-Dieter Mathes, "Tāranātha's 'Twenty-One Differences with regard to the Profound Meaning' – Comparing the Views of the Two *gŽan stoṅ* Masters Dol po pa and Śākya mchog ldan." *Journal of the International Association of Buddhist Studies* 27, no. 2 (2004): 285–328.

Thompson, Evan. *Waking, Dreaming, Being: Self and Consciousness in Neuroscience, Meditation, and Philosophy*. New York: Columbia University Press, 2015.

Thrangu Rinpoché. *Distinguishing Dharma and Dharmatā*. Translated by Jules Levinson. Delhi: Sri Satguru Publications, 2001.

Thrangu Rinpoché. *An Ocean of the Ultimate Meaning*. Translated by Peter Alan Roberts. Boston: Shambhala Publications, 2004.

Thurman, Robert. "Philosophical Nonegocentrism in the Works of Wittgenstein and Candrakīrti." *Philosophy East & West* 30, no. 1 (1980): 321–337.

Tillemans, Tom. "Serious, Lightweight, or Neither: Should Madhyamaka Go to Canberra?" In *How Do Mādhyamikas Think? And Other Essays on the Buddhist Philosophy of the Middle*, 221–241. Boston: Wisdom Publications, 2016.

Tilopa. *Ganges Mahāmudrā* (*phyag rgya chen po'i man ngag*). Tibetan edition and English translation by David Molk in Sangye Nyenpa, *Tilopa's Mahamudra Upadeshad*, 1–17. Boston: Snow Lion, 2014.

Toadvine, Ted. *Merleau-Ponty's Philosophy of Nature*. Evanston, Ill: Northwestern University Press, 2009.

Tsongkhapa (*tsong kha pa blo bzang grags pa*, 1357–1419). *Essence of Eloquence* (*drang ba dang nges pa'i don rnam par phye ba'i bstan bcos legs bshad snying po*). In *Tsongkhapa's Collected Works*, vol. 14 (*pha*), 321–502. Xining, China: Nationalities Press, 2015 [2008].

Tsongkhapa. *The Great Exposition of the Stages of Mantra* (*sngags rim chen mo*). Xining, China: Nationalities Press, 1995; English translation in Jeffrey Hopkins, translator and editor, *Tantra in Tibet*. London: George Allen & Unwin, 1977.

Tsongkhapa. *Great Exposition of the Stages of the Path* (*lam rim chen mo*). Xining, China: Nationalities Press, 2000 [1985]; English translation in Lamrim Chenmo Translation Committee, edited by Joshua W. C. Cutler, *The Great Treatise on the Stages of the Path to Enlightenment*, vols. 1–3. Ithaca, NY: Snow Lion Publications, 2000–2004.

Tsongkhapa. *Middling Stages of the Path* (*byang chub lam rim 'bring ba'i sa bcad kha skong dang bcas pa*). Byllakuppe, India: Sera Je, 2005.

Tsongkhapa. *Ocean of Reason* (*dbu ma rtsa ba'i tshig le'ur byas pa shes rab ces bya ba'i rnam bshad rigs pa'i rgya mtsho*). *Tsongkhapa's Collected Works*, vol. 15 (*ba*), 3–311. Xining, China: Nationalities Press, 1998; English translation in Garfield, Jay, and Geshe Ngawang Samten, *Ocean of Reasoning*. Oxford: Oxford University Press, 2006.

Tsongkhapa. *Thoroughly Illuminating the Viewpoint* (*dgongs pa rab gsal*). *Tsongkhapa's Collected Works*, vol. 16, 443–751. Xining, China: Nationalities Press, 1998.

Tsongkhapa. *Three Principal Aspects of the Path* (*lam gyi gtso bo rnam gsum*). Xining, China: *sku 'bum byams pa gling*, 2001.

Utpaladeva. *Īśvarapratyabhijñākārikā*. In *The Īśvarapratyabhijñākārikā of Utpaladeva with the Author's Vṛtti*, edited and translated by Rafaelle Torella. Rome: IsMEO, 1994.

van der Kuijp, Leonard. "An Early Tibetan View of the Soteriology of Epistemology: The Case of 'Bri-gung dJig-ldan mGon-po." *Journal of Indian Philosophy* 15 (1987): 57–70.

van Schaik, Sam. *Approaching the Great Perfection*. Boston: Wisdom Publications, 2004.

Wallace, Vesna. *Inner Kālacakra*. Oxford: Oxford University Press, 2001.

Wallace, Vesna. *The Kālacakratantra: The Chapter on the Individual Together with the Vimalaprabhā*. Treasury of Buddhist Sciences Series. New York: Columbia University Press, 2004.

Wangchuk Gyeltsen (*dbang phyug rgyal mtshan*, fifteenth c.). *Biography of Nāropa* (*mkhas grub mnyam med dpal ldan nā ro pa'i rnam par thar pa dri med legs bshad bde chen 'brug sgra*). Bir, India: tsondu senghe yorey tsang, 2006.

Watson, Alex. *The Self's Awareness of Itself: Rāmakaṇṭha Bhaṭṭa's Arguments Against the Buddhist Doctrine of No-Self*. Wien: De Nobili, 2006.

Westerhoff, Jan. "On the Nihilist Interpretation of Madhyamaka." *Journal of Indian Philosophy* 44, no. 2 (2016): 337–376.

Whitehead, A. N. "Immortality." In *The Philosophy of Alfred North Whitehead*, vol. 3, edited by Paul Schilpp, 682–744. Evanston, Ill: Northwestern University Press, 1941.

Whitehead, A. N. *Science and the Modern World*. Cambridge: Cambridge University Press, 2011.

Wittgenstein, Ludwig. *Philosophical Investigations*. Translated by G. E. M. Anscombe. Malden, MA: Blackwell Publications, 2001 [1953].

Wylie, John. *Landscape*. New York: Routledge, 2007.

Zahavi, Dan. *Subjectivity and Selfhood: Investigating the First-Person Perspective*. Cambridge: MIT Press, 2005.

Zahavi, Dan, and Josef Parnas. "Phenomenal Consciousness and Self-Awareness: A Phenomenological Critique of Representational Theory." *Journal of Consciousness Studies* 5, no. 5–6 (1998), 687–705.

Zhang, Yisun, ed. *The Great Tibetan-Chinese Dictionary (bod rgya tshig mdzod chen mo)*. Beijing: Nationalities Press 1998 [1993].

Index

www.ingramcontent.com/pod-product-compliance
Lightning Source LLC
La Vergne TN
LVHW020220180225
803987LV00015B/138

9780197616598